AppleScript
The Definitive Guide

Other Macintosh resources from O'Reilly

Related titles

AppleWorks 6: The Missing Manual

Learning Cocoa with Objective-C

Learning Unix for Mac OS X

Mac OS X for Unix Geeks

Mac OS X Hacks

Mac OS X Hints

Mac OS X in a Nutshell

Mac OS X: The Missing Manual

Office X for Macintosh: The Missing Manual

Switching to the Mac: The Missing Manual

Building Cocoa Applications: A Step-by-Step Guide

Mac OS X Unwired

Macintosh Books Resource Center

mac.oreilly.com is a complete catalog of O'Reilly's books on the Apple Macintosh and related technologies, including sample chapters and code examples.

A popular watering hole for Macintosh developers and power users, the Mac DevCenter focuses on pure Mac OS X and its related technologies, including Cocoa, Java, AppleScript, and Apache, to name just a few. It's also keenly interested in all the spokes of the digital hub, with special attention paid to digital photography, digital video, MP3 music, and QuickTime.

Conferences

O'Reilly & Associates brings diverse innovators together to nurture the ideas that spark revolutionary industries. We specialize in documenting the latest tools and systems, translating the innovator's knowledge into useful skills for those in the trenches. Visit *conferences.oreilly.com* for our upcoming events.

Safari Bookshelf (*safari.oreilly.com*) is the premier online reference library for programmers and IT professionals. Conduct searches across more than 1,000 books. Subscribers can zero in on answers to time-critical questions in a matter of seconds. Read the books on your Bookshelf from cover to cover or simply flip to the page you need. Try it today with a free trial.

AppleScript
The Definitive Guide

Matt Neuburg

O'REILLY®

Beijing · Cambridge · Farnham · Köln · Paris · Sebastopol · Taipei · Tokyo

AppleScript: The Definitive Guide
by Matt Neuburg

Copyright © 2004 O'Reilly & Associates, Inc. All rights reserved.
Printed in the United States of America.

Published by O'Reilly & Associates, Inc., 1005 Gravenstein Highway North, Sebastopol, CA 95472.

O'Reilly & Associates books may be purchased for educational, business, or sales promotional use. Online editions are also available for most titles (*safari.oreilly.com*). For more information, contact our corporate/institutional sales department: (800) 998-9938 or *corporate@oreilly.com*.

Editor:	Chuck Toporek
Production Editor:	Genevieve d'Entremont
Cover Designer:	Ellie Volckhausen
Interior Designer:	Melanie Wang

Printing History:

November 2003:   First Edition.

ISBN: 0-596-00557-1

Table of Contents

Part III. AppleScript In Action

Part IV. Appendixes

Preface

From a technological and historical perspective, AppleScript is one of the greatest innovations and distinguishing features of the Mac OS. The System provides not only a mechanism for applications to communicate with one another, ordering one another about, getting information from one another, and generally collaborating to avail themselves of one another's strengths and abilities, but also a way for ordinary users to take advantage of this mechanism programmatically. The user can write and execute code in the AppleScript language as a way of automating the behavior of applications, reducing many steps to one, throwing the burden of repetition and calculation onto the computer, and combining the powers of multiple applications into a seamless united workflow. AppleScript is a labor-saving device that lets ordinary users program the computer for themselves; and, after all, labor-saving and programming are just what computers are all about.

Although AppleScript was long treated by Apple itself as something of an unwanted, troublesome step-child—and has even (according to apocryphal legend) at times come perilously near being tossed onto the scrapheap—it has lately prospered, and is now perhaps entering a kind of Golden Age. AppleScript has been embraced and acknowledged and is starting to take its rightful place in the firmament of Apple's star technologies. It is noticed on Apple's own web pages as a major aspect of Mac OS X (for example, see *http://www.apple.com/macosx/overview/*). The Script Editor has been rewritten as a Cocoa application. Scripts may be run from a System-wide menu. More and more of Apple's own new applications are scriptable. Integration with Unix scripting has been provided. AppleScript can even be used to drive applications that are not technically scriptable at all. And users can actually write a genuine application with a full-fledged Aqua user interface—windows, menus, buttons, text fields, scrolling lists, and more—using AppleScript as their programming language, thanks to the astounding AppleScript Studio. And it all comes for free as part of Mac OS X.

In this context, with interest in AppleScript waxing anew, the need for a complete explanatory manual and reference is greater than ever. In that spirit, this book is offered. It is hoped that it will prove helpful to AppleScript's beginning and veteran users alike. No prior knowledge of AppleScript is assumed, nor any previous programming experience, so that the complete beginner can use this book to learn AppleScript from the ground up; at the same time, the book aims at such a degree of technical depth and completeness as will satisfy the needs of those who wish only to consult it to check some point of syntax, or to gain a firmer understanding of such advanced arcana as how the scoping rules operate, how terminology is resolved, or what an Apple event really is.

The Scope of This Book

What should be the scope of a book about AppleScript? This is a tricky problem, and one that earlier books, in my view, have not always dealt with satisfactorily. The trouble is that AppleScript is really two subjects. First, there is what one may call AppleScript itself, a "little language," not particularly useful or powerful on its own, but ready to talk to scriptable applications and to take advantage of *their* utility and power. Second, there is AppleScript as extended and implemented by particular scriptable applications: how to use AppleScript to talk to the Finder, how to use AppleScript to talk to Adobe Photoshop, how to use AppleScript to talk to QuarkXPress, and so forth.

On the whole, this book makes no attempt to treat this second aspect of AppleScript. This may be surprising to readers accustomed to some earlier books, but I believe it to be the right decision nonetheless. AppleScript as implemented by particular applications is a massive, encyclopedic subject. It would be easy to write an entire book of techniques, tricks, and tips for scripting just *one* major application. And the scope of any attempt to do this for *every* scriptable application would be open-ended, since it is impossible to know what scriptable applications the reader has or might acquire, and since new applications, any of which might be scriptable, are being developed all the time. Also, such treatment is largely unnecessary. Every scriptable application includes a dictionary telling the user about how it extends the language; and the user can employ this, together with trial and error, and possibly examples from documentation and the Internet, to obtain pretty fair mastery over the art of scripting that application. There might even be books on the exact subject the reader is interested in. (Thus, for example, it is far better that the reader should consult Ethan Wilde's book *Adobe Illustrator Scripting with Visual Basic and AppleScript* than that the present book should attempt to compress a treatment of the same material into some reduced and undoubtedly inadequate form.)

My choice, therefore, is between concisely teaching the reader to fish and giving the reader a large pile of possibly quite unnecessary fish. Readers who know anything of my work (or anything about fish) will know instantly which choice I would make! Rather than trying to encompass the details of scripting every application, my approach in this book has been to explain the AppleScript language itself, and to describe how a dictionary works and what a user can and can't learn from it, providing examples from across the range of applications that I actually use, so that the reader will be mentally equipped and educated and able independently to study and experiment with scripting any application.

Besides, books about the first aspect of AppleScript—about AppleScript itself—have been surprisingly few and far between. It is here that the need exists. The fact is that I have never seen the AppleScript language taught, explained, and documented in what I would regard as a clear, rigorous, and helpful way. Considering how long AppleScript has been around, it is hard to explain this lack. It may have partly to do with the lack of clear explanation from Apple itself. After all, Apple wrote Apple-Script, and only the folks at Apple have access to AppleScript's inner workings. Yet the only Apple manual of AppleScript, the *AppleScript Language Guide*, generally lacks explanatory depth.

There is a kind of unspoken myth—we may call it the "ease of use" myth—that tries to give the impression that AppleScript is so easy and intuitive that it doesn't really *need* explanation. Apple possibly didn't want users to see AppleScript as a full-fledged programming language, with all the precision, complexity, and sophistication that this entails, because that would be something that users would have to learn, exercising those parts of their brain to which a Macintosh, with its windows and icons and colorful buttons, isn't supposed to appeal. Instead, AppleScript is supposed to be so simple, so thin, so easy, so English-like, so intuitive, that there is hardly anything to learn in the first place; just pick up an application and its dictionary and presto, you're ready to script it.

Nothing could be further from the truth. First you must learn the language; only then will a dictionary make sense and be useful. AppleScript is not a mere veneer, an intuitive and obvious "glue" for hooking together the terms from an application's dictionary into sentences that will script that application as the user desires. On the contrary, it's a real programming language—a really interesting programming language (not least because it's fairly cranky, opaque, quirky, and oddly designed). To conceal this fact from the potential user of AppleScript does that user no favor whatever. Every day I see on the Internet users who are starting AppleScript, who seem to imagine that they're just going to "pick it up"—that their AppleScript code will somehow just write itself. Well, it won't. A beginning user who expects to cut to the chase, to pick up an application's dictionary and just start scripting, is likely to give up in frustration. As Socrates said of virtue, AppleScript isn't just something we all somehow are born knowing; it must be learned, and therefore it must be taught. There is nothing about AppleScript that makes it any less susceptible to scrutiny, careful description, and ordered, Euclidean explanation than any other language.

In this light, I have written the AppleScript book that I have for so long myself wished to read. Also, I have always found myself rather confused about Apple-Script—I could use it with reasonable effectiveness, but I was always somewhat hazy on the details—so writing this book has been an opportunity for me to dispel my own confusion. The result is a reasoned, rigorous, step-by-step presentation of the AppleScript language, intended for instruction and for reference, a studious, patient, detailed, ordered exposition and compendium of the facts. This book presents AppleScript as a programmer, a student, a thinker would learn it. In short, it's just what I've always wanted! This book has helped me tremendously: before I wrote it, I didn't really quite understand AppleScript; now I believe I do. I hope reading it will do the same for you.

Versions

Things change. All things change. And software often changes faster than the ability of printed books to keep up with it. It may therefore be useful for the reader to know what versions of software I was looking at when I wrote this book. The first draft was written using Mac OS X 10.2.6 ("Jaguar") and AppleScript 1.9.1. While polishing the final draft I had access to a preview version of Mac OS X 10.3 ("Panther"), with AppleScript 1.9.2 and Script Editor 2.0 v41, and the book treats these as the standard. Screen shots were redone using Panther. There may be further changes in Panther, and possibly even in AppleScript, by the time the book goes to print, but if so, it seems unlikely that these will affect the book's content; still, the reader should be alert to the possibility of slight discrepancies between what I describe and the now current state of things.

The book is written entirely from the perspective of Mac OS X. This is a deliberate design decision. There is an important sense in which Mac OS 9 really is frozen, if not downright moribund: very few new applications of any importance are being written for it, it is not likely to evolve further to any significant extent, and Apple has begun to produce computers which won't even boot in it. If you are not using Mac OS X, this book might still be useful to you, but please keep in mind that it isn't geared primarily to your situation.

How This Book Is Organized

This book is divided into four sections:

Part I, AppleScript Overview

Part I consists of general introductory material, explaining what AppleScript is, motivating the reader with examples of various ways and means for putting AppleScript to use, and defining fundamental terms that the reader will need to understand.

Chapter 1, *Ways to Use AppleScript*
> Provides some motivational guidelines and real-life examples intended to answer such big existential questions as what AppleScript is good for and why you would want to use it anyway.

Chapter 2, *Places to Use AppleScript*
> Surveys the various areas of the computer where AppleScript can be employed— for example, by running a script in the Script Editor, by calling into AppleScript from some application's internal scripting language, or by way of a Unix scripting language like Perl.

Chapter 3, *The AppleScript Experience*
> A brief hands-on tutorial or walk-though, illustrating what it's like to plan and implement a task using AppleScript in real life.

Chapter 4, *Basic Concepts*
> An explanation of the technologies underlying AppleScript and a glossary of fundamental terms. This is where the technical discussion starts. If you already know something about AppleScript and don't need to be motivated to use or learn it, you might skim or skip the first three chapters, but you should definitely read this one, since the rest of the book depends upon it.

Part II, The AppleScript Language

Part II develops AppleScript as a programming language. Learners should read the chapters in order; experienced users may employ this section as a linguistic reference.

Chapter 5, *Introducing AppleScript*
> A subjective description of what AppleScript is like as a language, just to give you a sense of what you're getting into.

Chapter 6, *Syntactic Ground of Being*
> Describes some fundamental externals of the language, such as lines and comments.

Chapter 7, *Variables*
> Discusses aspects of variables, such as how to assign and declare them, and how scoping and persistence work.

Chapter 8, *Handlers*
> Discusses handlers (subroutines)—in particular, such matters as how to declare and call them, how their scoping works, and how they operate as values.

Chapter 9, *Script Objects*
> Discusses script objects (scripts within scripts), including how to refer to them, how their scoping works, how to load and save them dynamically, and how inheritance works.

Taken together, Chapters 6 through 9 comprise a survey of the constituent parts of an AppleScript program.

Chapter 10, *Objects*
> Describes how objects and their attributes (properties and elements) are referred to.

Chapter 11, *References*

Describes how the way in which objects and their attributes are referred to can be encapsulated into a value.

Chapter 12, *Control*

Surveys the linguistic structures for determining the flow of an AppleScript program, such as branching, looping, and error handling.

Chapter 13, *Datatypes*

A guide to the built-in classes of variable value (such as integers, strings, lists, and records) and how they work.

Chapter 14, *Coercions*

Explains how one datatype may be turned into another datatype explicitly or implicitly.

Chapter 15, *Operators*

Catalogues the various ways to test and combine values, such as addition, comparison, and concatenation.

Chapter 16, *Global Properties*

Catalogues some built-in variables, such as pi. (You didn't know pi was a variable, did you?)

Chapter 17, *Constants*

Catalogues some built-in enumerations and classes that behave as reserved words.

Chapter 18, *Commands*

Catalogues those few built-in verbs not previously covered.

Part III, AppleScript in Action

Part III describes aspects of AppleScript in practice and in relation to the wider world.

Chapter 19, *Dictionaries*

Talks about the mechanism whereby applications make themselves scriptable through AppleScript by extending the AppleScript language, and explains how terminology is resolved, how to read a dictionary, and what a dictionary is good for and not good for.

Chapter 20, *Scripting Additions*

Talks about code resources that extend the AppleScript language without reference to any particular application. It surveys the built-in scripting additions and provides some additional technical details.

Chapter 21, *Scriptable Applications*

Explains how to drive applications with AppleScript, whether they are on the same or a different computer, including certain kinds of web services. It also mentions a few useful scriptable applications that come with Mac OS X but that the reader might not otherwise be aware of.

Chapter 22, *Unscriptable Applications*

Talks about how AppleScript can be used together with the System's Accessibility API to automate the interface of applications that are not directly scriptable.

Chapter 23, *Unix*

Talks about how AppleScript can call the Unix shell command line and how Unix scripting languages can call AppleScript.

Chapter 24, *Writing Applications*

Discusses ways to turn an AppleScript program into a standalone application, ranging from a simple applet to a full-fledged application with a true user interface written in AppleScript Studio.

Part IV, Appendixes

Appendix A, *The 'aeut' Resource*

Presents a listing of AppleScript's own hidden dictionary, where the terms of the language itself are embodied.

Appendix B, *Tools and Resources*

A list of references and further readings. If this book mentions an application you've never heard of, or you want to know how to learn more about AppleScript, this appendix is the place to come.

Conventions Used in This Book

The following conventions are used in this book:

Italic

Used for file and folder names, URLs, and new terms when they are defined

`Constant width`

Used for code examples and the names of variables, handlers, and commands

`Constant width italic`

Used for placeholders in code, where the programmer would supply the actual name of something

`Constant width bold`

Used in code examples, for user input from the command line; often seen in conjunction with $, which symbolizes the shell prompt

`-- code comment in italic`

Used in code examples, for my comments to the reader about the code or its effect

`-- code comment in bold`

> Used in code examples, to represent the result (output) of executing the line

`vertical bar |`

> Used in syntax templates to indicate alternatives

`[square brackets]`

> Used in syntax templates to indicate that something is optional

¬

> This character indicates a line of code that continues; these lines will be unbroken in your code but were too long to fit on the printed pages of this book.

This icon represents a tip relating to the nearby text.

This icon represents a warning relating to the nearby text.

How to Contact Us

The book-writing process is long and arduous, and the examples have been tested and retested. However, mistakes do creep in from time to time. If you find any errors in the text or code examples, please write to:

> O'Reilly & Associates, Inc.
> 1005 Gravenstein Highway North
> Sebastopol, CA 95472
> 800-998-9938 (in the United States or Canada)
> 707-829-0515 (international/local)
> 707-829-0104 (fax)

We have a web page for the book, where we list any additional information. You can access this page at:

> *http://www.oreilly.com/catalog/applescpttdg/*

To comment or ask technical questions about this book, send email to:

> *bookquestions@oreilly.com*

For more information about our books, conferences, software, Resource Centers, and the O'Reilly Network, see our web site at:

> *http://www.oreilly.com*

Acknowledgments

In a completely just world, Mark Alldritt of Late Night Software would probably have his name on the cover of this book. In fact, he really ought to have written the book himself, since in all probability no one outside of Apple knows more about AppleScript than he does. I have benefited from his knowledge in three ways: he wrote Script Debugger, without which much of AppleScript's behavior would have remained opaque to me; he provided untiring assistance and advice while I was writing; and he performed a thorough and valuable technical review of the first draft.

Paul Berkowitz also acted as technical reviewer, a task which he performed with brilliance and insight, combining a long and thoughtful experience of AppleScript with diligence and critical perspicacity. He corrected many errors of fact, and gave excellent advice from the perspective of a model reader. Those who find this book useful should know that much of the credit is his. Chuck Sholdt also made several helpful suggestions and provided much-needed encouragement.

All the members of the AppleScript team at Apple who were present at Apple's 2003 WWDC were extremely generous with their time despite the many other demands upon it. Some of them provided important technical advice that has greatly increased the book's accuracy.

It remains only to add that the responsibility where I have not taken or understood the advice of my technical reviewers must rest with me.

My editor, Chuck Toporek, did all the right things. He assigned me the book, he monitored the signals emerging from Apple, he enabled me to attend Apple's 2003 WWDC and put me in touch with the AppleScript team, and he displayed forbearance, confidence, and patience while I was writing, leaving me to wrestle with problems of form and content on my own, never criticizing an early draft that he knew I would eventually rip to shreds myself, while at the same time providing encouragement when needed and advice when requested. Having as copyeditor my old friend Nancy Kotary made this stage of the process a pleasure instead of a trial; she brought to the task her characteristic combination of sound judgement, sharp eyes, and a kind heart, and a number of passages read more clearly thanks to her intervention. Genevieve d'Entremont oversaw the production in a thoroughly professional manner. My thanks to them and to all at O'Reilly & Associates who participated in the making of this book.

AppleScript Overview

Part I introduces AppleScript. What is it? How does it work? Where can I use it? What can I do with it? These are the sorts of questions this part answers.

If you already have a notion of what AppleScript is and just want to get on with studying the language, you can skip most of this section; but you should read Chapter 4, because it contains fundamental information and definitions that are not repeated later, and on which the rest of the book depends.

The chapters are:

Chapter 1, *Ways to Use AppleScript*
Chapter 2, *Places to Use AppleScript*
Chapter 3, *The AppleScript Experience*
Chapter 4, *Basic Concepts*

Ways to Use AppleScript

If you've never used AppleScript before, you probably have two questions at the outset. You might like to know: "What is AppleScript?" And you also might like to know: "And why should I care, anyway?" This chapter gives general answers to both questions, by focusing on the question: "What is AppleScript *for*?" The chapter classifies the main kinds of use for AppleScript, and provides some examples showing AppleScript being put to these various kinds of use.

The purpose of this chapter is as much motivational as informative. By demonstrating AppleScript in action, in some typical real-life contexts, I hope to get you thinking by extension about ways in which you might now or in the future want to use AppleScript in your own life. If you can mentally formulate some appropriate tasks you actually want to perform with AppleScript, you'll have more reason to learn it, and you'll learn it more easily and more enjoyably.

The Nature and Purpose of AppleScript

As you know, you've got various applications on your computer, and you typically make them do things by choosing menu items and clicking buttons and generally wielding the mouse and keyboard in the usual way; and you get information from them by reading it off the screen, or you can communicate information from one application to another by copying and pasting.

With AppleScript, you can make applications do things, not with the mouse and keyboard and screen, but *programmatically*—by writing and executing a little program that gives an application commands and fetches information from it. In the chain of actions that you make the application perform, the program that you write takes the place of your brain; the program's power to give commands to the application takes the place of your hands on the mouse and keyboard, and its power to ask the application questions takes the place of your eyes reading the screen. Thus, you can automate the sorts of things you're accustomed to making applications do manually. Instead of your doing something with the mouse, then reading the screen, then thinking about what this means and what you should do next, and so forth, the computer does the doing, the reading, and the thinking. This means that your hands and eyes and brain are freed from having to perform repetitive or tiresome activities better suited to the computer itself.

Suppose, for example, you've got a folder full of image files and you want to change their names in a systematic way to *image01.jpg*, *image02.jpg*, and so forth. It isn't as if you don't know how to do this. You select the first image file with the mouse, press Return to start editing its name, type image01.jpg, and press Return again. Now you select the next image file with mouse, and do it again. The business of doing it again rapidly becomes tiresome and error-prone. You have to remember where you are ("What was the number I assigned to the previous image file I renamed?"), think what to do next ("What do I get when I add 1 to the previous number?"), and do it (click, Return, type, Return). It isn't long before you're making mistakes clicking or typing, or your eyes are starting to go out of focus, or you are just plain bored out of your skull.

How many files would there have to be before you'd regard this as a daunting or boring or error-prone task? A thousand? A hundred? To me, the prospect of manually renaming even *ten* files in this way seems an annoying waste of my time and brainpower. I've got better things to do than repetitively to click and type and add 1! With AppleScript, you can just write a little program that accomplishes the same thing automatically, and it doesn't matter how many files the folder contains—the program will do the job for you, and it won't make *any* mistakes.

And that, of course, is just a tiny example. When I was editing *MacTech* magazine, AppleScript was an essential part of our workflow; we had massive tasks, tying together several major applications such as Microsoft Word and QuarkXPress, with information moving from one application and being fed into another and then being formatted and prepared in all sorts of clever, complicated ways—and these tasks were automated, freeing the human user from the burdens of tedium and accuracy and casting those burdens onto the computer itself, thanks to AppleScript.

The name "AppleScript" denotes both the language in which you write the program that automates your existing applications and the underlying System-level technology that supports and executes it. AppleScript is present as part of the System. You get it for free, so you may as well take advantage of it. And you know it will be present on any Mac OS computer, so if you write an AppleScript program that might be useful to others, you can share it. Or, just the other way around, you can find lots of AppleScript programs floating around on the Internet that might be useful to you. There's an entire community and culture of AppleScript users, sharing their work and benefiting from one another's experience.

I don't want to give the impression, however, that AppleScript lets you tell *every* application programmatically to do *everything* it is capable of. That, alas, is not so. It lets you tell *some* applications programmatically to do *some* of the things they are capable of. The way AppleScript works is by sending messages to the applications you are automating; these messages are called *Apple events*. You cannot send just any old Apple event to any old application. (Well, you can, but it might not have any effect.) The application you're sending an Apple event to must recognize that Apple event and must have a way of responding to it. Such an application is said to be *scriptable*.

Based on these considerations, we can now enunciate some general principles about what AppleScript is good for:

- AppleScript is appropriate primarily when you have a *scriptable application* that you want to automate.
- AppleScript is good for expressing *calculated* and *repetitive* activity.
- AppleScript is a good means of *reduction*, combining multiple steps into a single operation.
- AppleScript is a way of *customizing an application*.
- AppleScript gives you the opportunity to *combine specialties* (you could also think of this as *divide and conquer*): by automating more than one application, you make them work together, letting each application do what it's good at and uniting their several powers.

In general, if you're looking for ways to use AppleScript, my advice is to leave your mental annoyance meter turned on. When the computer annoys you, that's a sign that perhaps you should call upon AppleScript to help you. Does something feel slow, repetitious, clumsy, boring, error-prone? Do you feel that a program isn't quite doing what you want? Does a series of steps need to be reduced to one? Has the computer got you trained, like some sort of laboratory animal, to perform a sequence of set tasks in a certain way? That's just not right. The computer should work for you— not the other way round! Maybe AppleScript can turn the tables.

Is This Application Scriptable?

Our first rule of thumb for when AppleScript is appropriate is that you should have a scriptable application that you want to automate with it. That's because Apple-Script, although it is a genuine programming language with some interesting and useful features, is intended for use with other applications, which are expected to provide the real muscle. Thus AppleScript's numeric abilities are limited (it has no built-in trigonometric or logarithmic functions) and its text processing facilities are fairly rudimentary (it doesn't support regular expressions and isn't even very good at extracting substrings). So, for example, if I wanted to remove a text file's HTML markup, or extract the headers and bodies of all the messages in an *.mbox* file, I'd be far happier using Perl. On the other hand, AppleScript can drive Perl (and vice versa), so in your AppleScript code you can take advantage of Perl's powers (and vice versa); we'll see several examples later in the book. Thus success might simply be a matter of combining specialties appropriately.

Using AppleScript with a scriptable application is not itself a panacea. First you need a scriptable application that has the capabilities to do what you want. And even such an application might not provide a way to script those particular capabilities. Still, you can't worry about that if you don't know whether an application is scriptable in the first place!

Here's the most reliable way to ascertain whether an application is scriptable. Start up Apple's Script Editor program. (It's in */Applications/AppleScript*.) Choose File → Open Dictionary. This shows you a list of applications on your computer that the Script Editor thinks are scriptable. Initially, this list might omit some applications, so you can press the Browse button to locate an application using the standard Open dialog. If an application is dimmed here, it isn't scriptable. To double-check, choose and open an application. If a Dictionary window appears, the application is probably scriptable; but this could be a false positive. Make sure that the left side of the Dictionary window lists commands other than the "required" commands open, print, and quit—that it lists commands that actually *do* something. As a rule of thumb, the more items you see listed on the left side of the window, the more scriptable the application is, though this really is a gross over-simplification. Later in the book we'll go into much more detail about the Dictionary and what it tells you (Chapter 19 and Appendix A).

The scriptable applications I use with some regularity include many of those supplied by Apple as part of Mac OS X, such as Address Book, AppleWorks, iCal, iTunes, Mail, Safari, TextEdit, Apple System Profiler, and the Finder. Then there are important third-party programs like Microsoft Word and Excel, FileMaker Pro, Internet Explorer, Interarchy, Mailsmith, BBEdit, StuffIt Deluxe, GraphicConverter, and Frontier. You might also have QuarkXPress or Photoshop. Of course there are many others.

It is sometimes possible to drive even a nonscriptable application, by using AppleScript to simulate a "ghost" user who can physically choose menu items, push buttons, and so forth. This approach should probably be used only as a last resort, but it's important to know about, so I'll demonstrate it later in this chapter, and there's a further chapter devoted to it (Chapter 22).

Calculation and Repetition

Computers are good at calculation and repetition—which happen to be exactly the things humans are not good at. Humans are liable to calculate inaccurately, and repetitive activity can make them careless and bored. The whole idea of having a computer is to have it take over in these situations.

Here's an example. Someone on the Internet writes: "I want to rename a whole lot of image files based on the names of the folders they're in." One can just picture this user's eyes glazing over at the thought of doing this by hand. This is just the sort of thing a computer is for.

The task would make a good droplet. A *droplet* is a kind of applet, which is a little application you write with AppleScript, such that you can drop the icons of files and folders onto the droplet's icon in order to process those files and folders in some way. (See "Applet and Droplet" in Chapter 4, and "Applets" in Chapter 24.) So here's the AppleScript code for a droplet where you drop a folder onto its icon and it renames all the files in that folder as the name of the folder followed by a number:

```
on open folderList
    repeat with aFolder in folderList
        tell application "Finder"
            if kind of aFolder is "Folder" then
                my renameStuffIn(aFolder)
            end if
        end tell
    end repeat
end open
on renameStuffIn(theFolder)
    set ix to 0
    tell application "Finder"
        set folderName to name of theFolder
        set allNames to name of every item of theFolder
        repeat with aName in allNames
            set thisItem to item aName of theFolder
            set ix to ix + 1
            set newName to folderName & (ix as string)
            try
                set name of thisItem to newName
            end try
        end repeat
    end tell
end renameStuffIn
```

The parameter folderList is handed to us as a list of whatever is dropped onto the droplet. We process each dropped item, starting with a sanity check to make sure it's really a folder. The actual renaming is done by extracting the names of the things in the folder and cycling through those names.

Here's another example. The email client Mailsmith has a spam-reporting feature, which submits a spam message to the SpamCop service (*http://www.spamcop.net*). This service operates in three stages: the user submits the message, via email; Spam-Cop replies with an email message giving a URL; the user goes to that URL in a web browser and presses a final Submit button. The Report to SpamCop feature in Mail-smith performs the first stage, and SpamCop performs the second; the problem is to get from the second stage to the third. After a while, I have several email messages from SpamCop, each containing a URL; I now need to go to all of those URLs in my browser. To do so, I run the following script:

```
tell application "Mailsmith"
    set allMessages to every message of incoming mail ¬
        whose subject begins with "SpamCop has accepted"
    repeat with aMessage in allMessages
        set theBody to get contents of content of aMessage
```

```
            set theParas to every paragraph of theBody
            repeat with aPara in theParas
                if aPara begins with "http://spamcop.net/sc" then
                    open location aPara
                    exit repeat
                end if
            end repeat
        end repeat
    end tell
```

The script finds all messages that come from SpamCop, and in each of those it finds the line that's the URL I'm supposed to go to and sends that URL to my web browser with the magic open location command.

Reduction

A script is a means of *reduction*: it combines multiple steps into a single operation. Instead of doing one thing, then another, then another, you do just *one* thing—run the script. I particularly like using AppleScript for reduction. Having worked out a series of steps to accomplish a task, I often realize that not only do I not want to have to go through them all again later, but also I fear I won't even remember them again later! My AppleScript program remembers the steps for me.

Here's an example. From time to time I have to reboot my computer into Mac OS 9. The drill is: open System Preferences, switch to the Startup Disk pane, click the Mac OS 9 System folder, hold the Option key, click Restart. Too much work! Too many steps, too much waiting, too much hunting for the right thing to click on, too much clicking. Here's the script that does it for me:*

```
    try
        do shell script ¬
            "bless -folder9 'Volumes/main/System Folder' -setOF" ¬
                password "myPassword" with administrator privileges
        tell application "System Events" to restart
    end try
```

I've got that script saved as an *applet*, which is a little application written with Apple-Script. To run the script in an applet, you just open the applet like any application. So this applet is sitting right on my desktop, where I can't miss it. To restart into Mac OS 9, I just double-click it. Now *that's* something I can remember.

Here's another example. A journal for which I occasionally write articles requires me to submit those articles in XML format. It happens that the XML editor I use inserts line breaks; the magazine doesn't want those. In practice the problem arises only between <Body> tags. So this BBEdit script post-processes my XML output, removing the line breaks between <Body> tags just before I send an article off to the magazine:

---

* This code is inspired by an original from Thomas Neveu; see *http://www.nonamescriptware.com*.

```
tell application "BBEdit"
    activate
    repeat
        find "<Body>([\\s\\S]*?)</Body>" ¬
            searching in text 1 of text window 1 ¬
            options {search mode:grep, starting at top:false, ¬
            wrap around:false, reverse:false, case sensitive:false, ¬
            match words:false, extend selection:false} ¬
            with selecting match
        if not found of the result then
            exit repeat
        end if
        remove line breaks selection of text window 1
    end repeat
end tell
```

There's nothing very complicated about that script, and I don't use it very often, but when I do use it, it's tremendously helpful. For one thing, it saves me from having to remember the regular expression used to do the find. For another, it takes over the repetition of finding, then removing line breaks, then finding again, then removing line breaks again, and so forth. (Clearly the notions of reduction and repetition can be closely allied.) The example may seem very specialized, but that's fine, because the whole point of AppleScript is that you are the programmer and can write the code that solves your own real-life problems. And it does illustrate some important general principles, such as using a scriptable application to process text more power-fully than AppleScript alone can easily do it.

The next example is about URLs. Often, working in some application or other, one sees a URL and wants to click on it and have the right thing happen: if it's an http URL, one's default browser should open and fetch it; if it's an email address, one's email program should create a new message to that address; and so forth. In some applications, such as a web browser, URLs are automatically clickable in this way; but in other applications you sometimes have to deal with the URL manually. This involves starting up the right helper program yourself, and then doing something with the URL: in a browser, paste it and press Return; in an email program, make a new message and paste it into the address field. With this AppleScript solution, I just copy the URL and let the computer do the rest:

```
tell application "System Events"
    set theProc to (get process 1 where it is frontmost)
    tell application "Finder"
        activate
        delay 1 -- give time for clip to convert from Classic
        copy (the clipboard) to theURL
        ignoring application responses
            try
                open location theURL
            end try
        end ignoring
    end tell
```

```
        set the frontmost of theProc to true
    end tell
```

The switch to the Finder is to force the clipboard contents to convert themselves to a usable form (and the delay is to give this time to happen); this seems to be needed particularly when working in a Classic application. System Events is called upon at the end to switch back to the application I was using at the outset. The heart of the script is the magic open location command, which does the "right thing" with the URL.

Customization

It's hard to write an application that meets everyone's desires and expectations; perhaps it's impossible. It's not just a matter of features; it's a matter of psychology. The software developer can't anticipate exactly how you'd like to use the software. By making the software scriptable, the developer can greatly reduce this problem. Instead of berating developers for not including that one menu item that would do just what you want, you get to applaud them for making the application scriptable and letting you implement the functionality yourself. If an application is scriptable, there may be much less reason for you to complain that it can't do a certain thing; quite possibly, by means of scripting, it can.

For example, Mailsmith can filter incoming email messages, and can perform various actions as part of this filtering process—but saving an email message to disk, as a text file, is not one of them. Now, you could look at this as meaning that Mailsmith can't save an email message to a file as part of a filter; but that's not really true, because Mailsmith can be scripted to save a message to a file. I subscribe to a number of mailing lists in digest form, and I like to save these as files to particular folders on my hard drive. So I have a script (not shown here) that runs through every message in the "incoming mail" mailbox, looks to see if it belongs to a mailing list, and if it does, saves it to the corresponding folder on disk and deletes it from the mailbox.

Some scriptable applications provide a means for customization at an even deeper level, by letting you modify what happens when you choose one of the application's own menu items or perform some other action in that application. For example, the Finder can be set up with Folder Actions that take over when you do things such as move a file into a certain folder. (See "Automatic Location" in Chapter 2 and "Folder Actions" in Chapter 24.)

Combining Specialties

Different applications are good at different things. You typically don't perform every task in a single application. Some applications do attempt to behave as "Swiss army knives" and be all things to all people (for example, Microsoft Word, a word processor, includes image-processing facilities); but on the whole, applications are specialized. Very often the point of using AppleScript is to get two or more applications working together. By sharing data, each application can contribute its own particular excellence to an operation's workflow.

Here's an example. In order to design the stop list for a web-based search engine, I needed to know the most frequently used words in each web page on the site. The web pages were easily stripped of their HTML, but then the question was how to count the occurrences of each word in a file and record the totals for the 30 most frequent words. The counting, I decided, could best be done with Ruby, a Unix scripting language I'm fond of. I wrote a little Ruby script that could be called from the command line with a file's pathname as argument:

```ruby
#!/usr/bin/ruby
class Histogram
    def initialize
        @tally = Hash.new(0)
    end
    def analyze(s)
        s.split.each do |word|
            myword = word.downcase.gsub(/[^a-z0-9]/, "")
            @tally[myword] = @tally[myword] + 1 if !myword.empty?
        end
        @tally.sort { |x,y| y[1]<=>x[1] }
    end
end
analysis = Histogram.new.analyze(File.new(ARGV[0]).read)
```

The hash of words and their frequencies has now been sorted by frequency and is sitting in the variable analysis. But what to do with this data? It was decided that the most flexible approach would be to store it in an Excel worksheet for later retrieval, manipulation, and analysis. So the Ruby script now goes on to hand the data over to Excel, using AppleScript. Here's the second part of the same Ruby script:

```ruby
counter = 1
oneline = ""
analysis[0..29].each do |entry|
    oneline = oneline + "set the value of cell 1 of " +
        "row #{counter.to_s} to \"#{entry[0]}\"\n"
    oneline = oneline + "set the value of cell 2 of " +
        "row #{counter.to_s} to #{entry[1].to_s}\n"
    counter = counter + 1
end
script = <<DONE
    tell application "Microsoft Excel"
        activate
        tell worksheet 1
            #{oneline}
        end tell
    end tell
DONE
`osascript -ss -e '#{script}'`
```

The strategy here, typical when using AppleScript from a Unix script, is to construct the entire AppleScript code as a string and then hand it over to osascript for execution. (We'll come back to this in Chapter 23.) The script sets one cell at a time in the Excel worksheet until a two-by-thirty range of cells is filled up, showing the thirty most frequently used words and the number of times each occurs (Figure 1-1).

	A	B
1	the	207
2	pg	120
3	of	91
4	to	89
5	and	85
6	a	64
7	in	56
8	that	52
9	for	52
10	on	40
11	macintosh	35
12	as	30
13	with	30
14	is	30
15	be	29
16	you	27
17	or	26
18	it	26
19	have	24
20	updates	24
21	apple	24
22	system	23
23	this	22
24	new	22
25	an	21
26	10	20
27	drives	20
28	by	20
29	from	19
30	are	18

Figure 1-1. Data communicated to Excel by Ruby

I next wrap an AppleScript frontend around this Ruby script. The reason is that AppleScript has the ability to present to the user a dialog from which to choose the file to be analyzed. So it presents this dialog, transforms the pathname of the chosen file to a Unix-type pathname, and calls the Ruby script with that pathname as argument:

```
set thePath to POSIX path of (choose file)
tell application "Microsoft Excel" to Create New document
set s to "ruby ~/Desktop/histoChart.ruby '" & thePath & "'"
do shell script s
```

At this point someone has a great idea. (I hate when that happens.) It might be useful to include in this worksheet a graph of the data. So having called the Ruby script, which has inserted the data into the Excel spreadsheet, the script proceeds to talk to Excel directly. This is the second half of the AppleScript code:

```
tell application "Microsoft Excel"
    tell Worksheet 1
```

```
Select Range "A1:B30"
set c to Create New Chart
set Type of c to xlBar
set HasTitle of c to true
set text of Characters of ChartTitle of c to "30 Most Frequent Words"
set HasLegend of c to false
ApplyDataLabels c Type xlShowLabel without LegendKey
set numAxes to count Axes of c
repeat with ix from 1 to numAxes
    set thisAxis to Axis ix of c
    set HasMajorGridlines of thisAxis to false
    set HasMinorGridlines of thisAxis to false
    set HasTitle of thisAxis to false
end repeat
set Size of Font of DataLabels of Series 1 of c to 14
set HasAxis of c to {{false, false}, {false, false}}
end tell
end tell
```

First we select the range of cells where we know the Ruby script has just deposited the data; then we generate and format a chart of that data (Figure 1-2).

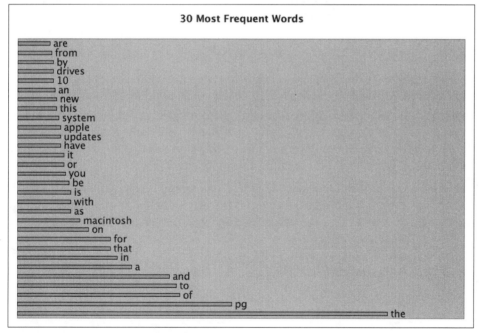

Figure 1-2. Excel chart generated with AppleScript code

Let's sum up the example. We start with AppleScript. The script puts up a dialog where we choose a file (because that's something AppleScript is good at). The script takes the pathname of that file and calls the Ruby script. The Ruby script makes a histogram of word usage in the file (because that's something Ruby is good at). The

Ruby script then constructs and calls some AppleScript code to store the first 30 rows of the histogram in Excel (because storing and dealing with this kind of data is something Excel is good at). The Ruby script ends, and it's now back to Apple-Script; here, we tell Excel to graph the data (because that's something else Excel is good at).

There are many other ways to solve the given problem, but the virtue of this approach is that it was easy to assemble using the tools, knowledge, and resources I had on hand. Ruby and Excel and AppleScript were all right there waiting to be used, so I used them. Furthermore the pieces of the problem were solved one at a time, in the order shown, without knowing precisely what else I might want to do. Apple-Script thus acts as a kind of flexible glue, allowing me to assemble code modules into a workflow that performs some larger task.

An interesting variation on the theme of combining specialities arises when one of the specialized applications isn't on your computer. This is possible because Apple-Script can send messages to remote applications. Details on the different ways this can be done appear later in this book (Chapter 21). For this example, we'll have the remote application be a web service. AppleScript supplies a built-in way to talk to any web service that implements an XML-RPC or SOAP interface.

 A good clearinghouse for finding SOAP-enabled web services is *http://www.xmethods.net*.

Sometimes, in sending an email message, I want to append a random quotation to the end of the message instead of my normal signature. I happen not to have a random quotation generator on my computer—and I don't need one, because there are several on the web. I'll just choose one of them for this example.

The script starts by creating a new outgoing email message, using Mailsmith. Then it goes out on the Web and uses SOAP to fetch today's random quote from a random quotation web service; it formats the results and inserts them into the email message.

```
tell application "Mailsmith"
    set m to make new message window
    set use signature of m to false
end tell
set sig to ""
try
    tell application ¬
    "http://www.swanandmokashi.com/HomePage/WebServices/QuoteOfTheDay.asmx"
        set returnValue to call soap ¬
            {method name: ¬
                "GetQuote", ¬
            method namespace uri: ¬
                "http://www.swanandmokashi.com", ¬
            SOAPAction: ¬
                "http://www.swanandmokashi.com/GetQuote"}
```

```
        end tell
        set sig to return & "------------------------------------"
        set sig to sig & return & quoteoftheday of returnValue
        set sig to sig & return & "         -- "
        set sig to sig & author of returnValue & return
    end try
    tell application "Mailsmith"
        copy sig to after text of m
        select insertion point before character 1 of m
    end tell
```

In this example, the call soap command takes a record of three items. That's the material in curly braces; an AppleScript record is a list of paired names and values (Chapter 13). To learn what the values of those items needed to be, I consulted the web service's documentation (see *http://www.swanandmokashi.com/HomePage/ WebServices/QuoteOfTheDay.asmx?op=GetQuote*). The result arrives into the variable returnValue as another record, consisting of two items called quoteoftheday and author. The script extracts the two items, formats them into a nice string, and appends them to the email message back in Mailsmith. If anything goes wrong, it goes wrong inside a try block, so there's no harm done: an empty string is appended to the message. The selection point is then set to the start of the message, ready for me to type. Figure 1-3 shows the result of running the script.

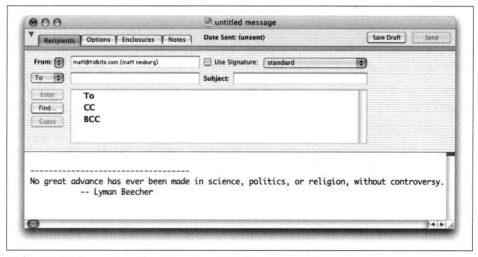

Figure 1-3. Mail message with a quotation supplied by a web service

For another example of combining specialties, see the section "Internally Scriptable Application" in Chapter 2. In the example there, the tasks of database and mail client are assigned to two different applications, FileMaker Pro and Mailsmith, so that each program can do what it does best; the two applications are able to share data, so that for purposes of a particular task—sending an email message to someone in the database—they cooperate and act as one.

CHAPTER 2

Places to Use AppleScript

In the previous chapter you learned about the kinds of thing you can do with Apple-Script. But *where* can you do these things? You're going to write and run some AppleScript code; where are you going to write it, and where are you going to run it? This chapter answers these questions, by surveying the many areas of your computer where AppleScript is available to you.

We've seen that the main reason for using AppleScript is in order to drive a scriptable application. AppleScript does this by sending messages, which are actually Apple events, to the scriptable application. So the scriptable application is the receiver (or *target*) of these messages; AppleScript, and by extension the host environment where AppleScript code is being run, is the *sender*. So this chapter is about the various kinds of environment you might use as a sender.

As you will see in more detail in Chapter 4, there are three stages in the life of an AppleScript program:

1. The AppleScript code starts life as *text*.
2. Then that text is *compiled* into a different form, one that humans can't read but that AppleScript can execute. The compiled code can optionally be saved at this point, as a compiled *script file*.
3. Finally, the compiled code is *executed*, or *run*.

We are really concerned in this chapter only with the last stage—the kinds of place where compiled AppleScript code can be executed—though it happens that many such places can also compile AppleScript code, transforming it from raw text into executable form.

(In general I have had to make up some descriptive terms in order to taxonomize the kinds of sender described in this chapter, but I define those terms immediately, and I don't think this makes the taxonomy any less helpful. The example scripts in this chapter are for the most part deliberately simple and somewhat contrived; they are not intended to provide any serious illustration of the actual uses to which Apple-Script might be put. That, after all, was the task of the previous chapter.)

Script Editor

By *script editor* I don't mean just Apple's Script Editor application—though that is in fact an example of a script editor. I mean a dedicated application intended as a general environment for the user to create, edit, compile, develop, and run AppleScript code. Typically such a program will have the following features:

- A script can be edited within a convenient interface.
- There is a facility for displaying the dictionary of any scriptable application, so that the programmer can learn something about how to speak to that application.
- If a target application is recordable, user actions in that application can be recorded into a script.
- A script may be compiled.
- A compiled script is formatted ("pretty-printed") according to AppleScript's internal settings for fonts, syntax-coloring, and so forth.
- A compiled script can be run.
- When a script is run, if it yields a result, that result can be displayed.
- A script can be saved in any of the standard formats: as text, as a compiled script, or as an applet.
- A script can use any installed OSA language, not just AppleScript.

(Terms in that list that may be strange to you are explained in Chapter 4. That's where I'll formally introduce dictionaries, explain what it means for an application to be recordable, describe the standard AppleScript file formats, and talk about the OSA, or Open Scripting Architecture.)

Apple Computer provides a script-editing application of this kind, called (logically enough) Script Editor. It's free, and is part of the default installation of Mac OS X. It is located in */Applications/AppleScript*.

Figure 2-1 shows a very short script being edited in Script Editor. The script has been compiled using the Compile button, which appears at the center of the toolbar at the top of the window; thus the script is "pretty-printed" with syntax coloring. The script has also been run, using the Run button in the toolbar; the result is shown in the lower half of the window. The script asks the Finder for the names of all mounted volumes. Technically, the response is a list of strings; the curly braces indicate a list, and the double quotes indicate strings (Chapter 13).

The lower pane of the window consists of three tabs; the second tab, the Result tab, is showing in Figure 2-1. Another tab, Event Log, keeps a record of all outgoing

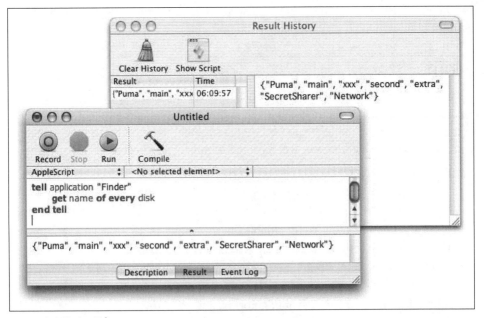

Figure 2-1. Script Editor

commands and incoming replies—that is, of all lines of AppleScript that equate to Apple events sent to other applications, and the replies returned by those applications. The Event Log is operative only if the Event Log tab is selected when a script is run; but another window (not shown), the Event Log History window, can be set to operate even when not open. The first tab, Description, is a place where the user can enter a comment to be stored with the script. At the top of the window is a popup menu where the user can choose the installed OSA language to be used for compiling and running the script, and another popup menu for navigating among handlers (subroutines) within the script. Also shown is the Result History window, which logs the result of every execution of every script. Both the Event Log History window and the Result History window are particularly useful while developing and testing a script.

The Script Editor offers some helpful shortcuts for entering commonly used text such as control structures (Chapter 12) and built-in commands. One is the contextual menu that appears when you Control-click in the window; it gives access to various utility scripts. The Script Editor is itself scriptable, and these utility scripts drive it to modify the text appearing in the script window. You can modify these scripts, and can add utility scripts of your own; they live in */Library/Scripts/Script Editor Scripts*. Another text-entry shortcut is the Script Assistant; when this feature is turned on, the Script Editor performs autocompletion as you type, and you can accept or choose among its offerings with the Edit → Complete menu item (default shortcut F5).

Figure 2-2 shows an application's dictionary as displayed by the Script Editor—in this case, the dictionary of the Finder, the application targeted by the example script in Figure 2-1. The window behaves as a kind of browser. The classes and events (the nouns and verbs constituting the application's vocabulary) are clumped into groups on the left; when a particular class or event is selected, the information for it is displayed on the right. Here, the information for the disk class is displayed. (Dictionaries, and how to interpret the information about them displayed in a window such as this, are the subject of Chapter 19.)

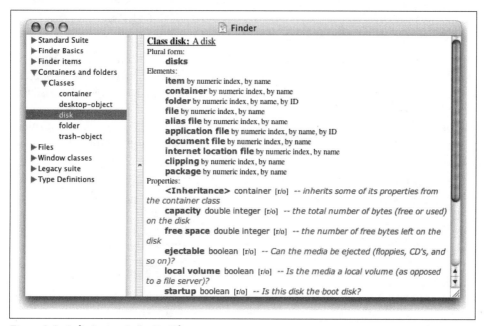

Figure 2-2. A dictionary in Script Editor

Another free script editing program is Smile. It provides an excellent working environment, including splendid text-editing and navigation facilities, full scriptability, and some remarkable features to help you in developing scripts, including:

- Execution of selected text
- Automatic persistence of variables and readily accessible global context
- Translation to raw four-letter codes
- Display of AppleScript's own dictionary
- Terminology-searching through all relevant dictionaries with a single command
- Integrated facilities for constructing and saving custom dialogs and for graphics display

(Four-letter codes, and AppleScript's dictionary, are discussed in Chapter 19.)

A commercial alternative is Late Night Software's Script Debugger. Its primary advantage, as the name suggests, is that it provides a full-fledged AppleScript debugger, making it a genuine development environment. It is completely scriptable, provides many shortcuts for entering and navigating code, and includes:

- A debugging environment with breakpoints, stepping, tracing, watchpoints, expression watching, live display and editing of variables, and browser windows for display of complex variable values

- Sophisticated dictionary display, with incorporation of inherited attributes, hierarchical class charts, and display of actual attributes of running applications

- An event log with display of Apple events

Figure 2-3 shows a script that has been edited, compiled, and run in Script Debugger (Version 3.0.6). At the top of the first window is a pane displaying the properties associated with this script. (Properties are a kind of global variable, discussed in Chapters 7 and 9.) The second window displays the result of the script, in a hierarchical format. The first line states explicitly the type of the result—it's a list. The values of the list's items are displayed on subsequent lines, with icons indicating their types.

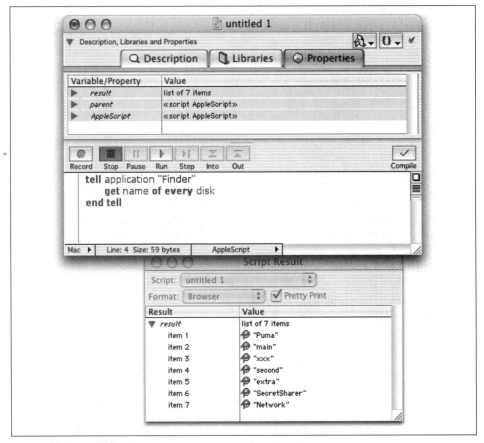

Figure 2-3. Script Debugger

Figure 2-4 shows the Finder's dictionary as shown in Script Debugger, in one of three available views. In this particular view, the hierarchy of actual current Finder objects is presented. Thus one can see directly that among the Finder's top-level elements are its disk objects. The listing for one disk object has been opened to show its attributes (Chapter 10); among these one can see its various elements and their counts, such as the fact that it has three folder objects, and its various properties, such as its name property, whose value is shown. In contrast to Figure 2-2, which is an abstract display of facts about Finder disk objects in general, Figure 2-4 is a concrete display of the Finder's actual disk objects at this moment; this a very powerful and informative way to explore the repertory of things one can say to a scriptable application.

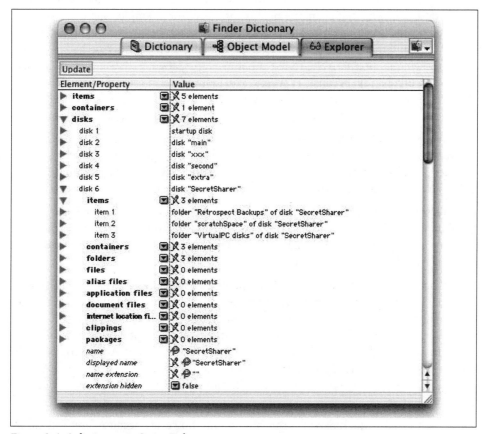

Figure 2-4. A dictionary in Script Debugger

You don't have to feel confined to one particular script editor; compiled scripts are a standard format, so any script editor can read the files of any other. (Though as of this writing this is a bit less true than it used to be, because Apple has just introduced two new script formats, the script bundle and the application bundle, and the other editors have not yet caught up.) So if you find yourself wishing to switch among script editors, it's more or less effortless to do so. Some script editor program will probably be the main way you'll work with AppleScript.

Scripting Environment

The term *scripting environment* is meant to denote a small class of applications dedicated primarily to letting the user edit and run scripts in some language other than AppleScript, while secondarily providing a way to enter and run AppleScript code.

In the pre–Mac OS X world, a good example of such a program was HyperCard. HyperCard's main purpose was to allow the user to construct an interface and to associate scripts with the elements of this interface; for example, one could write a script to be run when a button was clicked. These scripts were usually in Hyper-Card's own internal scripting language, HyperTalk; but each script had a popup menu allowing it, alternatively, to use other available languages such as AppleScript. This was very handy because it meant you could use HyperTalk for the things HyperTalk was good at (such as driving the HyperCard interface) and AppleScript for the things AppleScript was good at (such as driving other scriptable applications).

A similar program is UserLand Frontier. Frontier also has a much less expensive "little brother," Radio UserLand; for our purposes the two programs are interchangeable. Frontier is meant to store and run scripts in UserLand's own scripting language, User-Talk; but a Frontier script can use other available languages, including AppleScript.

(The reason HyperCard and Frontier can "see" and incorporate AppleScript is that these are OSA-savvy applications: they can see and incorporate any OSA language, and AppleScript is an OSA language. "The Open Scripting Architecture" in Chapter 4 explains what this means.)

Figure 2-5 shows some AppleScript code being run in Radio UserLand. The Apple-Script code is in the middle window, the one whose language popup (at the bottom of the window) is set to AppleScript. You should ignore the triangles at the left of each line, which are a feature of Frontier's outline-based script editing environment. In Figure 2-5, the UserTalk code in the bottom window calls the AppleScript code in the middle window and displays the result in the top window. The purpose of this arrangement is to show you how UserTalk and AppleScript can interact transparently in Frontier.

There isn't usually much need for this interaction, however, because UserTalk all by itself can drive scriptable applications through Apple events, just as AppleScript can. To prove this, Figure 2-6 demonstrates UserTalk obtaining the same information from the Finder (the name of every mounted volume) without any AppleScript at all. The UserTalk code generates and sends to the Finder the very same Apple event that AppleScript would generate and send; the Finder's experience is identical regardless of whether the user employs AppleScript or UserTalk to communicate with it.

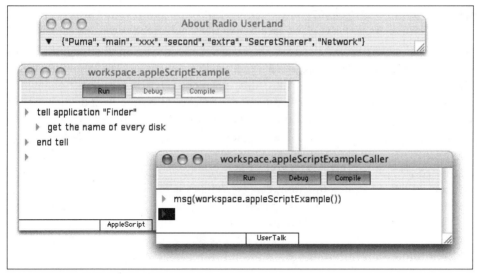

Figure 2-5. Radio UserLand

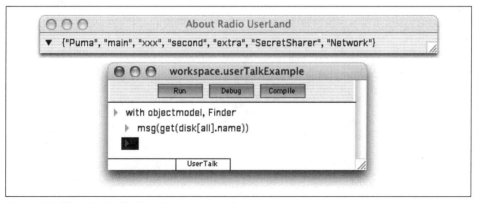

Figure 2-6. How Radio UserLand expresses Apple events natively

Internally Scriptable Application

A number of applications are *internally scriptable*. By this I mean that the application contains its own internal mechanism, possibly a proprietary language, for automating just that application. When such an application is developed for Mac OS, it sometimes happens that its developers would like to provide it with a means of communicating with other applications. That means Apple events, and AppleScript is a convenient way to send Apple events (convenient both for the developers and for the end user), so a typical approach is to let the internal scripting language treat text as AppleScript code. Such applications are not very good places to develop your Apple-Script code, since you usually have no way to edit and test that code coherently inside the application. A typical approach is to develop the code in a dedicated script editing environment such as the Script Editor, and then copy it into the other application.

An example is Microsoft Word. Word comes with its own internal scripting language, Visual Basic for Applications (VBA), whose purpose is to automate Word itself. The Mac OS version of VBA also includes the MacScript function, which accepts a string and compiles and runs it as AppleScript on the fly. For more about using VBA in Word, see Steven Roman's *Writing Word Macros* (O'Reilly).

Constructing your AppleScript code in VBA is rather a trying experience, because you have to pass through VBA's rules about generating strings. Since AppleScript is a line-based language, line breaks in the code must be expressed explicitly; the way to do this in VBA is to call a function, Chr(13). The calls to this function must be concatenated with the rest of your string to form the AppleScript code. Quotation marks are also a cause of concern and possible confusion.

Figure 2-7 shows a Word document and the Macro dialog; we are about to run the CallASExample macro. Figure 2-8 shows the result of running this macro. The macro has placed the names of my disks at the insertion point. The way Word found out the names of the disks was by constructing and running some AppleScript code.

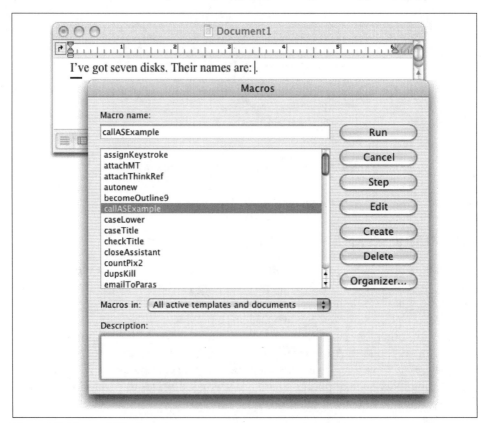

Figure 2-7. Microsoft Word

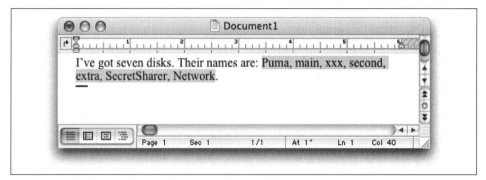

Figure 2-8. Word inserts the result of an AppleScript call

Here's the VBA code of the CallASExample macro:

```
Sub callASExample( )
    s = "tell application ""Finder""" + Chr(13)
    s = s + "get the name of every disk" + Chr(13)
    s = s + "end tell"
    Selection.InsertAfter Text:=MacScript(s)
End Sub
```

The AppleScript code is assembled into the string variable s; as promised, this is a fairly hideous operation. The code is concatenated from literals representing each line, separated by the Return characters generated by calling Chr(13). In order to express the double-quoted literal "Finder" inside a VBA string literal, the double quotes must themselves be doubled, since this is how VBA "escapes" a quote character. Once the script text is assembled, it is handed to the MacScript function. This returns a string, which is yet another problem: AppleScript is capable of returning a variety of datatypes, but your script must limit itself to a result that can be expressed as a string, possibly coercing or reformatting it somehow before returning it. Finally, the VBA macro inserts that string result into the document.

A program that behaves similarly is the database application FileMaker Pro. It has internal scripting facilities, and one of the things its internal scripting language can do is take some text and execute it as AppleScript. This text can be static; alternatively, it can be the contents of a field, and since field values in FileMaker can be "calculated," the text can be dynamically constructed. Here's an example that illustrates both approaches.

Figure 2-9 shows two programs, FileMaker Pro and Mailsmith. The FileMaker window (in front) shows a database of contacts. In this window is a "To" button; pressing this has just caused Mailsmith to create a new email message (in back) using the email address from the current FileMaker record. So in this scenario FileMaker Pro is the sender and Mailsmith is the target; FileMaker tells Mailsmith to create a new email message, using the value of a field in the current record as the addressee of this new message. The idea is that AppleScript lets the two programs work together, each doing what it does best: a database program is good for storing and finding information, whereas a mail client is good for constructing and sending mail messages (see "Combining Specialties" in Chapter 1).

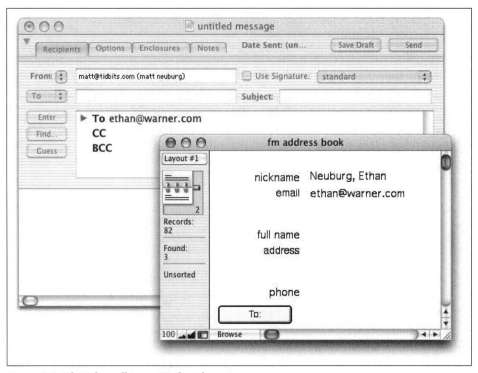

Figure 2-9. FileMaker talking to Mailsmith

The FileMaker script that's triggered by pressing the "To" button consists of two text snippets executed as AppleScript. Figure 2-10 shows the first snippet, which is static and has simply been typed directly into a dialog box.

Figure 2-11 shows how the second snippet is generated dynamically through a calculated field. Some literal text is combined with the value of the expansion field to construct the string that will be executed as AppleScript:

```
"tell application ""Mailsmith"" to tell message window 1
to make new to_recipient at end with properties
{address:""" & expansion & """}"
```

The challenges here are similar to those of the Microsoft Word example just preceding. In the AppleScript code, quotation marks must surround the string value drawn from the expansion field; to indicate these in a string literal, they have to be "escaped" by doubling them, and this happens to occur at the boundaries of two literals, necessitating the bizarre triple-double-quotes toward the end of the text.

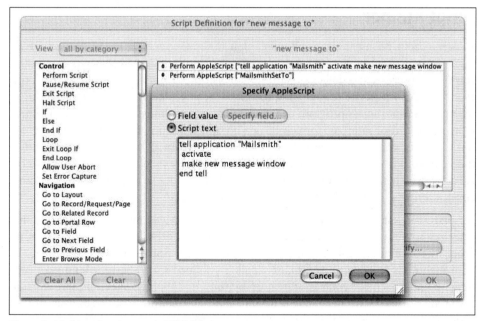

Figure 2-10. Literal script text in FileMaker

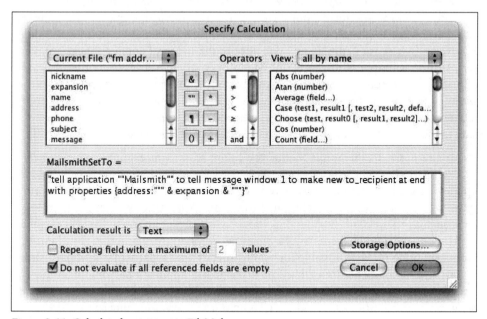

Figure 2-11. Calculated script text in FileMaker

Script Runner

By *script runner* I mean an application that accepts compiled script files and runs them. It typically has no facilities for editing or compiling scripts; you create and compile the scripts in a dedicated editor such as the Script Editor, and save the script as a compiled script file. Usually the file must then be placed in a particular location where the script runner program can find it. The script runner program typically provides some sort of interface for selecting a compiled script; when you select one, the script runner causes it to be executed. Since the script is compiled beforehand, a time-consuming step (compilation) is skipped, and execution thus typically proceeds considerably faster in a script runner than it does in an internally scriptable application where the code must be compiled on the fly.

An extreme example of a script runner is the Script Menu provided by Apple. It's extreme because a script runner is all it is; it has no other purpose, and it has no other interface apart from the menu of scripts. If you don't see the Script Menu in your menu bar (it appears as a black scrolled s-shaped icon), Script Menu isn't running on your machine; you can start it up by running */Applications/AppleScript/Install Script Menu*. The menu items in the Script Menu represent the folders and script files inside */Library/Scripts* and *~/Library/Scripts*; you can toggle the visibility of the menu items representing */Library/Scripts* with the Show/Hide Library Scripts menu item. To add an item to the menu, put a compiled script file inside one of these directories. The menu is global, but if you create a folder *~/Library/Scripts/Applications/AppName* (where for "AppName" you supply the name of some application), then scripts in it will appear in the Script Menu only when AppName is the frontmost application.* To run a script, choose the corresponding menu item from the menu. Many of the scripts in the Script Menu are worth studying as examples of scripting techniques. (Some of them are shell scripts or Perl scripts; in general these are outside the scope of this book, but it's nice that the Script Menu can run them as well.)

As an alternative to the Script Menu, you might want to use some sort of *launcher*. This term covers various kinds of utility that can be used to open things (folders, applications, files); such a utility may have other powers as well, but the important thing here is that it can run a compiled script file. A launcher will give you an interface, such as a keyboard shortcut or a "dock" with clickable icons, that you can associate with an action; these would then be ways to run a script. Furthermore, launchers often make it possible for you to specify that a particular keyboard shortcut or dock should be active only in a particular application. Some examples of launchers are iKey (*http://www.scriptsoftware.com/ikey/*), Keyboard Maestro (*http://www.keyboardmaestro.com*), and DragThing (*http://www.dragthing.com*).

---

* A similar utility is FastScripts: *http://www.red-sweater.com/RedSweater/FSFeatures.html*. An alternative that uses contextual menus is *http://ranchero.com/bigcat/*.

There are also various applications that are script runners in a secondary sense; they are intended for something else entirely, but they also act as script runners. Typically the point is to give you a convenient way to customize the application itself. The Script Editor is an example. Recall that the Script Editor provides a contextual menu that lists the contents of the */Library/Scripts/Script Editor Scripts* folder. These contents are compiled scripts, and choosing an item from the contextual menu executes the corresponding script. Script Editor is thus a script runner. Of course the compiled scripts that appear in the Script Editor's contextual menu can do anything you like, but the primary purpose of this menu is as a repository for scripts that target Script Editor itself, like the ones that are already there.

Another example is BBEdit, which has a Scripts menu in the menu bar. Again, whatever compiled scripts you place in a particular location (in this case it's the *Scripts* folder in the *BBEdit Support* folder) will appear as menu items in this menu and can be run by choosing the corresponding menu item. Furthermore, you can assign keyboard shortcuts to these menu items, which makes it even more convenient to access these scripts (as in a launcher). BBEdit is quite heavily scriptable, so this is a very convenient way to store and run scripted actions that customize BBEdit.

(This convention, where a scriptable application has a Scripts menu so you can easily access scripts that drive that application, is an excellent one, and in my view is not sufficiently widespread. Some other applications that work this way are Script Debugger, Smile, Microsoft Entourage, Mailsmith, Tex-Edit Plus, and various Adobe applications.)

BBEdit can also run scripts in other ways. Two more folders, *Startup Items* and *Shutdown Items*, are repositories for scripts that BBEdit will run automatically when you launch it and when you quit it. And scripts that you put in the *Menu Scripts* folder will be run before and after you choose from any of BBEdit's built-in menus. Thus BBEdit, by functioning as a script runner, lays itself open to a considerable amount of automation and customization by the user.

It isn't uncommon, when applications work this way, for the developers to "seed" the Scripts menu by including some sample scripts in it by default. These can be worth studying as examples of how to drive the application with AppleScript. Some applications go even further, and actually incorporate scripts as normal menu items—that is to say, the application is scriptable and uses its own scriptability to implement some of the functionality present by default in the menu bar. Mail's Import Mailboxes menu item is said to work this way, and in Canto Cumulus more than a dozen standard menu commands are actually scripts.

Automatic Location

An *automatic location* can be thought of as a highly specialized type of script runner: it's a place where you can put a compiled script to have it run automatically when certain events take place.

On Mac OS X, if you want a script to run automatically when you start up, you could save it as an applet and list it in the Startup Items tab of the Accounts pane, in System Preferences. A compiled script wouldn't do here, though; it would be opened, not executed, because Startup Items is not a script runner.

A primary example of an automatic location on Mac OS X is the Finder, where you can associate scripts with particular folders by means of *folder actions*. Folder actions are a mechanism whereby scripts run if certain things happen, in the Finder, to the folder to which they are attached: that folder's window is opened, closed, or moved, or something is put into or removed from that folder. Naturally you don't have to respond when all of those things happen; your script will contain a specific handler for each type of action you want to respond to. (See *http://www.apple.com/applescript/folder_actions/*.)

Folder actions are described at length in Chapter 24, but here's a quick explanation of how to set one up. Create *~/Library/Scripts/Folder Action Scripts* if it doesn't exist already. Create a script and save it as a compiled script file in that folder. Now go to a folder in the Finder and in its contextual menu choose Enable Folder Actions and then Attach a Folder Action, and in the Open dialog select your script. You can also manage the relationships between folders and scripts with the Folder Actions Setup application, which is in */Applications/AppleScript*.

In this example, we'll make a folder automatically decode any *.hqx* files as they are put into it. Here's the script:

```
on adding folder items to ff after receiving L
    tell application "Finder"
        repeat with f in L
            set n to the name of f
            if n ends with ".hqx" then
                tell application "StuffIt Expander" to expand f
            end if
        end repeat
    end tell
    tell application "System Events"
        if process "StuffIt Expander" exists then
            tell application "StuffIt Expander" to quit
        end if
    end tell
end adding folder items to
```

The handler, on adding folder items to, is automatically called when files are put into the folder to which this script is attached. The script runs when *any* file is put into that folder, but it has no effect except upon *.hqx* files. We examine the name of each file that is being added; if it ends in *.hqx*, we call StuffIt Expander to decode it. This leaves StuffIt Expander running, so at the end we look to see if StuffIt Expander is running, and if it is, we quit it. The folder thus functions as a kind of magic decoder drop box for *.hqx* files.

Application

By *application* I mean here an application you write yourself. There are various ways to incorporate use of AppleScript into an application, and various reasons why you might do so.

Let's start with an applet. An *applet* is just a compiled script saved with a tiny application framework wrapped around it; you can make one in any script editor application. I can think of three main reasons for saving a script as an applet:

- You want to be able to run the script from the Finder, by double-clicking it.
- You want your script to process files and folders when you drop their icons onto the script's icon; an applet that does is this called a *droplet*.
- You want to be able to run the script from some other environment that can launch things but isn't a script runner.

We have already seen that if you want a script to be a Startup Item, so that it runs automatically at startup, it has to be an applet. As another example, consider the toolbar and sidebar at the top and left side of a Finder window. You can put any item you like in these places; clicking an item opens it, in the sense of launching it, as if from the Finder. So items in the toolbar or sidebar cannot be mere compiled scripts if you want to run them; they must be applets (or droplets—dropping a file or folder onto a toolbar or sidebar droplet works just fine). Apple supplies a number of examples at *http://www.apple.com/applescript/toolbar/*.

Moving up the ladder of complexity and sophistication, we arrive at another way you can create an application using AppleScript—with AppleScript Studio. AppleScript Studio itself isn't exactly an application; it's an aspect of two applications, Xcode (formerly known as Project Builder) and Interface Builder. AppleScript Studio allows you to use AppleScript as the underlying programming language inside what is effectively a Cocoa application, instead of the standard language, Objective-C. Thus you can combine all the power of Mac OS X–native windows and interface widgets with your knowledge of AppleScript to write a genuine application. Even more amazing, it's free. AppleScript Studio doesn't give you AppleScript access to everything that Cocoa can do, not by a long chalk; but if you have some AppleScript code and you want to wrap an interface around it, AppleScript Studio can be an easy and rapid way to do so. The result will look and act like an ordinary Cocoa application; it might not even be possible for users to tell that you wrote it with AppleScript.

 You must install the Developer Tools in order to get these applications. Always use the latest version; to obtain it, sign up for ADC membership (it's free at the lowest level; see *http://connect.apple.com*) and download it from Apple.

If you've never seen AppleScript Studio you might be wondering what I'm talking about, so here's a simple example of what it's like. (There's another example in Chapter 24.)

We'll write an application that displays the names of your hard disks as the rows of a Table View widget. You start up Xcode and make a new project, designating it an AppleScript Application, and when the project window appears, find the *MainMenu.nib* listing and double-click it. You are now in Interface Builder, where you design your interface. Figure 2-12 shows me dragging a Table View into the main window; this is where the names of the disks will be displayed.

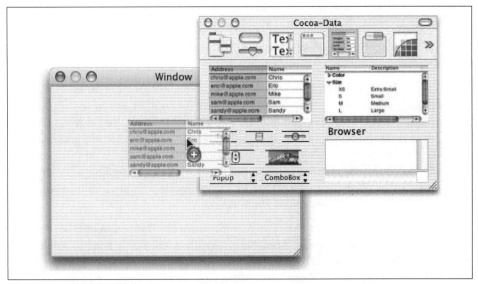

Figure 2-12. Making an interface in AppleScript Studio

After resizing the Table View and the window, I set the Table View to have just one column, and give the column a heading "Your Disks". Then I name the column disks; to do so, I select the column, press ⌘-7 to bring up the AppleScript pane of the Info palette, and type "disks" as the column's name. Now it's just a question of seeing that some code runs to populate the table. There are many places to put this code; since I'm already looking at the column's AppleScript info, I decide to put it in the column's awake from nib handler, which runs as the window comes into existence. Figure 2-13 shows me ticking the checkboxes that specify this handler.

I then press the Edit Script button at the bottom of the Info palette, and am thrown back into Xcode, where my script window opens with the awake from nib handler already created, waiting for me to add my code to it. Here it is:

```
on awake from nib theObject
    tell application "Finder" to set L to (name of every disk)
    set ds to make new data source at end of data sources
    set tv to table view 1 of scroll view 1 of window 1
```

Figure 2-13. Creating a handler in AppleScript Studio

```
    set col to make new data column at end of data columns of ds ¬
        with properties {name:"disks"}
    repeat with aName in L
        set aRow to make new data row at end of data rows of ds
        set contents of data cell "disks" of aRow to aName
    end repeat
    set data source of tv to ds
end awake from nib
```

The first line of this script gathers the information from the Finder; the rest of the script is devoted to dealing with the interface. The script creates a kind of object called a datasource, populates it with the disk names gathered from the Finder, and attaches it to the Table View. The Table View automatically displays the contents of its data source. I can now build and run my application. Figure 2-14 shows what the application's window looks like when the application starts up; as expected, the names of my hard disks are displayed.

Another way you might find yourself incorporating AppleScript into an application you write yourself is when you're writing the application in some other programming language but want to avail yourself secondarily of AppleScript's special abilities. Typically this is because you need your application to function as a sender and have it drive some other application as a target.

In REALbasic the way you incorporate AppleScript is to write and compile your AppleScript code elsewhere, and then save it as a compiled script and import this compiled script into your REALbasic project. (As of this writing, REALbasic can't read compiled script files saved by the Script Editor; until this is fixed, you need to save the compiled script in the older format, with the script data in the resource fork. Script Debugger can save the file this way.) Your REALbasic code can then call the compiled script. The script must have a run handler if you want to pass any parameters. Every parameter must be a string or an integer, and the result can only be a string.

Figure 2-14. A Cocoa application written with AppleScript Studio

To illustrate, we'll write the REALbasic equivalent of the AppleScript Studio application developed a moment ago. First we create our AppleScript code and save it as a compiled script:

```
on run {}
    tell application "Finder"
        name of every disk
    end tell
end run
```

We drag the compiled script file into the REALbasic project window; now we can call the script using the name under which we saved it, which happens to be *finderTest*. Now, in REALbasic, we drag a ListBox into the main window and put this REALbasic code into its Open event handler:

```
Sub Open( )
  dim L as string
  dim i,u as integer
  L = finderTest( )
  me.columnAlignment(0) = 2
  u = countFields(L,", ")
  for i = 1 to u
    me.addRow nthField(L,", ",i)
  next
End Sub
```

That handler is called automatically as the application starts up and the window opens. The call to finderTest( ) runs our AppleScript code; what's returned is like what was returned in the Microsoft Word example earlier, a string consisting of the disk names separated by a comma and a space. We parse that string to populate the

ListBox. When we compile and build the application, the *finderTest* file is incorporated into it and no one ever knows we used AppleScript. Figure 2-15 shows the application running.

Figure 2-15. A REALbasic application using AppleScript

In Cocoa/Objective-C you have a choice of techniques for incorporating AppleScript through the NSAppleScript class. You can start with a string and compile and execute it, or you can start with a compiled script and execute that.

I'll illustrate both techniques. Our application's interface looks just like the Apple-Script Studio and REALbasic examples: it's a one-column NSTableView in a window. Our controller class, instantiated in the nib, is the NSTableView's datasource. It has one instance variable, an NSArray called diskList. Here's the Objective-C code for the controller class:

```
-(int)numberOfRowsInTableView:(NSTableView*)tv {
    if (!diskList) return 0;
    return [diskList count];
}

-(id)tableView:(NSTableView*)tv
    objectValueForTableColumn:(NSTableColumn*)c row:(int)r {
    return [diskList objectAtIndex:r];
}

-(void)awakeFromNib {
    NSAppleScript* scpt;
    NSAppleEventDescriptor* result;
    NSDictionary* error;
    NSString* s;
    NSMutableArray* arr = [NSMutableArray array];
    s = @"tell application \"Finder\" to get name of every disk";
    scpt = [[NSAppleScript alloc] initWithSource: s];
```

```
                    result = [scpt executeAndReturnError: &error];
                    if ([result descriptorType] == 'utxt')
                        [arr addObject: [result stringValue]];
                    else if ([result descriptorType] == 'list') {
                        int i,u = [result numberOfItems];
                        for (i=1; i<=u; i++)
                            [arr addObject: [[result descriptorAtIndex: i] stringValue]];
                    }
                    diskList = [[NSArray arrayWithArray: arr] retain];
                }
```

The first two methods simply deal with the interface; they are the datasource routines that populate the NSTableView from the diskList array. The awakeFromNib method is where the action is. As the application starts up, our controller class will be instantiated and this awakeFromNib method will be called; its job is to populate the diskList array. We create our AppleScript code as a string, use this string to create a new NSAppleScript instance, and tell that instance to compile and execute the string. (At this point there should be some error checking, but I've optimistically omitted it.) The result is an NSAppleEventDescriptor, and now the question is what to do with it. To parse it properly, we should look to see what type it is: if it's just text (there was only one disk so the result is simply its name), we append that text to a local array; if it's a list, then we cycle through the items of that list, appending the text from each of those to our local array. The main trick here is to realize that list indexes in an Apple event are 1-based! Now we have an array of the names of the disks; we copy that array into diskList, and the datasource routines take care of displaying it in the NSTableView.

The other way to do this, probably faster to execute, would be to compile the Apple-Script code beforehand and incorporate the compiled script file into the project, rather as one does in REALbasic. Let's suppose the compiled script is called *askFinder.scpt*. (Now the problem is the other way around from the REALbasic example; if the script is to be saved with Script Debugger, you must be sure to specify that the script data should be in the data fork. The old-style compiled script using the resource fork won't work.) I'm sure you know how it goes:

```
    tell application "Finder"
        return name of every disk
    end tell
```

We add *askFinder.scpt* to our project, so it will be built into the application. The awakeFromNib code, after the declarations, now starts out a little differently, because we're initializing the NSAppleScript instance from a file, not an NSString:

```
    s = [[NSBundle mainBundle] pathForResource: @"askFinder" ofType: @"scpt"];
    NSURL* url = [NSURL fileURLWithPath: s];
    scpt = [[NSAppleScript alloc] initWithContentsOfURL: url error: &error];
```

The rest is as before. The built Cocoa application running looks absolutely identical to Figure 2-14.

Unix

By the term *Unix* I mean the command line and other shell-related environments such as Perl and Ruby scripts. Here the important word to know is osascript. This verb is your key to leaping the gulf between Unix and AppleScript. You should read the relevant manpages. (Further details are provided in Chapter 23.)

osascript can execute a compiled script file or can compile and execute a string. The option -e signals that it's a string, not a script file, and of course if you're going to type a literal string, this raises all the usual problems of escaped characters. In the Terminal you can usually bypass these problems by single-quoting the string.

The following little conversation in the Terminal illustrates the difference in the formatting of the output depending on whether you supply the -ss flag. I generally prefer this because it does a better job of showing you what sort of reply you've really got. The curly braces and the double quotes show clearly that it's a list of strings:

```
$ osascript -e 'tell app "Finder" to get name of every disk'
xxx, main, second, extra
$ osascript -ss -e 'tell app "Finder" to get name of every disk'
{"xxx", "main", "second", "extra"}
```

In a Perl script it's rather easy to tie oneself in knots escaping characters appropriately so as to construct the correct string and hand it off to osascript. The difficulties are even worse than in the Microsoft Word example earlier in this chapter, because two environments, Perl and the shell, are going to munge this string before it gets to AppleScript. This line of Perl shows what I mean:

```
$s = `osascript -e "tell app \\"Finder\\" to get name of every disk"`;
```

The Perl backtick operator hands its contents over to the shell for execution, but first there's a round of variable interpolation within Perl; during that round, the escaped backslashes are mutated into single backslashes, and these single backslashes correctly escape the double quotes around "Finder" in the string that the shell receives as the argument to osascript. (Obviously I could have single-quoted that string and avoided the backslashes, but that wouldn't have illustrated the problem so well.)

A more humane approach—and much more common because it allows you to construct multilined, legibly formatted AppleScript code easily—is to take advantage of your language's "here document" facility and do your variable interpolation there. You then hand the AppleScript code to the shell, single-quoted. By way of illustration, here's a rather silly Perl program intended to be run in the Terminal; it asks the user for the number of a disk and then fetches the name of that disk:

```
#!/usr/bin/perl
$s = <<"END_S";
    tell application "Finder"
        count disks
    end tell
END_S
```

```
chomp ($numDisks = `osascript -ss -e '$s'`);
print "You have $numDisks disks.\n",
    "Which one would you like to know the name of?\n",
    "Type a number between 1 and $numDisks: ";
while (<>) {
    chomp;
    last if $_ < 1 || $_ > $numDisks;
    $ss = <<"END_SS";
        tell application "Finder"
            get name of disk $_
        end tell
END_SS
    print `osascript -ss -e '$ss'`,
        "Type a number between 1 and $numDisks: ";
}
```

Observe that the result of osascript has an extra return character appended to it, which has to be chomped if that isn't what we wanted. Here's the game in action, played in the Terminal:

```
$ ./disker.pl
You have 7 disks.
Which one would you like to know the name of?
Type a number between 1 and 7: 3
"xxx"
Type a number between 1 and 7: 4
"second"
Type a number between 1 and 7: bye
```

Communication in the reverse direction, calling the shell from AppleScript, is handled through the do shell script command, which is dealt with in Chapter 23.

CHAPTER 3

The AppleScript Experience

This chapter illustrates informally the process of developing AppleScript code. The idea is to help the beginner gain a sense of what it's like to work with AppleScript, as well as to present some typical stages in the development of an AppleScript-based solution. My approach is to demonstrate by example, letting you look over my shoulder as I tackle a genuine problem in my real life. This chapter doesn't actually teach any AppleScript; that comes later. But the procedures and thought processes exemplified here are quite typical of my own approach to writing AppleScript code, and probably that of many other experienced users as well; as such, the neophyte may benefit by witnessing them. Besides, if you've never programmed with Apple-Script before, you're probably curious about what you're getting yourself into.

Think of this chapter, then, as a nonprogrammer's introduction to the art of Apple-Script development. It's the art that's important here. The particular problem I'll solve in this chapter will probably have no relevance whatever to your own life. But the way I approach the problem, the things I do and experience as I work on it, contain useful lessons. At the end of the chapter we'll extract some general principles on how to approach a task with AppleScript.

The Problem

I have just completed, working in Adobe FrameMaker, the manuscript for a book about AppleScript. This manuscript is now to be submitted to my publisher. My publisher can take submissions in FrameMaker, which is what the production office uses in-house; and there is a checklist enumerating certain details of the form the manuscript should take. Looking over this checklist, I find an entry from the illustration department informing me that I'm supposed to follow certain rules about the naming of the files that contain the illustrations, and that I'm to submit a list of illustrations providing the number, name, and caption of each figure. Table 3-1 presents the example the illustration department provides.

Table 3-1. How the O'Reilly illustration department wants figure files named

Fig. No.	Filename	Caption (or description)
1-1	*wfi_0101.eps*	Overview of the Windows NT operating system environment.
1-2	*wfi_0102.eps*	Name space presented by the Object Manager.
1-3	*wfi_0103.eps*	Filter drivers in the driver hierarchy.
2-1	*wfi_0201.eps*	Local File System.
2-2	*wfi_0202.eps*	Hierarchical name space for directories and files.

As the example shows, the illustration department would like each illustration file named according to its place in the book. Each name starts with some letters identifying the book, followed by an underscore. Then there are two digits signifying the number of the chapter in which the figure appears. Then there are two more digits signifying the relative position of the figure within the chapter. Finally, there's the suffix indicating what kind of file it is. The illustration department would also like me to attach a list that looks like the table, associating figure numbers, filenames, and captions.

Naturally, as I've been writing the book, I haven't done any of that. It wouldn't have made sense, because I didn't know, as I wrote the book, exactly how many chapters there would be and what order they would be in, and exactly what illustrations there would be and what order *they* would be in. I've been cutting and pasting and rearranging right up until the last moment. My illustration files simply have whatever names I gave them at the time of creation; these names are generally pretty meaningless, and in the Finder they appear in alphabetical order, which is not at all the order in which they appear in the book. For example, here are the names of the illustration files for Chapter 2, as they appear in the Finder:

> *fileMaker1.eps*
> *fileMaker2.eps*
> *fileMaker3.eps*
> *ib.eps*
> *ib2.eps*
> *ib3.eps*
> *radio.eps*
> *radio2.eps*
> *RB.eps*
> *scriptDebugger.eps*
> *scriptDebuggerDict.eps*
> *scriptEditor3.eps*
> *scriptEditorDict.eps*
> *word3.eps*
> *word4.eps*

Now, however, the last moment has arrived. So it's time for me to grapple with the illustration department's requirements. The problem, therefore, is to rename these files in accordance with the chapter in which they appear and the order in which they appear within it. Clearly I'm going to have to work in two places at once. In FrameMaker, I need to look at each illustration in order, and see what file on disk it corresponds to. In the Finder, I need to change the name of that file. Then, back in FrameMaker, I need to change the reference for each illustration, so that it points to the correct file under its new name.

This promises to be a massively painful, tedious, and error-prone task—not something I'm looking forward to. Then I get an idea. Adobe FrameMaker is scriptable; in fact, it's extraordinarily scriptable. And so is the Finder. Perhaps this task can be automated using AppleScript.

A Day in the Life

Although I know that FrameMaker is scriptable, I have no idea how to script it. I haven't the slightest notion how to talk to FrameMaker, using AppleScript, about the illustrations in my manuscript. So the first thing I need to do is to try to find this out.

Caught in the Web of Words

My starting place, as with any new AppleScript programming task, is the *dictionary* of the application I'm going to be talking to. The dictionary is where an application lists the nouns and verbs I can use in speaking to it with AppleScript. To see FrameMaker's dictionary, I start up Apple's Script Editor, open the Library window, add FrameMaker to the library, and double-click its icon in the Library window. The dictionary opens, as shown in Figure 3-1.

This is a massive and, to the untrained eye (or even to the trained eye), largely incomprehensible document. What are we looking for here? Basically, I'd like to know whether FrameMaker gives me a way to talk about illustrations. To find out, I open each of the headings on the left, and under each heading I open the Classes subheading. A *class* is basically a noun, the name of a type of thing in the world of the application we're talking to. So what I'm trying to find out is what things FrameMaker knows about, so that I can guess which of those things is likely to be most useful for the problem I'm facing. In particular, I'd like to find a class that stands a chance of being what FrameMaker thinks my illustrations are.

The fact is, however, that I don't see anything that looks promising. The trouble is that I don't really understand what an illustration is, in FrameMaker's terms. I know that to add an illustration to a FrameMaker document, using the template my publisher has set up, I begin by inserting a *table*. And sure enough, there is a table class in the FrameMaker dictionary. But then, to make the reference to an illustration file,

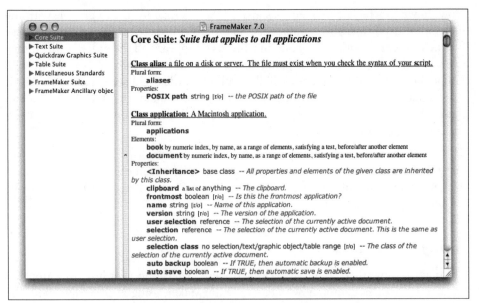

Figure 3-1. FrameMaker dictionary

I choose the Import File menu item, and it is not at all clear to me what kind of entity I generate as a result.

At this point an idea strikes me. Perhaps I should start with an existing illustration and see if I can find a way to ask FrameMaker, "What's this?" In fact, very near the start of FrameMaker's dictionary—and you can see this in Figure 3-1—there's a listing called selection. This suggests that perhaps if I select an illustration manually in FrameMaker and then use AppleScript to ask FrameMaker for its selection, I will learn what sort of thing an illustration is.

The word selection is listed as a property of the application class. A *property* is a feature of a class that you can refer to with the word of followed by an instance of the class. For example, if you have a reference to a paragraph and the paragraph class has a font property, you can refer to the "font of" this paragraph. However, the application class is special; it's the ultimate reference, and you don't need any "of" to talk about its properties when you're already talking to that application.

To talk to an application in AppleScript, you embed your code in a tell block, like this:

```
tell application "FrameMaker 7.0"
    ...
end tell
```

Whatever I say inside that block will be addressed to the named application, which in this case is FrameMaker. The way you ask for the value of a thing in AppleScript is with the verb get. So, in FrameMaker, I manually select an illustration; then, in Script Editor, I make a new script window and enter this code:

```
tell application "FrameMaker 7.0"
    get selection
end tell
```

I run that code, and the result comes back in the lower part of the script window, in the Result tab (I've reformatted the result here to emphasize its structure):

```
inset 1
    of anchored frame 43
        of document "extra:applescriptBook:ch02places.fm"
            of application "FrameMaker 7.0"
```

Wow! All of a sudden I'm getting someplace. I now have a chain of ofs showing the classes needed to refer to an illustration. So it turns out there's a class called inset, and that an inset belongs to another class called anchored frame. I certainly would never have thought of any of that on my own; even with the help of the dictionary I would never have realized that these were the classes I needed. Now that I know, of course, I see that these classes are indeed listed in the FrameMaker dictionary.

In particular, looking at the dictionary listing for the inset class, I see that it has a property inset file, which is described as follows:

```
inset file alias -- The file where the graphic originated
```

This could be just what I'm after—the link between an illustration in FrameMaker and the illustration file on disk. To find out, I'll ask for the inset file property of the same illustration I just selected a moment ago. So I make a new script and enter some new code and run it. Everything here is based on the reply I just received from AppleScript a moment ago; however, for convenience and clarity I've reversed the order of everything, and I'm using nested tell blocks instead of the word of. (Tell blocks and the word of are almost the same thing, except that they work in the opposite order.)

```
tell application "FrameMaker 7.0"
    tell document "extra:applescriptBook:ch02places.fm"
        tell anchored frame 43
            get inset file of inset 1
        end tell
    end tell
end tell
```

And here's the answer that comes back:

```
"extra:applescriptBook:figures:ch02:fileMaker1.eps"
```

Perfect! This is sensational. I've started with a way of referring to an illustration inside FrameMaker, and I've ended up with the pathname of the corresponding illustration file on disk—the very file I'm going to want to rename. Clearly I'm on the right track. I set this script aside and move on to the next part of the problem.

One for All and All for One

I now have some idea of how I'm going to refer to an illustration in FrameMaker and how I'm going to mediate between that reference and the pathname of the file on disk that the illustration comes from. So, having solved this piece of the puzzle for one illustration, I move on to the problem of generalizing. I'm going to want to do this for *every* illustration in the document. How, using AppleScript, am I going to talk about *every* illustration?

In the previous code, I specified a particular illustration by talking about "anchored frame 43." This sort of reference is not a property; it specifies an *element*. An element is very like a property, except that with a property there is just one of a thing; with an element, there can be many things of a certain class, and you have to say which one you want. So if the class that represents my illustrations is the anchored frame class, perhaps the way I'm going to solve the problem is by cycling through the anchored frame elements of my document—that is, by talking about "anchored frame 1," then "anchored frame 2," and so on. I'm a little surprised, however, by how the numbers are working here. I don't have 43 illustrations in this document, so why am I talking about "anchored frame 43"? However, I press on regardless; we'll cross that bridge when we come to it.

Let's see if I can list the inset files for *all* the illustrations in the document. To do so, I'll start by gathering up a list of all the anchored frame elements; if FrameMaker will let me, I should be able to do that using the word every. Let's try it:

```
tell application "FrameMaker 7.0"
    tell document "extra:applescriptBook:ch02places.fm"
        get every anchored frame
    end tell
end tell
```

Here's the response:

```
{anchored frame 1 of document "extra:applescriptBook:ch02places.fm"
    of application "FrameMaker 7.0",
 anchored frame 2 of document "extra:applescriptBook:ch02places.fm"
    of application "FrameMaker 7.0",
 anchored frame 3 of document "extra:applescriptBook:ch02places.fm"
    of application "FrameMaker 7.0",
 ...
}
```

I've left out most of it, but you get the idea. This seems to be working nicely so far. What I've gotten back is a list—that's what the curly braces around the response mean—and each item of this list, separated by commas, is a reference to one of the anchored frames in the document. So I should be able to run through this list and ask each anchored frame for the inset file property of its "inset 1" element, just as I did with anchored frame 43 earlier.

The way you run through a list in AppleScript is with a repeat block. I'll start by making a variable allFrames to store the list in—in AppleScript, you define the value of a variable using the verb set—and then I'll see if I can run through it:

```
tell application "FrameMaker 7.0"
    tell document "extra:applescriptBook:ch02places.fm"
        set allFrames to get every anchored frame
        repeat with oneFrame in allFrames
        end repeat
    end tell
end tell
```

That code runs, which is good. First I've made a variable allFrames to hold the list; then I've made another variable oneFrame to represent each item of that list as I run through it. But the code doesn't do anything, because I haven't said yet what I want to do with oneFrame; there is no code inside the repeat block.

What I'll do now is create yet another variable, allPaths, to hold my file paths. I'll start this variable as an empty list, which in AppleScript is symbolized by empty curly braces; every time I get a file path, I'll append it to the list, which you do in AppleScript with the verb set end of. So here's my code:

```
tell application "FrameMaker 7.0"
    tell document "extra:applescriptBook:ch02places.fm"
        set allPaths to {}
        set allFrames to get every anchored frame
        repeat with oneFrame in allFrames
            set end of allPaths to inset file of inset 1 of oneFrame
        end repeat
    end tell
end tell
```

I run this code, and...it doesn't work! I get an error message:

```
FrameMaker 7.0 got an error: Can't get inset file of inset 1 of anchored frame 1
    of document "extra:applescriptBook:ch02places.fm".
```

I don't really know what this error message means. That sort of thing happens a lot when you're working with AppleScript; stuff goes wrong, but you don't get a very helpful error message explaining why. However, I do see that we didn't get far in the list; right at the start, with anchored frame 1, we had a problem. Now, we know that this is going to work for anchored frame 43, so maybe the problem is related to the mystery of the numbering of the anchored frames. Maybe I've got two kinds of anchored frame: those that represent illustrations and those that don't, which apparently is the same thing as saying those that have an inset file and those that don't.

Since I believe this code should work when I get up to anchored frame 43, I'd like to ignore the problem with anchored frame 1 and any other anchored frames that may not be relevant here. There's an easy way to do this: I'll wrap the code in a try block. A try block is AppleScript's form of error-handling. I expect I'll still get an error, but now the code won't stop; it will shrug off the error and keep going. In this way I hope to cycle far enough through the list of anchored frames that I get to the ones where I don't get an error. Here's the code now:

```
tell application "FrameMaker 7.0"
    tell document "extra:applescriptBook:ch02places.fm"
        set allPaths to {}
        set allFrames to get every anchored frame
        repeat with oneFrame in allFrames
            try
                set end of allPaths to inset file of inset 1 of oneFrame
            end try
        end repeat
    end tell
end tell
```

I run that code, and there's no error. However, I'm not getting much of a result, either; here's what I get:

```
"extra:applescriptBook:figures:ch02:RB.eps"
```

That's the pathname of an illustration file, all right, but it's not what I was expecting; I wanted a list of *all* the pathnames of *all* the illustration files. Oh, wait, I see what I did wrong. I constructed the list, as the variable allPaths, but I forgot to ask for that list as the final result of the script. The result that you see in the Result pane of the Script Editor after you run a script is the value of the last command that was executed. So the way to display, as your result, the value of a variable you're interested in is to say the name of that variable as the last executable line of your code. Let's try again, like this:

```
tell application "FrameMaker 7.0"
    tell document "extra:applescriptBook:ch02places.fm"
        set allPaths to {}
        set allFrames to get every anchored frame
        repeat with oneFrame in allFrames
            try
                set end of allPaths to inset file of inset 1 of oneFrame
            end try
        end repeat
    end tell
end tell
allPaths
```

And here's the result:

```
{"", "", "", "", "", "",
"extra:applescriptBook:figures:ch02:fileMaker1.eps",
"extra:applescriptBook:figures:ch02:fileMaker2.eps",
"extra:applescriptBook:figures:ch02:fileMaker3.eps",
"extra:applescriptBook:figures:ch02:ib.eps",
"extra:applescriptBook:figures:ch02:ib2.eps",
"extra:applescriptBook:figures:ch02:scriptEditor3.eps",
"extra:applescriptBook:figures:ch02:scriptEditorDict.eps",
"extra:applescriptBook:figures:ch02:scriptDebugger.eps",
"extra:applescriptBook:figures:ch02:scriptDebuggerDict.eps",
"extra:applescriptBook:figures:ch02:radio.eps",
```

```
"extra:applescriptBook:figures:ch02:radio2.eps",
"extra:applescriptBook:figures:ch02:word3.eps",
"extra:applescriptBook:figures:ch02:word4.eps",
"extra:applescriptBook:figures:ch02:ib3.eps",
"extra:applescriptBook:figures:ch02:RB.eps"}
```

Well, that's pretty good. I have no idea what those first six items are, the ones that just show up as empty strings (symbolized by empty pairs of quotation marks). But in my final code I guess I could just ignore the empty strings, so that's not really a problem. And then we've got 15 pathnames, which is exactly right because the chapter has 15 illustrations.

But there's a problem. A really big problem. *The pathnames are in the wrong order.*

Remember, our entire purpose is to rename these files in accordance with the order in which they appear in the document. But this is *not* the order in which they appear in the document. I don't know what order it is, but I do know that the first illustration in the document is *scriptEditor3.eps*. This is a disaster. Our efforts so far have probably not been a total waste, but there's no denying that we're completely stuck. The "every anchored frame" strategy is a failure.

Seek and Ye Shall Find

At this point I'm exhausted and frustrated, so I do something else for a while and brainstorm subconsciously about the problem to see if I can come up with a new angle. Instead of gathering up all anchored frame references as FrameMaker understands them, we want to run forward through the document itself looking for anchored frames, just as a user would. Hmm…as a user would….

This gives me an idea. How would I, as a user, run through the illustrations in a FrameMaker document? I'd use the Find dialog. Perhaps FrameMaker lets me do the same thing with AppleScript. Yes, by golly; looking in the dictionary, I discover there's a find command. Here's the dictionary entry:

find: *Find text, objects, or properties in a Frame document.*
   find **text/text having paragraph tag/text having character tag/marker/**
      marker having type/marker containing text/variable/variable having name/
      anchored frame/table/table having tag/footnote/xref/xref having format/
      unresolved xref/autohyphen -- *The type of object or property to be found.*
   [with value **string**] -- *The value of the text, tag, type, format, or name being found.*
   [with properties **a list of list**] -- *The properties of the text to be found.*
         Most text properties will work here. Finding both value and properties
         is unlikely to work, and some combinations of properties don't work
         well together.
   in **reference** -- *The document in which to find.*
   [using **use case/whole word/use wildcards/backwards/no wrap/**
         find next] -- *The options to be applied to the find.*
   Result: **reference** -- *to the object that was found.*

The words "anchored frame" in the first paragraph leap right off the screen at me. I can find an anchored frame! I create a new script window in Script Editor, and try it.

```
tell application "FrameMaker 7.0"
    find anchored frame
end tell
```

No, when I run that it generates an error. What's gone wrong? Oh, I see: I've left out the in parameter. I have to tell FrameMaker what document to look in.

```
tell application "FrameMaker 7.0"
    find anchored frame in document "extra:applescriptBook:ch02places.fm"
end tell
```

It works! The first illustration is selected, and the result is a reference to it, just as the dictionary promises:

```
anchored frame 48 of document "extra:applescriptBook:ch02places.fm"
    of application "FrameMaker 7.0"
```

So now it begins to look like I can use find repeatedly to get a succession of references to the anchored frames in the document in the order in which they actually appear. To test this idea, I'll just make an artificial loop by using the repeat command without worrying for now about how many times I would have to loop in real life:

```
tell application "FrameMaker 7.0"
    set allPaths to {}
    repeat 5 times
        set oneFrame to find anchored frame ¬
            in document "extra:applescriptBook:ch02places.fm"
        set end of allPaths to inset file of inset 1 of oneFrame
    end repeat
end tell
allPaths
```

Here's the result:

```
{"extra:applescriptBook:figures:ch02:scriptEditor3.eps",
 "extra:applescriptBook:figures:ch02:scriptEditor3.eps",
 "extra:applescriptBook:figures:ch02:scriptEditor3.eps",
 "extra:applescriptBook:figures:ch02:scriptEditor3.eps",
 "extra:applescriptBook:figures:ch02:scriptEditor3.eps"}
```

Oops. We're not moving forward through the document; we're just finding the same illustration repeatedly. In FrameMaker itself, hitting the Find button over and over keeps finding the *next* match, which is what we want; in AppleScript, though, it appears that giving the find command over and over keeps finding the *same* match. But wait; the find command has a using parameter where I can specify find next. Let's try that:

```
tell application "FrameMaker 7.0"
    set allPaths to {}
    repeat 5 times
        set oneFrame to find anchored frame ¬
            in document "extra:applescriptBook:ch02places.fm" using find next
        set end of allPaths to inset file of inset 1 of oneFrame
    end repeat
end tell
allPaths
```

Darn it; this generates the same result. I guess "find next" simply means to find forwards as opposed to backwards. The trouble is I'm *not* finding forwards. It appears that once I've selected something, finding again just finds that same thing again. All right, then, maybe if I can just somehow move the selection point forward a little after finding an illustration, I'll be able to find the next illustration instead of the current one. So now I have to figure out how to move the selection point forward. I start by selecting some text, and then comes a long round of experimentation, of which I'll spare you the details, at the end of which I come up with this:

```
tell application "FrameMaker 7.0"
    select insertion point after selection
end tell
```

This works just fine when the selection is some text. Unfortunately, as I soon discover, when the selection is an illustration, I get an error message. This is so frustrating! Just when I thought I had the problem solved, I'm completely blocked again, simply because I don't know how to move the selection off an illustration.

Turning the Tables

At this point I remember that every illustration is embedded in a table. According to FrameMaker's dictionary, the find command has an option to find a table. Perhaps this will work better if I start by dealing with tables instead of anchored frames. So I try this:

```
tell application "FrameMaker 7.0"
    find table in document "extra:applescriptBook:ch02places.fm"
    select insertion point after selection
end tell
```

Gee, there's no error. Could it be that this is actually working? To find out, I'll try to cycle through several tables, collecting references to them to see if I'm finding different ones:

```
tell application "FrameMaker 7.0"
    set allTables to {}
    repeat 5 times
        set oneTable to find table ¬
            in document "extra:applescriptBook:ch02places.fm"
        set end of allTables to oneTable
        select insertion point after selection
    end repeat
end tell
allTables
```

Here's the result:

```
{table 52 of document "extra:applescriptBook:ch02places.fm"
    of application "FrameMaker 7.0",
 table 53 of document "extra:applescriptBook:ch02places.fm"
    of application "FrameMaker 7.0",
 table 51 of document "extra:applescriptBook:ch02places.fm"
```

```
        of application "FrameMaker 7.0",
    table 54 of document "extra:applescriptBook:ch02places.fm"
        of application "FrameMaker 7.0",
    table 55 of document "extra:applescriptBook:ch02places.fm"
        of application "FrameMaker 7.0"}
```

That's great. The numbers are once again mystifying; I have no idea why FrameMaker thinks there are at least 55 tables in this document, and of course it is numbering them in a different order than they appear in the document, just as it did with anchored frames. But the important thing is that those are five *different* tables. That means I really can cycle through the tables of the document this way.

Now I need to prove to myself that having found a table I can get to the anchored frame—the illustration—inside it. This could be tricky, but surely there's a way. Examining the table class listing in the dictionary, I see that a table has cell elements. Well, for a table representing an illustration, that should be simple enough; there's only one cell. Let's see:

```
tell application "FrameMaker 7.0"
    tell document "extra:applescriptBook:ch02places.fm"
        tell table 55
            get cell 1
        end tell
    end tell
end tell
```

Yes, that runs without error. Now, what's inside a cell? Looking in the cell class listing in the dictionary, I see that it has various possible elements, including paragraph, word, and text. Let's try paragraph:

```
tell application "FrameMaker 7.0"
    tell document "extra:applescriptBook:ch02places.fm"
        tell table 55
            tell cell 1
                get paragraph 1
            end tell
        end tell
    end tell
end tell
```

Yes, that too runs without error. But can I get from this paragraph to the anchored frame, the actual illustration? There's only one way to find out—try it:

```
tell application "FrameMaker 7.0"
    tell document "extra:applescriptBook:ch02places.fm"
        tell table 55
            tell cell 1
                tell paragraph 1
                    get anchored frame 1
                end tell
            end tell
        end tell
    end tell
end tell
```

Here's the result:

```
anchored frame 52 of document "extra:applescriptBook:ch02places.fm"
    of application "FrameMaker 7.0"
```

Son of a gun, it worked. Starting with a reference to a table, I've found a way to refer to the anchored frame inside it. But in that case—dare I say it?—the problem is essentially solved. I know that in principle I can cycle through all the tables in a document, in the order in which they appear. I know that in principle I can get from a reference to a table to a reference to an anchored frame. I know that, given an anchored frame, I can obtain the pathname for the file on disk that is the source of the illustration. So I should be able to put these abilities all together and get the pathnames for the illustration files, in the order in which the illustrations appear in the document.

Let's try it. I'll start things off at the top of the document by selecting the first paragraph. Then I'll cycle through the tables. As I come to each table, I'll get the anchored frame, and from there I'll get the pathname to its source file and append it to a list. I'll continue my policy of cycling some arbitrary number of times, because I don't want to worry yet about the real question of how many times to do it; I just want to prove to myself that I *can* do it.

The first thing is to learn how to select the first paragraph. This turns out to be somewhat tricky. I try this, but it doesn't work:

```
tell application "FrameMaker 7.0"
    tell document "extra:applescriptBook:ch02places.fm"
        select paragraph 1
    end tell
end tell
```

By once again using my trick of selecting the first paragraph manually and then asking FrameMaker for its selection, so as to learn how it thinks of a paragraph, I finally come up with this:

```
tell application "FrameMaker 7.0"
    tell document "extra:applescriptBook:ch02places.fm"
        select paragraph 1 of text flow 1
    end tell
end tell
```

Now I'm ready to put it all together:

```
tell application "FrameMaker 7.0"
    tell document "extra:applescriptBook:ch02places.fm"
        set allPaths to {}
        select paragraph 1 of text flow 1
        repeat 5 times
            set oneTable to find table in it
            set end of allPaths to inset file of inset 1 ¬
                of anchored frame 1 of paragraph 1 of cell 1 of oneTable
            select insertion point after selection
        end repeat
```

```
        end tell
    end tell
    allPaths
```

A change you'll notice here is the use of the word it. In AppleScript, that's how you refer to a thing when you're already inside a tell block addressing that thing. This is needed because the find command requires a reference to a document, but all the other commands are already being addressed to that document.

Here's the result:

```
{"extra:applescriptBook:figures:ch02:scriptEditor3.eps",
 "extra:applescriptBook:figures:ch02:scriptEditorDict.eps",
 "extra:applescriptBook:figures:ch02:scriptDebugger.eps",
 "extra:applescriptBook:figures:ch02:scriptDebuggerDict.eps",
 "extra:applescriptBook:figures:ch02:radio.eps"}
```

That's the right answer: those are the pathnames to the first five illustrations in the document, *in the order in which they appear.* For the first time since starting to work on the problem, I now believe I'm going to be able to solve it.

Refiner's Fire

Now let's make a few refinements. First, it occurs to me that I'm doing something rather stupid here; I'm finding every table. That's going be troublesome, because some tables are illustrations but some are just ordinary tables. I want to find illustration tables only. I know that in my FrameMaker template these are tables whose tag (or style name) is "Figure". The find command, according to FrameMaker's dictionary, lets me find a table having tag. So that's the way I should find my tables. After a short struggle to understand the syntax of this command, I come up with the following new version of my script:

```
tell application "FrameMaker 7.0"
    tell document "extra:applescriptBook:ch02places.fm"
        set allPaths to {}
        select paragraph 1 of text flow 1
        repeat 5 times
            set oneTable to find table having tag with value "Figure" in it
            set end of allPaths to inset file of inset 1 ¬
                of anchored frame 1 of paragraph 1 of cell 1 of oneTable
            select insertion point after selection
        end repeat
    end tell
end tell
allPaths
```

The result is just the same, so I haven't wrecked the successes I've already had (known in the programming business as a "regression"), and I believe I've eliminated some possible false positives from the find.

Next, let's worry about how to know how many times to loop. By changing "5 times" to "20 times", which is more times than the number of illustrations in the document, and then running the script again, I discover that when I get to the end of the document the search wraps around and starts from the top once more. I try to fix this by adding the option using no wrap to the find, but it doesn't help. Therefore I'd like to know *beforehand* exactly how many times to loop.

Now, I know from the dictionary that a table has a table tag property. AppleScript has a construct (called a "boolean test specifier") that allows me to specify particular objects of a class in terms of the value of one of that class's properties; not every scriptable application implements this construct when you'd like it to, but the only way to find out whether FrameMaker does in this case is to try it, so I do. After some stumbling about, I realize that a document has a text flow element that I have to refer to before I can refer to a table, and I come up with this:

```
tell application "FrameMaker 7.0"
    tell document "extra:applescriptBook:ch02places.fm"
        tell text flow 1
            get tables whose table tag is "Figure"
        end tell
    end tell
end tell
```

That works. But I don't really want this entire list; I just want to know how many items it contains. In AppleScript, the size of a list can be obtained with the count command:

```
tell application "FrameMaker 7.0"
    tell document "extra:applescriptBook:ch02places.fm"
        tell text flow 1
            count (get tables whose table tag is "Figure")
        end tell
    end tell
end tell
```

The result is 15. That's correct. So I should be able to use this approach before starting my loop in order to know just how many times to loop. Here's my new version of the script:

```
tell application "FrameMaker 7.0"
    tell document "extra:applescriptBook:ch02places.fm"
        tell text flow 1
            set howMany to count (get tables whose table tag is "Figure")
        end tell
        set allPaths to {}
        select paragraph 1 of text flow 1
        repeat howMany times
            set oneTable to find table having tag with value "Figure" in it
            set end of allPaths to inset file of inset 1 ¬
                of anchored frame 1 of paragraph 1 of cell 1 of oneTable
            select insertion point after selection
        end repeat
    end tell
end tell
allPaths
```

And here's the result; it's absolutely perfect, the correct names of the correct illustrations in the correct order:

```
{"extra:applescriptBook:figures:ch02:scriptEditor3.eps",
 "extra:applescriptBook:figures:ch02:scriptEditorDict.eps",
 "extra:applescriptBook:figures:ch02:scriptDebugger.eps",
 "extra:applescriptBook:figures:ch02:scriptDebuggerDict.eps",
 "extra:applescriptBook:figures:ch02:radio.eps",
 "extra:applescriptBook:figures:ch02:radio2.eps",
 "extra:applescriptBook:figures:ch02:word3.eps",
 "extra:applescriptBook:figures:ch02:word4.eps",
 "extra:applescriptBook:figures:ch02:fileMaker1.eps",
 "extra:applescriptBook:figures:ch02:fileMaker2.eps",
 "extra:applescriptBook:figures:ch02:fileMaker3.eps",
 "extra:applescriptBook:figures:ch02:ib.eps",
 "extra:applescriptBook:figures:ch02:ib2.eps",
 "extra:applescriptBook:figures:ch02:ib3.eps",
 "extra:applescriptBook:figures:ch02:RB.eps"}
```

Naming of Parts

Let's now turn our attention to the business of deriving the new name of each illustration. This will involve the chapter number. How can we learn this number?

It happens that in the FrameMaker template I'm using, every chapter document has exactly one paragraph whose tag (paragraph style) is "ChapterLabel," and that the text of this paragraph is the chapter number. So if FrameMaker gives me a way to refer to this paragraph, I should be home free. The dictionary tells me that the paragraph class has a paragraph tag property. Using the same sort of boolean test specifier construct I used a moment ago to find only those tables with a particular table tag, I try to find just those paragraphs that have this particular paragraph tag, expecting there to be just one:

```
tell application "FrameMaker 7.0"
    tell document "extra:applescriptBook:ch02places.fm"
        tell text flow 1
            get paragraphs whose paragraph tag is "ChapterLabel"
        end tell
    end tell
end tell
```

This doesn't give me an error, but the result is not quite what I expected:

```
{""}
```

I guess the problem is that the paragraph itself is empty; the chapter number is generated automatically through FrameMaker's autonumbering feature, and doesn't really count as its text. The dictionary lists a couple of paragraph properties that look promising here:

autoNum string **string** -- *The automatic numbering format string.*
paragraph number **string** -- *The formatted string representation of the paragraph number.*

The second one looks like what I'm after, so I try it:

```
tell application "FrameMaker 7.0"
    tell document "extra:applescriptBook:ch02places.fm"
        tell text flow 1
            get paragraph number of paragraphs ¬
                whose paragraph tag is "ChapterLabel"
        end tell
    end tell
end tell
```

The result is this:

```
{"Chapter 2"}
```

That's the right answer! It's a list because I asked for all such paragraphs, but it's a list of just one item because there is only one such paragraph, and the string "Chapter 2" provides the chapter number for this chapter. Now, of course, I need to extract just the "2" from this string, but that's easy, because AppleScript understands the concept of a word:

```
tell application "FrameMaker 7.0"
    tell document "extra:applescriptBook:ch02places.fm"
        tell text flow 1
            set chapNum to (get paragraph number of paragraphs ¬
                whose paragraph tag is "ChapterLabel")
        end tell
    end tell
end tell
set chapNum to word -1 of item 1 of chapNum
chapNum
```

The element item 1 extracts the single string "Chapter 2" from the list, and the element word -1 extracts the last word of that. The result is "2", which is perfect.

I want this number formatted to have two digits. Now, this is a piece of functionality I'm going to need more than once, so I write a little handler (a subroutine). The idea of a handler is that repeated or encapsulated functionality can be given a name and moved off to another location; this makes your code cleaner. This handler's job is to accept a string and pad it with zero at the front until it is two characters long. Having written the handler, I add some code to call the handler and test it, twice, because I want to make sure it works for a string that is either one or two characters long.

```
on pad(s)
    repeat while length of s < 2
        set s to ("0" & s)
    end repeat
    return s
end pad
log pad("2")
log pad("22")
```

The pad handler makes use of concatenation (via the ampersand operator) to assemble the desired string. Those last two lines do two things:

- The pad command calls the pad handler that appears earlier in the code.
- The log command puts the result of the pad command into the Event Log History window. The Event Log History window must be opened manually before running the script.

Logging like this is a good approach when you want to test more than one thing in a single running of a script. The result looks good:

```
(*02*)
(*22*)
```

Those parentheses and asterisks are comment delimiters; I don't quite understand why the log window uses them, but it doesn't matter.

Another problem is that the new name of each illustration is going to be based partly on its old name. I need to break up the illustration file's pathname into its components, and I need to break up the last component, the actual name of the file, into the name itself and the file-type suffix, because the only part of the pathname I want to change is the name itself.

The typical AppleScript way to break up a string into fields based on some delimiter is to set a special variable called text item delimiters to that delimiter and then ask for the string's text items. So I'll do that twice, once with colon as the delimiter and again with period as the delimiter. Once again, I'll make this a handler, just because it makes the script so much neater. I'll have the handler return both results, the list of pathname components together with the list of filename components, combined as a single list. That way, when I call this handler, I will have all the pieces and can reassemble them the way I want:

```
on bust(s)
    set text item delimiters to ":"
    set pathParts to text items of s
    set text item delimiters to "."
    set nameParts to text items of last item of pathParts
    return {pathParts, nameParts}
end bust
bust("disk:folder:folder:file.suffix")
```

The result shows that the right thing is happening:

```
{{"disk", "folder", "folder", "file.suffix"}, {"file", "suffix"}}
```

Now I'm ready to practice renaming an illustration file. I'll write a handler that takes two numbers and the current pathname of the illustration file and generates the new pathname for that file:

```
on pad(s)
    repeat while length of s < 2
        set s to ("0" & s)
    end repeat
```

```
        return s
    end pad
    on bust(s)
        set text item delimiters to ":"
        set pathParts to text items of s
        set text item delimiters to "."
        set nameParts to text items of last item of pathParts
        return {pathParts, nameParts}
    end bust
    on rename(n1, n2, oldPath)
        set bothLists to bust(oldPath)
        set extension to last item of item 2 of bothLists
        set pathPart to items 1 thru -2 of item 1 of bothLists
        set newFileName to "as_" & pad(n1) & pad(n2)
        set newFileName to newFileName & "." & extension
        set text item delimiters to ":"
        return (pathPart as string) & ":" & newFileName
    end rename
    rename("2", "3", "disk:folder:folder:oldName.eps")
```

The expression as string when applied to a list, as in the very last line of the rename handler, assembles the items of the list, together with the text item delimiters between each pair of items, into a single string. And here's the result:

```
    "disk:folder:folder:as_0203.eps"
```

Got it right the first time! It's hard to believe, but I am now ready for a practice run using an actual FrameMaker document.

Practice Makes Perfect

If I've learned one thing about programming over the years it's to practice before doing anything drastic. I'm going to run through the document and *pretend* to change the illustration names. Instead of really changing them, I'll log a note telling myself what I *would* have changed the name to if this had been the real thing. So, putting it all together, here's my practice script:

```
    on pad(s)
        repeat while length of s < 2
            set s to ("0" & s)
        end repeat
        return s
    end pad
    on bust(s)
        set text item delimiters to ":"
        set pathParts to text items of s
        set text item delimiters to "."
        set nameParts to text items of last item of pathParts
        return {pathParts, nameParts}
    end bust
    on rename(n1, n2, oldPath)
        set bothLists to bust(oldPath)
        set extension to last item of item 2 of bothLists
        set pathPart to items 1 thru -2 of item 1 of bothLists
```

```
            set newFileName to "as_" & pad(n1) & pad(n2)
            set newFileName to newFileName & "." & extension
            set text item delimiters to ":"
            return (pathPart as string) & ":" & newFileName
    end rename
    tell application "FrameMaker 7.0"
        tell document "extra:applescriptBook:ch02places.fm"
            tell text flow 1
                set howMany to count (get tables whose table tag is "Figure")
                set chapNum to (get paragraph number of paragraphs ¬
                    whose paragraph tag is "ChapterLabel")
            end tell
            set chapNum to word -1 of item 1 of chapNum
            set allPaths to {}
            select paragraph 1 of text flow 1
            set counter to 1
            repeat howMany times
                set oneTable to find table having tag with value "Figure" in it
                set thisFile to inset file of inset 1 ¬
                    of anchored frame 1 of paragraph 1 of cell 1 of oneTable
                set newName to ¬
                    my rename(chapNum, (counter as string), thisFile)
                log "I found " & thisFile
                log "I'm thinking of changing it to " & newName
                select insertion point after selection
                set counter to counter + 1
            end repeat
        end tell
    end tell
```

Observe that I have put in the variable counter, which starts at 1 and is incremented in every loop; this is how I know how many times I've done the find, and therefore tells me the number of the current illustration. I must admit that it took me a couple of tries to get this script to run. When I first tried to run it, I got an error at the point where I call the rename handler. This was because I had forgotten to put the magic word my before it; this word tells AppleScript that even though I'm talking to FrameMaker I want to call a handler in my own script. And then, after I made that change and ran the script again, I got another error: it appeared that the rename handler was called but was now choking. The reason was that the variable counter was a number, and the rename handler was passing this on to the pad handler, which was expecting a string. The phrase counter as string converts the number to a string for purposes of passing it to the rename handler.

Here are the relevant entries of the resulting log:

```
(*I found extra:applescriptBook:figures:ch02:scriptEditor3.eps*)
(*I'm thinking of changing it to
    extra:applescriptBook:figures:ch02:as_0201.eps*)
(*I found extra:applescriptBook:figures:ch02:scriptEditorDict.eps*)
(*I'm thinking of changing it to
    extra:applescriptBook:figures:ch02:as_0202.eps*)
(*I found extra:applescriptBook:figures:ch02:scriptDebugger.eps*)
```

```
(*I'm thinking of changing it to
    extra:applescriptBook:figures:ch02:as_0203.eps*)
(*I found extra:applescriptBook:figures:ch02:scriptDebuggerDict.eps*)
(*I'm thinking of changing it to
    extra:applescriptBook:figures:ch02:as_0204.eps*)
(*I found extra:applescriptBook:figures:ch02:radio.eps*)
(*I'm thinking of changing it to
    extra:applescriptBook:figures:ch02:as_0205.eps*)
(*I found extra:applescriptBook:figures:ch02:radio2.eps*)
(*I'm thinking of changing it to
    extra:applescriptBook:figures:ch02:as_0206.eps*)
(*I found extra:applescriptBook:figures:ch02:word3.eps*)
(*I'm thinking of changing it to
    extra:applescriptBook:figures:ch02:as_0207.eps*)
(*I found extra:applescriptBook:figures:ch02:word4.eps*)
(*I'm thinking of changing it to
    extra:applescriptBook:figures:ch02:as_0208.eps*)
(*I found extra:applescriptBook:figures:ch02:fileMaker1.eps*)
(*I'm thinking of changing it to
    extra:applescriptBook:figures:ch02:as_0209.eps*)
(*I found extra:applescriptBook:figures:ch02:fileMaker2.eps*)
(*I'm thinking of changing it to
    extra:applescriptBook:figures:ch02:as_0210.eps*)
(*I found extra:applescriptBook:figures:ch02:fileMaker3.eps*)
(*I'm thinking of changing it to
    extra:applescriptBook:figures:ch02:as_0211.eps*)
(*I found extra:applescriptBook:figures:ch02:ib.eps*)
(*I'm thinking of changing it to
    extra:applescriptBook:figures:ch02:as_0212.eps*)
(*I found extra:applescriptBook:figures:ch02:ib2.eps*)
(*I'm thinking of changing it to
    extra:applescriptBook:figures:ch02:as_0213.eps*)
(*I found extra:applescriptBook:figures:ch02:ib3.eps*)
(*I'm thinking of changing it to
    extra:applescriptBook:figures:ch02:as_0214.eps*)
(*I found extra:applescriptBook:figures:ch02:RB.eps*)
(*I'm thinking of changing it to
    extra:applescriptBook:figures:ch02:as_0215.eps*)
```

That looks as good as I could wish.

Finder's Keepers

I must not change only the file reference of each illustration within FrameMaker; I must change also the name of the actual illustration file. This involves speaking to the Finder. As a test, I create a file and run a little code to make sure I know how to tell the Finder how to change the name of a file.

```
tell application "Finder"
    set name of file "xxx:Users:mattneub:Desktop:testing.txt" to "itWorked"
end tell
```

This works, and now we are ready to run our original script for real. Before doing so, we make sure we have backup copies of everything involved, in case something goes wrong. Even with backups, it's a scary business making such possibly disastrous changes, both in a FrameMaker document and on disk, so I start by running the script against a document that has just one illustration—in fact, I run it against this very chapter, Chapter 3.

To make the script work for real, I change it in two places. First, at the start I add another little handler to extract the final component from a pathname, so that I can obtain the new name that the Finder is to give to the illustration file:

```
on justName(s)
    set text item delimiters to ":"
    return last text item of s
end justName
```

Second, I replace the two "log" lines from the previous version with this:

```
set newShortName to my justName(newName)
tell application "Finder" ¬
    to set name of file thisFile to newShortName
set inset file of inset 1 ¬
    of anchored frame 1 of paragraph 1 of cell 1 of oneTable ¬
    to newName
```

The first two lines are simply a rewrite of the Finder file-renaming code we just tested a moment ago, with the values coming from variables in the script instead of being hardcoded as literal strings. The second line actually changes the name of the illustration file on disk. Observe that we can talk to the Finder even inside code where we are already talking to FrameMaker. The last line is the only one that makes an actual change in the FrameMaker document—the crucial change, the one we came here to make, altering the illustration's file reference to match the new pathname of the illustration file. I run the script against Chapter 3 and it works: the illustration file's name is changed, and the illustration's file reference in the FrameMaker document is changed to match.

I've Got a Little List

Recall that one of our purposes is to generate the figure list requested by the illustration department, as shown in Table 3-1. I already know the chapter number, the illustration number, and the illustration file's name. The only missing piece of information is the illustration's caption. The FrameMaker dictionary shows that a table has a title property that looks like what I want. A quick test against a specific table shows that it is:

```
tell application "FrameMaker 7.0"
    set theTitle to (get title of table 46 of document ¬
        "extra:applescriptBook:ch03handson.fm")
end tell
```

This works, but because of the way the template is constructed, it includes an unwanted return character at the start of the result. To eliminate this, I use an Apple-Script expression that extracts all but the first character of a string:

```
tell application "FrameMaker 7.0"
    set theTitle to text from character 2 to -1 of ¬
        (get title of table 46 of document ¬
        "extra:applescriptBook:ch03handson.fm")
end tell
```

That works; the result is this:

```
"FrameMaker dictionary"
```

That is indeed the caption of the first illustration of this chapter. AppleScript can write to a file, so all I need now is a handler that appends to a file, nicely formatted, a line containing the information for the illustration currently being processed. Here, then, is the final version of the script, including this handler and a call to it:

```
on pad(s)
    repeat while length of s < 2
        set s to ("0" & s)
    end repeat
    return s
end pad
on bust(s)
    set text item delimiters to ":"
    set pathParts to text items of s
    set text item delimiters to "."
    set nameParts to text items of last item of pathParts
    return {pathParts, nameParts}
end bust
on rename(n1, n2, oldPath)
    set bothLists to bust(oldPath)
    set extension to last item of item 2 of bothLists
    set pathPart to items 1 thru -2 of item 1 of bothLists
    set newFileName to "as_" & pad(n1) & pad(n2)
    set newFileName to newFileName & "." & extension
    set text item delimiters to ":"
    return (pathPart as string) & ":" & newFileName
end rename
on justName(s)
    set text item delimiters to ":"
    return last text item of s
end justName
on writeInfo(n1, n2, theName, theTitle)
    set s to return & n1 & "-" & n2 & tab & theName & tab & theTitle & return
    set f to open for access file "xxx:Users:mattneub:figs" with write permission
    write s to f starting at (get eof of f)
    close access f
end writeInfo
tell application "FrameMaker 7.0"
    tell document "extra:applescriptBook:ch03handson.fm"
        tell text flow 1
```

```
                    set howMany to count (get tables whose table tag is "Figure")
                    set chapNum to (get paragraph number of paragraphs ¬
                        whose paragraph tag is "ChapterLabel")
            end tell
            set chapNum to word -1 of item 1 of chapNum
            set allPaths to {}
            select paragraph 1 of text flow 1
            set counter to 1
            repeat howMany times
                    set oneTable to find table having tag with value "Figure" in it
                    set thisFile to inset file of inset 1 ¬
                        of anchored frame 1 of paragraph 1 of cell 1 of oneTable
                    set newName to my rename(chapNum, (counter as string), thisFile)
                    set newShortName to my justName(newName)
                    tell application "Finder" to set name of file thisFile to newShortName
                    set inset file of inset 1 ¬
                        of anchored frame 1 of paragraph 1 of cell 1 of oneTable ¬
                        to newName
                    set theTitle to text from character 2 to -1 of (get title of oneTable)
                    my writeInfo(chapNum, (counter as string), newShortName, theTitle)
                    select insertion point after selection
                    set counter to counter + 1
            end repeat
        end tell
    end tell
```

There is just one thing I don't like about that script, namely this line:

```
tell document "extra:applescriptBook:ch03handson.fm"
```

That line hardcodes the pathname of the document file. This works, but it means
that I have to change the script manually for each file I process. That's not so terri-
ble, since only about eight chapters of this book have any illustrations at all, but it
would be nice not to have to do it at all, if only because it seems a possible source of
error. Nevertheless, I think we can save this matter for some future round of refinements, and for now at least, consider the problem solved.

Conclusions, Lessons, and Advice

You'll no doubt have noticed that most of my time and effort working on this problem was spent wrestling with the particular scriptable application I was trying to automate. In general, that's how it is with AppleScript. AppleScript itself is a very small
language; it is extended in different ways by different scriptable applications. Trying
to work out what a particular scriptable application will let you say and how it will
respond when you say it constitutes much of the battle of working with AppleScript.

Another feature of the struggle is that AppleScript's error messages aren't very helpful, and it lacks a debugging environment (unless you use Script Debugger as your
script editor application), so it's important to proceed with caution and patience.
When you try to execute a script, all you really know is that it worked or it didn't; if
it didn't, finding out why isn't easy. You can see that I developed my final script

slowly and in stages, testing each piece as I went along. I knew that the pieces worked before I put them into place; that way I could be pretty confident that I knew what the script as a whole would do.

Here, to conclude, are a few apophthegms to live by, derived from the foregoing. I hope you'll find this advice helpful in your own AppleScript adventures:

Use the dictionary.

> The biggest problem you face as you approach driving a scriptable application is that you don't know the application's "object model"—what sorts of thing it thinks of itself as knowing about, what it calls these things, and how the things relate to one another. In this regard, nouns (classes) are much more important than verbs (events). Most scriptable applications, especially if they are scriptable in a deep and powerful way, have lots of nouns and relatively few verbs. Notice how I did almost everything in the script with the basic built-in verbs get, set, and count; even select is fairly standard. The only unusual verb I ended up using was find. I spent almost all of the time worrying about the nouns. The biggest problem in AppleScript is referring to the thing you want to talk about, in the manner that your scriptable application expects and accepts.

Don't expect too much from the dictionary.

> Try to think of other ways to learn how to construct the desired reference. FrameMaker's dictionary let us down quite severely on several occasions; I was much more successful in asking for the selection and letting FrameMaker describe a thing in its own terms than in trying to construct a reference from scratch based on the dictionary. In fact, although I didn't say anything about it at the time because the matter is rather technical, FrameMaker's dictionary is massively faulty; although I learned by experiment that an anchored frame can be an element of a paragraph or of a document, the dictionary doesn't say this at all. Had it done so, I would have had a much easier time.

Think outside the box.

> When FrameMaker wouldn't just hand me references to every anchored frame in the order in which they occur in the document, I was frustrated but I didn't give up; I tried to think of another way. The find command looks broken to me, but I didn't worry about this; I figured out how to move the selection point forward to work around the problem. If you waste your time and energy bewailing things that you feel are broken or quirky or inadequate in AppleScript or in some particular scriptable application, you won't get any work done. Face reality and tighten your belt another notch.

Start small.

> Look at how much of the time was taken up testing very short snippets of code over and over just to learn how to construct a reference or to see what some operation would do. Part of the problem here is that you don't know until you try it what an application will permit you to do; the dictionary can't really tell you. Another part of the problem is that AppleScript has no built-in facilities for

debugging. Therefore you need to develop the program one line at a time, building it up from individual lines that you already know work (because you've tested them). Don't try to write an entire program in AppleScript and then figure out why it didn't work; you'll never manage it. By the time you put the whole program together, you should be like a lawyer cross-examining a witness in court: ideally, you should never ask a question to which you don't already know the answer.

Test every step.

When you don't know the answer to some question your code is asking in the course of your script, find out. Use the result of running a script. Use logging. You want to know at every step, as you develop a script, whether what's happening is what you want and expect.

Don't be ashamed to experiment.

Don't be ashamed to guess! A lot of AppleScript code development is guesswork. As Aristotle said, it is a mark of wisdom to ask from a subject only so much precision as that subject admits of.

Solve the single case before expanding to "every."

Solve the single case before expanding to a loop. Solve an artificial loop before worrying about the boundary cases (that is, before figuring out how to know exactly how many times to loop).

Don't try to understand AppleScript's mysterious error messages.

The important thing isn't what went wrong but where it went wrong. Knowing where the problem is will usually suffice, because you know where you need to make a change, even if you're just guessing when you make it. If you think the error isn't important, use error-handling (a try block) to ignore it, so that it won't stop your code from executing.

Write a practice script before writing the final version of the script.

AppleScript has the power to do very far-reaching things, such as deleting files and wrecking your document. You want to be very sure things are working before you throw the switch that says, "This is not a drill."

Know the language.

It's true that in the course of development I did a lot of guessing about FrameMaker's object model; but I didn't guess about the language itself. I couldn't have written this program at all if I hadn't known already what my and it mean, and how to use tell and of, and how to form a boolean test specifier, and what the difference is between a property and an element. AppleScript may look like English, and that might make you think you already know AppleScript because you already know English. If you think that, you're wrong. AppleScript is a rule-based programming language like any other. It is rigorous, choosy, and precise. This book can't teach you to write that one special script you'd like to write, but it can and does teach you the language.

CHAPTER 4

Basic Concepts

This chapter explains how AppleScript works. Its purpose is to provide you with a mental picture of what's really going on when you use AppleScript. It also acts as a kind of glossary, defining the basic terms and concepts needed for an understanding of AppleScript, but the concepts are presented in an expository order rather than alphabetically.

All subsequent chapters will presuppose some familiarity with the terms and concepts presented in this chapter. You don't have to grasp everything immediately, and you don't need to read every section with equal care. But you should at least skim this chapter in order to get your conceptual bearings. You can always come back later and reread a section if you need a refresher on the details.

Apple Event

Apple events lie at the heart of what AppleScript is and why you're going to use it, and having a sense of what they are will be of tremendous help to you in your Apple-Script adventures.

Apple events are the Macintosh's system-level way of letting one running application communicate with another. Such communication is called *interapplication communication*. Apple events were introduced in 1991 as part of System 7. I refer to the two parties in an interapplication communication as the *sender* (the application that sends the message) and the *target* (the application that receives the message); I find this clearer and more instructive than the more technical terms "client" and "server."

An Apple event is an astonishingly powerful thing. Hermes-like, it crosses borders. Two completely independent applications are talking to each other. What's more, Apple events work across a network, including the Internet, so these two applications can be on different computers. Or it can be the opposite; an application can send an Apple event to itself. (Why would it want to do that? You'll find out, in the section "Recordable," later in this chapter.)

Moreover, the range of what may be expressed in an Apple event is remarkably broad. Apple events actually have a kind of grammar: there are (so to speak) verbs and nouns and modifiers, and these are so cleverly and flexibly devised that single Apple events can be constructed to say surprisingly complicated things, such as (speaking to a word processing program), "Look at the text of your first window and give me a reference to every line of it whose second word begins with the letter t," or (speaking to an email program), "Look in the mailbox where the incoming mail is, find the first mail message with a subject that starts with the word 'applescript', and move it into the 'AppleScript' mailbox."

Command, Query, and Reply

An interapplication communication can be thought of as either a *command* or a *query*. There is no real technical distinction here; either way it's the same kind of message. But as human beings we naturally tend to feel that these are broadly the reasons for sending an interapplication communication: either we tell the target to do something or we ask the target a question. In either case, there will be a *reply*. The reply to an Apple event is itself an Apple event.

You might think that if an interapplication communication is a command, there wouldn't need to be a reply. But that's not so. Apple events tend to use the reply to hand back useful information; for example, you saw in Chapter 3 that telling FrameMaker to find, which sounds like a command, also nets us a reference to what was found. What's more, even if the sender couldn't care less about the content of the reply, the reply itself is still important. Remember, these two applications are running independently, so they have to be coordinated somehow if they are to interact coherently. The sender, having sent a command to the target, typically doesn't want to proceed to its own next step until the target has finished obeying that command. The reply informs the sender that the command has been carried out (or not, if an error has occurred).

When two independently running applications communicate with each other, things can go wrong. The sender sends a message to the target, and then what? The target application might try to obey the message, and crash. It might obey the message, but require a great deal of time to do so. It might be busy or otherwise not in a position to receive the message. The sender needs a way to hedge his bets in order to cope with such possibilities. Apple events provide some bet-hedging mechanisms.

- The sender may attach to the message a *timeout* value, a statement of how long he is willing to wait for an answer. If a reply doesn't come back within the specified time, the sender receives a reply anyway—a reply saying that, for one reason or another, no reply came back in time. This can permit the sender to proceed to the next step. (Meanwhile the target is probably still performing his time-consuming task, blissfully unaware that the sender has lost interest.)

- The sender may specify that he isn't interested in the reply at all: he doesn't care about its value (which implies that this is a command, not a query); he doesn't care to know even whether there is a reply, or whether the command was carried out. In this case the sender does not wait; the message is sent, and the sender immediately proceeds to the next step of his own process. The sender will never find out in any direct way what became of the Apple event. This devil-may-care approach is rather rarely used, but there are times when it comes in very handy.

Scriptability

Not just any old Apple event can be sent to any old application. Well, it can, but the result could easily be an error message instead of the desired result. The target application needs to have been written in the first place in such a way that the particular Apple event you send is one to which it is prepared to respond. Such an application defines internally a *repertory* of Apple events that it understands. The application is then said to be *scriptable*.

A given scriptable application's repertory of acceptable Apple events doesn't necessarily resemble that of any other scriptable application. This presents something of a problem for the sender, since every possible target application is picky in a different way about what can be said to it. This problem washes over into AppleScript, and is in fact one of the single greatest challenges facing the AppleScript programmer. (You already saw this in Chapter 3.)

The knowledge of what Apple events a scriptable application can respond to, and what it will do in response to them, is an implicit fact built into its workings, not an explicit fact written somehow on its face. How, then, is it possible to know what a scriptable application's repertory is? Some secondary device is clearly needed to expose this information. In the AppleScript world, this device is the application's *dictionary*, which is a kind of built-in public document describing the application's repertory. There is a section about dictionaries later in this chapter, and an entire chapter devoted to them later in the book (Chapter 19).

The Life of an Apple Event

There's obviously more to the story of interapplication communications than just the sender application and the target application. For example, earlier it was said that the sender normally receives a reply even if the target isn't even listening. How is that possible? It's possible because the System itself functions as the intermediary through which all interapplication communications happen. The sender doesn't speak directly to the target, but to the System. It is the System that is responsible for passing the message on to the target, and for letting the sender know how things went.

Figure 4-1 shows in more detail the process whereby an Apple event is sent and a reply is returned.

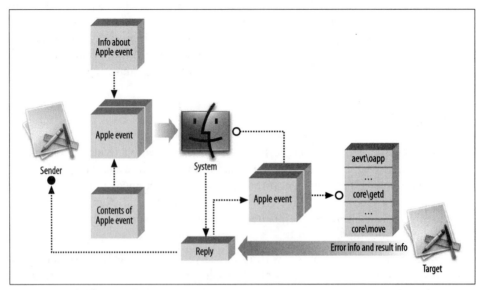

Figure 4-1. Life of an Apple event

1. The sender application (on the left of the figure) constructs the Apple event. The Apple event is rather like a letter inside an envelope that you post in the mail. It has information about how it is to be directed—who the target application is, and whether the sender intends to wait around for the reply, and if so, what the timeout value is. This information is intended for the System, and is rather like the stuff that goes on the outside of the envelope. Then there is the content—the details as to what kind of Apple event this is and the particular data that it involves. This information is intended for the target application, and is rather like the letter that's inside the envelope.

2. The sender application calls the System (in the middle of the figure) and hands it the Apple event. The System, rather like the postal service, examines the Apple event and looks at the information about how it is to be directed. Using this information, the System tries to locate the target application. Let's presume that it succeeds in doing this.

3. The target application (on the right of the figure) is portrayed as having a repertory of Apple events to which it is prepared to respond. These Apple events are listed using pairs of four-letter codes. (Apple events really are identified by pairs of four-letter codes, as explained in Chapter 19, and the Apple events listed in the diagram are genuine, common Apple events.)

4. The System calls the target application, handing it the Apple event supplied by the sender. The System also attaches to this Apple event a reply Apple event. It is rather is if, when the post office delivers a letter to you, it were to provide a

stamped addressed envelope for you to put your reply into. The System holds out this reply event to the target application, but doesn't let go of it.

5. The target application does whatever the Apple event tells it to do, and puts the result into the reply event. There are two parts to this result. First, the target application must return a value signifying whether or not things succeeded. Second, the target application may put into the reply any other information to be returned. If there was an error, it can put in a text message describing the problem. If things succeeded and a result is expected, it can put in that result.

6. The target application now signs off, and the System is left holding the reply Apple event (which, as we said, it never let go of). The System now delivers the reply Apple event to the sender application, and the story ends.

What an Apple Event Looks Like

By now the reader is probably eager to see an Apple event. What does one look like? Actually, an Apple event was never meant for human eyes. It is meant to be machine-constructible and machine-parsable. It doesn't really even have, in a strict sense, any appearance at all. Nevertheless, as a kind of linguistic shortcut for expressing and understanding Apple events, there is a textual format called AEPrint that shows you what an Apple event looks like. Example 4-1 displays, in AEPrint format, the second of the two Apple events I mentioned earlier, the one addressed to a mail program.

Example 4-1. A raw Apple event

```
core\move{
    insh:insl{
        kobj:obj {
            form:'name',
            want:'Mbox',
            seld:"appleScript",
            from:'null'()
        },
        kpos:'end '
    },
    ----:obj {
        form:'indx',
        want:'cobj',
        seld:1,
        from:obj {
            form:'test',
            want:'msg ',
            from:obj {
                form:'prop',
                want:'prop',
                seld:'unBX',
                from:'null'()
            },
            seld:cmpd{
                relo:'bgwt',
```

Example 4-1. A raw Apple event (continued)

```
                            obj1:obj {
                                form:'prop',
                                want:'prop',
                                seld:'subj',
                                from:exmn($$)
                            },
                            obj2:"applescript"
                    }
                }
            }
        }
```

Go and Catch an Apple Event

We have seen that the System plays the central role of postman whenever an Apple event is sent. Now imagine that Apple events are secret messages, and that we are international spies who would like to get a look at them when they are sent. In effect, we would like to waylay the postman, bonk him over the head, snatch the letter out of his hand, and glance at its contents. It turns out that there is a way to do this.

Here's how. First, open the Console; that's where any Apple events are going to be reported to us. Next, go into the Terminal and enter the following:

```
$ setenv AEDebug 1
$ setenv AEDebugSends 1
$ setenv AEDebugReceives 1
```

Or, in bash (the default shell in Panther), you'd say:

```
$ export AEDebug=1
$ export AEDebugSends=1
$ export AEDebugReceives=1
```

This turns on the environment settings that cause Apple events to be intercepted and reported. These settings will apply only within this shell session, and only with respect to applications that are launched from within this process. So, let's launch one:

```
$ open /Applications/Safari.app
```

Now any Apple events sent to Safari will be logged. Let's send one:

```
$ open http://www.apple.com
```

(I'm assuming here that Safari is your default browser.) This causes two things to happen. First, within the Terminal, the process started by the open command sends an Apple event, and this fact is reported within the Terminal. Second, Safari receives this Apple event, and this fact is reported within the Console. The two Apple events are exactly the same event, so there's no point examining both of them—here it is as it's reported in the Console, when Safari receives it:

```
AE2000 (556): Received an event:
------oo start of event oo------
{ 1 } 'aevt': GURL/GURL {
```

```
        return id: 38666240 (0x24e0000)
     transaction id: 0 (0x0)
  interaction level: 112 (0x70)
     reply required: 0 (0x0)
  target:
    { 1 } 'psn ':  8 bytes {
      { 0x0, 0x3e0001 } (open)
    }
  optional attributes:
   < empty record >
  event data:
    { 1 } 'aevt':  - 1 items {
      key '----' -
        { 1 } 'TEXT':  20 bytes {
          "http://www.apple.com"
        }
    }
}

------oo  end of event  oo------
```

This is quite a bit more verbose than simple AEPrint format, and more informative. I won't analyze it for you, but you can see immediately that the first half is information about the Apple event (its identifier, its target, whether a reply is expected, that sort of thing) and the second half is the content of the Apple event (the actual URL that Safari was asked to open).

Let's do another. In the Terminal, say this:

```
$ osascript -e 'tell app "Finder" to get disks'
```

(The osascript command was mentioned under "Unix" in Chapter 2, and is formally discussed in Chapter 23.) This causes the Terminal to spew out large amounts of information. The bulk of this information has to do with the fact that we've just asked the Terminal to compile and run a line of AppleScript, and may be ignored here. The important thing for our purposes is the Apple event that is ultimately sent to the Finder. You'll see it, along with the Finder's reply, at the very end of the output. Here it is:

```
AE2000 (811): Sending an event:
------oo start of event oo------
{ 1 } 'aevt':  core/getd {
        return id: 53149700 (0x32b0004)
     transaction id: 0 (0x0)
  interaction level: 64 (0x40)
     reply required: 1 (0x1)
  target:
    { 2 } 'psn ':  8 bytes {
      { 0x0, 0xc0001 } (Finder)
    }
  optional attributes:
    { 1 } 'reco':  - 1 items {
      key 'csig' -
```

```
            { 1 } 'magn':  4 bytes {
              655361 (0x10000)
            }
          }
      }

  event data:
    { 1 } 'aevt':  - 1 items {
      key '----' -
        { 1 } 'obj ':  - 4 items {
          key 'form' -
            { 1 } 'enum':  4 bytes {
              'indx'
            }
          key 'want' -
            { 1 } 'type':  4 bytes {
              'cdis'
            }
          key 'seld' -
            { 1 } 'abso':  4 bytes {
              'all '
            }
          key 'from' -
            { 4 } 'null':  null descriptor
        }
      }
  }

  ------oo  end of event  oo------
```

Without going into the details of this Apple event, you can once again recognize its two main constituent parts.

What All This Has to Do with AppleScript

A raw Apple event, as portrayed in the preceding sections, is not by any means completely incomprehensible to a human being. Nevertheless, you'll surely admit that if raw format were the only available way of expressing Apple events, your attitude would probably be: "In that case, forget it." And rightly so. Raw Apple events are meant primarily for computers to construct and to read, not for humans.

But Apple wants ordinary users to be able to take direct advantage of Apple events. They want Apple events to be human-readable and human-writable. And that's why there's AppleScript. The very same Apple event seen in Example 4-1 can be constructed and presented in a different textual form, one which looks rather more familiar, intuitive, and accessible to a human being:

```
move item 1 of (every message of incoming mail ¬
    whose subject begins with "applescript") ¬
    to end of mailbox "appleScript"
```

That's AppleScript. One of the chief purposes of AppleScript—perhaps *the* chief purpose—is to provide an English-like way of expressing Apple events.

The Open Scripting Architecture

In 1992–93, the founders of AppleScript had to decide where the language should live. They could have made AppleScript the internal language of a single application, like HyperCard's HyperTalk; the user would then compile and run AppleScript code entirely from within this one application. But this approach was unacceptable. Rather, they wanted AppleScript to be available everywhere. Thus the language would have to be part of the System. In creating a place within the System to put it, they generalized this place to be somewhere that not only AppleScript but any scripting language could live in. The resulting structure is the *Open Scripting Architecture* (OSA).

Components

Under the OSA, a scripting language is implemented by a something called a *component*. (Components were not invented specially for the OSA; they existed already in connection with QuickTime.) Think of a component as a piece of self-contained functionality made available at system level so that any program can hook up to it and use it. One thing that's special about components is that they can be installed and uninstalled dynamically. So an OSA-savvy program doesn't necessarily think in terms of any particular scripting language; it asks the System—in particular, the Component Manager—what scripting languages are presently installed, and if it wants to use one, the Component Manager provides access to it.

Since components are installed dynamically, this installation must actually take place while the computer is running. AppleScript is installed as the computer starts up and simply left in place, so that it's always available. You may recall that under Mac OS 9 there was an extension called AppleScript (in the Extensions folder of the System Folder). Its job was to install AppleScript as a component under the OSA as the computer started up. On Mac OS X, the same function is performed by *AppleScript.component*, which is in */System/Library/Components*; this type of file is called a *component file*.

A nice consequence of this architecture is that Apple can easily release upgrades to AppleScript, and the user can easily install them, with no effect on any other part of the System. AppleScript itself has a version number, which refers to the version number of the component that is installed to implement it; you can find out what this is by running the following one-word script in the Script Editor:

```
version
```

At the time of this writing, the result is "1.9.2".

Components are special in another way, too: when a program is given access to a component by the Component Manager, it gets, in effect, its own private copy of that component, with its own persistent storage. This means, among other things, that multiple programs can use a component without interfering with one another.

This has important consequences for how the AppleScript language behaves, and we'll come back to it.

Other Scripting Languages

The Open Scripting Architecture is meant to accommodate scripting languages in general; but AppleScript is the only one supplied by Apple. In fact, AppleScript is designated the *default scripting component*, the one that is used when no particular scripting component is specified. Still, there *can* be other scripting languages. So where are they?

There have never been many other OSA scripting languages, perhaps because developers have not felt much need to supply them. I know of just four:

- UserLand Frontier (under Mac OS 9 and before) installed its internal scripting language, UserTalk, as an OSA component dynamically whenever Frontier was running.
- CE Software's QuicKeys (under Mac OS 9 and before) installed its scripting language, QuicKeys Script, as an OSA component at startup, by means of an extension.
- Late Night Software's JavaScriptOSA installs JavaScript as a system-wide scripting language at startup, by means of a component file.
- Late Night Software's Script Debugger installs a debuggable version of Apple-Script, called AppleScript Debugger, at startup, by means of a component file.

JavaScriptOSA is free, so you might like to look into it. A cool feature of it is that it adds classes to the JavaScript language that allow Apple events to be expressed. Thus it can be used where you would use AppleScript, and for the same purposes. Java-Script has some nice linguistic features (such as powerful string handling and object orientation), so it makes an interesting alternative to AppleScript. To learn more, see *http://latenightsw.com/freeware/JavaScriptOSA/index.html*.

If you were to download JavaScriptOSA and copy it to */Library/Components* and then log out and log in, JavaScript would be present as a scripting language on your machine. You would observe this in the Script Editor, where "JavaScript" would appear in the scripting languages popup at the top of the window. You would be able to write, compile, and run scripts written in JavaScript from within the Script Editor. This illustrates the dynamic and generalized nature of the Open Scripting Architecture.

Talking to a Scripting Component

There are two approaches that a program can take when it wants to gain access to a scripting component. An OSA-savvy program like the Script Editor wants to be able to access any scripting component at all, indiscriminately. For this purpose, the OSA supplies a special component called the *Generic Scripting Component* (GSC). The program asks the Component Manager to let it talk to the GSC, and after that the GSC routes communications between the program and the appropriate scripting component such as AppleScript. Alternatively, a program might ask the Component Manager for direct access to one particular scripting component; such a program would not implement OSA scripting in a general way, but rather would be accessing just that one scripting language. Either way, once a program is in communication with the appropriate scripting component, the program can do scripting in that scripting language.

Now comes the really interesting part. The program itself doesn't do any of the work, and doesn't need to have any knowledge of the scripting language; that's the job of the component. For example, earlier we said, in the Terminal:

```
$ osascript -e 'tell app "Finder" to get disks'
```

The phrase 'tell app "Finder" to get disks' is an AppleScript expression; and when we gave this command in the Terminal, it was obeyed—references to all mounted volumes were displayed in the Terminal. But the Terminal doesn't know Apple-Script. The shell, to which we're talking in the Terminal, doesn't know AppleScript. And the osascript program, which we call from the shell, doesn't know AppleScript either. So who does know it? The AppleScript scripting component, of course.

Figure 4-2 diagrams a typical chain of events by which a program turns text into a runnable script, runs it, and is able to display the result, under the OSA.

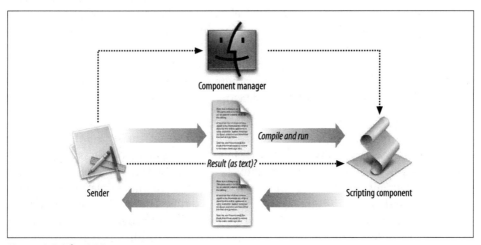

Figure 4-2. The OSA in action

1. The program asks the Component Manager to put it in touch with the scripting component.

2. The program obtains some text and hands it to the scripting component with instructions to compile and run it. If any of the expressions in this script are

equivalents of Apple events, those Apple events will be generated and sent, and we will then be in the world of Figure 4-1.

3. The program asks the scripting component for the result as text; the scripting component complies.

Figure 4-2 is how a script-editing application such as the Script Editor works. The Script Editor does *not* know any AppleScript. It merely serves as a front end to the AppleScript scripting component, where all the work of compiling and running scripts actually takes place. (There are some additional details having to do with how scripts are compiled, saved, and decompiled, and we will get to them in the course of this chapter.)

Maintenance of State

Step 3 in the discussion of Figure 4-2 contains a very remarkable statement: the program "asks the scripting component for the result." The startling implication is that the scripting component has a memory! We say that components *maintain state*. In fact, the component to which a program gets a connection is like an instance in the world of object-oriented programming: state is maintained *individually for each connection*. This is one of the things that makes components special.

Here's an analogy to help you visualize what's going on. Imagine the AppleScript scripting component as a kind of little universe, a universe where the knowledge of AppleScript resides. And imagine that this universe can make copies of itself. When a program asks the Component Manager for access to the AppleScript scripting component, as at the top of Figure 4-2, it isn't simply given a telephone line to the one master copy of the AppleScript universe sitting in the System; instead, it's as if the Component Manager makes a copy of the AppleScript universe and gives the program a telephone line to that copy. The program now has its *own private AppleScript universe*. This private copy of the AppleScript universe is technically an *instance* of the AppleScript scripting component.

The AppleScript scripting component instance can maintain state without getting confused at some global level, because it isn't operating at a global level. It's operating at a local level—local to the program that summoned it. Suppose we have two different programs, each of which gets a connection to the AppleScript scripting component and asks it to compile and execute a script. The AppleScript component does not get all flustered and say, "Oh, gosh, two different programs are trying to get me to do two different things at once!" Rather, there are in effect at that moment two different AppleScript component instances, the one that the first program is talking to and the one that the second program is talking to. Each program asks its own instance of the AppleScript component to compile and execute its script, and there is no conflict or confusion at all.

So each instance of the AppleScript scripting component maintains state. In terms of our analogy, each AppleScript universe remembers what goes on in it. Thus a program is able to return again and again to its same AppleScript universe and refer back to things that happened earlier. Thus, in the middle section of Figure 4-2, let's introduce a pause. Let's say the program hands the text to the AppleScript component and asks it just to compile it. The AppleScript component succeeds, reports this success, and stops. Now let some time pass. Then the program comes back to the AppleScript component and says: "Say, remember that script I had you compile a little while ago? Now I'd like you to run it." The AppleScript component can do this. The program does not hand the compiled version of the script over to the Apple-Script component to be run; the program doesn't have the compiled version of the script. The AppleScript component still has it. When it compiles a script, the Apple-Script component remembers the compiled version. Thus, when the program comes back and asks that the compiled script be run, there is no overhead of handing across a lot of compiled code, and the AppleScript component is ready to rock and roll (as a computer scientist would say) with no further ado.

The internal memory of an AppleScript scripting component instance will not persist forever. The lifetime of one of these instances can be no longer than that of the application that summoned it. When that application quits, any of these little component universes that it may have created must also fade away, and all the stuff that a component instance has been remembering trickles away like the air escaping from a deflating balloon.

So if a program asks the AppleScript scripting component to compile a script and then wants the compiled version to persist somehow after the program quits, it must take special steps to obtain the compiled version from the AppleScript component and save it in some way. This in fact is just what a program such as the Script Editor does when you save a compiled script. I'll talk more about that later in this chapter.

Script

A number of terms that are common in connection with AppleScript are used in a somewhat bewildering variety of senses. The word "script" is particularly liable to be tossed loosely about. This is unfortunate, especially since some of the meanings of "script" are important and rather technical. It's not a word one can do completely without, and so it is all the more crucial that its meaning not be blurred. This section tries to clarify the main ways in which the word "script" is used.

Script as Drive

To "script" an application is to automate it, to drive it, to target it. People say, "I'd like to script the Finder to rename some files automatically." There is an implication that the Finder already has the power to do things to files, and that we are merely taking advantage of this power by dictating programmatically a sequence of actions that Finder should take.

This sense of "script" is formalized in the way some sources define a "scripting language." This quotation comes from the ECMAScript Language Specification (*http://www.ecma-international.org/publications/standards/ECMA-262.htm*):

> A scripting language is a programming language that is used to manipulate, customise, and automate the facilities of an existing system. In such systems, useful functionality is already available through a user interface, and the scripting language is a mechanism for exposing that functionality to program control. In this way, the existing system is said to provide a host environment of objects and facilities, which completes the capabilities of the scripting language.

That is a perfect description of AppleScript. It has few powers of its own; it is meant primarily for controlling the powers of existing applications.

Script as Program

The preceding quotation from ECMA continues:

> A scripting language is intended for use by both professional and nonprofessional programmers. To accommodate non-professional programmers, some aspects of the language may be somewhat less strict.

This leap is common enough, but in my view it is unwarranted. Most languages that are commonly referred to as scripting languages are full-fledged programming languages, and make no particular concession to informality or inexperience. There is arguably nothing easy, and certainly nothing simplistic, about Tcl, Perl, or Scheme. As far as ease of use is concerned, any distinction between a scripting language and a programming language is a distinction without a difference.

Unfortunately this false distinction has played a major role in the history of AppleScript. To this day, Apple's main web page on AppleScript (*http://www.apple.com/applescript/*) leaps through extraordinary verbal hoops to avoid the word "program," which never appears. AppleScript can make "script files," it can "think," it can "automate," it's something you "use." The term "script" has ended up as an acceptable synonym for the politically incorrect "program." You do not program with AppleScript; you script with it. What you write are not programs; they're scripts. You're not a programmer; you're a scripter. This, I feel, is silly. AppleScript is a programming language (and, I happen to think, not a particularly easy one). You are a programmer, and you will write programs with AppleScript.

Script as Script Object

There is a rigorous sense in which it is right to speak of an AppleScript program as a script. To understand what that sense is, you need first to be aware that many AppleScript programs that you write or read will contain the term script used to demarcate part of their code. Here's an example:

```
script myScript
    display dialog "Hello from " & (get my name) & "!"
```

```
end script
run myScript -- dialog says: Hello from myScript!
```

Such a section of code is often called a *script object*, but the AppleScript language itself calls it a script.

Now, the interesting thing is that an AppleScript program as a whole is itself a script object. This may sound confusing, but in fact it's quite a cool and sophisticated aspect of AppleScript. Thus it is reasonable to speak of an AppleScript program as a whole as a script, not as a way of avoiding the fact that it is a program, but as a way of expressing its ontological status within the world of AppleScript. As you'll learn later, a script as a whole and a script object within a script have exactly the same ontological status. The script-as-a-whole does have some special features of its own, because it is the ultimate container of any other script objects; it is the top-level script object. But it is not different in kind from script objects that it may contain. So it is a "script," as any script object that it contains is also a "script." We'll fully explore the details of script objects later in the book, especially in Chapter 9.

Script as Scripting Component Operand

In a completely technical and rigorous sense, the term "script" refers to a unit of operation between a frontend program that asks for some AppleScript code to be compiled or executed and the scripting component that does the actual work. When such a program sends the scripting component a bunch of text for compilation, as in Figure 4-2, that bunch of text is assigned an identifying number. This number points to the code that is being remembered by the scripting component, and is called its *script ID*. It is by this arrangement that the frontend program and the scripting component can continue to talk about the script while it persists over time, as described earlier in this chapter ("Maintenance of State"). The code itself, the thing being remembered by the scripting component, is thus technically a script, because that's what the scripting component itself calls it. A script is a kind of entity that the scripting component holds on to and can perform various operations on, such as compiling it or executing it.

Script as File

The individual code file is an important and meaningful unit in AppleScript. Unlike some programming environments, where multiple files are assembled through a "make" or some other build process into a complete program, with AppleScript the individual file *is* the complete program. An AppleScript program and the file containing it are thus coterminous. But, as we have just seen, an AppleScript program is a script. Therefore it is natural to speak of the file in which your code is saved as itself a script. The script file icon in the Finder seems to represent the script. One says, "Double-click the script to open it in the Script Editor." The Script Editor itself speaks of saving your code as a script.

Compiling and Decompiling

Before an AppleScript program can be run, it must be compiled. To *compile* something means to transform it, behind the scenes, from text—the form in which a human user is able to read and edit the code—to a form consisting of actual executable instructions intended for a machine.

Compiling

The nature of compiled code depends upon the nature of the engine that runs it. In the case of a C program written for a Macintosh, the engine is the Macintosh's central processing unit (CPU); so the compiled code must consist of machine-language instructions in accordance with the CPU chip's specifications. Such machine-language instructions, indeed, are the only instructions your computer can really execute, because the computer's ultimate "brain" *is* the CPU.

In the case of AppleScript, the engine is the AppleScript scripting component, and compiled code does not consist of anything so low-level. AppleScript compiled code is *bytecode*: roughly, the nouns and verbs of the original text are translated into some sort of compressed, coded equivalent (called *tokens*). These tokens are meaningful only to the AppleScript scripting component's run-engine. When it runs the code, the engine still has to parse whatever tokens it meets along its path of execution, accumulating them into chunks and translating these chunks further in order to execute them. It is usual to describe a language that is compiled and executed in this way as being *interpreted*.

There isn't necessarily anything shameful about being an interpreted language. (After all, Java is an interpreted language, and yet some people take it seriously.) Being an interpreted language does mean that running AppleScript code is relatively slow, since the compiled code must be processed further while being run before it can *really* be run, and there is a heavy layer of operation (the runtime engine) between the compiled code and the CPU. Whether you'll perceive this slowness depends on the nature of the script and the speed of your computer; typically the observable bottleneck will be the time required for communicating with the target scriptable application and for that application to process commands and queries, not the overall speed of the AppleScript runtime engine.

If running even a compiled script is slow, why bother to compile beforehand? Well, for one thing, the nature of bytecode is such that it can be executed in linear fashion; tokens are not interpreted until and unless execution reaches them, and they can be interpreted by gathering them up in order. With raw text, on the other hand, you could be saying anything at all—you could be saying nonsense—and AppleScript would have to work very hard to find this out. By doing that hard work at compile time, not at execution time, AppleScript makes execution faster. The AppleScript compiler is what's called a *single-pass compiler*; this is a fairly simple-minded approach to compilation, but it helps to ensure that your script has a certain level of legality and overall consistency *before* runtime. (Of course, even a legal, successfully compiled script could still choke at runtime, but this would be for a different kind of reason; we'll see many examples in the course of the book.)

Also, the use of compilation makes AppleScript a better language. For instance, the following AppleScript code is legal:

```
sayHowdy( )
on sayHowdy( )
    display dialog "Howdy"
end sayHowdy
```

In this code, we call a handler, sayHowdy( ), *before we've defined it*. If AppleScript code were not compiled ahead of time, this would not be possible, because upon encountering this reference to a handler it has not yet met, the runtime engine simply wouldn't know what to do.

Decompiling

In the Script Editor, an uncompiled script, or those regions of the script that have been edited since the last compilation, will appear in a single font and size without any automatic indentation. A compiled script is *pretty-printed*; different kinds of word may appear in various colors, fonts, and sizes (depending upon your formatting preferences), and there is automatic indentation in accordance with the script's structure. This pretty-printing is performed by the AppleScript scripting component; the Script Editor merely shows it to you, by asking the AppleScript component for the compiled version in a form suitable for display to a human user.

The AppleScript scripting component, however, remembers the compiled script as bytecode, not as human-readable text. In order to respond to the Script Editor's request to supply the compiled script in human-readable form, the AppleScript scripting component must transform the bytecode into text. This is called *decompiling*. So the pretty-printed text that you see when you compile your text in the Script Editor is not merely a colorful version of *your* text; it's a completely *different* text, supplied by decompiling the compiled script.

A curious consequence of this is that some of the words constituting your script may differ before and after compilation. For example, suppose you type this code:

```
tell app "Finder" to get ref disk 1
```

It compiles, but in the process it is transformed into this:

```
tell application "Finder" to get a reference to disk 1
```

The reason is that some AppleScript terms have synonyms that are acceptable for purposes of compilation, but the scripting component does not remember, in the compiled bytecode, that you used one of these synonyms. It substitutes, at compile time, a token signifying the canonical form of the term; thus, when it decompiles the bytecode, what you see is the canonical form.

When AppleScript reformats your script in the course of pretty-printing it, it may render it harder to read rather than easier. For example, AppleScript allows you to break long lines into shorter lines through the use of a continuation character (¬); at compile time AppleScript will sometimes undo your attempts to use this feature, removing your continuation characters or putting them somewhere else. If I compile this code:

```
do shell script "echo 'hi'" ¬
    password "myPassword"
```

AppleScript rebreaks it like this:

```
do shell script ¬
    "echo 'hi'" password "myPassword"
```

This looks like a trivial annoyance, but if the line were longer it wouldn't be so trivial. The problem stems from the fact that the bytecode contains no information about whitespace, so the new formatting imposed by the decompilation process may not correspond to your original whitespace. Fortunately, the new version of the Script Editor wraps long lines, which makes this much less of a problem than it used to be.

External Referents Needed at Compile Time

AppleScript is a little language, leaving it up to various external entities such as scriptable applications (or scripting additions) to extend the language as needed. When the time comes to compile a script, if it makes any use of such externally defined extensions to the language, those external entities *must be present*, and AppleScript *must be able to locate them*, so that it can ascertain whether the words you're using in your code correspond to extensions to the language defined in these external entities, and if so, how to translate them into bytecode.

To see what I mean, let's start with code like this:

```
get disk 1
```

If that's all your script says, it won't compile at all, because the notion "disk" used as a class (which is how it's being used here) isn't part of the AppleScript language. You can use this phrase only with reference to some external entity, such as a scriptable application, that does define the notion "disk" used as a class, as part of its way of extending the AppleScript language. Now, suppose we just make up such an application:

```
tell application "NoSuchApp" to get disk 1
```

When you try to compile this, you're presented with a dialog listing every application, and posing the question: "Where is NoSuchApp?" AppleScript has realized that although, in the AppleScript language proper, the notion "disk" is meaningless the way you're using it, it might be meaningful in the context of this application NoSuchApp. AppleScript therefore attempts to find the application. (I do not know the exact steps used in the search.) But NoSuchApp can't be found, because there's no such app. If you cannot at this moment provide AppleScript with a pointer to NoSuchApp, the script will simply not compile.

Interestingly, you can nominate *any* application as NoSuchApp; it doesn't have to be called NoSuchApp. This makes sense because the problem might merely be that the name has changed or you've typed it wrong. For example, you could claim that NoSuchApp is Address Book. However, having investigated Address Book's vocabulary, AppleScript concludes that Address Book doesn't know what a "disk" is, and the script still won't compile.

Now suppose we try again, and this time, when AppleScript asks us about NoSuchApp, we tell it that NoSuchApp is the Finder. The script now compiles successfully, because the Finder does know what a "disk" is; and in the compiled script (that is to say, the decompiled script) the name "NoSuchApp" is changed to "Finder".

To repeat: you cannot compile a script in the absence of the necessary external entities. AppleScript will look for these entities, and will consult you for assistance if it can't find them; but if neither AppleScript nor you can locate them, that's the end of the story.

We'll return to the business of how AppleScript knows about particular applications' privately defined vocabulary, later in this chapter ("Dictionary") and again later in the book (Chapter 19).

Saving Compiled Scripts

Compilation takes some time—several seconds, in the case of a lengthy script. Thus, with a script that will not change and that one intends to execute at some future time, it would be nice, at runtime, to skip compilation altogether, avoiding any initial delay and permitting the runtime engine to leap into action immediately. The current instance of the AppleScript scripting component remembers the compiled script and is ready to run it at a moment's notice; but the current instance of the AppleScript scripting component goes out of existence when we quit the host application (such as the Script Editor). Therefore we would like a way for the compiled script to outlive the current instance of the AppleScript scripting component. AppleScript allows this; it is possible to save a script in its compiled form. The result is a compiled script file (see "Script as File" earlier in this chapter).

 A saved compiled script file has extension *.scpt* on Mac OS X and is of type 'osas' on previous systems. The Script Editor saves such a file with both features, and the resulting file can be opened, edited, and executed on both Mac OS X and Mac OS 9 (the latter only if the version of Script Editor is sufficiently recent). There is also a new "script bundle" format with extension *.scptd*, which is not backward-compatible to before Mac OS X 10.3 ("Panther").

The reason for the caveat about the version of the Script Editor is that there are two ways to save the compiled script data—in the resource fork or in the data fork. Early versions of the Script Editor saved it as a resource. Recent versions of the Script Editor save it in the data fork, and you don't have to go back very far in time before you get to a version of the Script Editor that can't cope with this. So there are really three compiled script file formats: the old format with the script data in the resource fork, the new format with the script data in the data fork, and the really new format with the script data as a file inside a bundle. This is something to be careful of. We already saw in Chapter 2 that REALbasic couldn't read the new formats and that Xcode's NSAppleScript class couldn't read the old format.

In the Script Editor, when you save a script, you're offered a choice of format in which to save it: you can save it as text (or "script text," depending what version of the Script Editor you're using), or as a script (a compiled script file). The former saves just the current text appearing in the window, even if not yet compiled. The latter attempts to compile the script if it contains any uncompiled changes, and then, if compilation was successful, saves the bytecode (also called the *script data*). You can confirm this by getting a hex dump of a saved compiled script:

```
$ vis -otw -F 60 myScript.scpt
FasdUAS\0401.101.10\016\000\000\000\004\017\377\377\000\
\001\000\002\000\003\001\377\377\000\000\015\000\001\000\
[... and so on ...]
```

Nothing legible here. It's bytecode, all right. But of course when you open this compiled script in the Script Editor, it shows up legibly. The mechanism, as you have surely guessed, is that the saved bytecode is handed to the AppleScript scripting component, and then decompiled for display.

You cannot save as a compiled script file code that, for whatever reason, will not compile. This seems tautological, but it can be surprising nevertheless, so it is worth mentioning.

References to applications

When you open a compiled script file, and the saved bytecode is handed to the AppleScript scripting component, and the scripting component decompiles the script for display, the script faces issues with regard to any external information parallel to what happens when it is compiled originally. If a compiled script targets a particular application, that application must be located; if it cannot be located, the compiled script can't be decompiled, and it can't be opened in the Script Editor.

Enough information about the application is stored with the compiled script to enable the AppleScript scripting component to find it under most circumstances. The compiled script contains an alias to the application; an *alias* is a very clever kind of pointer, such that if you change the application's name, or move it to a different folder on the same volume, the compiled script will continue to keep track of the application, and will open with no problem in the Script Editor. But if you move the application to a different volume, the compiled script may lose track of it, so that when you try to open it in the Script Editor, you'll get the dialog asking you to locate it. If you don't, the compiled script won't open. If you do, then the compiled script will open; the script is now modified within the AppleScript scripting component, so that the reference to the application points at it in its new location.* There's more about this decompilation process, and about what happens if you lie to AppleScript and nominate the wrong application as the missing application, in Chapter 19.

In many situations, you can hand a compiled script file over to some application for execution without asking that the text of the script be displayed to you—that is, without decompiling it. (See, for some examples, "Script Runner" in Chapter 2.) As the compiled script executes, if it refers to externals, it may face some issues parallel to those that it would face at compilation and decompilation time; but these issues do not arise until execution is underway and code that targets an application is actually encountered. If at that point the AppleScript scripting component can't find the target application, what happens depends upon the context. Ideally we would like to be presented with the dialog asking for the application, and this does usually happen; but sometimes it doesn't. In the case of the Script Menu, for example, a script that targets an application that can't be found will simply fail silently. Furthermore, having helped the AppleScript scripting component find the application, you'd like that information to be saved back into the script so that next time the script will run without assistance. Again, sometimes this happens and sometimes it doesn't, depending upon the context.

Run-only scripts

A compiled script can optionally be saved as *run-only*. Normally, a compiled script actually contains two kinds of information:

- The tokens (bytecode) needed to run the script
- Further information needed to decompile the script and display it to the user

For example, let's say you put a comment into your script. This comment is nothing that the runtime can execute; that's what it means to be a comment. But clearly you don't want this comment thrown away merely because you compile the script; the bytecode retains it, so that when the script is decompiled, you can still read the comment. Similarly, the names of variables are intended entirely for humans; as far as bytecode is concerned, it would be sufficient to assign them numbers, and that's probably what AppleScript bytecode does. But you don't want your variable names

---

* But this does not "dirty" the script file itself, so you can then close it, and it will not ask whether you want to save it, and will not retain this knowledge of the application's new location; you'll have to go through the whole rigmarole again the next time you open the script file. I regard this as the fault of AppleScript, which apparently has no way to alert the Script Editor that the compiled script has changed.

to be lost, so they are saved as part of the bytecode, even though they aren't needed for execution.

When you save a compiled script as run-only, the tokens needed merely to decompile the script and display it to the user are thrown away. This makes the compiled script much smaller and probably causes it to run a bit faster, but the compiled script can never again be displayed to the user. If you have not saved another copy, you will never again be able to read or edit that script.

If a run-only script loses track of an external referent, such as an application, there is no way to show the script where the referent is and recompile. In the case of an application reference, the dialog asking where the application is will appear, the user can then show AppleScript the application, and the script will then continue executing; but this information cannot be saved back into the script, so the next time the script runs, the dialog will appear again. Because of this you may want to think twice before saving a script as run-only. You're probably saving it this way because you want to keep it from prying eyes—you want to be able to send the script to other people so they can use it, without their being able to read it. But you should weigh against this the possibility that you will anger your users when the script doesn't work properly and they can't do anything about it.

In my tests, it was possible at least sometimes to open a run-only script within the Script Editor, though of course no text appeared. It was then possible to press the Run button, but nothing would happen. This entire situation is very confusing, and I regard it as a bug (presumably in Script Editor); it should not be possible to open a run-only script in an editor at all.

Script Text File

The Script Editor offers the option to save a script as text (or "script text," depending what version of the Script Editor you're using). A script text file is simply a text file, such as can be opened by any word processor. No bytecode is saved into the file. (But the Script Editor does also try to compile the script even when you save it as text, which seems unnecessary.)

A script text file consists of ordinary text in the default system encoding (usually MacRoman). It has file extension *.applescript* on Mac OS X and is of type 'TEXT' on Mac OS 9 and earlier. The Script Editor saves such a file with both features, and it can be opened on both platforms.

A script text file can be opened with a dedicated editor such as the Script Editor. The situation is then exactly as if you had just typed the code into the Script Editor: if the code is valid and all external referents can be found, the code can be compiled and run.

A script text file cannot generally be run from a script runner application, such as the Script Menu, because the script is not compiled and the application is not prepared to do the compilation for you.

Since a compiled script file can be decompiled and edited further, as well as executed directly, what's the good of a script text file? Apple's documentation implies that it isn't much good, and calls it a "last resort" format; Apple's advice would seem to be that a compiled script file is the standard and most readily usable and communicable format, the format you would use when sending a script to someone else to be run on another machine.

However, I'm not so sure that a compiled script is so very communicable, or that it is better for such purposes than a script text file. There are various formats of compiled script file, and the new ones aren't backward-compatible: a compiled script file saved by the current version of the Script Editor can't be opened by some older versions of the Script Editor, and a compiled script bundle isn't backward-compatible to any system before Mac OS X 10.3 ("Panther"). Plus, as mentioned in the previous section, it is possible for a compiled script to face difficulties with regard to external referents that it can't locate; if these external referents can't be located at all, the script can't even be opened for editing, let alone executed. By contrast, a text file can always be opened under any system and on any machine; AppleScript and the Script Editor are present on every machine, so it is always possible, with valid code, to compile the script afresh.

Not infrequently I have seen AppleScript utterly confused about a reference to an application when a compiled script is moved to a different computer. For example, recently I downloaded from the Internet a compiled script that, when I tried to run it, generated a mysterious error message and didn't work, so I opened it and found references in it to an application that wasn't an application at all (it was just some file buried deep in /usr/share/emacs). Clearly what had happened was that the compiled script had lost track of the application it was supposed to be pointing at, but it was so confused that it didn't even realize this, and instead of asking me for the application's location, had substituted for the name of this application the name of a completely different file. The really devilish part of this situation was that there was no way for me to learn the name of the application the script was really supposed to be pointing to (since the name had been changed in the course of decompilation). Had this script been text, there would have been no difficulty at all, because the name of the application in the text would have been preserved, and I would have been able to compile, save, and execute the script on my own machine without any problem.

(In this regard, a valuable feature of Late Night Software's Script Debugger is that when it saves a compiled script file it also saves the original text into the file, as a TEXT resource. In a pinch, therefore, the text can be recovered and used to help fix problems with external referents.)

Applet and Droplet

An *applet* is a compiled script file format that functions as an executable. A dedicated editor such as the Script Editor offers the option to save a compiled script as an applet (or "application," depending on your Script Editor version). When you open an applet from the Finder, it launches as if it were an application and its code runs. Furthermore, an applet is scriptable. In short, an applet is a simple, easy way for someone who knows AppleScript to write a little application. This application has just about no user interface to speak of (unless some is added by way of a scripting addition). But the disadvantages of this can easily be outweighed by the simplicity of writing one.

> An applet is an application. It is saved in Mac OS X with file extension *.app*, and in Mac OS 9 it has file type 'APPL' and creator 'aplt'. The Mac OS X Script Editor saves the applet with both features. There is also a new "application bundle" format, also with file extension *.app*, which is not backward-compatible with systems prior to Mac OS X 10.3 ("Panther").

A *droplet* is a form of applet; the difference is that a droplet does something when file or folder icons are dragged-and-dropped onto its icon in the Finder. Typically it then proceeds to process those files or folders in some way. Technically, a droplet is simply an applet whose script contains an open handler for dealing with the drop. Indeed, the very same script application can operate both as an applet (it does something when it is opened by launching) and as a droplet (it does something when files or folders are dragged-and-dropped onto its icon). A droplet has a different creator type from an applet ('dplt'), and it has a different icon, which looks like an applet's icon with the addition of a downward arrow. The Script Editor makes this distinction when you save the file, based on the presence or absence of an open handler.

Since opening an applet from the Finder launches it as an application, the applet needs to be opened in some other way in order to edit its script. For example, you can choose Open from the File menu within the Script Editor and select the applet, or drop the applet's icon onto Script Editor's icon. If the applet's script was not saved as run-only, the compiled script will then be decompiled and will be displayed for further editing, exactly as if this were just an ordinary compiled script file. A running applet may also display a menu item offering a chance to edit it. Thus, saving a compiled script as an applet does not prevent you from continuing to edit and develop the script—nor does it hide the script from prying eyes (for that, you must also save the script as run-only).

An applet contains a very small amount of genuine executable code—just enough to qualify it as a true application. This code, called the *bootstrap code*, is what initially runs when the applet is launched. It summons a scripting component called the Script

Application Component. This component does the rest, handing the applet's compiled script over to the AppleScript scripting component for execution, and taking care of such things as putting up the applet's description window if there is one. The applet also contains the other resources necessary to make it a scriptable application.

In earlier versions of the Mac OS 9 Script Editor there was an option to save as a Mac OS X applet, but in my experiments a Mac OS X applet saved in this way wouldn't open successfully in Mac OS X. The most recent version of the Mac OS 9 Script Editor abolishes this distinction, and offers to save simply as an "application"; the resulting applet runs under either Mac OS X or Mac OS 9.

In earlier versions of the Mac OS X Script Editor (such as version 1.9), an applet could be set to "require Classic"; in this case the applet was saved as a Classic-only application and the Get Info option to toggle between opening in Mac OS X and opening in Classic was absent. An applet (but not an applet bundle) saved using the current Script Editor in Mac OS X can be launched in a previous system.

For further details about how to make and write applets and droplets, as well as to learn how to use AppleScript Studio to write more sophisticated applications with a user interface, see Chapter 24.

Scripting Addition

A *scripting addition* is a code library, loaded by the AppleScript scripting component instance, that implements vocabulary extending the AppleScript language. Behind the scenes, communication with a scripting addition uses Apple events, just as does communication with a scriptable application. The difference, from the AppleScript programmer's point of view, is a linguistic one: the scripting addition's vocabulary is available to scripts compiled and run on that machine with no need to target any particular application. In other words, the extended vocabulary implemented by a scripting addition appears to the programmer to be built into AppleScript itself.

Scripting additions are typically written in a compiled lower-level language such as C. Their purpose is usually to bring to AppleScript some functionality that can be implemented in this lower-level language (possibly by calling into the Macintosh Toolbox) but is otherwise missing from AppleScript itself.

 A scripting addition on Mac OS 9 is a resource file of type 'osax'. On Mac OS X it can also be a bundle with extension *.osax*. A scripting addition is often referred to as an *osax* (plural *osaxen*). On Mac OS 9, osaxen live in the System Folder, in its Scripting Additions subfolder. On Mac OS X the supplied osaxen live in */System/ Library/ScriptingAdditions*; the user may add osaxen to */Library/ ScriptingAdditions* or to *~/Library/ScriptingAdditions*, according to the domain of their desired availability.

AppleScript is a little language, and at a very early stage it was felt to be a bit *too* little; so certain sorely missed features were added by Apple itself, implemented through scripting additions present on every machine. This got more confusing as more such "official" scripting additions were added. In recent times the situation has been simplified considerably by the incorporation of most of these scripting additions into a single scripting addition called *Standard Additions* (or, on Mac OS X, *StandardAdditions*).

Other developers are welcome to write scripting additions, and many have done so; there is a large body of freeware, shareware, and commercial scripting additions available. Typically the reason for writing a scripting addition rather than an application is simply that its extensions to the language are present universally without launching or targeting an application. On the other hand, this universal presence can be a problem, because it is possible for vocabulary terms implemented in different scripting additions to conflict with one another or with the vocabulary implemented by particular applications or even AppleScript itself. This point is taken up again in Chapter 19.

Dictionary

A scriptable application defines a repertory of Apple events to which it is prepared to respond, and to be scriptable with AppleScript, it must publish information about this repertory, so that when a script targeting the application is compiled or decompiled, the AppleScript scripting component can confirm that the English-like words of its code really are defined by the application, and can translate between those English-like words and the Apple event structures that will actually be used when communicating with that application as the script runs. Such publication is performed through a dictionary. Not just scriptable applications must have a dictionary; scripting additions must have one too. And AppleScript itself has a dictionary (displayed in Appendix A).

Physically, a dictionary may take one of two forms:

- In Mac OS 9, and optionally on Mac OS X (typically under Carbon), a dictionary is a resource of type 'aete'. The format of an 'aete' resource ('aete' stands for Apple Event Terminology Extension) is formally defined in:

  /System/Library/Frameworks/ApplicationServices.framework/Versions/A/ Frameworks/AE.framework/Versions/A/Headers/AEUserTermTypes.h

  and is documented at *http://developer.apple.com/documentation/mac/IAC/IAC-308.html*.

- In a Cocoa application, a dictionary is a set of XML (property list) text files inside the application's package, with file extensions *.scriptSuite* and *.scriptTerminology*. For the *.scriptSuite* and *.scriptTerminology* file formats, see:

  http://developer.apple.com/documentation/Cocoa/Conceptual/Scriptability/Tasks/ SuiteDefs.html

A new XML format, the *.sdef* file, is currently under development; it will represent within a single file all the information in both a *.scriptSuite* file and a *.scriptTerminology* file. You can learn more about it from the sdef manpages.

A dictionary may be published statically or dynamically. It is published statically if AppleScript can read the dictionary right off the disk; it can do this with an 'aete' resource. It is published dynamically if AppleScript must ask the running application for its dictionary (which it does by sending the application an Apple event, of course). A Cocoa application implements scriptability by publishing its dictionary dynamically, because AppleScript can't read the *.scriptSuite* and *.scriptTerminology* files directly. An advantage of the dynamic approach to dictionary publication is that the dictionary may be dynamically constructed—that is, the application can actually vary its own dictionary in response to particular circumstances. A disadvantage is that the application must be running in order for AppleScript to acquire its dictionary (and so it must be launched merely in order for AppleScript to compile or decompile a script that targets it).

A dictionary contains two kinds of information:

Machine-readable information

The dictionary describes its repertory of Apple events in a manner intended primarily for the AppleScript scripting component, and not for a human user, since the whole idea of AppleScript is to shield the user from having to gaze upon raw Apple events. Still, you're allowed to look at it, and this can be useful if you need to know what's going on behind the scenes when you talk to a particular application. An easy way to get a look at this part of the dictionary is to use Script Debugger, which provides an option to show a dictionary in terms of Apple events.

Human-readable information

The part of the dictionary specifically intended for human eyes lists the actual English-like words you may use when targeting the application, along with comments that can contain additional information about what these words do and how you are to use them. The comments are intended for human beings only, but the listing of English-like terminology is also used by AppleScript when compiling or decompiling, to translate between English-like words and Apple events.

A raw dictionary, in and of itself, is not intended to be particularly readable by a human being. Under Mac OS 9 and before, in fact, it can be quite a chore to inspect a raw dictionary; the best way is to use a dedicated 'aete' resource editor. A very good free one is Gary McGath's EightyRez (*http://www.panix.com/~gmcgath/EightyRez.html*). A Cocoa application's dictionary is just text, and can be studied with the Property List Editor (included with the Developer Tools) or with any word processor. For example, take a look in */System/Library/Frameworks/Foundation.framework/Resources* at *NSCoreSuite.scriptSuite* and *NSCoreSuite.scriptTerminology*. You might not understand everything you're seeing, but you'll get a fair idea of what goes on in a dictionary.

Usually, the way you look at a dictionary is through some utility that knows how to parse it and present it in a human-readable fashion. A dedicated script editor is an example of such a utility. That's because when you're writing a script you are likely to want to study the dictionary of the application you're targeting, so that you know what to say to it; indeed, it may be said that nine-tenths of the art of programming with AppleScript is figuring out what a targeted application expects and permits you to say to it (as we saw in Chapter 3). You might think that this would be no art at all, since there's the dictionary giving you this information straight out. But it turns out that a dictionary is a remarkably poor device for communicating to a human user the information that is really needed. A dictionary can be well or badly written, and in any case it doesn't really tell you how much of the AppleScript language the application implements, how well it implements it, and (most important) how you're supposed to combine the vocabulary listed in the dictionary into expressions that will cause the application to do what you want. A great many trees will have to die so that we can mull over the implications of this difficulty in Chapter 19.

Scriptable, Recordable, Attachable

These three adjectives refer to three levels on which an application can be scriptable. They aren't really levels, but they seem to form a natural progression. That progression seems to have diminishing returns, since very few scriptable applications are also recordable, and *very* few scriptable applications are also attachable.

Scriptable

An application is *scriptable* by means of AppleScript if it defines a repertory of Apple events to which it is prepared to respond, and publishes that repertory in a dictionary. So, the usual way to learn whether an application is scriptable is to try to open its dictionary with an editor such as the Script Editor. If it has a dictionary, it's scriptable.

(At least, that's how things are supposed to work. We're assuming here that all the pieces of the mechanism are behaving properly. It's possible for an application to lie. For example, it could publish a dictionary giving the impression that it responds to Apple events it doesn't respond to. At the furthest extreme, an application could *look* scriptable, in the sense that it publishes a dictionary, but not actually *be* scriptable. Yes, I've seen applications that do that.)

Recordable

The idea of a scriptable application's being *recordable* is that the application can help the user learn to drive it with AppleScript by constructing a script in reverse: the user performs ordinary actions in the application, choosing from menu items, pushing buttons, or whatever, and meanwhile these actions are translated into the code that would be used to accomplish the same effect via AppleScript.

To try this out, start with a recordable application; here, we'll use BBEdit. Start it up. Now use a dedicated script editor such as the Script Editor. In the Script Editor's main window, there's a Record button. Press it. Now switch to BBEdit and type ⌘-N to make a new window. Now return to the Script Editor and press the Stop button. You will notice that the following text has magically appeared in the Script Editor window:

```
tell application "BBEdit"
    activate
    make new text window
end tell
```

That is the AppleScript code you would have to execute in order to cause the same actions to occur through a script.

Recording is implemented partly by AppleScript and partly by the application. Pressing the Record button in Script Editor signals to AppleScript that it should start watching for recordable events. When it sees a recordable event, AppleScript decompiles it and sends the decompiled text to Script Editor, which displays the text. The only question is then what constitutes a recordable event. The answer turns out to be surprisingly simple: it's any Apple event that an application sends to itself. In fact, an application is allowed to send itself a "fake" Apple event just so that if recording happens to be turned on, this Apple event will be detected and treated as the AppleScript equivalent for whatever else is happening in the application.

An application can deal elegantly both with recordability and with scriptability by being written in a factored style. A *factored* application is one that triggers its own functionality (or at least some portion of it) by sending itself Apple events. For example, in BBEdit when you type ⌘-N (or choose New from the File menu), BBEdit responds by sending itself the Apple event that commands a new text window to be created; it then receives this Apple event and responds to it by creating a new text window.* Under this architecture, it makes no difference to BBEdit whether a user working inside BBEdit types ⌘-N or whether a script tells it to "make new text window," because ultimately BBEdit receives the same Apple event in either case, without knowing or caring whether it came from itself or from a script. So in a factored application, scriptability is built in at a deep level, and the user interface is wrapped around that. A factored application has some advantages for the developer, making it easier to continue modifying the application while maintaining scriptability; plus, of course, it makes the application recordable "for free."

---

* Wittgenstein asked, "What is left over when I subtract the fact that my arm goes up, from the fact that I raise my arm?" Now we know: an Apple event.

There is no way to find out whether an application is recordable, if you don't know in advance, other than by trying to record it. Very few applications are recordable on Mac OS X. As of this writing, there is some indication that the Finder may be recordable in Mac OS X 10.3; if so, this should please users accustomed to the Finder's recordability in Mac OS 9 and before, who have missed this feature in earlier versions of Mac OS X.

Attachable

An *attachable* application gives the user the opportunity to interfere with certain incoming Apple events by means of a script. This means that the user can customize what happens when an Apple event arrives. If the application is scriptable, then the user may be able to customize the effect of scripting the application. If the application is factored, then the user may be able to customize the effect of performing an action within the user interface. The only applications I know that are strongly and deeply attachable in this canonical sense are Script Debugger and Smile.

There are no standards for how attachability is to be implemented, however, and as a result it is not entirely clear what constitutes attachability. Perhaps one should distinguish between degrees of attachability. For example, folder actions (see "Automatic Location" in Chapter 2 and "Folder Actions" in Chapter 24) may be seen as a mild form of attachability, since you are customizing what happens when certain events take place in the Finder's user interface. On that definition, one could also call BBEdit's factored menu implementation a form of attachability: when you choose a menu item in BBEdit, if there is an appropriately named script in the *BBEdit Support/ Menu Scripts* folder, that script is called, so you can customize what happens in response to the menu item.

The AppleScript Language

Part II is the heart of the book; it describes the AppleScript programming language.

This part is intended for use both as a reference and as a source of instruction. The order of exposition is pedagogical, and the chapters are meant to be read in order.

The chapters are:

CHAPTER 5

Introducing AppleScript

This chapter describes the AppleScript language in very general terms. What sort of language is it? What is it like to learn and to use? The chapter is informal, opinionated, and personal. It is also nonessential, so readers who don't want to know my thoughts about what AppleScript "feels like" and just want to get on with the facts can skip this chapter.

Why include such a chapter at all? Simply because the AppleScript language itself seems to call for some explanation. It's full of contradictions. Users frequently express a certain degree of exasperation with AppleScript. Often, it seems to make easy things hard and hard things all but impossible; a program that should take five minutes to write takes an hour. Yet at the same time AppleScript has some remarkably sophisticated features.

To learn a computer language is to sense, in some measure, the mental makeup of its creator. I don't really know who invented AppleScript or what the reasoning process was, but one definitely senses certain aims and ideas floating about in the background. They are great ideas, but they don't always seem quite to fit together, and there are some odd holes in how some of them have been implemented. It is this combination of characteristics in this particular way that gives AppleScript its peculiar flavor. This chapter tries to describe that flavor.

A "Little Language"

The "little language" philosophy, as expressed in computer languages such as LOGO, Smalltalk, and Scheme, comes in various forms; but the very words, "little language," tell you most of what you need to know. Littleness can be a virtue in a number of ways. A little computer language can fit in a small space and be run by a small interpreter. A little computer language can be easy to learn. A computer language is a tool to make tools, so the initial tool itself can be quite minimal, provided it has the power to make any other tools that may prove necessary.

All of these notions apply to AppleScript. AppleScript was to be easy for users to learn, so the less there was of it, the better. AppleScript appeared at a time when the idea of a computer with as much as four megabytes of random-access memory still felt rather strange and extravagant. To minimize expenditure of resources of time and space, it had to be compilable with just a single pass. In these days of hundreds of megabytes of RAM and dozens of processes running simultaneously, it's easy to forget that AppleScript comes from a day when running more than one application at once on your Macintosh was a relatively new experience, and liable to tax the computer's resources to the utmost. At the time, AppleScript itself needed to be small simply to stay out of the way of other applications. The first version of AppleScript could load a scripting component instance and run a heavily recursive script in less than 300K of RAM.

And after all, those other applications were the whole point. The purpose of Apple-Script was to tell *other* programs to do things. Thus AppleScript itself could afford to be so minimal as to have next to no power of its own. AppleScript has minimal string-munging and number-crunching facilities, but then AppleScript is not intended for munging strings or crunching numbers—it's made for driving applications, and *they* can munge the strings and crunch the numbers if need be.

So *is* AppleScript's littleness a virtue? Well, if you're used to a full-fledged scripting language—Perl, for instance—AppleScript comes as something of a disappointment. Perl has some hundreds of built-in functions; AppleScript has about a dozen. Perl has built-in support for regular expressions and trigonometry; AppleScript doesn't. The "little language" philosophy seems very cute just until you actually need to get something done. On the other hand if you don't try to misuse it, AppleScript seems quite adequate, especially since it can avail itself directly of the power of Perl and other built-in Unix tools. As I said in Chapter 1, success may simply be a question of combining specialities appropriately.

Extensibility and Its Perils

As part and parcel of its power to communicate with other applications, AppleScript concedes to those applications an ability to extend the language. Such linguistic extensions appear temporarily to be part of AppleScript, only for just so long as your program is talking to the application that provides them. We thus have a language that grows and shrinks and mutates depending on what application it is talking to. For example, AppleScript itself knows nothing of a disk or a folder, but the Finder does. So as long as your AppleScript code is talking to the Finder, it can talk about a disk or a folder. The moment it is no longer talking to the Finder, it can't.

This architecture, as we saw in Chapter 4, has its practical consequences. An Apple-Script program that talks to a particular application becomes something of a nonentity in the absence of that application. If you send your friend a compiled script file that talks to BBEdit and your friend doesn't have BBEdit, the result isn't just that your friend can't run the script—your friend can't even *read* the script. Similarly, even if you know all about BBEdit and how it extends the AppleScript language, you can't write and compile any AppleScript code that talks to BBEdit unless you have BBEdit present on your machine at the time.

For the programmer, the main consequence of AppleScript's extensibility is that it is not one language but many—as many as there are applications to which you might wish to speak. We saw this consequence in action in Chapter 3, where all my knowledge of AppleScript was as nothing compared to my ignorance of how to talk to FrameMaker. Thus the AppleScript programmer, no matter how expert, remains something of a perpetual neophyte. To learn to talk to a new scriptable application is to learn a new language. Just the other day I had an email from an AppleScript-savvy friend expressing an unwillingness to try a new application just because "I hate trying to figure out the scripting quirks of every app." AppleScript thus displays some tendency to frighten its most devoted users from doing the very thing it was intended to do.

The "English-likeness" Monster

As we have already seen, AppleScript is English-like. Its vocabulary appears to be made up of English imperative verbs, nouns, prepositional phrases, and even an occasional relative clause.

Whether this English-likeness is a good thing or not is debatable. It is probably responsible for attracting users who would otherwise be frightened by the rigid-looking pseudo-mathematical terseness of a language like Perl, with its funny variable names, its braces and brackets and semicolons. Personally, though, I'm not fond of AppleScript's English-likeness. For one thing, I feel it is misleading. It gives one the sense that one just knows AppleScript because one knows English; but that is not so. It also gives one the sense that AppleScript is highly flexible and accepting of commands expressed just however one cares to phrase them; and that is *really* not so. This sense is reinforced by AppleScript's abundance of synonyms. For example, instead of saying:

```
if x <= y
```

you can say:

```
if x is less than or equal to y
```

You are also allowed to use the word "the" wherever it feels natural. And nouns even come with plurals:

```
get the first word of "hello there"
get the words of "hello there"
```

Nevertheless, none of this is due to AppleScript's knowing any English. AppleScript actually has no natural language intelligence at all. AppleScript is every bit as mathematically structured, rigid, and unforgiving as Perl or any other computer language. If you step outside its rules by a tiny fraction of an inch, AppleScript slaps your hand just as any computer language would. The trouble here, I suggest, is that it was AppleScript's English-likeness that tempted you (subconsciously perhaps) to break the rules in the first place.

For example, later in the book I will have to leap up and down and wave my arms wildly to warn the reader not to confuse these two constructs:

```
get words 1 thru 4 of "now is the winter of our discontent"
get text from word 1 to word 4 of "now is the winter of our discontent"
```

The natural tendency to meld these two constructs (which do very different things) into an illegal blend such as "get words 1 to 4" or "get text from words 1 thru 4" is almost overwhelming. That's because in English these notions are too similar to one another. If they were represented by harsh mathematical symbols, there would be no danger of confusing them; but because they look like English, the part of one's brain that speaks English takes over and tries to soften the boundaries between these expressions in the same way that the boundary between them is soft in the world of natural language.

It is often the case, too, that AppleScript vocabulary looks like a certain English part of speech when it can't in fact be used as that part of speech would be. For example, in the Finder there is an application file property called has scripting terminology, which naturally leads one to try to say something like this:

```
if theApplication has scripting terminology
```

That won't compile; rather, you have to say this very un-English-like phrase:

```
if has scripting terminology of theApplication
```

Another problem with AppleScript's English-likeness is that with so many English words floating around the language, it can be hard to think up a meaningful variable name that isn't already in use for something else. The following lines of code are all illegal:

```
set name to "Matt"
set feet to 7
set count to 9
set center to 1.5
```

The trouble here is that so much of the English language has been reserved for AppleScript's personal use.

Then there is the fact that English is verbose. In most computer languages, you would make a variable x take on the value 4 by saying something like this:

```
x = 4
```

In AppleScript, you must say something wordy like one of these:

```
copy 4 to x
set x to 4
```

Doubtless not everyone would agree, but I find such expressions tedious to write and hard to read. In my experience, the human mind and eye are very good at parsing simple symbol-based equations and quasi-mathematical expressions, and I can't help feeling that AppleScript would be much faster to write and easier to read at a glance if it expressed itself in even a slightly more abstract notational style.

Object-likeness

In many computer languages, values are things that you talk about. In AppleScript, values are things that you talk *to*. The following is a legal way to add 4 and 5 in AppleScript:

```
tell 4
    get it + 5
end tell
```

The use of tell (we are addressing the number 4), get (we are ordering the number 4 about), and it (which means "whoever I am now addressing") shows the nature of the idiom. It is not actually necessary to talk this way; one can add 4 and 5 by saying something much simpler:

```
4 + 5
```

But this works because, behind the scenes, AppleScript is supplying the tell and the get for you, to make your life simpler. In AppleScript, whether you know it or not, you are *always* talking to some value and telling it to do something.

One might therefore suppose that AppleScript is an object-oriented language and that all values in AppleScript are objects. Perhaps, one thinks, AppleScript will turn out to be like Smalltalk, where "everything is an object." AppleScript also has certain values that are explicitly called "objects," and refers to the datatypes of all values as "classes." Plus, in a couple of areas AppleScript implements a kind of "inheritance" between one object (or class) and another. All of these things add to the impression that AppleScript might be object-oriented.

Personally, I remain doubtful as to whether AppleScript is really an object-oriented or even an object-based language. Apple's own documentation says flatly that it is, but I've come to think of AppleScript as merely having values with certain *object-like* aspects. Perhaps the reason for the object-likeness of AppleScript's values has something to do with the fact that AppleScript is all about sending messages (Apple events) to scriptable applications ("Apple Event" in Chapter 4). Having devised a syntax for representing this message-sending architecture in an English-like way, AppleScript's inventors seem to have generalized this syntax to pervade the language.

LISP-likeness

A number of features of AppleScript seem to suggest that someone on the original AppleScript team was fond of LISP (or some LISP dialect such as Scheme). Since I, too, am fond of Scheme, I rather like these features.

For example, AppleScript has lists, which are ordered collections of any values whatever. It provides certain primitive operations for dealing these lists, such as taking the first element, taking everything but the first element, and joining two lists into one (like Scheme's car, cdr, and cons). And AppleScript permits recursion (a subroutine calling itself).

Thus, it is possible to write AppleScript code that bears an extraordinary resemblance to Scheme code. To give an example, here's a little Scheme program that defines a routine for removing the *n*th element from a list, and then tests it:

```
(define remvix
    (lambda (ix ls)
        (cond
            ((null? ls)
                '())
            ((= ix 1)
                (cdr ls))
            (else
                (cons (car ls) (remvix (- ix 1) (cdr ls)))))))
(remvix 2 '(mannie moe jack))
```

And here's the same thing done in just the same style in AppleScript:

```
on remvix(ix, ls)
    if ls is {} then
        return {}
    else if ix is 1 then
        return rest of ls
    else
        return {item 1 of ls} & remvix(ix - 1, rest of ls)
    end if
end remvix
remvix(2, {"Mannie", "Moe", "Jack"})
```

Even if you don't know any Scheme or any AppleScript, the structural and stylistic similarity between these approaches is hard to miss; they are in fact move for move identical, the only differences between them being matters of syntactic detail. To be sure, I've stacked the deck by deliberately writing the AppleScript routine in a Scheme-like style; but the point is that AppleScript is capable of that style, and invites it.

AppleScript also can generate closures (subroutines that remember their global environment). And there is a sense in which all the components of a script—variables, handlers, and script objects—possess the same first-class status; for example, any of them can be passed as a parameter to a subroutine. All of this has a markedly LISP-like flavor.

The Learning Curve

In case you're beginning to worry that AppleScript is hard, don't; it isn't! Apple-Script is a straightforward computer language, and can be taught and learned in a straightforward manner; if I didn't believe that, this book wouldn't exist. Apple-Script is extensible, so this book will tell you how to read a scriptable application's dictionary, warn of possible pitfalls, and give plenty of examples. AppleScript is English-like, so the book will teach a clean, concise style, and will wave a red flag when an analogy with natural language threatens to mislead. AppleScript values are object-like; this book tells you how to talk to them. AppleScript has some LISP-like features; this book elicits these features where they are relevant, but where they seem too advanced you can always skip a section and return to it later on. If this book occasionally comments on the odd way AppleScript does certain things, it is not to frighten or frustrate the reader, but rather to gain the reader's trust. It's just my way of saying, "Don't worry if this seems weird; it *is* weird."

So approach AppleScript without fear. It deserves respect, appreciation, and perhaps a little wonder. After all, it's amazingly old. The Mac OS X revolution has let Apple thoroughly modernize a System that was breaking under its own accumulated weight of years; yet AppleScript remains, to all intents and purposes, its same old self. The fact that AppleScript works at all in this brave new world of Unicode text and POSIX paths is simply amazing. But it does, and until a new broom comes along to sweep it clean, having to negotiate some accumulated quirks and cobwebs dating from the creation seems a small price to pay.

CHAPTER 6

Syntactic Ground of Being

This chapter is about the basic facts of AppleScript language syntax. These are the facts you must know before you can read or write any AppleScript code at all.

Lines

AppleScript is a line-based language. There is no visible command terminator, such as a semicolon; a command ends with and is separated from the next command by a line break. For example:

```
set x to 1
copy x + 1 to y
display dialog y
```

In a script text file (or other text to be treated as AppleScript code) it doesn't matter whether the line break character is the Macintosh line break (\r), the Unix line break (\n), or the Windows line break (\r\n). Presuming the code is valid, AppleScript will be able to compile it regardless; all line breaks are expressed as Macintosh line breaks on decompilation.

It is legal for a line to be completely blank. Extra whitespace (spaces, tab characters) is legal and will be ignored.

Line Break Characters in Literal Strings

It is legal to type a line break in a literal string (that is, between matched pairs of double-quotes). This represents a line break character within the string. For example:

```
set pep to "Manny
Moe
Jack"
display dialog pep
```

Exactly what line break character is represented in this way depends upon the editing environment. In the old Script Editor:

```
set pep to "Manny
Moe"
pep contains (ASCII character 13) -- true
pep contains (ASCII character 10) -- false
```

In the new Script Editor:

```
set pep to "Manny
Moe"
pep contains (ASCII character 13) -- false
pep contains (ASCII character 10) -- true
```

A returned string value containing a line break character will be displayed (in most contexts) with a visible line break at that point. For example:

```
set pep to "Manny" & return & "Moe"
```

The result is displayed like this:

```
"Manny
Moe"
```

The same is true of a decompiled string literal containing an "escaped" return character. (Escaped characters in string literals are discussed under "String" in Chapter 13.) For example, if you type this:

```
set pep to "Manny\rMoe"
```

then when you compile you'll see this:

```
set pep to "Manny
Moe"
```

This is generally agreed to be annoying behavior on AppleScript's part. The line break character represented by the keyword return is a Macintosh line break character (\r), which can confuse the display in a Unix context. This is purely a cosmetic issue. For example (in the Terminal):

```
$ osascript -e 'set pep to "Manny" & return & "Moe"'
Moeny
$ osascript -e 'set pep to "Manny" & (ASCII character 10) & "Moe"'
Manny
Moe
```

What happened in the first reply is that "Moe" overprinted "Manny".

Continuation Character

Long lines can be broken into multiple lines by typing the continuation character. This character appears as the "logical not" sign; it is MacRoman codepoint 194, Unicode (and WinLatin1 and ISOLatin1) codepoint 172. This character is usually typed on Macintosh as Option-l (that's option-ell); but as a convenience, in a script editing application, typing Option-Return enters both the logical-not character and a return character, and is the usual way of continuing a line.

For example:

```
set a to ¬
    1
```

It is a compile-time error for anything to follow the continuation character on the same line other than whitespace.

It is a compile-time error for the line following the continuation character to be blank, unless what precedes the continuation character is a complete command, as in this very silly example:

```
set a to 1 ¬

set b to 2
```

A continuation character inside a literal string is interpreted as a literal logical-not character. To break a long literal string into multiple code lines for legibility without introducing unwanted return characters into the string, you must concatenate multiple literal strings:

```
set s to "one very long line " & ¬
    "deserves another"
```

Under some circumstances, AppleScript will move or remove your continuation characters at compile time. There's nothing you can do about this; it's an effect of the decompilation process. See "Decompiling" in Chapter 4.

 In this book, long lines are manually broken for legibility. Continuation characters are inserted to indicate such breaks, without regard for whether AppleScript would move or remove these continuation characters in a compiled version of the script.

Result

At runtime, every line of AppleScript code that actually executes an expression—that is, it isn't blank, a comment, or mere flow control (looping and branching)—generates a *result*. This result is some sort of value; the particular value depends upon what the line does and what values it does it with.

The line need not be a "complete sentence"; any valid AppleScript expression constitutes a valid line, even if it does nothing (that is, even if it doesn't have what a computer science person would call "side effects"). For example, this is a valid line of AppleScript code, and it has a value (can you guess what it is?):

```
5
```

A line's result may be captured in two ways: explicitly or implicitly.

Explicit Result

The result of a line after it is executed may be captured explicitly by using the keyword result in the next line that is executed. For example:

```
5
display dialog result -- 5
```

One sees this technique used typically after fetching a value in a context of interapplication communication. For example, this is a fairly common style of coding:

```
tell application "Finder"
    get the name of every folder
end tell
set L to the result
```

Here's another example:

```
tell application "Finder"
    count folders
end tell
set c to the result
```

The reason why people use this technique appears to be twofold. First, it may be a habit left over from HyperTalk, where this sort of thing was pretty much standard practice. Second, there seems to be a sense that a line is more legible and understandable if it consists of a single command. This technique is never actually necessary, though. If you want to capture the result of a command, you can do it in the same line:

```
tell application "Finder"
    set L to (get the name of every folder)
    set c to count folders
end tell
```

Furthermore, there is an argument to be made that use of result is a bad idea, since you may not know what it represents as well as you think you do. For example:

```
set L to {"Mannie", "Moe"}
set end of L to "Jack"
```

After these two lines, L is {"Mannie", "Moe", "Jack"}, but result is "Jack". If you were expecting result to be the same as L, you'll be wrong, and code that depends upon this assumption won't work. That's a simple example; for more complicated code, the chances increase that you may be mistaken about what result represents. The problem is simply that you are dependent upon AppleScript's rules about what a statement's result is. But there is no need to be dependent upon these, or even to bother knowing what result a line generates, because it is never necessary to use result.

Also, result is volatile. It changes after the execution of every expression. If you get into the bad habit of not capturing values when they are generated, because you intend to pick them up later using result, you are just asking for trouble when another expression is executed in the meantime and the value you needed has been lost. This can easily happen, because you might insert a line in the course of developing your code; this kind of mistake is very difficult to debug.

Implicit Result

The result of a line's execution is captured implicitly if it is the last line executed in a handler or script. This means that in theory there is no need to return a value explicitly from a handler or script using return. For example, instead of this:

```
on add(x, y)
    return x + y
end add
display dialog add(1, 2)
```

it is possible to say this:

```
on add(x, y)
    x + y
end add
display dialog add(1, 2)
```

This technique suffers from the same drawbacks as using result. The keyword return has the great advantage that you know exactly *what* you're returning (because that's the value of whatever follows the word return) and *when* you're returning it (because the handler exits the moment return is encountered). To rely on an implicit result is to know neither of these things. A line's result, as we've seen, may not be what you think it is. And the value returned by a handler or script is not the value of its physical last line, but rather the value of whatever line happens to be executed last; where there is flow control (loops and branches), you might not know what line this will be.

In actual fact, I do tend to use the implicit result in one particular context—when developing or testing a script. A script editing program always displays the result after executing a script. Thus you can see whether the script is working as expected, by specifying the final result:

```
on add(x, y)
    x + y
end add
set z to add(1, 2)
z
```

The last line here is just a way of causing the value of z to show up as the result of the script after execution, to make sure it's being set as expected. Here it may be argued that the use of the implicit result is actually the best approach, and here's why. Suppose you return the result explicitly, like this:

```
on add(x, y)
    x + y
end add
set z to add(1, 2)
return z
```

You now proceed with developing the script, adding code after this snippet, and are very surprised when it doesn't work as expected. The reason is that you've accidentally left this line in the script:

```
return z
```

When that line is encountered, execution terminates; the code that follows it is never executed. You might think this sort of mistake unlikely, but I speak from extensive experience. By contrast, the nice thing about this line:

```
z
```

is that it has no effect at all on the behavior of your script, even if subsequent code is added later.

Comments

AppleScript permits two kinds of comment: single-line comments and delimited comments. Everything including and after two successive hyphens on a line is a *single-line comment*. For example:

```
set a to 1 -- this a comment on the same line as a command
-- this a comment on a line by itself
```

The *comment delimiters* are (* and *). Everything between comment delimiters is a comment. Such a comment may span multiple lines. This code contains three stretches of text that are legally commented out with comment delimiters:

```
set a to 1 (* because we feel like it;
tomorrow we may not feel like setting a to 1 *)
(* in fact things could be very different tomorrow,
but I really can't speak to that issue just now *)
set b to 2 (* this seems a good idea too *)
```

A comment delimited with comment delimiters may *not* interrupt a command, nor precede a command on the same line. Neither of these lines will compile:

```
set a to (* because we feel like it *) 1
(* here's a good idea *) set a to 1
```

Comment delimiters attempt to be "intelligent." Comments may be nested, in which case the delimiters must match in pairs. The value of this is that you can easily comment out a stretch of script that already contains some comments:

```
(* outer comment
(* inner comment *)
rest of outer comment *)
```

A rather weird side effect of this "intelligence" is that quotation marks and vertical bars inside comment delimiters must also match in pairs:

```
(* "this works fine" and so does |this| *)
```

If you remove one quotation mark or one vertical bar from inside that comment, the code won't compile.

Single-line comments attempt no such "intelligence"; they simply cause the rest of the line to be ignored, and they take precedence over everything. Thus if you insert comment delimiters to comment out a block of code, you must be careful not to place either delimiter within a single-line comment. This won't compile:

```
(* set a to 1 -- and why not? *)
```

That's because the closing comment delimiter is itself commented out as part of the single-line comment, so the opening comment delimiter is unbalanced.

Abbreviations and Synonyms

Many AppleScript terms permit other terms to be substituted for them. For example, the following expressions are equivalent in pairs, assuming a and b are defined:

```
a is less than b
a < b

a is b
a = b
```

Some terms have a very large number of equivalents. For example, these expressions amount to the same thing:

```
a ≤ b
a <= b
a less than or equal b
a is less than or equal to b
a is not greater than b
a isn't greater than b
a does not come after b
a doesn't come after b
```

To add to the confusion, on decompilation, AppleScript might substitute one equivalent for another (see "Decompiling" in Chapter 4). So the code in the previous example compiles, but afterwards it looks like this:

```
a ≤ b
a ≤ b
a is less than or equal to b
a is less than or equal to b
a is not greater than b
a is not greater than b
a does not come after b
a does not come after b
```

I call terms that are functionally equivalent to one another *synonyms*. I call terms that are replaced by other terms on decompilation *abbreviations*.

Code in this book is compiled before being pasted into the page, so you won't see any abbreviations in the book's code examples (except, as here, with the explicit purpose of displaying an abbreviation). In fact, this book does not even list abbreviations except where I find them particularly handy when typing code. For example, I habitually type less-than-or-equal as <= even though in the compiled code what will appear is ≤, so I tell you about this abbreviation (under "Comparison Operators" in Chapter 15).

I don't tell you about all synonyms either, and on the whole I try not to use them. I feel that it's good style, and makes your AppleScript code more legible, to adopt just one synonym for each term and stick with it. In general my personal preference is the shortest synonym, but not always; for example, of the following two expressions, I prefer the second:

```
a ≠ b
a is not b
```

And in a very small number of cases I do use two synonyms indiscriminately. For example, I'm equally likely to use either of these expressions:

```
a = b
a is b
```

To sum up: wherever there are synonyms, I have a favorite (or, in a very small number of cases, a couple of favorites). My favorites are the versions of each term that I tell you about, and they are the ones I use in code.

Blocks

A *block* is one or more lines of code demarcated from its surroundings as having a separate nature or purpose. A block is announced by a line stating what type of block it is; then comes the code of the block; and finally the block is terminated by a line starting with the keyword end. Blocks can occur within blocks.

It's very easy to spot a block in AppleScript code, because at compile time the code lines are indented from the announcement line and the termination line. For example:

```
myHandler( )
on myHandler( )
    repeat 3 times
        display dialog "Howdy"
    end repeat
end myHandler
```

That code contains two blocks. One is announced with the on myHandler( ) line, and is terminated by the end myHandler line; everything in between them is the code of that block. That code consists of another block, announced with the repeat line and terminated by the end repeat line; the line of code in between them is the code of that block.

In this book I frequently refer to such blocks by their announcement keyword or type; for example, I might say "an on block" or "a repeat block".

The only blocks you can make in AppleScript are those for which keywords are supplied; you cannot indent arbitrarily for clarity, as you can in UserTalk or C. So for example in UserTalk you can say this:

```
local (x)
bundle
    x = 4
msg (x)
```

The keyword bundle here does nothing except to allow some code to be indented for clarity and to provide a further level of local scope. In AppleScript the scoping issue doesn't arise (as we shall see), but a way of indenting for clarity might still be nice. To achieve it you would need to misuse an existing block type. For example:

```
local x
repeat 1 times
    set x to 4
end repeat
display dialog x
```

The

AppleScript allows you to use the word the before almost anything. This is pure syntactic sugar, and I never use it. For example, this is perfectly legal:

```
set the x to the 9
display dialog the (get the the the the x + the 1)
```

Now, really.

CHAPTER 7

Variables

This chapter describes the rules for declaration, typing, initialization, naming, scoping, and lifetime of variables in the AppleScript language.

A *variable* is a binding between a name and a value. You can think of it as a shoebox with a label on it, into which something is placed for storage. The shoebox's label is the variable's name; what's inside the shoebox is the variable's value. For example, when we say:

```
set x to 5
```

it is as if we had a shoebox labeled "x" into which we place the number 5.

Assignment and Retrieval

To *assign* a value to a variable is to put something into the shoebox. If the variable already has a value, that value is replaced. Assignment is performed with one of two commands: set or copy, described here.

---

set

Syntax

```
set variableName to value
```

Description

Assigns *value* to *variableName*.

Example

```
set x to 5
```

There is a synonym using the word returning instead of set, with the parameters in reverse order, like this: 5 returning x. But I have never seen this used.

---

copy

Syntax

copy *value* to *variableName*

Description

Assigns *value* to *variableName*.

Example

```
copy 5 to x
```

An abbreviation for copy is put; an abbreviation for to is into. Thus you could type put 5 into x, although it would still come out as copy 5 to x. This is doubtless to accommodate HyperCard users, who were habituated to this syntax.

In these expressions, *variableName* can optionally be a list of variable names, allowing multiple assignments in one command. The *value*, too, will then be a list—a list of the values to be assigned. The first item in the *value* list is assigned to the first item in the *variableName* list, the second to the second, and so forth. If the *value* list is longer than the *variableName* list, the extra values are not assigned to anything; if the *value* list is shorter than the *variableName* list, there is a runtime error. This remarkably elegant feature is probably under-utilized by beginners. (For a parallel construction involving assignment to a record, see "Record" in Chapter 13.) For example:

```
set {x, y, z} to {1, 2, 3}
z -- 3, and can you guess what x and y are?
```

It sounds from their descriptions as if set and copy must be completely interchangeable. In most cases, they are; but with regard to four types of value—lists, records, dates, and script objects—they are not. This point will be covered in subsequent chapters. For other datatypes, you may use whichever command you prefer; I prefer set.

There is no simple assignment operator, such as equals sign (=). You cannot, for example, perform an assignment like this:

```
x = 5
```

That is a comparison, and returns a boolean result revealing whether x is already 5. The fact that such code is legal (and therefore does not cause a compile-time error) but is not an assignment (as any mildly experienced programmer would expect) is a frequent cause of bugs in my scripts. See "The "English-likeness" Monster" in Chapter 5.

To *retrieve* the value of a variable (or *fetch* the value, or *use* the value, or whatever you want to call it), simply use the variable's name in code. As with most computer languages, there is no problem retrieving from and assigning to the same variable in a single statement:

```
set x to x + 1
```

There is no circularity, because first the value of x is retrieved, and 1 is added to that value; then the result of this addition is assigned to x, replacing the original value.

The result of a line consisting of just the name of a variable is the value of that variable. So, for example:

```
set x to 5
x
```

The result of that script is 5. This can be useful when you want to employ the implicit result of a script as a way of testing or debugging (see "Implicit Result" in Chapter 6).

It is possible to retrieve a variable's value by using the get command:

```
set x to (get x) + 1
```

But no one ever talks this way in real life, and as far as I know this use of get with a variable adds nothing. However, get with an object reference is another matter; see "Get" in Chapter 10.

Declaration and Definition of Variables

There is no requirement in AppleScript that variables be declared explicitly. The rule is basically that if you use a word that AppleScript doesn't understand, the word is assumed to be the name of a variable. The following code, as a complete script, will compile just fine:

```
set x to x + 1
```

Definition

The code in that last example, as a complete script, will compile, but it won't run; at runtime, it generates an error. That's because x has never been assigned a value. The error message reads: "The variable x is not defined." The problem is *not* that the variable x has never been declared! There is no need to declare it. AppleScript understands (or assumes) that x is supposed to be a variable. Nor is the problem that you are trying to assign to it. The problem is that you are trying to fetch its value, and it has no value. An AppleScript variable is not defined until you first give it a value explicitly. To continue our shoebox analogy, there is no "x" shoebox to fetch the contents of, because you've never put anything into it.

This code both compiles and runs:

```
set x to 5
set x to x + 1
```

During execution of the first line, AppleScript observes that you're putting something into the "x" shoebox, but there is no such shoebox as yet. No problem;

AppleScript creates the shoebox, labels it "x", and puts 5 into it. Now the second line runs fine, because there is a shoebox "x" from which to fetch a value.

Once a variable has been defined in the course of running a script, it generally stays defined until its scope finishes executing, as discussed later in the chapter. There is no command explicitly letting you "undefine" a variable or assign the "undefined" value to it. However, you can undefine a variable by assigning to it the result of a command that has no result. This is typically an accident: you were expecting a command to return a value, but it doesn't. Code for doing it on purpose appears under "Returned Value" in Chapter 8.

There is no way to ask whether a variable's value is defined; all you can do is fetch its value and see if you get an error. It would then be up to your code to handle this error ("Errors" in Chapter 12); otherwise your script will simply stop running at that point.

Initialization

A variable is *initialized* (given its first value) when you explicitly assign it its first value. There is no auto-initialization of variables in AppleScript, and there is no special syntax for initializing variables. A variable is undefined until you assign it a value; at that moment it is defined and initialized—the variable now exists, it has a value, and it is possible to fetch that value.

The exception is a *script property*. A script property is a kind of global variable, and it is declared and initialized in the same line of code. Script properties have some other interesting features, which are discussed later in this chapter.

Typing

A variable in AppleScript has *no fixed type*. By this I mean simply that it is permissible to assign any variable any value, any time. The following code is legal:

```
set x to 5
set x to 5.2
set x to "hello"
set x to string
set x to {"fee", "fie", "fo", "fum"}
set x to (path to current user folder)
```

In that code, x becomes successively an integer, a real, a string, a class, a list, and an alias. A defined variable (one that has a value) has a type, called its *class*; this is simply the class (datatype) of its current value, and it changes if a value of a different class is assigned to it.

The various built-in datatypes, and the ways in which AppleScript lets you coerce implicitly and explicitly from one to another, are discussed later in this book (Chapters 13, 14, and 15).

Explicit Declaration

Although it is not *necessary* to declare a variable, it is *possible* to declare a variable, and there are three ways to do so:

- As a script property:

```
property x : 5
set x to x + 1
```

- As a global:

```
global x
set x to 5
set x to x + 1
```

- As a local:

```
local x
set x to 5
set x to x + 1
```

The meanings of these declarations are explained later in this chapter.

> It is almost always best to declare your variables. Your code will be easier to understand, and the scoping rules are simpler and clearer, if all your variables are declared. Unfortunately there is no way to have AppleScript to warn you when a variable is not declared.

Variable Names

The name of a variable must begin with a letter or underscore and must consist entirely of alphanumeric characters or underscore. So a variable name must begin with a character in the character set [a-zA-Z_] and must consist entirely of characters in the character set [a-zA-Z0-9_].

Variable names are *case-insensitive at compile time*. That means the following code will compile and run:

```
set myVar to 5
set myvar to myvar + 1
```

AppleScript assumes that myvar in the second line is the same variable as myVar in the first line. Furthermore, as a reflection of this assumption, AppleScript rewrites the variable names after compilation so that their case matches the first usage of the name:

```
set myVar to 5
set myVar to myVar + 1
```

This suggests a trick that can help you spot undeclared variables: in your declarations, use an uppercase letter somewhere in every variable name; elsewhere, never use an uppercase letter in a variable name. Then, after compilation, any variable name without an uppercase letter must be an undeclared variable. For example, here's some code that I typed following these rules, after compilation:

```
local myVar
set myVar to 5
set mybar to myVar + 1
```

In that code I have accidentally created and set the value of an unwanted variable mybar in the last line. I meant to say myvar, but I mistyped it. This won't cause Apple-Script to generate any error, and the script will misbehave. The chances that I will spot my mistake are increased by my use of the case trick.

Once a script has been compiled for the first time, its variable names are remembered as they appear at that moment. (Recall that AppleScript has a memory. See "Maintenance of State" in Chapter 4.) Suppose you compile this script:

```
local avariable
set avariable to 7
```

You then change your mind and decide to use the inner capitalization trick, so you edit the script to give the variable names inner capitalization:

```
local aVariable
set aVariable to 7
```

When you compile, you find your efforts are in vain; AppleScript removes the inner capitalization!

```
local avariable
set avariable to 7
```

The reason is that when AppleScript first saw the variable name avariable—the first occurrence during the first compilation of the script—it had no capitalization, and that's how the name is remembered from then on.

What's more, this rule washes over to other scripts that you edit during the same session! To see this, start up your script editor program and compile this script:

```
set myvar to 7
```

Now open a new, different window and compile this script:

```
local myVar
set myVar to 7
```

Your variable names are changed in this second script! It ends up looking like this:

```
local myvar
set myvar to 7
```

This bizarre behavior is caused by the combination of two facts: variable names are remembered at global level in the AppleScript scripting component, and there is just one AppleScript scripting component instance per script editor session. (You did reread "Maintenance of State" in Chapter 4, didn't you?) This instance is shared by all the scripts you compile during that session, so the variable names in one script affect the variable names in another. This phenomenon persists until you quit the Script Editor program. Two different applications don't share the same AppleScript scripting component instance, though, so your variable names in Script Editor do not affect your variable names in Script Debugger at the same moment.

You can force an illegal variable name to be legal by surrounding it with vertical bars, also known as "pipes" (|). So, for example:

```
set |1| to 2
if |1| is 2 then
    display dialog "The laws of logic are suspended."
end if
```

The laws of logic aren't really suspended; 1 and 2 have not become the same number. A variable named "1" has been assigned the value 2, that's all. This device is good also for variable names in languages other than English:

```
set |monZéro| to 0
```

or for spaces in a variable name:

```
set |my big long variable name with spaces| to 7
```

A variable name surrounded by pipes *is case-sensitive*. This script will compile, but it won't run:

```
set |MyVar| to 5
set |MyVar| to |Myvar| + 1 -- error
```

The reason is that |Myvar| is not the same variable as |MyVar| and has never been given a value, so its value can't be fetched. AppleScript will not touch the case of names in pipes after compilation.

A variable name surrounded by pipes may include a backslash as an "escape" character. The legal escape expressions in this context are \n, \r, \t, \|, and \\.

The real meaning of pipes is to tell AppleScript to suspend its compile-time parsing rules and turn what's inside the pipes into a token. The main reason this is genuinely useful is to avoid a conflict between a token name and a reserved word. For example:

```
set |is| to "ought"
```

You couldn't do that without the pipes, because is is a reserved word, a part of the AppleScript language.

Now, you might say: "So what? I'll never need to worry about that; I just won't use any names that conflict with reserved words." But even though *you* might not use such names, some entity with which you need to communicate might do so. For example, some unwary developer could use a reserved word as part of the vocabulary defined by a scriptable application (even though they're not supposed to), and you would then need pipes in order to use that word to talk to the application. (See "Resolution Difficulties" in Chapter 19.)

Scoping of Variables

The notion of *scoping* has to do with where an entity is visible. Your code consists of regions; these regions are each continuous, and some of them may be inside others, but they do not partially intersect—given two regions, either one is entirely inside the other or they are completely distinct. The region in which a variable is visible is called its *scope*. A variable that is visible at a certain point is said to be *in scope* at that point.

Scoping of variables in AppleScript is extraordinarily complicated (in my opinion). It's also very important to understand, so don't skip this section.

How Scoping Is Meaningful

Before we can talk about the scoping of variables in particular, you must understand the basic principles of AppleScript scoping in general. These are:

- The top level of all scope is the script as a whole.
- The regions of scope are handlers and script objects (and the top level).
- A script object may contain a handler. A handler may contain a script object. A script object may contain a script object. But a handler may not (directly) contain a handler.

Let's start with the first rule. Your script as a whole is itself the ultimate region of scope, containing everything else. So, let's say that your script consists of just the following code:

```
set x to 7
```

In terms of scope, where are we when this code executes? This is all the code there is, and we're not in a handler or a script object, so we are at the top level of all scope, the script as a whole.

Now I will illustrate the second and third rules, even though I have not yet explained rigorously what a script object or a handler is; all you need to know is that in code a script object is a block declared by the word script and a handler is a block declared by the word on. This code, then, is legal:

```
on handlerOne( )
    script scriptOne
    end script
end handlerOne
script scriptTwo
    on handlerTwo( )
    end handlerTwo
    script scriptThree
    end script
end script
```

Everything you see in that code is inside the top-level script. Within the top-level script are handlerOne and scriptTwo. Within handlerOne is scriptOne. Within scriptTwo are handlerTwo and scriptThree.

Along with the top level, these handlers and script objects are the regions of scope. Each region starts with the declaration of the handler or script object, and ends with the corresponding end line. Into this code may be inserted further code, and every line of this further code is in some definite region of scope.

The question we want to answer, then, is how variables in these various regions of scope are visible to code within other regions of scope.

Explicit Locals

An *explicit local* is a variable declared with the keyword local. It is legal to declare more than one variable local in the same command, by separating them with commas. So:

```
local x
local y, z
```

In general, an explicit local is visible *only within the scope where it is declared.* (There is one exception, which I'll mention in a moment.)

Different local variables in different scopes can thus have the same name without trampling on one another. Suppose a script object starts like this:

```
script myScript
    local x
```

The moment that local declaration for x is encountered, it means that from now on when code in this script object's scope says x it means this local x and no other. Other scopes may declare their own local x, they may declare a global x, they may bang the floor and have a temper tantrum, but they absolutely will not be able to have any effect upon myScript's x, nor will anything myScript does with its x have any effect upon them.

Here's an example of a local variable in action:

```
local x
set x to 5
script myScript
    display dialog x
end script
run myScript -- error
```

(The code inside a script object does not run when the script object is defined. To run the code inside a script object, you tell that script object to run. This is formally explained in Chapter 9. So in this example, first we define myScript, then we run it.)

That code compiles, but it won't run; it stops with a runtime error at the display dialog x command, objecting that x is not defined. There is a variable called x and it is defined, but it is declared local and therefore is visible only within its own scope. In this case, that scope is the top-level script. The `display dialog x` command is in a different scope, that of the script object `myScript`. Therefore AppleScript takes this to be a different x, and this different x has never been assigned a value.

Now let's do it the other way round:

```
on myHandler( )
    local x
    set x to 5
end myHandler
myHandler( )
display dialog x -- error
```

(The code inside a handler does not run when the handler is defined. To run the code inside a handler, you say its name followed by parentheses. This is formally explained in Chapter 8. So in this example, first we define `myHandler`, then we run it.)

This code stops with a runtime error at the `display dialog x` command, objecting that x is not defined. There is a variable x that has been defined, but that happened inside the scope of the handler `myHandler`, where this x was declared local. The `display dialog x` command is in a different scope, namely the top level. Therefore AppleScript takes this to be a different x, and this different x has never been assigned a value.

There is, however, this one great exception to the rule about the scope of local variables: *a script object defined in a handler can see the handler's local variables.* For example:

```
on myHandler( )
    local x
    set x to 5
    script myScript
        display dialog x
    end script
    run myScript
end myHandler
myHandler( ) -- 5
```

This remarkable exception to the local scoping rule will permit us to pass a handler as a parameter to another handler and call it ("Handlers as Parameters" in Chapter 8). We will also combine it elegantly with a handler's ability to return a script object ("Script Object as Handler Result" in Chapter 9).

Global Declarations: The Downward Effect

Our next topic will be variables declared with the keyword global. It is legal to declare more than one variable global in the same command, by separating them with a comma. So:

```
global x
global y, z
```

For clarity, I'm going to discuss the effect of a global declaration in two stages. First I'm going to explain what I call the *downward effect* of a global declaration. By this I mean the effect a global declaration has on code in the same scope as the declaration, or a deeper scope within that scope.

Here's the rule. A variable declared global is visible *subsequently in the same scope* as the declaration, and within all handlers and scripts defined subsequently in the same scope, *to an infinite depth*.

For example, this code runs:

```
global x
set x to 5
on myHandler( )
    display dialog x
end myHandler
myHandler( ) -- 5
```

The variable x is declared global; it is then visible downward into the scope of myHandler, because myHandler is defined subsequently in the same scope as x. (Do you see why I call this the downward effect of the declaration?)

In that example, I proved that code inside myHandler could see x by having that code fetch its value. But such code can equally well set its value:

```
global x
on myHandler( )
    set x to 5
end myHandler
myHandler( )
display dialog x -- 5
```

That's important. Code exposed to a variable by a global declaration is very powerful. The code gains full access to the variable.

Let's prove that the downward visibility created by a global declaration operates to a greater depth (it operates, as I said earlier, "to an infinite depth," but I don't see how to prove that):

```
global x
on myHandler( )
    script myScript
        on mySecondHandler( )
            set x to 5
        end mySecondHandler
    end script
    myScript's mySecondHandler( )
end myHandler
myHandler( )
display dialog x -- 5
```

The line where x is given a value appears in a handler within a script object within a handler. Nevertheless that line can see the variable x declared global in the first line, and the script runs successfully.

Now let's concentrate on the word "subsequently." A variable not declared global until after the definition of a script object or handler cannot be seen by code within that script object or handler. The following code does not work:

```
on myHandler( )
    script myScript
        on mySecondHandler( )
            set x to 5
        end mySecondHandler
    end script
    myScript's mySecondHandler( )
end myHandler
global x
myHandler( )
display dialog x -- error
```

The variable x was not declared global until after the definition of the handler myHandler. Therefore code within myHandler cannot see x. The line set x to 5 was executed, but it failed to set the global variable x's value; therefore when we reach the last line, the global variable x has no value and a runtime error occurs.

(You might now be wondering: "Okay, the line set x to 5 didn't set the value of the global variable x, but it didn't cause a runtime error either; so what did it do?" I'll get to that, I promise.)

Naturally, any downward scope may shield itself from the downward effect of a global declaration at a higher level, simply by declaring the same variable name as local for its own scope. For example:

```
global x
set x to 5
script myScript
    local x
    on myHandler( )
        set x to 10
    end myHandler
    myHandler( )
    set x to 20
end script
run myScript
display dialog x -- 10 (not 20)
```

The dialog displays 10, not 20. The global x declaration in the first line has a downward effect on myScript and, within it, on myHandler. But myScript then shields itself from this effect with a local x declaration. The variable x declared global in the first line is thus visible at top level and at the third level in myHandler, but at the second level in myScript it is not visible, and the x referred to there is a different x. When myHandler sets x to 10, that is the same x as at the top level. When myScript then sets x to 20, that's a different x and this has no effect on the value displayed in the last line.

Global Declarations: The Upward Effect

We are now ready to talk about what a global variable really is. In the previous section, in talking about the downward effect of a global declaration, I was talking about just the declaration; a global declaration can appear anywhere. But now we're talking about the actual variable named by a global declaration—a global variable. The rule is: *a global variable actually exists at the top level*.

However, it turns out that a global variable, even though it exists at top level, *cannot automatically be seen in every scope*. In order for a global variable to be seen in a scope other than top level, it must be explicitly declared.

There are two ways for a global variable to be declared so as to be visible in a scope other than top level. One we have already seen: the top level may declare it, which makes it visible subsequently downwards. The other way is for the deeper scope to ask to see the global variable; it does this with a global declaration in its own scope.

The upward effect of declaring a variable global is to *identify the declared variable with the top-level global variable of the same name*. This top-level global variable may or may not exist already; if it doesn't exist, we may say that the declaration also creates it. (But the global variable doesn't *really* exist until it is defined by being assigned a value.)

To illustrate:

```
on setX( )
    global x
    set x to 5
end setX
on getX( )
    global x
    display dialog x
end getX
setX( )
getX( ) -- 5
```

When setX runs, its declaration of x as global creates the global variable x at top level (because no such global variable exists previously), and identifies this x with that x; thus, in setting the value of x, it sets the global's value. Then when getX runs, its declaration of x as global identifies this x with the now existing global variable x at top level. Thus, when it displays the value of x, it is the global's value that it displays. Both setX and getX have access to the very same global variable x; and they have that access because they each asked for it, with a global declaration.

It goes without saying (said he, saying it) that such a global declaration, by virtue of its downward effects, also gives to all downward scopes the same powers over a top-level global that it gives its own scope (unless, of course, they deliberately shield themselves from this power by means of a local declaration, as in the example at the end of the previous section). For example, this code works:

```
script myScript
    global x
```

```
    on myHandler( )
        set x to 5
    end myHandler
    myHandler( )
end script
on getX( )
    global x
    display dialog x
end
run myScript
getX( ) -- 5
```

By the time we come to the last line, the script object myScript has run, and its handler myHandler has executed the line set x to 5. Because there has been a higher-level global declaration of x, this x is that global x. (That's the downward effect of the global declaration.) But this x is also the top-level global x. (That's the upward effect of the global declaration.) Therefore, even though it contains no global declaration within itself, myHandler is able to set the value of the top-level global x. Then when getX runs, since it starts with a global declaration for x, it sees the same top-level global variable, and displays its value.

Undeclared Variables

We come now to the question of undeclared variables. Say that at compile time, a variable name is encountered, and this name has not been declared for this scope—that is, it has not been declared as local in this same scope, and it has not been declared as global in the same or a higher scope. Now, a variable can only be local or global. *What will AppleScript do?*

It turns out that there are two different answers, depending on where the code occurs—at the top level, or elsewhere.

Undeclared variables at top level

Code at the top level of the script is special. (Technically, what I mean here is "code at the top level of the run handler." See "The Run Handler" in Chapter 8.) Code at the top level of the script doesn't need a global declaration in order to create, set, or see a global variable. An undeclared variable name at top level is *treated as global*. But lacking the explicit global declaration, it *lacks the downward effect* that an explicit global declaration would have. We may call such a variable an *implicit global*.

So, for example:

```
set x to 5
on getX( )
    global x
    display dialog x
end getX
getX( ) -- 5
```

In the first line, the previously undeclared x was created as a top-level global, implicitly, and given a value. When getX runs, it is able to access that value with a global declaration, and can display it.

Now let's do the converse:

```
on setX( )
    global x
    set x to 5
end setX
setX( )
display dialog x -- 5
```

By the time we get to the last line, setX has run; it has created a top-level global variable x, and has set its value. In the last line, the previously undeclared x spoken of at top level is an implicit global, so it is that same top-level global variable x. Thus the value 5 is displayed.

But this code fails with a runtime error, unless the first line is uncommented:

```
-- global x
set x to 5
on getX( )
    display dialog x
end getX
getX( ) -- error, unless you restore the global x declaration
```

The presence of the global x declaration has a downward effect, enabling code inside the getX handler to see x without a global x declaration of its own. Without such an explicit global x declaration anywhere, x is still global, but code in getX can't see it.

It is perfectly possible for code at the top level to shut off its own access to a global variable, just as any other scope may do, by declaring a local variable of the same name. For example:

```
local x
set x to 5
on setX( )
    global x
    set x to 10
end setX
setX( )
display dialog x -- 5
```

This displays 5, not 10. That's because there has been a declaration that the x spoken of at top level is a local. It's true that setX set a top-level global to 10, but that's a different variable! The top-level code isn't accessing that variable; it closed off its access to it, through the local declaration.

Undeclared variables not at top level

An undeclared variable name *not* at top level is treated *exactly as if that variable had been declared local in its scope.* We may call such a variable an *implicit local.*

For example:

```
set x to 5
script myScript
    set x to 10
end script
run myScript
display dialog x -- 5
```

The dialog displays 5. You should now understand why. Each set x line creates a different x—the first creates an implicit global at top level, the second creates an implicit local in its own scope. Thus the x that is set to 10 is a different x from the x that was set to 5; it is the x that was set to 5 that is displayed in the last line. There was no runtime error; no one tried to access the value of an undefined variable. But myScript's x was wasted; it was set to 10 and then was immediately destroyed as it went out of scope, with no effect on anything else in the code.

Declare your variables

Sounds like "eat your vegetables," doesn't it? Well, it should. Each motto is good advice, no matter how unpalatable it may seem at first. I strongly advise you (once again) to declare all your variables—even your locals.

Now that you understand what happens when variables are not declared, you can imagine the sorts of confusion that can arise. If you let yourself become lulled into a false sense of security by the fact that there's no need to declare your variables, then you can be surprised when some other scope tramples them.

For example, imagine that your script starts like this:

```
set x to 5
```

That's top-level code, so you've just implicitly declared x a global. This means that any other handler or script object anywhere in this script can access your x and change its value, just by saying this:

```
global x
```

This other code may not have intended to trample on your x; perhaps it was trying to establish a global of its own, possibly in order to communicate its value to code at a lower level. But the damage is done, because of the upward effects of a global declaration. And to think you could have prevented this, just by declaring your x local to start with.

In the case of script objects the problem is particularly insidious, because it is possible to run a script object whose code you can't see, by loading it from a compiled script file on disk. There will be more about that later (Chapter 9), but here's a quick example:

```
set x to 5
run (load script alias "myHardDrive:aScriptFile.scpt")
display dialog x
```

The frightening fact is that x could now be anything! If the script in the file *aScriptFile.scpt* happens for any reason to declare global x, it can freely change the value of your x.

The converse is also true. Pretend you have a large script and that this code occurs somewhere within it:

```
on myHandler( )
    set x to 5
end
```

Is x a local or a global here? You don't know! It depends upon the context. If x has previously been declared global at a higher level, this x is global (by the downward effect of that declaration). If not, this x is local. But it is intolerable that you should have to look elsewhere to learn the scope of x within myHandler! All you have to do is explicitly declare it global or local, right here in myHandler, and then you'll know for sure.

Free Variables

An entity defined outside a handler or script object but globally visible within it, and not overshadowed by a declaration of the same name, is called a *free variable* with respect to that handler or script object. For example:

```
global x, y, z
script myScript
    property x : 1
    local y
    yy
    z
end script
```

Within myScript, x is explicitly defined as a property (as explained later in this chapter in "Script Properties") and y is explicitly defined as a local, so neither is a free variable. The variable yy isn't explicitly defined within myScript, but it isn't defined outside it either, so it is an implicit local and not a free variable. But the variable z is globally visible within myScript (from the global declaration at the start of the code), and the name is not redeclared within myScript, so z within myScript is a free variable, and is identified with the global z declared in the first line.

A free variable takes its value within the handler or script object *at the time the code runs*, not at the time the handler or script object is defined. For example:

```
set x to 5
on myHandler( )
    global x
    display dialog x
end myHandler
set x to 10
myHandler( ) -- 10 (not 5)
```

The dialog displays 10, not 5. It doesn't matter that x had been set to 5 when myHandler was defined; it only matters what its value is when the code inside myHandler actually runs. By that time, x has been set to 10.

It is important here (as we saw earlier) that x has been declared global in code that appears *before* the code where myHandler speaks of it. Free variables' values are determined at runtime, but the identification of a variable as a free variable, and its association with some particular globally visible variable, is performed during compilation (and AppleScript's compilation is single-pass, remember). This way of resolving the meaning of free variable names is called *lexical scoping*.

For example:

```
set x to 5
on myHandler( )
    display dialog x
end myHandler
global x
myHandler( ) -- error
```

It's true that x is declared global before (temporally) myHandler runs. But that's not good enough. We must declare x global before (physically) myHandler speaks of it; otherwise, myHandler's x isn't the global x, and the code fails with a runtime error because myHandler's x isn't defined.

Redeclaration of Locals and Globals

It is a compile-time error to redeclare an implicit global as local:

```
set x to 5
local x -- compile-time error
```

It is a compile-time error to redeclare an implicit local as global:

```
on getX( )
    display dialog x
    global x -- compile-time error
end getX
```

It is a compile-time error to redeclare as local a variable declared global in the same scope (except at top level):

```
on getX( )
    global x
    local x -- compile-time error
end getX
```

It is a compile-time error to redeclare as global a variable declared local in the same scope (except at top level):

```
on getX( )
    local x
    global x -- compile-time error
end getX
```

At top level, it is *not* an error to declare a variable local and then declare it global in the same scope. But it doesn't have any effect within the top-level scope either. For example:

```
local x
global x
set x to 5
on setX( )
    set x to 10
end setX
on getX( )
    display dialog x
end getX
setX( )
getX( ) -- 10
display dialog x -- 5
```

Once x is declared global, both setX and getX have automatic access to a top-level global variable x. But the code in the top level does not have such access. There, x has already been declared local; nothing can change this. Once a local, always a local. The x that is set to 5, and that is displayed at the end, is this local x, which is different from the global x.

At top level, it is *not* an error to declare a variable global and then declare it local in the same scope. But access to the global variable is lost in the top-level scope. For example:

```
global x
set x to 5
local x
on getX( )
    display dialog x
end getX
getX( ) -- 5
display dialog x -- error
```

After the first two lines, there is a top-level global variable x and its value is 5, and code at a deeper level can access it; the subsequent local declaration has no effect on this fact, even though it precedes the definition of the deeper-level code. But the top-level code has lost its access to this global variable, and can never recover it.

Script Properties

A *script property* (often just called a *property*) is a script-level global variable with initialization. A script property must be declared, and an initial value must be supplied as part of the declaration. The syntax is:

```
property propertyName : initialValue
```

For example:

```
property x : 5
```

The abbreviation for property is prop.

A property declaration can appear only at top level or at the top level of a script object. For example:

```
property x : 5
script myScript
    property y : 10
    -- other stuff
end script
-- other stuff
```

A property is a variable, so its value can be set and fetched in the normal way. For example:

```
property x : 10
display dialog x -- 10
set x to 5
display dialog x -- 5
```

Scoping of Properties

A property is a kind of global variable, and a property declaration has the *same downward effect as a global declaration*:

```
property x : 10
script myScript
    display dialog x
end script
on myHandler( )
    display dialog x
end myHandler
run myScript -- 10
myHandler( ) -- 10
```

Both myScript and myHandler can see the property x, because the property declaration works like a global declaration with respect to its downward effects.

The big difference between a global variable and a script property is in the upward effect of their declaration. A property's scope is *confined to the script object where it is declared*. The property is automatically visible downwards, as if the property declaration had been a global declaration; but it is not automatically visible anywhere else. Different script objects may declare a property by the same name, and these properties will be separate variables.

For example:

```
property x : 5
script scriptOne
    property x : 10
    script scriptTwo
        property x : 20
        display dialog x
    end script
    display dialog x
```

```
        run scriptTwo
    end script
    script scriptThree
        property x : 30
        display dialog x
    end script
    script scriptFour
        display dialog x
    end script
    display dialog x -- 5
    run scriptOne -- 10, 20
    run scriptThree -- 30
    run scriptFour -- 5
```

Every property x in that code is a separate variable. Observe that this separateness
would be impossible using global declarations, because each global x declaration at
any level would refer to the very same top-level global variable. Of course, locals provide a similar separateness, but with locals you wouldn't get the downward effect of
a property declaration (used by scriptFour to see the top-level x). Thus we see that
the scoping effect of a property declaration is different from either a global declaration or a local declaration.

Furthermore a property, unlike a local, even in scopes where it isn't visible automatically, *is visible on demand wherever its script object is visible.* To speak of a property
from outside the scope where it is visible automatically, you must employ a special
syntax: either you use the of operator (or the apostrophe-ess operator) and the name
of the script object, or you use the keyword its within a tell block addressed to the
script object. You are then free both to fetch and to change the value of the property.

For example:

```
    script myScript
        property x : 10
    end script
    on myHandler( )
        set myScript's x to 20
    end myHandler
    display dialog x of myScript -- 10
    myHandler( )
    display dialog myScript's x -- 20
    tell myScript
        display dialog its x -- 20
    end tell
```

A difficulty arises, though, when a script object has a property but wishes to speak of
a top-level property of the same name:

```
    property x : 5
    script myScript
        property x : 10
        display dialog x -- but I want to speak of the top-level x
    end script
    run myScript -- 10, alas
```

The difficulty is that the top-level script is anonymous. Under normal circumstances, it may be referred to at any level as parent. For example:

```
property x : 5
script outerScript
    property x : 10
    script innerScript
        property x : 20
        display dialog parent's x
    end script
end script
run outerScript's innerScript -- 5 (not 10 or 20)
```

However, it is possible to subvert this by redefining a script object's parent. (This will be explained in "Inheritance" in Chapter 9.) For example:

```
property x : 5
script scriptOne
    property x : 10
end script
script scriptTwo
    property x : 20
    property parent : scriptOne
    display dialog parent's x
end script
run scriptTwo -- 10 (not 5)
```

To get around this, the surest method, and therefore the surest method for accessing a top-level property in general, is to give the top level a name. This is done by assigning the value me to a global variable or property at top level. (For the formal explanation of me, see "Me" in Chapter 10.) So, for example:

```
property topLevel : me
property x : 5
script scriptOne
    property x : 10
end script
script scriptTwo
    property x : 20
    property parent : scriptOne
    display dialog topLevel's x
end script
run scriptTwo -- 5
```

Top-Level Properties Are Globals

There is no difference between a top-level global variable and a top-level property (except that the property is initialized). I will pause a moment to let this sink in.

One consequence of this is that in all the examples in the previous section where I declared a top-level property, I could have used a top-level global instead. This top-level global can be explicit (if I want the downward effects of the declaration) or implicit. For example, I'll just repeat the last example in a different guise:

```
global topLevel
script scriptOne
    property x : 10
end script
script scriptTwo
    property x : 20
    property parent : scriptOne
    display dialog topLevel's x
end script
set topLevel to me
set x to 5
run scriptTwo -- 5
```

In that version of the code, topLevel and x (at top level) are global variables, not properties. This changes essentially nothing. scriptTwo still speaks of toplevel's x, regardless. There is a declaration of topLevel as global, so that scriptTwo will be able to see it (the downward effect of the declaration), and it is assigned the value me so that scriptTwo can refer to the top level by name. x is an implicit global that comes into existence when it is set in the next-to-last line. The really interesting part of the example is this line:

```
display dialog topLevel's x
```

Here, scriptTwo can access the global variable x by referring to it in terms of the top level's name, just as if x were a property. And it can do this even though there has never been, and never will be, an explicit global declaration for x. This is because the compiler is satisfied by the specification topLevel's x; it knows just where to look for this x, and that's all the compiler wants to know. At runtime, by the time scriptTwo runs, the x in question has a value, and all is well.

The upward effect of a global declaration identifies the declared variable with a top-level property, just as it would with a top-level global variable. For example:

```
property x : 5
script outerScript
    property x : 10
    script innerScript
        global x
        display dialog x
    end script
end script
run outerScript's innerScript -- 5
```

The global declaration of x in innerScript identifies x in this scope with the top-level property of the same name. We thus have another way of jumping past the scope where x is 10 to see the x at top level.

Delayed Declaration of Properties

Because of the nature of AppleScript's one-pass compiler, a property declaration may appear anywhere in its scope, not just at the start. It still provides the initial value for the variable at the start of its scope, not merely from the point where the declaration appears.

So, for example, this script runs, and displays 10:

```
display dialog x
property x : 10
```

The property declaration is dealt with by the compiler, so before the script starts running x already exists and has the value 10. Thus the first line of the script works even though no definition of x precedes it. Even though it works, this is poor style and is to be discouraged.

Redeclaration of Properties

It is *not* a compile-time error to redeclare a property as a local or a local as a property; but access to the property is lost within that scope. For example:

```
script myScript
    property x : 4
    display dialog x
    local x
    display dialog x
end script
run myScript -- 4, then error
```

The second attempt to display x fails because by that point x has been redeclared as local, and this local has no value. But the downward effect of the property declaration remains, so the property remains accessible at a deeper scope. Thus:

```
script myScript
    property x : 10
    local x
    set x to 20
    on myHandler( )
        display dialog x
    end myHandler
    myHandler( )
    display dialog x
end script
run myScript -- 10, then 20
```

It is a compile-time error to redeclare as global a variable declared as a property in the same scope:

```
property x: 10
global x -- compile-time error
```

It is *not* a compile-time error to do it the other way round, redeclaring a global as a property. This is merely taken as a delayed declaration of the property, and the global declaration has no effect. So:

```
global x
set x to 10
script myScript
    global x
    set x to 5
    property x : 20
    display dialog x
end script
run myScript -- 5
display dialog x -- 10
```

Within myScript, x is a property throughout; the global declaration inside myScript has no effect. The property x starts out with the value 20 before myScript runs, but myScript then sets it to 5, and this is the value that is displayed in the first dialog. The second dialog shows that the global x is unaffected. This code was written and executed on a closed course by a trained driver; please, do not attempt.

Lifetime of Variables

The *lifetime* of a variable means just what you think it means—how long the variable lives.

A local variable is born when it first is assigned a value, and dies when the scope in which it was born stops executing. A variable that behaves this way is sometimes called an *automatic* variable, because it comes into existence and goes out of existence automatically. For example:

```
on myHandler( )
    local x
    set x to 5
    display dialog x
end myHandler
myHandler( ) -- 5
display dialog x -- error
```

Well, you already knew what would happen when that code runs. But what I'm saying now is something you can't see, and I can't quite prove, so you'll just have to believe me: by the time we get to the last line of that example, the local x inside myHandler isn't just unavailable, it's gone. It came into existence as myHandler was executing, and it went out of existence when myHandler finished executing.

A top-level entity other than a local variable is *persistent*. This means that its name and its value survives the execution of the script. This becomes interesting and relevant if you execute the same script twice.

Here's a simple example. Create this script in a script editor program and run it:

```
property x : 5
set x to x + 1
display dialog x -- 6
```

Now run it again, without doing anything else. Here's what happens:

```
property x : 5
set x to x + 1
display dialog x -- 7
```

This amazing result is possible because AppleScript has a memory. (You did reread "Maintenance of State" in Chapter 4, didn't you?) Your compiled script is in Apple-Script's memory. After the script is executed, AppleScript retains the compiled script, and along with it, all the top-level entities that resulted from its execution. This includes properties, so after the first execution of the script, AppleScript is remembering that the script has a property x and that its value is 6. Thus when you run the script a second time and x is incremented, it becomes 7.

Now, at this point, you are saying: "But wait! I can see x being initialized to 5 right in the first line of the script. So what about that line? Are you saying that, the second time the script is executed, AppleScript is ignoring that line?" Well, it's really just a matter of what *initialize* means. It means to give a value to something that has no value. The second time the script is executed, x has a value already, remembered from the previous execution. So the property declaration has all the usual downward effects of a property declaration; but the initialization part of it has no effect, because x doesn't need initializing.

You can do the very same thing with a top-level global variable, but it's a little trickier because you need a way to initialize the global—to give it a value if it doesn't have one, but not if it does. Obviously this won't do:

```
set x to 5
set x to x + 1
display dialog x -- 6
```

You can execute that over and over, and it just displays 6 over and over. The problem is that set is not a mere initialization; it sets x regardless. Thus you keep resetting x to 5 each time you execute the script. This means that you probably don't believe me when I say that the value of x is being remembered between executions. To get around this, we have to use stealth (and some syntax that hasn't been discussed yet—try blocks are explained in Chapter 12):

```
try
    set x to x + 1
on error
    set x to 5
    set x to x + 1
end try
display dialog x -- 6, then 7, and so forth
```

Run that repeatedly. Now do you believe me?

A script object defined at top level is a top-level entity, so it and all script objects defined within it, and therefore all their properties, also persist after execution. For example:

```
script outerScript
    script innerScript
        property x : 5
        on increment( )
            set x to x + 1
        end increment
    end script
    tell innerScript to increment( )
    display dialog innerScript's x
end script
run outerScript -- 6, then 7, and so forth
```

Now, nothing lives forever, so just how long does all this persistence persist? Well, for one thing, it all comes to an end if you edit the script. That's because altering the script means that the script must be recompiled, and at that point the contents of the old compiled script, including the values of the top-level entities from the previous execution, are thrown away from AppleScript's memory. That's why throughout this section I've been telling you to execute the script multiple times without doing anything else.

The really, *really* surprising part, though, is that this persistence can survive the saving and reloading of the script in a script file. Unfortunately you can't see this if you save or open the script file using the current Script Editor. It doesn't work with Smile, either. Smile has another way of implementing persistence between sessions. So try it with the old version of the Script Editor (1.9), or with Script Debugger. Create and run this script several times:

```
property x : 5
set x to x + 1
display dialog x
```

Now save the script as a compiled script file, and quit, just to prove to yourself that AppleScript's own memory of the value of x is well and truly erased. Now open the compiled script file again and execute it. The incrementing of x picks up right where it left off previously.

This mechanism is not automatic. AppleScript itself has no way to enforce file-level persistence, because AppleScript itself doesn't deal in files. It is up the environment that's talking to the AppleScript scripting component, after it asks AppleScript to run the compiled script file, to save AppleScript's copy of the compiled script back into the compiled script file after execution. If it doesn't do this, then the compiled script file won't contain the new values, and the values won't persist. Fortunately most environments, including applets, as well as script runners such as the Script Menu or BBEdit's Scripts menu, are well-behaved in this regard. But as we've just seen, the current version of Script Editor is not. This inconsistency can be troublesome.

CHAPTER 8
Handlers

A *handler* is a subroutine within a script. A handler is defined using a block of code that starts with the keyword on, with syntax of this sort:

```
on handlerName( )
    -- commands within the handler
end handlerName
```

A synonym for on is to.

 When typing a handler definition, don't bother to type the name of the handler a second time in the end line. Just type end for that line; the compiler will fill in the name of the handler.

A handler definition contains the code to be executed when the handler runs, but the mere presence of the definition does not itself cause such execution. A handler's code is run when an executed line of code *calls* the handler, using a corresponding syntax:

```
handlerName( )
```

The parentheses may not actually appear in the definition or the call; these are just vague syntax templates to get the discussion started. I'll explain the syntax of handler definitions and calls later in this chapter.

A handler is an important form of flow control, and leads to better-behaved, better-organized, more reusable, and more legible code. With a handler, the same code can be reused in different places in a script. Even if a handler is going to be called only once in the course of a script, it's a useful device because it names a block of code, and this name can be made informative as to the block's purpose.

Also, a handler can be called from elsewhere, so that only a specific part of a script or script object is executed. We saw this earlier in demonstrating folder actions, under "Automatic Location" in Chapter 2. The folder action script used as an example there consisted of a handler called adding folder items to:

```
on adding folder items to ff after receiving L
    -- ...
end adding folder items to
```

That script might have other handlers as well, but when files are added to the folder to which the script is attached, it is the adding folder items to handler that will be called. A handler thus serves as an *entry point* to execute part of a script. This is also how scriptability of an applet is implemented. We'll talk more about that in Chapter 24.

Returned Value

When a handler is executed, it may *return* a value. By this we mean that it generates a value which *becomes the value of the call* that executed the handler. We may speak of the returned value as the *result* of the handler.

 The term *result* is used here in a technical sense. A handler may do other things besides return a result, and these other things may be quite significant in the world outside of the handler; technically these are not the result of calling the handler, but its *side-effects*. Thus, if you call a handler that erases your hard drive and returns the number 1, you might say in ordinary conversation, "The result of calling the handler was that my hard drive was erased," but technically you'd be wrong: the result was 1; the erasure of your hard drive was a side-effect. (This shows that a side-effect can be much more important than a result.)

For example:

```
on getRam( )
    set bytes to system attribute "ram "
    return bytes div (2 ^ 20)
end getRam
```

The handler getRam( ) returns the amount of RAM installed on the user's machine, in megabytes. On my machine, it returns the number 384. This means that a call to getRam( ) can presently be used wherever I would use the number 384; in effect, it *is* the number 384. For example:

```
on getRam( )
    set bytes to system attribute "ram "
    return bytes div (2 ^ 20)
end getRam
display dialog "You have " & getRam( ) & "MB of RAM. Wow!"
```

The call to getRam( ) in the last line behaves exactly as the number 384 would behave in this context: it is implicitly coerced to a string and concatenated with the other two strings (as explained under "Concatenation Operator" in Chapter 15), and the full resulting string is displayed to the user.

The value returned by a handler is determined in one of two ways:

An explicit return

> The handler, in the course of execution, encounters a line consisting of the keyword return, possibly followed by a value. At that point execution of the handler ceases, and the returned value is whatever follows the return keyword (which could be nothing, in which case no value is returned).

An implicit result

> The handler finishes executing without ever encountering an explicit return. In that case, the returned value is the result of the last-executed line of the handler.

 For the same reason that I recommend that you not use the result keyword (see "Result" in Chapter 6), I recommend that you not use a handler's ability to return an implicit result. If you're going to capture a handler's result, use an explicit return statement wherever the handler ends execution.

If a handler returns no value, there is no error; but in that case it is a runtime error to attempt to use the call as if it had a value. The status of such a call is similar to that of a variable that has never been assigned a value (see "Declaration and Definition of Variables" in Chapter 7). So, for example, there's nothing wrong with this:

```
on noValue( )
    return
end noValue
set x to noValue( )
```

After that, even if x was previously defined, it is now undefined. Thus an attempt to fetch its value will generate a runtime error:

```
on noValue( )
    return
end noValue
set x to 1
set x to noValue( )
set x to x + 1 -- error
```

The result of a handler is volatile. It is substituted for the call, but the call itself is not storage (it isn't a variable), so the result is then lost. If you wish to use the result of a handler again later, it is up to you to capture it at the time you make the call. Of course, you could just call the handler again; but there are good reasons why this strategy might not be the right one:

- The handler might be such that, when called on different occasions, it yields different results; if you wanted the particular result of a particular call, calling it again won't do.

- The handler might do other things besides return a result (side-effects); to perform these side-effects again might not be good, or might not make sense.

- Storing a result and using it later is far more efficient than calling the handler a second time.

So, for example, this code works, but it is very poor code:

```
on getRam( )
    set bytes to system attribute "ram "
    return bytes div (2 ^ 20)
end getRam
set s to "You have " & getRam( ) & "MB of RAM. Wow! "
set s to s & getRam( ) & "MB is a lot!"
display dialog s
```

The handler is called twice to get the same unchanging result, which is very inefficient. The right way would be more like this:

```
on getRam( )
    set bytes to system attribute "ram "
    return bytes div (2 ^ 20)
end getRam
set myRam to getRam( )
set s to "You have " & myRam & "MB of RAM. Wow! "
set s to s & myRam & "MB is a lot!"
display dialog s
```

The second version calls the handler and immediately stores the result in a variable. Now it suffices to fetch the value from the variable each time it is needed.

The result of a handler may be ignored if the caller doesn't care about it (or knows that no value will be returned). In this case the handler is called entirely for its side-effects. Generally the call will appear as the only thing in the line:

```
eraseMyHardDisk( )
```

Parameters

A *parameter* is a value passed to a handler as it is called. A handler is defined to take a certain number of parameters; this can be any number, whatever the author of the handler feels is appropriate to what the handler does. (The details on the syntax of defining and calling a handler that has parameters are addressed in the next section; right now we're just talking about what parameters are.)

For example, here's a definition of a handler that takes two parameters, and a call to that handler:

```
on add(x, y)
    return x + y
end add
display dialog add(3, 2)
```

In the last line, the handler is called with the two parameters it requires. The value 3 is passed as the first parameter; the value 2 is passed as the second parameter. In the handler definition, names that effectively designate variables local to the handler have been declared. When the handler is called, and before it actually starts executing, these names are paired with the parameters that were passed, and the corresponding values are assigned. Thus, when add( ) is called on this occasion, it is as if it had a local variable x which has been initialized to 3, and a local variable y which has been initialized to 2.

Because the parameter names in the handler definition are local to the handler, they are invisible outside it. That's good. Any parameter names may be used within the handler without fear of confusion with other names outside the handler. For example:

```
on add(x, y)
    return x + y
end add
set x to 2
set y to 3
display dialog add(y, x)
```

In that code, what matters to the handler is that the value 3 is passed as the first parameter, and that the value 2 is passed as the second parameter. Thus, within the handler, the value 3 is assigned to x and the value 2 is assigned to y. Those are implicit locals; the handler knows nothing about the top-level names x and y (and vice versa).

A parameter name cannot be declared global within the handler, just as a local cannot be redeclared global (see "Redeclaration of Locals and Globals" in Chapter 7).

It is a runtime error to call a handler with fewer parameters than the definition of the handler requires. There is no way to declare a parameter optional in AppleScript. On the other hand, you really don't need a way to do this, because a parameter can be a list or a record, which can have any number of items.[*]

For example, here's a handler that calculates the area of a rectangle given the lengths of the two sides. If you pass the length of only one side, the rectangle is assumed to be a square:

```
on area(L)
    set a to item 1 of L
    if (count L) = 2 then
        set b to item 2 of L
    else
        set b to item 1 of L
    end if
    return a * b
end area
area({3, 4}) -- 12
area({3}) -- 9
```

[*] All we need is a shift command and this would be Perl!

Syntax of Defining and Calling a Handler

The parameters, if there are any, follow the name of the handler in both the definition and the call. In the definition, you're saying how many parameters there are, and supplying the names of the local variables to which they will be assigned; in the call, you're supplying their values. There are four syntactic cases that must be distinguished, depending on whether the handler has parameters and, if so, how they are specified. (Personally, I think the third and fourth ways to define a handler are silly, and I never use them. But you need to know about them anyway.)

 It is not an error to refer to a handler by its name alone, with no parentheses or parameters. This can be a useful thing to do, if you wish to refer to the handler as a value (see "Handlers as Values," later in this chapter); but it *doesn't call the handler*. If you refer to a handler by its name alone, intending to call it, your script will misbehave in ways that can be difficult to track down.

No Parameters

If a handler has no parameters, the name of the handler in the definition is followed by empty parentheses:

```
on handlerWithNoParameters()
    -- code
end handlerWithNoParameters
```

The call consists of the name of the handler followed by empty parentheses:

```
handlerWithNoParameters()
```

Unnamed Parameters

Unnamed parameters are sometimes referred to as *positional parameters*. This is because the pairing between each parameter value passed and the local variable in the handler that receives it is performed by looking at their respective positions: the first parameter is assigned to the first variable, the second parameter is assigned to second variable, and so forth.

If a handler has positional parameters, the name of the handler in the definition is followed by one or more variable names in parentheses, separated by comma:

```
on handlerWithOneParameter(x)
    -- code
end handlerWithOneParameter
on handlerWithFourParameters(a, b, c, d)
    -- code
end handlerWithFourParameters
```

The call then consists of the name of the handler followed by parentheses containing the parameter value or values, separated by comma:

```
handlerWithOneParameter(7)
handlerWithFourParameters("hey", "ho", "hey", "nonny no")
```

It is not an error to call a handler with more unnamed parameters than the handler requires, but the extra values are ignored.

Prepositional Parameters

Prepositional parameters are also called *labeled parameters*. Each parameter is preceded by a preposition drawn from a fixed repertoire. The use of prepositional parameters has two supposed advantages:

- The prepositions may give an indication of the purpose of each parameter.
- The prepositions are used to pair the parameter values with the variables in the handler, so the parameters may be passed in any order.

The preposition names from which you get to choose are limited to those listed in Table 8-1.

Table 8-1. The prepositions

above	beneath	into
against	beside	on
apart from	between	onto
around	by	out of
aside from	for	over
at	from	thru
below	instead of	under

In addition to the prepositions in Table 8-1, there is also a preposition of. This is used in a special way: if you use it, it must come first, and there must be more than one parameter. This odd rule seems to be due to a mistake in the original design of AppleScript. In AppleScript 1.0, the of parameter was intended as a way of distinguishing the "direct object" (the handler's main parameter). Then it was realized that where there was just one parameter and it was the of parameter, an unresolvable ambiguity with the of operator was introduced. So AppleScript 1.1 resolved the ambiguity by forbidding of to be used that way. But no alternative way of distinguishing the direct object was supplied, so in a sense this feature has been broken ever since.

If a handler has prepositional parameters, the name of the handler in the definition is followed by a preposition and a variable name, and then possibly another preposition and another variable name, and so on.

In the call, the name of the handler is followed by a preposition and a value, and then possibly another preposition and another value, and so forth. The prepositions used must match those of the definition, but they may appear in any order, except for of, which must be first if it appears at all.

Here are some examples of handlers with prepositional parameters and calls to them:

```
on firstLetter from aWord
    return character 1 of aWord
end firstLetter
display dialog (firstLetter from "hello")

on sum of x beside y
    return x + y
end sum
display dialog (sum of 1 beside 2)

on stopping by woods on aSnowyEvening
    return woods & aSnowyEvening
end stopping
display dialog (stopping on "horse" by "farm")
```

In the call, if the value you wish to pass is a boolean, you may use with or without (to indicate true and false respectively) followed by the preposition. If you don't use this syntax, AppleScript may use it for you when it compiles the script: any prepositional parameters for which you pass the literal value true or false will end up as with or without followed by the preposition. Multiple with clauses or without clauses can be joined using and. This looks quite silly when the labels are prepositions, but here goes:

```
on stopping by woods on aSnowyEvening
    if woods and aSnowyEvening then
        return "lovely, dark and deep"
    else
        return "ugly and shallow"
    end if
end stopping
display dialog (stopping with on and by)
display dialog (stopping with by without on)
```

It is a runtime error for the call to omit any defined prepositional parameter. It is not an error to toss some extra prepositional parameters into the call, but they are ignored by the handler.

The real value of labeled parameter syntax emerges when targeting scriptable applications. Application commands, unlike handlers in your scripts, can define their own labels beyond the list of prepositions in Table 8-1. For an example, see the dictionary listing for FrameMaker's find command under "Seek and Ye Shall Find" in Chapter 3, where the parameters are called with value, with properties, in, and using. It would be nice if handlers could do this too, but they can't. The closest they come is named parameters, described in the next section.

Named Parameters

Named parameters are a way to take advantage of labeled parameters while escaping the circumscribed repertoire of built-in prepositions. You get to make up your own names, though of course you mustn't use a word that's already reserved by the language for something else.

You may combine named parameters with prepositional parameters; if you do, the named parameters must come after the prepositional parameters.

The syntax for defining named parameters is this:

```
on handlerName ... given paramName1:varName1, paramName2:varName2, ...
```

The first ellipsis in that syntax schema is the definition for the prepositional parameters, if there are any. The second ellipsis is for as many further named parameters as you like.

The call works just the same way: the keyword given must appear, it must appear after all prepositional parameters if there are any, and the same colon-based syntax is used:

```
handlerName ... given paramName1:value1, paramName2:value2, ...
```

As with prepositional parameters, boolean values can be passed using with or without and the parameter name, and for these there is no need to say given. Again, AppleScript will use this syntax for you if you pass the literal value true or false.

Here are some examples of handlers with named parameters, and calls to them. For the sake of simplicity, none of these handlers also take prepositional parameters.

```
on sum given theOne:x, theOther:y
    return x + y
end sum
display dialog (sum given theOther:2, theOne:3)

on scout given loyal:loyal, trustworthy:trustworthy
    if loyal and trustworthy then
        return "eagle"
    else
        return "sparrow"
    end if
end scout
display dialog (scout with loyal and trustworthy)
```

The first example demonstrates that the order of parameters is free. The second example demonstrates the use of with, and also shows that the parameter labels can be the same as the local variable names.

Pass By Reference

Parameters passed to a handler, and the value returned from a handler, are normally *passed by value* in AppleScript. This means that a copy of the value is made, and it is the copy that arrives at the destination scope.

But four datatypes—lists, records, dates, and script objects—when they are passed as parameters to a handler, are *passed by reference*. This means that no copy is made; the handler's scope and the caller's scope both end up with access to the very same value, rather as if it were a global. Any change made to the parameter by the handler is also made back in the context of the caller. For example:

```
on extend(LL)
    set end of LL to "Jack"
end extend
set L to {"Mannie", "Moe"}
extend(L)
L -- {"Mannie", "Moe", "Jack"}
```

Notice that we didn't capture the value of the handler call extend( ). The handler extend was able to modify the list L *directly*. After the call, L has been changed in the caller's context, even though the caller didn't change it.

It makes sense that lists, records, dates, and script objects can be passed by reference, since these are the only *mutable* datatypes—the only datatypes whose values can be modified in place, as opposed to being replaced wholesale. But it is a little odd that they are passed by reference automatically. Passing by reference gives the handler great power over the parameter, which the handler can misuse. To prevent accidents, it is up to you to remember that list, record, date, and script object parameters are passed by reference, and that things you do in a handler to such parameters have an effect outside the handler.

What about values that are not lists, records, dates, or script objects? How can they be passed by reference? The nearest thing to a solution, which unfortunately works only when the variable in question is a global, is AppleScript's ability to pass (by value) a *reference* to a variable (see Chapter 11). The syntax consists of the phrase a reference to, followed by the name of a global. The handler must explicitly set the contents of the reference whose variable value it wants to change.

For example:

```
on increment(y)
    set contents of y to y + 1
end increment
set x to 5
increment(a reference to x)
display dialog x -- 6
```

Since only a global can be passed by reference in this way, it could be argued that one might as well use an actual global, and not bother passing anything at all:

```
on increment( )
    global param
    set param to param + 1
end increment
set param to 5
increment( )
display dialog param
```

This approach, however, depends on both scopes knowing the name of the global, so it lacks generality. Nevertheless, there are situations where a global is the best approach, as when a script must maintain state between calls to different handlers; we'll see examples in Chapter 24.

You cannot return a handler's value by reference. Well, you can, but it's usually pointless. It's true that this works:

```
on extend(LL)
        set end of LL to "Moe"
        return LL
end extend
set L to {"Mannie"}
set LLL to extend(L)
set end of LLL to "Jack"
L -- {"Mannie", "Moe", "Jack"}
```

It's clear that LLL has arrived by reference in the sense that changing it changes L. But the only reason this works is that we're just returning from extend( ) the very same reference that was passed in to start with! And we could have obtained that reference without calling the handler at all (in this case, simply by using set, as you'll see in "List" in Chapter 13). This was never a value local to the handler. It makes no sense to return by reference a value local to a handler, because by definition such a value is destroyed when the handler finishes executing; there is nothing for the reference to refer to.

Scoping of Handlers

A handler definition may appear only at the top level of a script or script object. (Therefore you can't nest handlers, except indirectly, by having a handler inside a script object inside a handler.)

A handler is visible to code in the scope where it is defined, even code that precedes the definition (see "Compiling" in Chapter 4). For example:

```
myHandler( ) -- Howdy
on myHandler( )
        display dialog "Howdy"
end myHandler
```

A handler is visible to scopes within the scope where it is defined. Remarkably, this works even before the handler is defined. For example:

```
script x
        myHandler( )
end script
run x -- Howdy
on myHandler( )
        display dialog "Howdy"
end myHandler
```

A handler is visible on demand from outside the script object where it is defined. Code that can see a script object can refer to its handlers, using essentially the same two kinds of syntax by which it would refer to its properties (see "Scoping of Properties" in Chapter 7). You don't need to use the word its to call a script object's handler from within a tell block addressed to that script object. This example illustrates both kinds of syntax:

```
script x
    on myHandler( )
        display dialog "Howdy"
    end myHandler
end script
x's myHandler( ) -- Howdy
tell x
    myHandler( ) -- Howdy
end tell
```

The comparison between handlers and properties is apt. The scoping of handlers is very similar to the scoping of properties. They are both top-level entities of a script or script object; they are visible on demand wherever that script or script object is visible; and they are automatically visible globally downwards.

Handler Calls Within Script Objects

A handler call within a script object is subject to a special rule: a handler is *not callable* from within a script object except by a name that is *defined as a global within that script object or its inheritance chain*. (The inheritance chain is explained under "Inheritance" in Chapter 9.) When I say "defined as a global" I mean that the name is the name of a handler, a property, or a global variable.

This is not really a rule about scope; it's a rule about how handler calls work. But this is the place to mention it, because your main interest in a handler's scope will be for purposes of calling the handler. The rule actually has to do with the fact that a script object is an object to which one can send messages. A handler call is such a message, so it falls under the targeting rules for object messages. A message sent from within an object, if no explicit target is given, is assumed to be targeting that same object. If a script object can't deal with a message, AppleScript looks up its inheritance chain for a script object that can.

Because of this rule, the following code generates a runtime error:

```
script x
    on myHandler( )
        display dialog "Howdy"
    end myHandler
    script y
        myHandler( )
    end script
    run y
end script
run x -- error
```

That's because the call to myHandler is in a script object y, and there is no explicit target, so the call is assumed to target the script object y; but myHandler is not a global defined in y. Now, if we move the definition of myHandler to top level, the code works just fine:

```
on myHandler( )
    display dialog "Howdy"
end myHandler
script x
    script y
        myHandler( )
    end script
    run y
end script
run x -- Howdy
```

That's because when myHandler is not found in y, we look up the inheritance chain, starting with y's parent. By default, the script as a whole is y's parent, and there we do indeed find myHandler as the name of a global (in particular, of a handler).

To show that this rule is not about scoping, I'll prove that myHandler, when defined in x, is in fact *visible* from within y even though it is not directly *callable* from within y. The proof involves treating a handler as a value, which isn't discussed until later in this chapter, but you should be able to make sense of it:

```
script x
    on myHandler( )
        display dialog "Howdy"
    end myHandler
    script y
        property localHandler : myHandler
        localHandler( )
    end script
    run y
end script
run x -- Howdy
```

The key point is that this line works:

```
        property localHandler : myHandler
```

That suffices to show that myHandler is visible from within y. The example also shows how myHandler *can* be called from within y, by referring to it through a name that *is* defined within y. Another technique is to specify explicitly the target for the call:

```
script x
    on myHandler( )
        display dialog "Howdy"
    end myHandler
    script y
        x's myHandler( )
    end script
    run y
end script
run x -- Howdy
```

Recursion

A handler is visible from within itself. This means that recursion is possible: a handler may call itself.

Explaining the elegances and dangers of recursion is beyond the scope of this book. The best way to learn about recursion is to learn a language like Scheme or LISP, where recursion is the primary form of looping. In fact, in conjunction with lists, AppleScript's recursion allows some remarkably Scheme-like (or LISP-like) modes of expression (see "LISP-likeness" in Chapter 5).

 The best way to learn Scheme is to read Harold Abelson et al., *Structure and Interpretation of Computer Programs*, 2nd Edition (MIT Press), the best computer book ever written.

For example, here's a recursive routine for filtering a list. We'll remove from the list everything that isn't a number:

```
on numbersOnly(L)
    if L = {} then return L
    if {class of item 1 of L} is in {real, integer, number} then
        return {item 1 of L} & numbersOnly(rest of L)
    else
        return numbersOnly(rest of L)
    end if
end numbersOnly
numbersOnly({"hey", 1, "ho", 2, 3}) -- {1, 2, 3}
```

The Run Handler

Every script has a run handler. When I say "every script," I mean either a script as a whole or a script object. When a script or script object is run, *what runs is its run handler*. This run handler may be implicit or explicit.

- If a script has any executable statements at its top level, the top level is the run handler. The script then has an *implicit run handler*.
- If a script has no executable statements at its top level, the run handler may be defined explicitly using the phrase on run. The script then has an *explicit run handler*.

Here is a script with an implicit run handler:

```
sayHowdy( )
on sayHowdy( )
    display dialog "Howdy"
end sayHowdy
```

The executable statement that makes the run handler implicit is the first line, the handler call. The handler definition that follows is not an executable statement and is not relevant to the matter.

Here is a script with an explicit run handler:

```
on run
     sayHowdy( )
end run
on sayHowdy( )
     display dialog "Howdy"
end sayHowdy
```

You will observe that the on run statement lacks any parentheses. The run handler is special and doesn't use parentheses. The effect of running this second script is exactly the same as running the first script.

To tell a script object to run its run handler (whether implicit or explicit), target the script object with the run command. This may be done using either of two syntaxes: the script object may be the run command's direct object, or the run command may occur in the context of a tell block targeting the script object.

This example illustrates both approaches:

```
script x
     on run
          display dialog "Howdy"
     end run
end script
run x -- Howdy
tell x
     run -- Howdy
end tell
```

Now we're going to talk about some special features of the run handler of a script (*not* a script object).

Variables defined implicitly in a script's top-level explicit run handler are implicit globals. In this respect, the explicit run handler is like the top level. For example:

```
on run
     set howdy to "Howdy"
     sayHowdy( ) -- Howdy
end run
on sayHowdy( )
     global howdy
     display dialog howdy
end sayHowdy
```

But in other respects an explicit run handler is not like the top level. It's a handler, so you can't define a handler directly within it. And scopes outside an explicit run handler are not somehow magically transposed to be within it, as if it really were the top level. For example, this doesn't work:

```
on run
     global howdy
     set howdy to "Howdy"
     sayHowdy( )
end run
```

```
on sayHowdy( )
    display dialog howdy -- error
end sayHowdy
```

Without its own global declaration for howdy, sayHowdy cannot see howdy any more; sayHowdy is not magically considered to be somehow inside the explicit run handler.

A script's explicit run handler may take parameters; these must be expressed as a single list. This is useful only under very special circumstances, and prevents the script from running at all under normal circumstances! For example:

```
on run {howdy}
    display dialog howdy
end run
```

That script is legal, but it won't run under normal circumstances because you have no way to pass the required single parameter to the run handler. But there are some contexts that give you a way to do it; for example, this is how you pass parameters to AppleScript code inside a REALbasic program. We'll see in Chapter 9 how you can pass parameters to a script's run handler.

Handlers as Values

A handler is a datatype in AppleScript. This means that a variable's value can be a handler. In fact, a handler definition *is* in effect the declaration (and definition) of such a variable. (That variable's status, as we have already seen, is essentially the same as that of a property.) The variable's name is the name of the handler, and its value is the handler's bytecode, its functionality.

A handler may thus be referred to like any other variable, and you can get and set its value. For example:

```
on sayHowdy( )
    display dialog "Howdy"
end sayHowdy
set sayHello to sayHowdy
sayHello( ) -- Howdy
```

In that example, we stored a handler as the value of a variable, and then called the variable as if it were a handler! This works because the variable *is* a handler.

The value of a handler can also be set. No law says you have to set it to another handler. For example, you could do this:

```
on sayHowdy( )
    display dialog "Howdy"
end sayHowdy
set sayHowdy to 9
display dialog sayHowdy -- 9
```

You can set one handler to the value of another, in effect substituting one entire functionality for another. Of course, the functionality has to be defined somewhere to begin with. For example:

```
on sayHowdy()
    display dialog "Howdy"
end sayHowdy
on sayHello()
    display dialog "Hello"
end sayHello
set sayHello to sayHowdy
sayHello() -- Howdy
```

Handlers as Parameters

At this point, you're probably thinking: "Wow! If I can store a handler as a variable, I can pass it as a parameter to another handler!" However, this code fails with a run-time error:

```
on sayHowdy()
    display dialog "Howdy"
end sayHowdy
on doThis(what)
    what()
end doThis
doThis(sayHowdy) -- error
```

We did succeed in passing the handler sayHowdy as a parameter to doThis(), but now we can't seem to call it; AppleScript refuses to identify the what() in the handler call with the what that arrived as a parameter. This is actually another case of the rule ("Handler Calls Within Script Objects," earlier in this chapter) that an unqualified handler call is a message directed to the current script object; AppleScript looks at the current script object, which is the script as a whole, for a global named what.

One obvious workaround is to use such a global:

```
on sayHowdy()
    display dialog "Howdy"
end sayHowdy
on doThis()
    global what
    what()
end doThis
set what to sayHowdy
doThis() -- Howdy
```

But globals are messy; we want a real solution. Here's one: we can pass instead of a handler, a script object. This is actually very efficient because script objects are passed by reference; and it works, because now we can use the run command instead of a handler call:

```
script sayHowdy
    display dialog "Howdy"
end script
on doThis(what)
    run what
end doThis
doThis(sayHowdy) -- Howdy
```

Alternatively, we can define a handler in a script object dynamically and *then* pass it. This is more involved, but it permits both the script and the handler that receives it as a parameter to be completely general:

```
script myScript
    on doAnything( )
    end doAnything
    doAnything( )
end script
on doThis(what)
    run what
end doThis
on sayHowdy( )
    display dialog "Howdy"
end sayHowdy
set myScript's doAnything to sayHowdy
doThis(myScript) -- Howdy
```

Observe that we can actually redefine a handler within a script object, from the outside!

My favorite solution is to pass a handler as parameter to doThis, just as in our first attempt, and to have a script object *inside* doThis waiting to receive it:

```
on sayHowdy( )
    display dialog "Howdy"
end sayHowdy
on doThis(what)
    script whatToDo
        property theHandler : what
        theHandler( )
    end script
    run whatToDo
end doThis
doThis(sayHowdy) -- Howdy
```

This is much like the technique used in "Handler Calls Within Script Objects," earlier in this chapter. It also depends upon the remarkable rule ("Explicit Locals" in Chapter 7) that a script object within a handler can see that handler's local variables. Thanks to this rule, our property initialization for theHandler can see the incoming what parameter and store its value—the handler. Now we are able to call the handler using the name theHandler, because this is the name of a global (a property) within this same script object.

For a useful application of this technique, let's return to the earlier example where we filtered a list to get only those members of the list that were numbers. The trouble with that routine is that it is not general; we'd like a routine to filter a list on *any* boolean criterion we care to provide. There are various ways to structure such a routine, but the approach that I consider the most elegant is to have filter( ) be a handler containing a script object, as in the preceding example. This handler accepts a list and a criterion handler and filters the list according to the criterion:

```
on filter(L, crit)
    script filterer
        property criterion : crit
        on filter(L)
            if L = {} then return L
            if criterion(item 1 of L) then
                return {item 1 of L} & filter(rest of L)
            else
                return filter(rest of L)
            end if
        end filter
    end script
    return filterer's filter(L)
end filter
on isNumber(x)
    return ({class of x} is in {real, integer, number})
end isNumber
filter({"hey", 1, "ho", 2, 3}, isNumber)
```

I consider that example to be the height of the AppleScript programmer's art, so perhaps you'd like to pause a moment to admire it.

Handlers as Handler Results

A handler may be returned as the result of a handler. Since you can't define a handler directly within a handler, you might have to define it as a handler within a script with the handler; but this is really no bother. So, for example:

```
on makeHandler( )
    script x
        on sayHowdy( )
            display dialog "Howdy"
        end sayHowdy
    end script
    return x's sayHowdy
end makeHandler
set y to makeHandler( )
y( )
```

In and of itself, however, this is not tremendously useful; in real life, you're more likely to return the entire script object rather than just one handler from it. We'll see why in the next chapter.

CHAPTER 9

Script Objects

A *script object* is a script within a script. In fact, a script really *is* a script object, but it also has a special status as the top-level script object—the script object that contains all others. A script object is defined using a block of code that starts with the keyword vertical barsscript, with syntax of this sort:

```
script scriptName
    -- commands within the script object
end script
```

 When typing a script definition, don't bother to type the full phrase end script in the end line. Just type end for that line; the compiler will fill in the word script.

A script object may be defined anywhere—at top level, within a script object, or within a handler. The mere presence of a script object definition does not itself cause execution of any code within the script object. A script object's code is run only on demand. (Later sections of this chapter, such as "Top-Level Entities" and "Script Object's Run Handler," discuss how to make such a demand.)

Like a script, a script object may contain script properties, handlers, script objects, and code. A script object is a device for organization of code and data. Related handlers, script objects, and variables can be packaged in a single self-contained script object. Also, a compiled script file can be accessed as a script object by a running script; thus a script object can function as a library of commonly needed code, or as persistent storage for variable values.

Together with variables and handlers, script objects complete a script's "map of the world." Handlers and script objects are AppleScript's regions of scope. Global variables, handlers, and script objects are the three types of persistent top-level attribute of a script (or a script object). Variables, handlers, script objects, and code constitute the entire structure of a script.

Scoping of Script Objects

The way a script object is scoped differs depending on whether it is defined in a script object (including a script as a whole) or in a handler. A script object *not* defined in a handler is the base case, so we start with that.

A script object (not defined in a handler) is visible to code in the scope where it is defined, even if that code precedes the definition of the script object. For example:

```
run myScript -- Howdy
script myScript
    display dialog "Howdy"
end script
```

A script object (not defined in a handler) is visible to scopes within the scope where it is defined, but not before the script object is defined. Thus the downward effect of a script object definition is like the downward effect of a property declaration. For example, this works:

```
run myScript -- Howdy
script myOtherScript
    property x : "Howdy"
end script
script myScript
    display dialog myOtherScript's x
end script
```

But this doesn't:

```
run myScript
script myScript
    display dialog myOtherScript's x -- error
end script
script myOtherScript
    property x : "Howdy"
end script
```

A script object's visibility is thus confined by default to the scope where it is defined. But a script object defined in another script object is visible on demand wherever that surrounding script object is visible; we'll come to that in a moment ("Top-Level Entities," later in this chapter).

Script Objects in Handlers

Within a handler, a script object definition must precede any reference to that script object. This is because until the handler actually runs, nothing within the handler definition happens—not even script object definitions. This rule is enforced by the compiler.

For example, this doesn't compile:

```
on myHandler( )
    run myScript
    script myScript -- compile-time error
        display dialog "Howdy"
    end script
end myHandler
myHandler( )
```

A script object defined in a handler can't be seen outside that handler. Again, this is because it doesn't exist except when the handler is executing.

A handler can return a script object, as we shall see later in this chapter.

Free Variables

Recall ("Free Variables" in Chapter 7) that an entity defined outside a handler or script object but globally visible and not redefined within it (a free variable) takes its value within the handler or script object *at the time the code runs*, not at the time the handler or script object is defined. In Chapter 7 our example of a free variable was a global variable. But it can also be a property, a handler, or a script object—in point of fact, any of the possible top-level entities of a script or script object.

Here's an example where the free variable is a property:

```
property x : 5
script myScript
    display dialog x
end script
script myOtherScript
    set x to 20
    run myScript
end script
set x to 10
run myScript -- 10
run myOtherScript -- 20
```

Here's an example where the free variable is the name of a handler:

```
run myScript -- Hello
set sayHello to sayGetLost
run myScript -- Get lost
on sayHello( )
    display dialog "Hello"
end sayHello
on sayGetLost( )
    display dialog "Get lost"
end sayGetLost
script myScript
    sayHello( )
end script
```

Top-Level Entities

There are three kinds of top-level entity in a script object—properties, handlers, and script objects (see Chapters 7 and 8 for script properties and handlers).

Accessing Top-Level Entities

Outside a script object, its top-level entities are *accessible on demand* to any code that can see the script object. This means that they can be both fetched and set by such code.

The syntax is as follows:

- Use the of operator (or the apostrophe-ess operator) to specify the top-level entity in relation to its script object. For example:

```
script myScript
    property x : "Howdy"
    on sayHowdy( )
        display dialog x
    end sayHowdy
    script innerScript
        display dialog x
    end script
end script
set x of myScript to "Hello"
myScript's sayHowdy( ) -- Hello
run innerScript of myScript -- Hello
```

- Alternatively, refer to the top-level entity within a tell block addressed to the script object. This requires the use of the keyword its, except in the case of a handler call. For example:

```
script myScript
    property x : "Howdy"
    on sayHowdy( )
        display dialog x
    end sayHowdy
    script innerScript
        display dialog x
    end script
end script
tell myScript
    set its x to "Hello"
    sayHowdy( )
    run its innerScript
end tell
```

In that last example, if you omit the keyword its from the line where you set x, you set an implicit global x, not the property of myScript. If you omit the keyword its from the line where you run innerScript, there is a runtime error, because no innerScript is in scope.

(It makes no difference whether or not the keyword its appears before the call to sayHowdy( ). This special treatment of handler calls is discussed under "Handler Calls Within Script Objects" in Chapter 8, and again later in this chapter.)

Persistence of Top-Level Entities

A top-level entity of a script object is persistent as long as you don't do something to reinitialize it. Typically, the top-level entity you're most immediately concerned with is a property. So, for example, the properties in this code persist and are incremented each time the script is run:

```
script myScript
    property x : 5
    script myInnerScript
        property x : 10
    end script
end script
tell myScript
    set its x to (its x) + 1
    tell its myInnerScript
        set its x to (its x) + 1
    end tell
end tell
display dialog myScript's x
display dialog myScript's myInnerScript's x
```

That code displays 6 and 11, then 7 and 12, and so forth, each time the script runs.

Script objects and handlers are top-level entities too, and they persist as well. Here's an example that illustrates this with a script object:

```
script myScript
    script myInnerScript
        display dialog "Hello"
    end script
    run myInnerScript
end script
script myNastyScript
    display dialog "Get lost"
end script
run myScript
set myScript's myInnerScript to myNastyScript
```

That code displays Hello the first time, but then it displays Get lost every time after that. The reason is that after the first time, myInnerScript has been replaced by myNastyScript, and this new version of myInnerScript persists.

As explained already under "Lifetime of Variables" in Chapter 7, if you edit a script and then run it, it is recompiled, so at that point persistence comes to an end: the script's top-level entities are reinitialized, and this includes its script objects, the script objects of those script objects, and so forth, along with all their top-level entities.

When a script object is defined within a handler, it has no persistence. The script object is created anew each time the handler runs.

Script Object's Run Handler

A script object has a run handler (see Chapter 8), which is executed when the script object is told to run. This run handler may be implicit or explicit.

To tell a script object to run its run handler, send the run message to it. You can do this by making the script object the direct object of the run command, or by saying run within a tell block targeting the script object.

If a script object's run handler is explicit, it is a handler, and rules about handlers apply to it. For example, you can't define a handler in a script object's explicit run handler; outside code can't see a script object defined in a script object's explicit run handler; and running a script object's explicit run handler reinitializes any script objects defined within it.

This example demonstrates that a script object defined in a script object's explicit run handler has no persistence:

```
script myScript
    on run
        script myInnerScript
            property x : 10
        end script
        tell myInnerScript
            set its x to (its x) + 1
            display dialog its x
        end tell
    end run
end script
run myScript -- 11
```

That code yields 11 every time it runs.

If a script object has no explicit run handler and has no executable statements in its implicit run handler, telling it to run can have unpredictable consequences. For example, this would be a bad thing to do:

```
script myScript
end script
run myScript -- stack overflow
```

This is almost certainly a bug.

Handler Calls

A handler call is special, because it is a kind of message. (See "Handler Calls Within Script Objects" in Chapter 8.) This message is directed to a particular target—a script object. If no target is specified explicitly, the target is the script object in which the handler call appears.

When a script object receives a handler call message, the handler is sought as a name *defined as a top-level entity within it* (that is, not a free variable and not a local variable). If there is no such name, the search passes to the script object's parent; this is the top-level script by default, though it can be changed ("Inheritance," later in this chapter).

In this example, the handler call is directed implicitly; the call appears within myScript so it is directed to myScript, which defines a handler by the right name:

```
script myScript
    on myHandler( )
        display dialog "Howdy"
    end myHandler
    myHandler( )
end script
run myScript -- Howdy
```

This example doesn't work, because myHandler isn't defined in myScript:

```
script outerScript
    on myHandler( )
        display dialog "Howdy"
    end myHandler
    script myScript
        myHandler( )
    end script
end script
run outerScript's myScript -- error
```

This example works, because we specify the correct target explicitly:

```
script outerScript
    on myHandler( )
        display dialog "Howdy"
    end myHandler
    script myScript
        outerScript's myHandler( )
    end script
end script
run outerScript's myScript -- Howdy
```

This works even though myHandler isn't defined in myScript:

```
script myScript
    myHandler( )
end script
on myHandler( )
    display dialog "Howdy"
end myHandler
run myScript -- Howdy
```

That works because myHandler is defined in myScript's parent, the top-level script. To prove that this explanation is correct, we'll pervert the inheritance chain so that myScript's parent *isn't* the top-level script. This is not easy, because if we make myScript's parent another script object, *that* script object's parent will be the top-level script. So we'll have to do something rather bizarre: we'll make myScript's parent something that isn't a script at all.

```
script myScript
    property parent : 3
    myHandler( )
end script
on myHandler( )
    display dialog "Howdy"
end myHandler
run myScript -- error
```

Script Objects as Values

A script object is a datatype in AppleScript. This means that a variable's value can be a script object. In fact, a script object definition basically *is* such a variable, one whose name is the name of the script object. You can refer to this variable, and get and set its value, just as you would any other variable. Here, we fetch a script object as a value and assign it to another variable:

```
script myScript
    display dialog "Howdy"
end script
local x
set x to myScript
run x -- Howdy
```

You can also assign a new value to a script object. No law says that this new value must be another script object; you're just replacing the value of a variable, as with any other variable. So, you could do this if you wanted:

```
script myScript
    display dialog "Howdy"
end script
set myScript to 9
display dialog myScript -- 9
```

You can assign a script object the value of another script object, in effect replacing its functionality with new functionality. Of course, that new functionality must be defined somewhere to begin with. For example:

```
script sayHowdy
    display dialog "Howdy"
end script
script sayHello
    display dialog "Hello"
end script
set sayHowdy to sayHello
run sayHowdy -- Hello
```

Set By Reference

When you use set (as opposed to copy) to set a variable to a value which is a script object, you set the variable *by reference*. This means that the script object is not copied; the variable's name becomes a new name for the script object, in addition to any existing names for the script object. This has two important implications:

- Setting a variable to a script object with set is extremely efficient, no matter how big the script object may be.
- If a script object has more than one name, then whatever is done to it by way of one name is accessible by way of its other names as well.

The second point is the vital one. Here's an example:

```
script sayHello
    property greeting : "Hello"
    display dialog greeting
end script
local x
set x to sayHello
set sayHello's greeting to "Howdy"
display dialog x's greeting -- Howdy
run x -- Howdy
```

In that example, we changed a property of the script object sayHello; the same property of the script object x was changed to the same thing. That's because sayHello and x are merely two names for the same thing. And *that's* because we used set to set x's value by reference to the script object that sayHello was already the name of.

When a script property is initialized to a value that is a script object, it too is set by reference. Let's prove it:

```
script addend
    property whatToAdd : 0
end script
script adder
    property z : addend
    on add(x)
        return x + (z's whatToAdd)
    end add
end script
set addend's whatToAdd to 2
display dialog adder's add(3) -- 5
```

In that example, we changed a property of the script object addend, and this affected the result of the handler add which refers to the same script object by way of the property z.

Pass By Reference

A script object passed as a parameter to a handler is passed by reference (Chapter 8). Let's prove it:

```
script myScript
    property x : 10
end script
on myHandler(s)
    set s's x to (s's x) + 1
end myHandler
display dialog myScript's x -- 10
myHandler(myScript)
display dialog myScript's x -- 11
```

In that example, myHandler never speaks explicitly of myScript; yet after running myHandler, we find that myScript's property x has been changed. This is because in passing myScript as a parameter to myHandler, we pass it by reference; myHandler has access, and can do whatever it wishes, to myScript.

Script Object as Handler Result

The result of a handler can be a script object. Normally, this script object is a copy, passed by value; it could not be passed by reference, since after the handler finishes executing there is no script object back in the handler for a reference to refer to. (Actually, if the returned script object is the same script object that was passed in as a parameter by reference, then it is returned by reference as well; still, that fact isn't terribly interesting, since at the time the script object was passed in, you must have had a reference to it to begin with.)

For example:

```
on scriptMaker( )
    script myScript
        property x : "Howdy"
        display dialog x
    end script
    return myScript
end scriptMaker
set myScript to scriptMaker( )
run myScript -- Howdy
```

In the last two lines, we acquire the script object returned by the handler scriptMaker, and run it. Of course, if we didn't want to retain the script object, these two lines could be combined into one:

```
run scriptMaker( ) -- Howdy
```

A handler can customize a script object before returning it. So, for example:

```
on scriptMaker( )
    script myScript
        property x : "Howdy"
        display dialog x
    end script
    set myScript's x to "Hello"
    return myScript
end scriptMaker
set myScript to scriptMaker( )
run myScript -- Hello
```

In that example, the handler scriptMaker not only created a script object, it also modified it, altering the value of a property, before returning it.

Obviously, instead of hardcoding the modification into the handler, we can pass the modification to the handler as a parameter:

```
on scriptMaker(s)
    script myScript
        property x : "Howdy"
        display dialog x
    end script
    set myScript's x to s
    return myScript
end scriptMaker
set myScript to scriptMaker("Hello")
run myScript -- Hello
```

Recall from "Explicit Locals" in Chapter 7 that, contrary to the general rules of scoping, a script object defined inside a handler can see the handler's local variables. This means that in the previous example we can save a step and initialize the property x directly to the incoming parameter s:

```
on scriptMaker(s)
    script myScript
        property x : s
        display dialog x
    end script
    return myScript
end scriptMaker
set myScript to scriptMaker("Hello")
run myScript -- Hello
```

The real power of this technique emerges when we retain and reuse the resulting script object. For example, here's a new version of the general list-filtering routine we wrote earlier ("Handlers as Parameters" in Chapter 8). In that earlier version, we passed a handler both a criterion handler and a list, and got back a filtered list. In this version, we pass just a criterion handler, and get back a script object:

```
on makeFilterer(crit)
    script filterer
        property criterion : crit
        on filter(L)
            if L = {} then return L
            if criterion(item 1 of L) then
                return {item 1 of L} & filter(rest of L)
            else
                return filter(rest of L)
            end if
        end filter
    end script
    return filterer
end makeFilterer
```

The script object that we get back from `makeFilterer` contains a `filter` handler that has been customized to filter any list according to the criterion we passed in at the start. This architecture is both elegant and efficient. Suppose you know you'll be filtering many lists on the same criterion. You can use `makeFilterer` to produce a single script object whose `filter` handler filters on this criterion, store the script object, and call its `filter` handler repeatedly with different lists. For example:

```
on makeFilterer(crit)
    // ... as before ...
end makeFilterer
on isNumber(x)
    return ({class of x} is in {real, integer, number})
end isNumber
set numbersOnly to makeFilterer(isNumber)
tell numbersOnly
    filter ({"hey", 1, "ho", 2, "ha", 3}) -- {1, 2, 3}
    filter ({"Mannie", 7, "Moe", 8, "Jack", 9}) -- {7, 8, 9}
end tell
```

Closures

A *closure* is one of those delightfully LISPy things that have found their way into AppleScript. It turns out that a script object carries with it a memory of certain aspects of its context at the time it was defined, and maintains this memory even though the script object may run at a different time and in a different place. In particular, a script object returned from a handler maintains a memory of the values of its own free variables.

For example, a script object inside a handler can see the handler's local variables. So a handler's result can be a script object that incorporates the value of the handler's local variables as its own free variables. This means we can modify an earlier example one more time to save yet another step:

```
on scriptMaker(s)
    script myScript
        display dialog s
    end script
    return myScript
end scriptMaker
set myScript to scriptMaker("Hello")
run myScript -- Hello
```

This is somewhat miraculous; in theory it shouldn't even be possible. The parameter s is local to the handler scriptMaker, and goes out of scope—ceases to exist—when scriptMaker finishes executing. Nothing in myScript explicitly copies or stores the value of this s; we do not, as previously, initialize a property to it. Rather, there is simply the name of a free variable s:

```
display dialog s
```

This s is never assigned a value; it simply appears, in a context where it can be identified with a more global s (the parameter s), and so it gets its value that way. Yet in the last line, myScript is successfully executed in a completely different context, a context where there is no name s in scope. In essence, myScript "remembers" the value of its free variable s even after it is returned from scriptMaker. myScript is not just a script object; it's a closure—a script object along with a surrounding global context that defines the values of that script object's free variables.

Here's an example where the value of the free variable comes from a property of a surrounding script:

```
on makeGreeting(s)
    script outerScript
        property greeting : s
        script greet
            display dialog greeting
        end script
    end script
    return outerScript's greet
end makeGreeting
set greet to makeGreeting("Howdy")
run greet -- Howdy
```

In that example, makeGreeting doesn't return outerScript; it returns just the inner script object greet. That script object uses a free variable greeting whose value is remembered from its original context as the value of outerScript's property greeting. In the last line, the script object greet runs even though there is no name greeting in scope at that point.

In the section "Context," later in this chapter, we explore further this ability of script objects to remember their global context.

Constructors

Another use for a script object as a result of a handler is as a *constructor*. Here we take advantage of the fact that when a handler is called, it initializes any script objects defined within it. So a handler is a way to produce a copy of a script object whose properties are at their initial value.

As an example, consider a script object whose job is to count something. It contains a property, which maintains the count, and a handler that increments the count. (This is using a sledgehammer to kill a fly, but it's a great example, so bear with me.) A handler is used as a constructor to produce an instance of this script object with its property set to zero. Each time we need to count something new, we call the handler to get a new script object. So:

```
on newCounter( )
    script aCounter
        property c : 0
        on increment( )
            set c to c + 1
        end increment
    end script
    return aCounter
end newCounter
-- and here's how to use it
set counter1 to newCounter( )
counter1's increment( )
counter1's increment( )
counter1's increment( )
set counter2 to newCounter( )
counter2's increment( )
counter1's increment( )
display dialog counter1's c -- 4
display dialog counter2's c -- 1
```

Compiled Script Files as Script Objects

A script can read a compiled script file and incorporate its contents as a script object. This provides a way for scripts in different files to refer to one another. You might use this facility as a means of persistent storage, in combination with the fact that top-level entities in scripts survive being saved as a compiled script file; or you might use it as a way of building a library of commonly needed routines.

This facility depends upon three verbs, described here, that are not part of Apple-Script proper; they are implemented in a scripting addition (Chapter 4) that is standard on all machines.

load script

Syntax

load script *aliasOrFile*

Description

Returns the top-level script of the compiled script file *aliasOrFile* as a script object.

Example

```
set myScript to load script alias "myDisk:myFile"
```

run script

Syntax

run script *aliasOrFile* [with parameters *list*]

Description

Tells the top-level script of the compiled script file or text file *aliasOrFile* to run, option-ally handing it the *list* as the parameters for its explicit run handler, and returns the result.

Example

```
run script alias "myDisk:myFile"
```

store script

Syntax

store script *scriptObject* [in file *path* [replacing yes|no]]

Description

Saves *scriptObject* to disk as a compiled script file. Returns no value. If no further parame-ters are supplied, presents a Save File dialog; if the user cancels, a runtime error is raised. If *path* is supplied, presents no Save File dialog, but if the file exists already, presents a dialog asking how to proceed; if the user cancels, a runtime error is raised. If replacing is supplied, this dialog is suppressed; if yes, the file is just saved, and if no, an error is raised if the file exists. The filename extension determines the format of the resulting file: *.scpt* (or nothing) for a compiled script file, *.scptd* for a script bundle, *.app* for an application bundle.

Example

```
store script sayHello in file "myDisk:myFile" replacing yes
```

(On aliases and file specifiers and the differences between them, see Chapter 13. The verb run script, instead of a file, can take a string, and it then functions as a kind of second level of evaluation; see Chapter 12.)

When you save a script object with store script, the lines delimiting the definition block (if any) are stripped, which makes sense. So, for example:

```
script sayHello
    display dialog "Hello"
end script
store script sayHello in file "myDisk:myFile" replacing yes
```

What is saved in *myFile* is the single line:

```
display dialog "Hello"
```

A compiled script file to be loaded with load script or run with run script could originate from a store script command, or it could have been saved directly from a script editor program. A text file to be run with run script could originate from any word processor that can save as text.

The run script command permits a run handler to have parameters. (See "The Run Handler" in Chapter 8.) For example, suppose you save this script as *myScript.scpt*:

```
on run {greeting}
    display dialog greeting
end run
```

You can't run that script on its own, but you can run it by way of run script, because this command can pass the needed parameter to the run handler:

```
run script file "myDisk:myScript.scpt" with parameters {"Hello"}
```

Library

A compiled script file may be used as a place to store commonly needed routines. A file used in this way is called a *library*. A running script can then access the contents of the library using load script. The library's top-level entities, including its run handler, are then available to the running script.

For example, suppose we have saved the handler makeFilterer (from page 170) in a compiled script file *makeFilterer.scpt*. We can then call makeFilterer from another script:

```
set s to load script file "myDisk:makeFilterer.scpt"
on isNumber(x)
    return ({class of x} is in {real, integer, number})
end isNumber
tell s's makeFilterer(isNumber) to filter ({"hey", 1, "ho", 2, 3})
```

That code assigns the entire script of the compiled script file *makeFilterer.scpt* to a variable s. Then the handler makeFilterer is accessed by way of s. Alternatively, since the compiled script file's top-level entities are available to us, we could have extracted the handler makeFilterer from the compiled script file *makeFilterer.scpt* and assigned *it* to a variable:

```
set makeFilterer to makeFilterer of (load script file "myDisk:makeFilterer.scpt")
on isNumber(x)
    return ({class of x} is in {real, integer, number})
end isNumber
tell makeFilterer(isNumber) to filter ({"hey", 1, "ho", 2, 3})
```

The advantage of a library is that it makes code reusable and maintainable. In this example, makeFilterer is a very useful handler. We don't want to have to keep copying and pasting it into different scripts. If its code lives in a library, it becomes accessible to any script we write. Furthermore, as we improve makeFilterer in its library file, those improvements are accessible to any script; a script that already calls makeFilterer by way of load script simply inherits the improvements the next time it runs.

On the other hand, a library reduces portability. In this case, we cannot just copy a script that calls makeFilterer to another machine, or send it to a friend, because it depends on another file, *makeFilterer.scpt*, and refers to it by a pathname that won't work on any other machine.

With Script Debugger, a trick for working around this problem is to load any library files as part of your script property initialization:

```
property makeFilterer : makeFilterer of (load script file "myDisk:makeFilterer.scpt")
on isNumber(x)
    return ({class of x} is in {real, integer, number})
end isNumber
tell makeFilterer(isNumber) to filter ({"hey", 1, "ho", 2, 3})
```

That code loads the compiled script file *makeFilterer.scpt* and initializes the property makeFilterer to the bytecode of the script file's handler makeFilterer—but only when the property makeFilterer needs initializing. After that, the handler is persistently stored as the value of the property makeFilterer. (Script Editor no longer performs this kind of persistent storage of properties; that's why this trick won't work with Script Editor. See "Lifetime of Variables" in Chapter 7.)

A script file created in this way with Script Debugger can be distributed to other machines, and it will still run. It must not, however, be edited on another machine! If the user on another machine edits the script and tries to compile it, the script is ruined: the value of the property makeFilterer is thrown away, AppleScript will try to reinitialize it, the load script command will fail because the file it refers to doesn't exist, and the script will no longer compile or run. In fact, the script is ruined if it is so much as opened with Script Editor. Script Debugger also helps you in this situation by allowing you to "flatten" a script so that it incorporates all library files on which it depends, and so has no load script dependencies.

Data Storage

We can use store script to take advantage of the persistence of top-level script object entity values ("Persistence of Top-Level Entities," earlier in this chapter). This can be a way of storing data on disk separately from the script we're actually running. You might say: "Why bother? Persistent data can be stored *in* the script we're actually running." Well, that's true for such environments as Script Debugger, or an applet; but it isn't true for the Script Editor. Besides, in any environment, persistence within a script comes to an end as soon as we edit and recompile the script. Storing the data separately circumvents such limitations.

In this example, we start by ascertaining the user's favorite color. This will be kept in a file *myPrefs*. The first thing we do is try to load this file. If we succeed, fine; if we fail, we ask the user for her favorite color and store it in *myPrefs*. Either way, we now know the user's favorite color, and we display it; and the information is now in the file *myPrefs*, ready for the next time we run the script. (See "Persistence" in Chapter 24 for a variant of this example using an application bundle.)

```
set thePath to "myDisk:myPrefs"
script myPrefs
    property favoriteColor : ""
end script
try
    set myPrefs to load script file thePath
on error
    set favoriteColor of myPrefs to text returned of ¬
        (display dialog "Favorite Color:" default answer ¬
            "" buttons {"OK"} default button "OK")
    store script myPrefs in file thePath replacing yes
end try
display dialog "Your favorite color is " & favoriteColor of myPrefs
```

If you run that script, entering a favorite color when asked for it, and then open the file *myPrefs* in a script editor program, you may be surprised to find that it doesn't actually seem to contain your favorite color:

```
property favoriteColor : ""
```

Don't worry! The information is there; it simply isn't shown in the decompiled version of the script. The decompiled version shows the actual bytecode, not the table of persistent data stored internally with the script.[*]

If you load a script as a script object with the load script command, and top-level entity values within this script object change, and you wish to write these changes back to disk, it is up to you do so, with store script.

The run script command does not save the script, so any changes in the script's top-level entity values do not persist.

Context

Recall from earlier in this chapter ("Closures") that a script object carries with it a memory of its global context. This applies when a script object is saved with store script and inserted into a different context with load script. As we've already said, there's more to a compiled script file than meets the eye; there's the decompilable bytecode, and there's the persistent data stored internally with the script. The persistent data isn't visible, but it is the *context* in which the script runs. The store script command saves a context into the compiled script file that it creates; the load script command loads this context, and the run script command runs within it.

---

[*] The only way I know of to get a look at the persistent data stored internally with a script is to use Script Debugger. Script Editor doesn't show it, and destroys it if you open and run the script directly.

The context comes into play when the script object refers to variables defined at a higher level (free variables). In particular:

- If a script object refers to a *top-level global*, then when the script object is loaded into another context with load script, the *fact* of the global variable is remembered but its *value* must be supplied by a global variable with the same name in the new context. No global declaration is needed.

- With load script, all *other* types of higher-level variable referred to in a script object simply keep the value they had when the context was saved.

- With run script, *all* higher-level variables referred to in a script object keep the value they had when the context was saved.

Suppose, for example, you run this script:

```
set thePath to "myDisk:myMessage"
global message
set message to "Howdy"
script myMessage
    display dialog message
end script
store script myMessage in file thePath replacing yes
```

The script object myMessage contains a reference to a top-level global (the variable message). That script object is saved into the file *myMessage*. Now we load *myMessage* into a different script, like this:

```
set thePath to "myDisk:myMessage"
set message to "Hello"
run (load script file thePath) -- Hello
```

The dialog appears, but it says Hello (not Howdy). The reference to a global variable message within *myMessage* adopts the value of the top-level global message in this new context, even without an explicit global declaration. But if we load *myMessage* into a context where there is *no* global message for it to identify its free variable message with, we get an error:

```
set thePath to "myDisk:myMessage"
run (load script file thePath) -- error
```

If we run the same *myMessage* with run script, on the other hand, it works even without a global message in the new context, because the script object remembers the global message from its original context:

```
set thePath to "myDisk:myMessage"
run script file thePath -- Howdy
```

Now we'll start all over again, generating a completely new *myMessage* file. This time the free variable message is identified with a property:

```
set thePath to "myDisk:myMessage"
property message : "Get lost"
script myMessage
    display dialog message
```

```
    end script
    store script myMessage in file thePath replacing yes
```

Now, this works:

```
    set thePath to "myDisk:myMessage"
    run (load script file thePath) -- Get lost
```

The script object has conserved the original context for the free variable `message`—both the property `message` and its value. The same is true when the original context involves a handler or script object. Suppose we generate *myMessage* like this:

```
    set thePath to "myDisk:myMessage"
    on sayHowdy( )
        display dialog "Howdy"
    end sayHowdy
    script myMessage
        sayHowdy( )
    end script
    store script myMessage in file thePath replacing yes
```

Then this works:

```
    set thePath to "myDisk:myMessage"
    run (load script file thePath) -- Howdy
```

We did not explicitly save the handler `sayHowdy`, but it was referred to in the script object `myMessage`, so it was stored as part of *myMessage*'s context, and is present when we load *myMessage* into another script.

Inheritance

Script objects may be linked into a *chain of inheritance*. If one script object inherits from another, the second is said to be the *parent* of the first. If a message is sent to a script object and it doesn't know how to obey it, the message is passed along to its parent to see whether *it* can obey it. A message here is simply an attempt to access any top-level entity.

To link two script objects explicitly into a chain of inheritance, *initialize the* parent *property of one to point to the other*.

 The parent property may be set only through initialization. You cannot use copy or set to set it.

In this example, we explicitly arrange two script objects, `mommy` and `baby`, into an inheritance chain (by initializing baby's parent property). We can then tell baby to execute a handler that it doesn't have, but which `mommy` does have. Here we go:

```
    script mommy
        on talk( )
            display dialog "How do you do?"
```

```
        end talk
    end script
    script baby
        property parent : mommy
    end script
    baby's talk( ) -- How do you do?
```

In that example, we told the child from outside to execute a handler that it doesn't have but the parent does. The child can also tell itself to execute such a handler:

```
    script mommy
        on talk( )
            display dialog "How do you do?"
        end talk
    end script
    script baby
        property parent : mommy
        talk( )
    end script
    run baby -- How do you do?
```

Getting and setting properties works the same way. In this example, we get and set the value of a property of baby that baby doesn't have:

```
    script mommy
        property address : "123 Main Street"
    end script
    script baby
        property parent : mommy
    end script
    display dialog baby's address -- 123 Main Street
    set baby's address to "234 Chestnut Street"
    display dialog mommy's address -- 234 Chestnut Street
```

Again, the same thing can be done from code within the child; but now the name of the property must be prefixed with the keyword my. Otherwise, since there is no property declaration in scope for this name, the name is assumed to be the name of a local variable. The keyword my says: "This is a top-level entity of the script object running this code." Thus, if AppleScript fails to find such a top-level entity in the script object itself, it looks in the script object's parent.

```
    script mommy
        property address : "123 Main Street"
    end script
    script baby
        property parent : mommy
        on tellAddress( )
            display dialog my address
        end tellAddress
    end script
    baby's tellAddress( ) -- 123 Main Street
```

Similarly, we can refer to a script object that the child doesn't have but the parent does:

```
script mommy
    script talk
        display dialog "How do you do?"
    end script
end script
script baby
    property parent : mommy
end script
run baby's talk -- **How do you do?**
```

Again, if the child wants to do this, it must use my:

```
script mommy
    script talk
        display dialog "How do you do?"
    end script
end script
script baby
    property parent : mommy
    run my talk
end script
run baby -- **How do you do?**
```

Polymorphism

When code refers to a top-level entity, the search for this top-level entity starts in the script object to which the message that caused this code to run was originally sent. This is called *polymorphism*. You may have to use the keyword my to get polymorphism to operate (and it's probably a good idea to use it in any case).

An example will clarify:

```
script mommy
    on tellWeight()
        display dialog my weight
    end tellWeight
end script
script baby
    property parent : mommy
    property weight : "9 pounds"
end script
baby's tellWeight() -- **9 pounds**
```

We ask baby to tell us its weight, but baby doesn't know how to do this, so the message is passed along to the parent, mommy. There is now an attempt to access my weight. But mommy has no top-level entity called weight. However, the search for weight starts with baby, because our original message was to baby (mommy is involved only because of inheritance). The property is found and the code works.

To see why my is important here, consider this code:

```
script mommy
    property weight : "120 pounds"
    on tellWeight()
        display dialog weight
    end tellWeight
end script
script baby
    property parent : mommy
    property weight : "9 pounds"
end script
baby's tellWeight() -- 120 pounds
```

There is no my before the name weight, and mommy's declaration for the property weight is in scope, so the name is simply identified with this property; polymorphism never has a chance to operate.

The reason for the "poly" in the name "polymorphism" is that the response to the parent's use of a term can take many different forms. A parent whose code is running because of inheritance has no idea of this fact, so it has no idea what its own code will do. For example:

```
script mommy
    property weight : "120 pounds"
    on tellWeight()
        display dialog my weight
    end tellWeight
end script
script baby
    property parent : mommy
    property weight : "9 pounds"
end script
script baby2
    property parent : mommy
    property weight : "8 pounds"
end script
mommy's tellWeight() -- 120 pounds
baby's tellWeight() -- 9 pounds
baby2's tellWeight() -- 8 pounds
```

In that example, the parental phrase my weight gets three different interpretations, depending solely on what script object was addressed originally.

Continue

A child can call an inherited handler by using the continue command. The syntax is the keyword continue followed by a complete handler call (parameters and all).

You might wonder why this is needed, since after all the child can just send a message directly to the parent by referring to the parent as parent. But there's a crucial difference. If a message is sent to the parent by referring to it as parent, that's a new message with a new target. On the other hand, the `continue` command takes place in the context of the current message and the current target; it passes the current flow of control up the inheritance chain. Thus, the one breaks polymorphism, the other does not.

This example demonstrates the difference:

```
script mommy
    property weight : "120 pounds"
    on tellWeight()
        display dialog my weight
    end tellWeight
end script
script baby
    property parent : mommy
    property weight : "9 pounds"
    parent's tellWeight()
    continue tellWeight()
end script
run baby -- 120 pounds, 9 pounds
```

The Implicit Parent Chain

A script object without an explicitly specified parent has as its parent the script as a whole.

We took advantage of this fact earlier (page 134) to refer to a top-level script property. Thus:

```
property x : 5
script myScript
    property x : 10
    display dialog my parent's x
end script
run myScript -- 5
```

But there's a parent beyond that. The script as a whole has as its parent the Apple-Script scripting component. This appears to your code as a script object called AppleScript.

The AppleScript script object has some properties that you can access. Normally you do this without having to refer to AppleScript explicitly, because these properties are globally in scope; it's as if every script were surrounded by another invisible script with property declarations for these properties. But in a context where a name overshadows the name of one of these properties, it would be necessary to be explicit, in order to jump past the current scope and up to the level of AppleScript:

```
set pi to 3
display dialog pi -- 3
display dialog AppleScript's pi -- 3.141592...
display dialog parent's pi -- 3.141592...
```

The AppleScript script object is also where the built-in verbs live. For example, when you say:

```
get 3 + 4
```

the get command travels up the inheritance chain until it reaches the AppleScript scripting component, which knows how to obey it.

The AppleScript scripting component has a parent too—the current application. This is the host application that summoned the AppleScript scripting component to begin with. The current application is the absolute top level, and can be referred to in code as current application. For example:

```
display dialog (get name of current application) -- Script Editor
```

To sum up:

```
script myScript
    my parent -- «script», the anonymous top level
    my parent's parent -- «script AppleScript»
    my parent's parent's parent -- current application
end script
run myScript
```

Observe that scope-wise containment is *not* implicit parenthood:

```
script myScript
    script myInnerScript
        my parent -- the anonymous top-level script, not myScript
    end script
    run myInnerScript
end script
run myScript
```

Nor can a contained script object be made to have a containing script object as its parent. AppleScript will balk if you try this:

```
script myScript
    script myInnerScript
        property parent: myScript -- compile-time error
    end script
end script
```

I think the reason for this restriction must be that the demands of parenthood would conflict irresolvably with the rules of scoping.

CHAPTER 10

Objects

Earlier chapters have quietly introduced the notion of sending messages to objects. In "Handler Calls Within Script Objects" in Chapter 8, and in "Handler Calls" in Chapter 9, a script object was treated as "an object to which one can send messages," with a handler call being such a message. In "Script Object's Run Handler" in Chapter 9, we spoke of "sending the run message to a script object." The object to which a message is sent was called its "target." The entire section "Inheritance" in Chapter 9 depended upon the idea of a message being sent to a particular target. In Chapter 7, and again more fully in Chapter 9, we described the use of the of operator (or apostrophe-ess operator) or a tell block to specify a target and send it a message. It is now time to formalize these notions.

A message originates as an imperative verb, a command of some sort. But there is a distinction to be drawn between a command and a message. The *command* is what you say in code. The *message* is the communication of that command to some *target*, which is supposed to obey the command. For example, count is a command, and in a certain context it can cause the count message to be sent to the Finder, while in some other context it can cause the count message to be sent to Mailsmith. An *object* is anything that can be targeted by a message.

Sending a message to a target object is the fundamental activity of all AppleScript code; everything that is said in AppleScript code involves some target object to which some message is being sent. Furthermore, every value in AppleScript can act as such a target. In this sense, every AppleScript value is an object. (See also "Object-likeness" in Chapter 5.)

This chapter deals with notions of message and target: how you specify the target object to which a message is to be sent, and how you go about actually sending it a message, along with various related syntactic features. Some relevant syntactic features, such as the keywords its and my, have already appeared informally in earlier chapters; now they too will be properly explained. The last part of this chapter is occupied with how objects may be related as attributes of one another called properties and elements, and talks about how to refer to one such object in terms of another.

Class

Every value is of some fixed type. I often refer to this as its datatype, but the Apple-Script term for a value's type is its *class*. You can assign a value of any class to any variable, but at any given moment a variable has only one value and that value has only one class (so it is customary to speak of a variable's class, meaning the class of the value it has at that moment).

You can inquire of any value what its class is, by asking for its class. For example:

```
class of 7 -- integer
class of "howdy" -- string
class of {"Mannie"} -- list
class of class of 1975 -- class
```

As the last line shows, even something's class is a value and therefore has to have a class, namely class.

Target

At every moment in AppleScript code, you are speaking to some object. That object is the *target*, to which, unless you specify otherwise, all messages will be sent. The target can be implicit, or you can specify an explicit target. Knowing what object is the target, and how to specify a desired target, is very important to your successful use of AppleScript.

The implicit target is the current script or script object. In this code, the implicit target of set is the script itself:

```
set x to 5
```

In this code, the implicit target of set is the script object myScript:

```
script myScript
    set x to 5
end script
```

There are two ways to specify an explicit target. Not coincidentally, they bear a strong resemblance to the two ways of accessing a script object's top-level entities (Chapter 9). You can specify an explicit target:

- With the of operator or its synonyms. A synonym for of is in. (I never use this.) Another synonym, for most purposes, is the apostrophe-ess operator: instead of saying *x* of *y*, you can say *y*'s *x*.

  The of operator specifies the target for just a single expression, and overrides all other targets, explicit or implicit.

- With a tell block. Instead of an actual block, one may apply tell to a single command ("Tell" in Chapter 12), but this is still just a special case of a tell block.

  In the context of a tell block, the object specified in the announcement is the default target for everything you say. This can be overridden by specifying a different target, using either an embedded tell block or an expression involving the of operator.

Here's an example of a tell block used to specify a target:

```
tell application "Finder"
    count folders
end tell
```

Here's the single-line version of that code:

```
tell application "Finder" to count folders
```

Both the count command and the word folders are within the context of a tell block directed at the Finder. Thus the count message will be sent to the Finder, and the Finder's folders will be counted.

(The tell block also makes a difference as to what the word folders *means*; it is the Finder that extends the AppleScript language to include this word. This, however, is a separate matter from the target. We'll come back to this matter under "Tell" in Chapter 12, and in Chapter 19.)

Here's an example of the of operator being used to specify a target:

```
using terms from application "Finder"
    count folders of application "Finder"
end using terms from
```

Thanks to the of operator, the Finder is the target of the count command; it will be sent the count message, and its folders will be counted.

(The using terms from block, which I refer to in this book as a "terms block," is present to allow the term folders to be interpreted correctly. This is also explained in Chapter 12 and Chapter 19.)

The Chain of Ofs and Tells

Objects, as we shall see in more detail later in this chapter, may be attributes of one another. It is actually this relationship that is specified with the of operator. That is why you can speak of a property myProp of a script object myScript like this:

```
get myProp of myScript
```

The top-level entities of a script object, including its script properties, are attributes of that script object. This relationship can be extended. For example, perhaps myScript contains a top-level definition for a script object myInnerScript that has a script property called myInnerProp; then you can say this:

```
get myInnerProp of myInnerScript of myScript
```

Thus we end up with a chain of ofs that is used to determine the target.

Since both tell and of perform the same function of determining the target, there is a sense in which tell and of are interchangeable. Thus it is possible to replace the chain of ofs by a chain of tells in the opposite order. This code is effectively identical to the previous example:

```
tell myScript
    tell its myInnerScript
        get its myInnerProp
    end tell
end tell
```

In determining the target, AppleScript actually works its way up the chain of ofs and then up the chain of tells until it assembles a complete target. (I am deliberately waving my hands over what I mean by "a complete target," but it means something like an application, a script, or a value within your script.) Thus it makes no difference whether you say this:

```
tell application "Finder"
    count folders of folder 1
end tell
```

or this:

```
tell application "Finder"
    tell folder 1
        count folders
    end tell
end tell
```

It is also perfectly possible for the of operator to appear in the announcement line of a tell block. It makes no difference whether you say this:

```
tell application "Finder"
    tell folder 1
        tell file 1
            get name
        end tell
    end tell
end tell
```

or this:

```
tell application "Finder"
    tell file 1 of folder 1
        get name
    end tell
end tell
```

See Chapter 3 for an extensive practical demonstration of the interchangeability of of with tell throughout the chain.

Multiple Assignments

Recall from Chapter 7 that it is possible to assign multiple values in a single command by using a list:

```
set {x, y, z} to {1, 2, 3}
```

You can use this syntax to fetch multiple properties, using either `tell` or `of`:

```
tell application "Finder"
    set {x, y} to {name, comment} of folder 1
end tell
{x, y} -- {"Mannie", "howdy"}
```

That code fetches `name of folder 1` and `comment of folder 1` from the Finder in a single command. You can use this construct to set multiple properties as well, but only in a tell block (trying to do it with `of` will cause a runtime error):

```
tell application "Finder"
    tell folder "Mannie"
        set {comment, name} to {"zowie", "Jack"}
    end tell
end tell
```

Be careful of the order in which you list the properties when assigning to them. The values are assigned from left to right. This wouldn't have worked:

```
tell application "Finder"
    tell folder "Mannie"
        set {name, comment} to {"Jack", "zowie"} -- error
    end tell
end tell
```

That would have set the name first, and afterwards there would no longer be a folder "Mannie" to set the comment of, so the attempt to set the `comment of folder` "Mannie" would have caused a runtime error.

Nesting Target Specifications

Once AppleScript has determined a complete target, it stops, ignoring any further `of`s or `tell`s that make up the rest of the chain. Consider, for example, the following:

```
tell application "Mailsmith"
    tell application "Finder"
        count folders
    end tell
end tell
```

Mailsmith is not in fact targeted in any way here; no message will be sent to it when the code runs. AppleScript works its way outwards from the `count` command until it reaches the Finder; now AppleScript has assembled a complete target, and stops. In fact, if you try to write the same thing this way:

```
count folders of application "Finder" of application "Mailsmith"
```

AppleScript literally throws away the mention of Mailsmith after compilation:

```
count folders of application "Finder"
```

Direct Object

Most commands have a *direct object*, which can be expressed right after the verb. Using of, you may include as much as you like of the target as the direct object of a command—all of it, none of it, or anything in between. Whatever you don't include in the direct object you can put in a tell.

So, in this example, the entire target appears as the direct object of the command:

```
using terms from application "Finder"
    count folders of application "Finder"
end using terms from
```

In this example, some of the target appears as the direct object, and some of it appears in a tell:

```
tell application "Finder"
    count folders
end tell
```

And here, the whole target appears in a nest of tells, and none of it appears as the direct object of the command:

```
tell application "Finder"
    tell folders
        count
    end tell
end tell
```

The keyword it represents the target. (See "It," later in this chapter.) You can include it as the direct object of the command if it doesn't otherwise have one, but this changes nothing:

```
tell application "Finder"
    tell folders
        count it
    end tell
end tell
```

Nothing stops you from putting something else as the direct object of the command—something that retargets it. For example:

```
tell application "Finder"
    tell folders
        count words of "hi there"
    end tell
end tell
```

In that code, no message is sent to the Finder! The phrase words of "hi there" is a complete target (a value). The tell blocks are ignored for purposes of this command.

Usually, you may use the word of to connect a command with its direct object. So you could say this:

```
tell application "Finder"
    count of folders
end tell
```

This usage of of is related to the special of that can mark the first parameter when using prepositional parameters in a handler call (Chapter 8). The apostrophe-ess operator is not a synonym for this usage.

Names in Scope

The rules for targeting do not override the scoping rules you have learned in the previous three chapters. You can say this:

```
set x to 10
tell application "Finder"
    get x
end tell
```

AppleScript knows that x is something meaningful in the context of the script itself, so it doesn't send any message to the Finder asking about x. That's a good thing, because the Finder doesn't know about anything called x. This is a thoroughly necessary mechanism, since without it a tell block would cut off access to the surrounding context and you wouldn't be able to use names that are in scope while explicitly targeting something.

You can therefore quite freely mingle names defined in the current context with names defined by the target. AppleScript is able to deal very nicely with this code:

```
set L to {"Mannie", "Moe", "Jack"}
tell application "Finder"
    count folders
    count L
end tell
```

The command count folders is sent to the Finder. The command count L is not; AppleScript knows that L is something belonging to the current context, not to the Finder, and the command is dealt with entirely within the script.

Here's another example with even more mingling:

```
set newname to "someFolder"
tell application "Finder"
    set oldname to name of folder 1
    set name of folder 1 to newname
end tell
display dialog oldname
```

In that example, folder and name are part of messages sent to the Finder, but oldname and newname are (implicit) globals within the script, and their values are set and retrieved without involving the Finder. In this line:

```
    set oldname to name of folder 1
```

AppleScript actually does two things; first it sends this message to the Finder (see the next section, "Get"):

```
    get name of folder 1
```

Then it uses the result to set the value of oldname. The mental picture I want you to have is one involving a clear division of labor: the Finder is sent messages telling it to do things involving the Finder, and the script is sent messages telling it to do things involving the script. The Finder does not somehow lay hands on any of your script's variables.

Thus, when it comes to terms you use that might be the names of entities in scope in your script, AppleScript must look in two places to resolve their meaning: in the targeted application, and in the script itself. This mechanism is actually quite subtle, and is discussed further in the section "Resolution of Terminology" in Chapter 19.

Do keep in mind that handler calls are special. A handler call is a message and will be sent to the target. This won't work:

```
on whatNumber( )
    return 1
end whatNumber
tell application "Finder"
    get folder whatNumber( ) -- error
end tell
```

The problem is that the Finder is sent the whatNumber message, but it knows of no whatNumber command. We'll see how to get around this later in the chapter ("Me").

Get

The default command is get. In other words, a sentence with no verb is assumed to have get as its verb. So, for example:

```
tell application "Finder"
    name of folder 1
end tell
```

The verb get is supplied here and is the actual message sent to the Finder. It's exactly as if you had said:

```
tell application "Finder"
    get name of folder 1
end tell
```

One even sees code written like this:

```
tell application "Finder" to name of folder 1
```

AppleScript can also supply get in the middle of a line where needed. As we have already seen, this code:

```
tell application "Finder"
    set oldname to name of folder 1
end tell
```

is actually treated by AppleScript as if it said this:

```
tell application "Finder"
    set oldname to (get name of folder 1)
end tell
```

Do not imagine, however, that it makes no difference whether you ever say get, and that you can blithely omit get for the rest of your life. On the contrary, it's probably better to err in the other direction and say get whenever you mean get. There are no prizes for obfuscated AppleScript, and you're most likely to confuse yourself (and impress no one else) if you get into bad habits. More important, omission of get from expressions of any complexity can cause runtime errors. For example, this:

```
tell application "Finder" to display dialog (name of folder 1) -- error
```

is not the same as this:

```
tell application "Finder" to display dialog (get name of folder 1)
```

In the first example, name of folder 1 is a reference to a property; that's not something that can be displayed by display dialog, so we get an error. In the second, the get command fetches the value of that property, a string, and all is well.

It

The keyword it represents the target. This can be useful in helping you understand who the target is. It can also be useful as an explicit target, in situations where Apple-Script would otherwise misinterpret your meaning. In situations where you would say of it after a word, you may say its before that word instead.

This example shows it used while debugging, to make sure we understand who the target is:

```
tell application "Finder"
    tell folders
        it -- every folder of application "Finder"
    end tell
end tell
```

We have already seen ("Accessing Top-Level Entities" in Chapter 9) the need for it when accessing a script object's top-level entities within a tell block addressed to the script object. Without it, this code fails:

```
script myScript
    property x : 5
end script
tell myScript
    display dialog x -- error
end tell
```

There is no x in scope, so there's a runtime error. Similarly, if there were an x in scope, AppleScript would identify this x with that x, rather than with myScript's property x, unless we use it:

```
script myScript
    property x : 5
end script
set x to 10
tell myScript
    display dialog its x -- 5, but 10 if we omit its
end tell
```

When targeting an application, however, there is generally no need for it used in this way. That's because, unlike a script object, an application has a dictionary, so Apple-Script knows when you're saying the name of a property of that application. For example, the Finder has a property home; there is no need for its to tell AppleScript that we mean the Finder's home rather than a variable in scope:

```
set home to "Ojai"
tell application "Finder"
    get home -- folder "mattneub" of folder "Users"...
end tell
```

In fact, here the problem is more likely to be how to refer to the variable home in the context of a tell block targeting the Finder. The next section ("Me") discusses this.

However, it is needed when targeting an application with a tell block in order to distinguish a property from a class, when (as often happens) these have the same name ("Properties and Elements," later in this chapter). The preceding example didn't display this problem, because home is not the name of a class. But consider this example:

```
tell application "Finder"
    tell folder 1
        get container -- container, a class
    end tell
end tell
```

This was not the desired result. To get the container property of a folder, we must use its or (what amounts to the same thing) the of operator:

```
tell application "Finder"
    tell folder 1
        get its container -- folder "Desktop" of...
    end tell
    get container of folder 1 -- folder "Desktop" of...
end tell
```

Another typical use of it when targeting an application appears toward the end of the section "Turning the Tables" in Chapter 3. Here the find command requires an in parameter specifying a document, but we are already in the context of a tell block targeting that document. Since the in parameter is the same as the target, we can express it as it.

Me

The keyword me represents the current script—the script or script object that is running the code where the keyword me appears. Thus:

```
script myScript
    me -- «script myScript»
end script
run myScript
me -- «script», the anonymous top-level script
parent of me -- «script AppleScript»
```

See also "The Implicit Parent Chain" in Chapter 9. In situations where you would say of me after a word, you may say my before that word instead.

We saw the keyword me used earlier ("Inheritance" in Chapter 9) as a way to force AppleScript to attempt to interpret a term as belonging to the current script object, so that it will use the inheritance chain.

The keyword me can be useful in a tell block, to specify the current script as the target instead of the tell block's target. For example, this doesn't work:

```
on reverseString(s)
    set the text item delimiters to ""
    return (reverse of characters of s) as string
end reverseString
tell application "Finder"
    set name of folder 1 to reverseString(get name of folder 1) -- error
end tell
```

The problem is that when we come to the handler call reverseString() in the next-to-last line, the target is the Finder. So AppleScript passes it along to the Finder, which doesn't know what to do with it. The target for reverseString needs to be me, even though the target of everything else in that line should be the Finder. This is just the kind of situation where me comes in handy:

```
set name of folder 1 to my reverseString(get name of folder 1)
```

But me won't also resolve a *terminology clash* between a name defined by the target and a name within your script. In that case, you'll have to use pipes around the name, to suppress its terminological interpretation in terms of the target. For instance, returning to an earlier example, how can we refer to the global variable home in the context of a tell block directed at the Finder, which has a property home? This doesn't work:

```
set home to "Ojai"
tell application "Finder"
    get my home -- error
end tell
```

The problem is not that my failed to retarget the message. It did retarget it! The problem is that the term home is still being resolved in accordance with the Finder's dictionary. So when the message arrives at our script, it doesn't speak of our variable home, but of some mysterious property that our script doesn't know how to interpret. Use of pipes solves the problem:

```
set home to "Ojai"
tell application "Finder"
    get |home| -- "Ojai"
end tell
```

There is no need for my, because the pipes cause AppleScript to take home as a name in scope within the script, and so it targets the script for us.

You may also encounter a need to use pipes around the name of a handler call, but now you must use me as well as the pipes. This is because a handler call is always directed at the target unless you explicitly say otherwise. In this example, the only way to call the script's entab( ) instead of Mailsmith's entab command is to put the name in pipes *and* use me:

```
on entab(s)
    return "tab" & s
end entab
tell application "Mailsmith"
    tell message window 1
        my |entab|("let")
    end tell
end tell
```

The pipes suppress the use of Mailsmith's terminology; the my routes the message to your script instead of Mailsmith. If you use me but no pipes, the message is sent to the script using Mailsmith's terminological encoding, and the script won't understand it; if you use pipes but no me, the message is sent to Mailsmith stripped of its terminological encoding, and Mailsmith won't understand it.

Properties and Elements

Two objects may stand in a relationship where one is an *attribute* of the other. It is this relationship of attribution that is specified by the chain of ofs and tells. Attributes are defined in terms of classes. (The term "attribute" is of my own devising, because the official AppleScript documentation lacks any comprehensive term for "property or element.")

For example, a list has a length attribute and an item attribute—these are facts about any list because they are facts about the list class. That is what makes this code legal:

```
set L to {"Mannie", "Moe", "Jack"}
length of L -- 3
item 1 of L -- "Mannie"
```

Recall this code from Chapter 3:

```
tell application "FrameMaker 7.0"
    tell document "extra:applescriptBook:ch02places.fm"
        tell anchored frame 43
            get inset file of inset 1
        end tell
    end tell
end tell
```

That code works because, in FrameMaker, the application has a document attribute, a document has an anchored frame attribute, an anchored frame has an inset attribute, and an inset has an inset file attribute. As we saw in Chapter 3, working out the chain of attributes so as to refer successfully to a desired object is a major part of working with AppleScript. An application's dictionary is supposed to help you with this, though it often falls short (Chapter 19). AppleScript's own dictionary is not typically visible, so this book describes the attributes of the built-in datatypes (Chapter 13).

An attribute is either a property or an element. A *property* is an attribute that this type of object has exactly one of. An *element* is an attribute that this type of object may have any number of, and in order to refer to one (or more) you have to say which one(s) you mean.

In the example about lists, length is a property; every list has a length, and that's the end of that. But item is an element; a list might not have any items, and if it does have some, it can have any number of them. To speak of an item or items we have to say which one(s) we mean, as in item 1. Similarly, in the FrameMaker example, inset file is a property but inset is an element.

A script object's top-level entities are effectively properties in this sense; that is why they can be referred to using the of operator. This is a bit confusing, because the word "property" is often used as shorthand for a script property, whereas script properties, script objects, and handlers can all be top-level entities of a script object. If there is ambiguity, we can call properties (of the sort under discussion in this section) *object properties*, to distinguish them from script properties. A script object cannot have elements.

Some properties are *read-only*. This means you can get but not set their value. For example:

```
tell application "Finder"
    get startup disk
    set startup disk to disk "second" -- error
end tell
```

Elements in general are read-only; you can't say set folder 1 to .... However, you can set an element's properties (except those that are read-only, of course), and applications often implement verbs permitting to you create and manipulate elements.

When you get a property or element, the value returned will be of some particular class. If this is one of AppleScript's built-in datatypes, what you get will usually be a copy. So, for example:

```
tell application "Finder"
    set s to name of disk 1
    set s to "yoho"
end tell
```

That code has no effect upon the name of the disk. A string came back and was stored in the variable s, and you then set the variable s to some other value, throwing away the string the Finder gave you.

But when the class of the returned value is an object type defined by and belonging to the application you're targeting, the value will usually be a reference (Chapter 11). Such a reference is a complete target. You can send a message to it, and you can get an element or property of it. You are not in control of what this reference looks like, and the way it looks may surprise you, but you shouldn't worry about that; it's a valid reference and a complete target, and that's all you should care about. For example:

```
tell application "Finder"
    set d to disk of folder 1
end tell
-- startup disk of application "Finder"
```

What I may have expected to see as a result of asking for this property doesn't matter; I must have faith that the Finder has given me a reference to what I asked for. To justify this faith, I can proceed to target this reference:

```
tell application "Finder"
    set d to disk of folder 1
end tell
get name of d -- "xxx"
```

That works. Since d is a complete reference to a Finder object, I can target it; in the last line, the get message is sent to the Finder, and the name of the disk comes back. The term name is understandable outside of a tell block targeting the Finder because it is defined within AppleScript itself (see Chapter 19).

Element Specifiers

To refer to a particular element, you must say which one you mean. To do this, you use an *element specifier* (or just *specifier* for short). A specifier has two components: the name of a class and some way of picking out the right one(s). AppleScript has eight built-in forms of specifier,* and these are the only ones you are allowed to use. The next eight sections describe those eight specifier forms.

The variety of specifier forms makes a specifier quite an interesting and complicated part of an Apple event. If you look back at the raw Apple event shown as

Example 4-1, you will see a repeated pattern involving four items called `form`, `want`, `seld`, and `from`. That pattern denotes a specifier.

In real life it will rarely be open to you to use just whichever specifier form you please. Given any particular application, object, and class of element, only certain specifier forms will work, and experimentation is the best guide as to which ones they are. An application's dictionary is supposed to help you here, but it might not be accurate ("Defective Element Specifiers" in Chapter 19).

Name

An element may have a name, which is some kind of string. To specify an element by name, say the class followed by the name:

```
tell application "Finder" to get disk "main"
```

You may insert the keyword `named` between the class and the name, but I never do.

Typically, there is also a `name` property, so that you can learn, based on some other element specifier, how to specify a particular element by name:

```
tell application "Finder" to get name of disk 2 -- "main"
```

Index

Elements may be ordered, and numbered in accordance with this ordering. The number is an index. The first element has index 1, the next element has index 2, and so forth. The last element can be referred to by index -1, the next-to-last by index -2, and so forth. (If you want to know just how many elements of this class there are, you have to find out in some other way, such as `count`.)

To specify an element by index, say the class followed by the index number:

```
tell application "Finder" to get disk 2
```

You may insert the keyword `index` between the class and the number, but I never do. Instead of a cardinal numeric value, you're allowed to say a wide variety of English-like ordinal numeric literals followed by the class name. So, for instance, you can say such things as `1st disk`, `third disk`, `last disk`, `front disk`, and `back disk`.

There is sometimes also an `index` property, so that you can learn, based on some other element specifier, how to specify a particular element by index; but this is not implemented anywhere near as often as one would like, and is sometimes buggy:

```
tell application "Finder" to get index of disk 2 -- 3, for heaven's sake
```

---

* Well, okay, there are actually nine element specifiers. I don't tell you about `middle` (returns the middle element), because it is rarely used. Plus, a reference to a property is actually a form of specifier, so that makes ten.

ID

Elements may have a unique ID, which is often a number but needn't be. An ID has the advantage of not changing. For example, in the Finder a folder's name can be changed, and its index may change if its name changes or the number of folders in its containing folder changes, but its ID would be constant, if it had one.

To specify an element by ID, say the class followed by the keyword id followed by the ID value. This value will have been obtained at some earlier point, typically by asking for an element's id property:

```
tell application "Mailsmith"
    set theMailboxID to id of mailbox 3 -- 162, if you must know
    --...
    get mailbox id theMailboxID
end tell
```

Some

A random element may be specified by saying some followed by the class:

```
tell application "Finder"
    name of some disk -- "extra"
    name of some disk -- "main"
    name of some disk -- "main"
end tell
```

Every

It may be possible to get a list of every element of a class. To ask for such a list, say the keyword every followed by the class; alternatively, you may be able to say just the plural of the class:

```
tell application "Finder" to get every disk
tell application "Finder" to get disks
```

If asking for just one element would result in a reference, the result in this case is a list of references.

Range

Elements may be ordered, and you may be able to obtain a list of contiguous elements (a range) by giving the first and last index number you're interested in. It is generally not important in what order you give these index numbers. To specify elements by range, say the class in a plural form (or every and the class) followed by an index number, the keyword thru (or through), and another index number. You can say beginning or end instead of an index number:

```
get words 1 thru 4 of "now is the winter of our discontent"
get words beginning thru 4 of "now is the winter of our discontent"
```

Alternatively you may be able to get a list of contiguous elements of a class where the range is marked off by two element specifiers for some *other* class. In this case you say the class in a plural form (or every and the class) followed by the keyword from, an element specifier for the starting point, the keyword to, and an element specifier for the ending point. Again, you can say beginning or end instead of an element specifier:

```
get words from character 12 to character 17 of "now is the winter"
get words from character 12 to character -1 of "now is the winter"
get words from character 12 to end of "now is the winter"
```

There is a tendency to confuse or conflate these two forms, and to try to say something like this:

```
get words 1 to 3 of "now is the winter of our discontent" -- error
```

You can't do that. "To" is not "thru"! Keep these two constructions straight. Practice them before going to bed.

Relative

Elements may be ordered, and it may be possible to refer to an element as the successor or predecessor of another element. To ask for an element in this way, say the name of the class, the keyword before or after, and an element specifier:

```
tell application "Tex-Edit Plus"
    tell window 1
        get word after word 1
    end tell
end tell
```

A synonym for before is in front of. Synonyms for after are behind and in back of.

In real life the main place this is used is in specifying something like an insertion point. For example, in BBEdit all text has insertion point elements lying between the characters. Thus you can say this:

```
tell application "BBEdit"
    tell text of window 1
        get insertion point before word 4
    end tell
end tell
```

The main use of an insertion point in BBEdit is that you can set its contents property to alter the text. So:

```
tell application "BBEdit"
    tell text of window 1
        set pt to insertion point before word 4
        set contents of pt to "great "
    end tell
end tell
```

Before running that script, the text in BBEdit's window said, "This is a test." After running it, it said, "This is a great test." If the insertion point reference doesn't need capturing, that whole script can be expressed as a single command:

```
tell application "BBEdit" to set contents of ¬
    insertion point before word 4 of text 1 of window 1 to "great "
```

There is also a class called insertion location defined by some applications. You'll see it in an application's dictionary referred to as a "location reference," and you usually can't get one directly; instead, you use it primarily in conjunction with the duplicate, make, and move commands, after the keyword at or to.

A location reference is specified using before or after and an element specifier (which yields wonderfully bizarre locutions such as at after); or using beginning of or end of and a reference to an object, or just beginning or end alone; or using just an element specifier.

Applications can be extraordinarily touchy* about how they respond to commands of this form, with results differing from application to application. Here are some examples, just to show the syntax in action; in each case I first show you some code and then describe its effect:

```
tell application "TextEdit"
    tell text of document 1
        make new word at after word 2 with data "not "
    end tell
end tell
```

That changes "this is a test" to "this is not a test".

```
tell application "TextEdit"
    tell text of document 1
        duplicate word 1 to end
    end tell
end tell
```

That changes "fair is foul and foul is " to "fair is foul and foul is fair".

```
tell application "TextEdit"
    tell text of document 1
        duplicate word 1 to beginning of word 3
    end tell
end tell
```

That changes "wonder of s, miracle of miracles" to "wonder of wonders, miracle of miracles".

```
tell application "TextEdit"
    tell text of document 1
        duplicate word 1 to word 7
    end tell
end tell
```

---

* Non-lawyers may read "buggy".

That changes "fair is foul and foul is foul" to "fair is foul and foul is fair".

```
tell application "Script Debugger"
    move window 2 to beginning
end tell
```

That brings the second window frontmost, and shows that this sort of locution is good for manipulating more than just text.

Boolean Test

It may be possible to get a list of those elements that satisfy a boolean test (the dictionary, if it lists this possibility, will say simply "satisfying a test"). What you test may be a property of the target, or it may be the target itself. The test may involve any boolean operator (see "Comparison Operators" and "Containment Operators" in Chapter 15).

A boolean test also involves an index-based specifier: index, range, or every (or some). This is because the boolean test yields a list, and you can ask for the whole list or for particular elements of it.

To specify elements by boolean test, say an index-based specifier and the keyword where, followed by a property of that class or the word it, followed by a boolean operator and any value that can function as that operator's second operand. In this context the target is each element as it is tested. Thus, the word it means the element to be tested. You can use it optionally to make your test read more like English. You can use whose instead of where, but this is mere syntactic sugar.

```
tell application "Finder" to get files where name begins with "s"
tell application "Finder" to get every file where name begins with "s"
tell application "Finder" to get files where name of it begins with "s"
tell application "Finder" to get files where its name begins with "s"
tell application "Finder" to get files whose name begins with "s"
```

Those are all equivalent. The index-based specifier is the every specifier, with file as its class. Then comes where or whose. Now every file will be tested, and name means the name property of the file being tested; the words of it or its are redundant but harmless. The boolean operator is begins with, and its second operand is the string "s".

When a boolean test specifier tests the value of a boolean property, you can say it is (or it is not) and the name of the property. This can make your expression more English-like, assuming the property name is an adjective:

```
tell application "System Events"
    get process 1 whose frontmost is true
    get process 1 where it is frontmost
end tell
```

The two formulations shown are equivalent, but most people prefer the latter, as being more English-like. Now let's have an example where you'd *need* it instead of a property name after where or whose:

```
tell application "TextEdit"
    tell text of document 1
        get every word where it contains "t"
        get words whose it contains "t"
    end tell
end tell
```

The two formulations shown are equivalent, but most people prefer the former, as being more English-like. AppleScript has no equivalent for where it, such as "which" or "that"; it doesn't let you be as English-like as all that.

That example works because when you ask TextEdit for words, you get a list of strings; each string then functions as the first operand of contains. But this is by no means how every application works. For example, in BBEdit, when you ask for words you get a list of references. To obtain the text of each word you ask for its contents, so you don't end up using it at all:

```
tell application "BBEdit"
    tell text 1 of window 1
        get every word whose contents contains "t"
    end tell
end tell
```

Finally, here's an example involving an index specifier other than every:

```
tell application "BBEdit"
    tell text 1 of window 1
        get word 1 whose contents contains "t"
    end tell
end tell
```

The only downside to that sort of formulation is what happens when no elements satisfy the test. When you use every, if no elements satisfy the text, you get an empty list. But when you specify the index, if that index doesn't exist, you get an error. (This is because you get an error if you ask for a nonexistent item of *any* list.) This is not much of a downside, since you can easily catch such an error and handle it (Chapter 12); it's just something to watch out for.

If the target application is willing, you may even be able to combine multiple boolean tests ("Boolean Operators" in Chapter 15). This requires that you supply another first operand for the second test, even if this is the same as the first operand of the first test:

```
tell application "Tex-Edit Plus"
    tell window 1
        words where it begins with "t" and it ends with "t" -- {"test"}
    end tell
end tell
```

The boolean test, where it works, is a very powerful specifier; with a single Apple event you're getting the target application to do a lot of thinking and testing for you. The only problem is that you never know whether it will work; only experimentation will show this.

AppleScript itself, most disappointingly, fails to implement boolean test specifiers for its own lists. The two halves of this example are deliberately parallel, yet the second half fails:

```
tell application "Finder"
    get every disk whose name begins with "M" -- "main"
end tell
set pepBoys to {"Mannie", "Moe", "Jack"}
tell pepBoys
    get every item whose text begins with "M" -- error
end tell
```

As a workaround, use the list-filtering handler developed earlier in this book ("Script Object as Handler Result" in Chapter 9).

Properties of Multiple References

When an element specifier would return a list of references, it may be possible to ask for a property of this list as a shorthand for asking for that property of each element of the list in turn.

For example, this works, and returns a list of strings, the names of each disk in turn:

```
tell application "Finder" to get name of every disk
```

Here's another example. Recall that when you ask BBEdit for a word, you get a reference. If you just want to know the word itself—that is, its text—you ask for its contents. You can combine these operations to get a list of words and translate them into their contents:

```
tell application "BBEdit"
    tell text 1 of window 1
        get contents of every word whose contents contains "t"
    end tell
end tell
```

Again, this a tremendously powerful construct where a single Apple event causes the target application to do a lot of work for you. And again, you can't be certain this construct will be implemented until you try it. If it isn't, the workaround is to obtain the list of references and then cycle through it yourself, obtaining the desired property for each reference one at a time. That involves many Apple events, though, so it's a poor substitute.

Object String Specifier

Objects of certain classes can be constructed in code using the name of the class followed by a string. Formally, this looks rather like an element specifier by name. But the object isn't an element of anything, and the string isn't exactly a name. There is no term for this construct in Apple's documentation, so I have coined the term *object string specifier* to denote it.

For example, AppleScript's built-in file class works this way; you can make a file object by using the word file followed by a string representing the pathname, as in the following code:

```
get POSIX path of file "myDisk:myFile"
```

The string doesn't have to be a literal; a variable will work just as well:

```
set f to "myDisk:myFile"
get POSIX path of file f
```

AppleScript also uses an object string specifier to represent a file object when reporting it as a value:

```
set f to "myDisk:myFile"
a reference to file f
-- file "myDisk:myFile" of «script»
```

AppleScript's application class works the same way; that is why I have been using this form of address throughout this chapter:

```
tell application "BBEdit"
```

Built-in classes that use object string specifiers will be duly noted as doing so, in Chapter 13.

CHAPTER 11

References

The notion of a reference has been informally used throughout the preceding chapters. In Chapter 3, an expression of this sort:

```
anchored frame 1 of document "extra:applescriptBook:ch02places.fm"
    of application "FrameMaker 7.0"
```

was described as a reference; building such an expression was called "constructing a reference," a command whose result was an expression of that sort was said to "return a reference," and a list of such expressions was called "a list of references." Much talk of the same sort appears in Chapter 10.

On the other hand, the word "reference" has also been used in another way. In various places we have referred to the setting and passing of values "by reference." That is *not* what this chapter is about. When you pass a list "by reference" as a parameter to a handler, you do not pass a reference; you pass a list (in a certain way). The identity of the terminology is unfortunate but unavoidable.

This chapter is about references in the first sense. As you might suspect from this, a *reference* is a complete chain of ofs, such as to specify a target. But this way of putting the matter makes it sound as if a reference is merely an expression, a stretch of words in your code. In AppleScript, a reference is more than that: it's a value embodying such an expression.

To see what I mean, let's imagine obtaining such a value in a way that's very common—as a result returned by a scriptable application. For example, suppose you say this:

```
tell application "Finder"
    set x to (get folder 1)
end tell
```

Now, what's x? On my machine, it's the following:

```
folder "Mannie" of desktop of application "Finder"
```

What can this mean? A folder is a thing in the Finder's world. Surely the Finder cannot have literally handed this folder to our script. Rather, the Finder has handed us some sort of *means of access* to this folder. That's a reference; x is a reference to a certain folder in the Finder. References are an important feature of AppleScript, and many values you'll encounter using AppleScript will be references.

References as Incantations

One very productive way to think of a reference is as an incantation. It's like frozen speech. It encapsulates a bit of phraseology, a particular utterance. If a variable's value is a reference, that value is something you can use to access the object it refers to. What I mean by "use" is "say": a reference is an encapsulation of the words you would have to utter (in your code, of course) in order to access the object. In a way, a reference is like a miniature package of suspended evaluation; it's a little phrase that isn't evaluated until you use it. When you do use it, it works just as if you'd said the phrase at that point in your code.

For example, consider this code:

```
tell application "Finder"
    set x to (get folder 1)
    display dialog (get name of x) -- Mannie
end tell
```

The dialog shows the name of the folder. Why does this work? As we have said, x is this reference:

```
folder "Mannie" of desktop of application "Finder"
```

This means that *using* x is like *using those words*. Therefore, when you say this:

```
get name of x
```

it's just like saying this:

```
get name of folder "Mannie" of desktop of application "Finder"
```

A reference answers the "What would I have to say...?" question. What would I have to say in order to speak of the Finder's folder 1? The Finder tells us one answer; I could say this:

```
folder "Mannie" of desktop of application "Finder"
```

You may be disconcerted at first by that fact that this is not what you *did* say. You said folder 1, referring to the folder by index number; the Finder said folder "Mannie", referring to it by name. You didn't say of desktop; the Finder did. You shouldn't worry about this. You just have to have faith, when an application gives you a reference, that this reference will access the thing you asked for access to.

Pre-Resolution of Terminology

When the time comes to use a reference, you don't have to be in the context of a tell. The reference is not only a complete target, it's a complete target whose vocabulary has *already been resolved* according to the context in which the reference was originally formed.

As a result, this works:

```
tell application "Finder"
    set x to (get folder 1)
end tell
name of x -- "Mannie"
```

(We looked a little at this phenomenon in Chapter 10; now we are in a position to discuss it properly.) How can this be? Look at just the last line of that code, in isolation:

```
name of x
```

That line contains no folder; it contains no Finder! But that line causes a message to be sent to the Finder asking for the name of a particular folder. The entire target:

```
folder "Mannie" of desktop of application "Finder"
```

is frozen into x. So the effect of the last line of that code is exactly—I mean *exactly*—as if you had said this:

```
tell application "Finder"
    get name of folder "Mannie" of desktop
end tell
```

The whole incantation involving the folder, the desktop, and the Finder is effectively frozen into x, ready to use. The terms folder and desktop have already been resolved, just as they would be in the context of a tell block targeting the Finder—because they were frozen into x in just such a context.

Being Careful with References

Keep in mind that a reference is full of hidden power. You can send an Apple event without realizing it, merely by using a reference. It's easy to be lulled into thinking you'll always know when you're sending an Apple event to a target application, because you'll see the chain of ofs and tells culminating in the name of the application. But with a reference, you won't see any of that; the whole chain is hidden inside the reference.

The Event Log in the script editor application can be a big help here, because it tracks Apple events. When you execute this code:

```
tell application "Finder"
    set x to (get folder 1)
end tell
name of x -- "Mannie"
```

the event log says this:

```
tell application "Finder"
    get folder 1
```

```
    get name of folder "Mannie" of desktop
end tell
```

That makes it very clear what's happening.

Another thing to bear in mind is that a reference is mere words, not a magic pointer. Consider the following:

```
tell application "Finder"
    set x to folder 1
    display dialog (get name of x) -- Mannie
    set name of x to "Moe"
    display dialog (get name of x) -- error!
end tell
```

The reason for the error is perfectly clear if you imagine a reference as an incantation. What's x during the first display dialog command? It's this:

```
folder "Mannie" of desktop of application "Finder"
```

And that's what it is during the second display dialog command, too; the incantation doesn't change. But at that point there is no folder "Mannie"—because we just changed the name of that folder to "Moe"! Our reference no longer works, because the incantation no longer speaks of the thing we want to speak of. The speech is frozen, while the world has changed.

Creating a Reference

We've already seen that a reference might be handed to you by some application; but you can also create one yourself. To do so, you use the a reference to operator. (An abbreviation is ref, which is a lot easier to type.) For example:

```
set x to 100
set y to a reference to x
```

When you create a reference, the phrase you use is effectively what gets frozen into the reference as an incantation:

```
tell application "Finder"
    set x to a reference to folder 1
end tell
x -- folder 1 of application "Finder"
```

What you say is what you get. And what you say doesn't have to exist, either; it doesn't even have to make sense! As long as the compiler can resolve the terminology, it will compile your phrase. The fact that it's unusable doesn't matter; you're *not* using it, you're just freezing it for later. Thus no error arises, no matter how silly your phrase may be. Of course, later on if you *do* try to use it, you'll find out if it's a valid thing to say:

```
tell application "Finder"
    set x to a reference to disk 99 of folder 1 of label "yoho"
end tell
get name of x -- error: Can't get name of disk 99 of folder 1 of label "yoho"
```

Identifying References

AppleScript goes to some lengths to hide the existence of references, making it remarkably difficult to find out that a value is a reference. Properly speaking, a reference is a class, a datatype like string or integer ("Class" in Chapter 10, and Chapter 13). If you ask a string about its class, it says string. If you ask an integer about its class, it says integer. But if you ask a reference about its class, it will never tell the truth and say reference.

```
set x to "hey"
set y to 9
tell application "Finder" to set z to folder 1
class of x -- string
class of y -- integer
class of z -- folder
```

Here are some tricks you can use to learn that a value is a reference. (I don't guarantee any of them, but they do seem mostly to work.)

The reference coercion trick

The only thing that can be coerced to a reference is a reference. If you try to coerce anything else to a reference, you'll get a runtime error. So try to coerce a value to a reference, and if there's no error, it is a reference. For example:

```
tell application "Finder" to set x to folder 1
x as reference -- no error; it's a reference
```

The editor result trick

If the script result, as shown in your script editor program, contains the word of, it is a reference. For example:

```
tell application "Finder" to set x to folder 1
x -- folder "Mannie" of...; it's a reference
```

The copy trick

A copy of a reference is the same reference. If you have two copies of something and they both provide access to the same thing (you may have to devise a further test in order to decide this question), they are both references. For example:

```
tell application "Finder"
    set x to folder 1
    copy x to y
    index of x is index of y and container of x is container of y -- true
end tell
```

When I'm debugging or developing a script, I like the second method best; I look at a variable's value and I can see right away whether it's likely to be a reference. If I'm writing code where the code itself needs to test whether something is a reference, I like the first method best. Here's a general handler that returns a boolean value telling whether its parameter is a reference:

```
on isRef(valueToTestAsRef)
    try
        valueToTestAsRef as reference
```

```
            return true
        on error
            return false
    end try
end isRef
-- and here's how to call it
tell application "Finder"
    set x to folder 1
end tell
isRef(x) -- true
set x to "haha"
isRef(x) -- false
```

Dereferencing a Reference

Once you have a variable whose value is a reference, AppleScript behaves with confusing inconsistency when you try to use it. In some cases, you can't use the reference without explicitly dereferencing the variable; in other cases, AppleScript
dereferences it for you implicitly when you use it. AppleScript can behave both ways
with one and the same reference.

When AppleScript performs implicit dereferencing, the reference is completely trans-
parent: it acts precisely as if you were saying the incantation that's frozen inside it.
This is exactly the same phenomenon noted in the previous section—you can't learn
from a reference that it is a reference, because it acts as if it were the thing referred to.

```
tell application "Finder"
    set x to folder 1
end tell
name of x -- Mannie
class of x -- folder
set name of x to "Moe"
```

None of that ought to be possible. A reference's class isn't folder, and a reference
doesn't have a name property that you can get and set. In this case, though, it happens that the reference is a reference to a thing whose class is folder and that has a
name property. AppleScript dereferences the reference implicitly; it treats the reference as if it were the thing referred to.

But in this example, an attempt to use the same reference transparently runs up
against a brick wall:

```
tell application "Finder"
    set x to a reference to the name of folder 1
end tell
set x to "Moe"
```

If you were hoping that this would set the name of the Finder's folder 1 to "Moe",
you're doomed to disappointment. It didn't: you set the variable x to the string "Moe"
(and you lost your reference).

The reason is that the transparency of references can't be permitted to destroy your access to your own variables. Thus, when you perform an assignment, not to a property of a variable that's a reference but to the variable itself, AppleScript stops treating the reference transparently. The assignment is an ordinary assignment to a variable: what's inside the shoebox is thrown away and a new value is put into the shoebox.

Similarly, the boolean equality and inequality operators do not treat references transparently by dereferencing them ("Comparison Operators" in Chapter 15). Here's a simple example:

```
set x to 3
set y to a reference to x
x = y -- false
y = 3 -- false
```

There's no implicit dereferencing here, and 3 is not the same a reference to x. With other operators, though, AppleScript does dereference, which makes for some paradoxical-looking results:

```
set x to 3
set y to a reference to x
x = y -- false
x + 0 = y + 0 -- true
x is not less than y and x is not greater than y -- true
```

In situations where AppleScript doesn't implicitly dereference a reference for you, you can dereference it yourself. The way you do this is with the contents of operator. So, this code renames a folder in the Finder:

```
tell application "Finder"
    set x to a reference to the name of folder 1
end tell
set contents of x to "Moe"
```

Here's another example:

```
set x to 10
set y to a reference to x
set contents of y to 20
x -- 20
```

Here's the equality example:

```
set x to 3
set y to a reference to x
x = contents of y -- true
```

The contents of operator works on any value. If the value isn't a reference, the result of applying the contents of operator is simply the value itself. In this example, the use of the contents of operator (twice) is essentially pointless; AppleScript basically just throws it away, and you end up saying the very same thing you'd say if you simply omitted the words contents of from the code:

```
set x to contents of "Mannie"
contents of x -- Mannie
```

You can take advantage of this in dealing with the equality example. Let's say you don't know which of x and y is a reference. That's okay; dereference them both, since it does no harm:

```
set x to 3
set y to a reference to x
contents of x = contents of y -- true
```

However, this is not to imply that you can simply use the words contents of capriciously. They do mean something, after all! So, this will cause a runtime error:

```
set x to "Mannie"
set contents of x to "Moe" -- error
```

This is like saying set "Mannie" to "Moe", which doesn't work, because "Mannie" is a literal, not the name of a variable.

If a value is a reference to an object belonging to an application, the contents of operator might get you another reference—or it might get you the same reference. So, for example:

```
tell application "Finder"
    set x to folder 1
end tell
x -- folder "Mannie" of desktop of application "Finder"
set x to contents of x
x -- folder "Mannie" of folder "Desktop" of folder "mattneub" of ¬
    folder "Users" of startup disk of application "Finder"
set x to contents of x
x -- folder "Mannie" of folder "Desktop" of folder "mattneub" of ¬
    folder "Users" of startup disk of application "Finder"
```

This is entirely up to the target application, and doesn't have any particular significance. In each case you're just telling the application to do a get whose direct object is the very same "phrase" the application handed back to you previously. Whether the application returns the same phrase or a different phrase referring to the same object is entirely its own business.

A problem arises when you're targeting an application whose dictionary defines a contents property for one of its object types. Applications shouldn't do this; it's bad behavior, because they're overlapping with a piece of AppleScript's own built-in vocabulary. In the context of a tell directed at such an application, this raises the question of whether the word contents will be seen as the contents of operator or the application's contents property.

 I'm told that the problematic nature of the contents property is actually an AppleScript bug.

An example of such an offender is BBEdit. BBEdit does something I consider very good: when you ask for a text element such as a word, it gives you a reference rather than a string. That's good, because it's then possible to access that element in its context and do things to it. But then BBEdit does something bad: it defines the contents property as your way of obtaining the actual string. (To be quite fair, the fault lies partly with AppleScript itself, which takes the lead by defining a contents property for its selection-object class.)

So, this works to obtain an actual string:

```
tell application "BBEdit"
    set w to contents of word 4 of window 1
end tell
w -- "test"
```

But this doesn't:

```
tell application "BBEdit"
    set w to contents of (get word 4 of window 1)
end tell
w -- characters 11 thru 14 of text window 1 of application "BBEdit"
```

And therefore neither does this:

```
tell application "BBEdit"
    set x to word 4 of window 1
    set w to contents of x
end tell
w -- characters 11 thru 14 of text window 1 of application "BBEdit"
```

The only way to access BBEdit's contents property is within a single expression, as in the first example. You can't apply it to a reference, as in the second two examples, because AppleScript sees that as dereferencing the reference.

The proper behavior would have been for the application to define some other term for obtaining the contents of a thing. Mailsmith, for example, uses a content property of its message class to represent the body of the message. No confusion arises; AppleScript doesn't know that this is the singular of contents. However, Mailsmith then bollixes the user in other ways. The result of asking for the content property is a record where the body text is in an item called contents (see "Pseudo-Classes" in Chapter 19). This accounts for the very odd verbiage we were forced to employ in "Calculation and Repetition" in Chapter 1:

```
set theBody to get contents of content of aMessage
```

In that line, the contents of operator never appears! First we get the content property of aMessage, which is a record; then we get the contents item of that record. Furthermore, Mailsmith does *also* let you say contents (instead of content) as the name of this property of the message class. So this code is possible:

```
tell application "Mailsmith"
    set r to a reference to message 1 of incoming Mail
end tell
get contents of contents of contents of r
```

In that code, every contents of is necessary in order to arrive at the desired string! The third one dereferences the reference, the second one gets the contents property of the message, and the first one gets the contents item of the resulting record.

Creating References to Local Variables

You can't make a reference to a local variable. Well, you can, but you won't be able to use it. For example:

```
local x
set x to {1, 2, 3}
set y to a reference to x
get item 1 of y -- error
```

This does not mean, however, that the only things you can create references to are top-level globals. You can make a reference to anything that isn't a local, such as a property:

```
script myScript
    property x : 5
    set y to a reference to x
    set contents of y to x + 1
    display dialog x
end script
run myScript -- 6
```

Reference as Parameter

You can pass a reference as a parameter to a handler, and it remains a reference. The fact that the variable where the reference is stored may be a local is irrelevant; so is the fact that the parameter is local to the handler.

So, for example:

```
local x
tell application "Finder"
    set x to folder 1
end tell
on setName(theRef)
    set name of theRef to "Jack"
end setName
setName(x)
```

In that code, x is a local, and theRef is too (because a handler parameter is local within the handler). But the code still works; it changes the name of a folder in the Finder.

But you can't pass a reference to a local, because you can't make a reference to a local. Well, you can, but you can't use it as a reference. That's why the reference to operator can't provide a general solution to the problem of passing by reference (see Chapter 8).

So, for example:

```
global x
local y
set x to 5
set y to 5
on doubleRef(theRef)
    set contents of theRef to 2 * theRef
end doubleRef
doubleRef(a reference to x)
display dialog x -- 10
doubleRef(a reference to y) -- error
```

The difference between x and y in this code is purely that x is global while y is local. Applying the contents of operator to x works; applying it to y causes an error.

The use of a reference as a parameter can permit a handler to perform dynamic targeting. As long as a handler doesn't use any vocabulary that depends on a specific target, it can target an application whose identity is not known until runtime. In this example, the same code in the same handler is able to target the Finder and Mailsmith indiscriminately:

```
on getNameOfAnything(theRef)
    return name of theRef
end getNameOfAnything
tell application "Finder" to set x to folder 1
tell application "Mailsmith" to set y to mailbox 1
getNameOfAnything(x) -- "Mannie"
getNameOfAnything(y) -- "(drafts)"
```

A handler or script object can also return a reference. Of course, this cannot be a reference to a local variable. It must be a reference to something that the handler or script object can obtain a reference to. For example, it can be a reference to a property:

```
script myScript
    property x : 3
    return a reference to x
end script
set y to run myScript
set contents of y to 10
myScript's x -- 10
```

Or it can be a reference obtained from a scriptable application:

```
on getFolderByNumber(n)
    local x
    tell application "Finder"
        set x to folder n
    end tell
    return x
end getFolderByNumber
getFolderByNumber(1) -- folder "Moe" of desktop of application "Finder"
```

And it can be a reference to a parameter that is a reference or was passed by reference. You can get some rather powerful effects that way:

```
on findInList(what, L)
    repeat with i from 1 to count L
        if item i of L is what then
            return (a reference to item i of L)
        end if
    end repeat
    return
end findInList
local pep
set pep to {"Mannie", "Moe", "Jack"}
set contents of findInList("Moe", pep) to "Larry"
pep -- {"Mannie", "Larry", "Jack"}
```

That's quite similar to return-by-reference in C++. The handler findInList returns a reference to a particular item of L; in this case, it returns the reference item 2 of {"Mannie", "Moe", "Jack"}. Thus we are now pointing at the desired item of the original list and can change that item, in place.

CHAPTER 12

Control

This chapter describes the control structures of the AppleScript language. These are not commands; rather, they dictate the flow of a script—how the next line or batch of lines should be interpreted, what line should be executed next, that sort of thing.

When typing any block in this chapter, in the termination line just type the word end. AppleScript fills in the missing term after compilation. This saves time and is helpful for confirming that you have correctly structured your blocks. So, for example, don't type end if; just type end.

Branching

The "intelligent" behavior of a computer program depends upon its ability to make choices at runtime. These choices generally take the form of evaluating some expression and executing a particular set of lines of code depending on how the evaluation turns out at that moment.

One major form of choice is *branching*. We have a line or block of code that can be executed optionally. The computer evaluates a boolean expression, called a *condition*. If the condition is true, the line or block of code is executed; if it isn't, the line or block of code is skipped, and execution jumps to the line that follows it.

In AppleScript, branching control is performed with if. There are several forms of *if block*.

When typing a multiline if block, don't bother to type the word then. AppleScript will add it at compile time.

The basic form is a block of code that is executed only if a condition is true. If the condition is false, the block is skipped, and execution resumes after the end if line.

```
if condition then
    -- what to do if condition is true
end if
```

It is also permitted to supply a second block, to be executed if the condition is false.
One or the other of the two blocks will be executed.

```
if condition then
    -- what to do if condition is true
else
    -- what to do if condition is false
end if
```

Another syntax lets you specify multiple conditions. AppleScript will execute the first
block whose condition is true, skipping the others. It is permitted to supply a final
block that will be executed if none of the conditions is true.

```
if condition1 then
    -- what to do if condition1 is true
else if condition2 then
    -- what to do if condition2 is true
-- ... same for condition3, condition4, etc.
[else]
    -- what to do if none of them is true
end if
```

So, for example:

```
set x to random number from 1 to 10
set guess to text returned of ¬
    (display dialog "Pick a number from 1 to 10" default answer "")
try
    set guess to guess as number
on error
    return
end try
if guess < 1 or guess > 10 then
    display dialog "I said from 1 to 10!"
else if guess < x then
    display dialog "Too small. I was thinking of " & x
else if guess > x then
    display dialog "Too big. I was thinking of " & x
else
    display dialog "Just right."
end if
```

There's also a single-line form:

```
if condition then whatToDo
```

In the single-line form, whatToDo is any valid expression or single-line command (it
can even be another single-line if).

Looping

The other major form of choice is *looping*, which involves branching back to the start of a block repeatedly. In AppleScript, looping is performed with repeat. There are several varieties of repeat, but *repeat blocks* all take same basic form:

```
repeat whatKindOfRepeat
-- what to do
end repeat
```

The big question with a repeat block is how you're going to get out of it. Obviously you don't want to repeat the repeat block forever, since this will be an infinite loop and will cause the computer to hang. Usually you deal with this through the nature of the *whatKindOfRepeat*, which typically provides a condition to be evaluated, as a way of deciding whether to loop again, or some other form of instruction governing how many times the block will be repeated.

There are also some special commands for hustling things along by leaping completely out of the repeat block. They can be used with any form of repeat block. Here they are:

return

This command leaves the repeat block by virtue of the fact that it terminates execution of the handler or script.

exit repeat

This command exits the innermost repeat block in which it occurs. Execution resumes after the end repeat line.

Repeat Forever

A repeat block with no *whatKindOfRepeat* clause repeats unconditionally, whence forever. Obviously you don't *really* want it to repeat forever, so it's up to you to supply a way out. I just told you two ways out. A third is to loop inside a try block and to throw an error; this method is illustrated later in this chapter, in "Catch."

```
repeat
    display dialog "Prepare to loop forever."
    exit repeat
end repeat
display dialog "Just kidding."
```

Repeat While

A repeat block where *whatKindOfRepeat* is the keyword while followed by a boolean expression tests the expression before each repetition. If the expression is true, the block is executed. If the expression is false, the block is not executed and that's the end of the loop; execution resumes after the end repeat line. The idea is that in the course of looping something will eventually happen that will make the expression false.

```
set response to "Who's there?"
repeat while response = "Who's there?"
    set response to button returned of ¬
        (display dialog "Knock knock!" buttons {"Enough!", "Who's there?"})
end repeat
```

Repeat Until

A repeat block where *whatKindOfRepeat* is the keyword until followed by a boolean
expression tests the expression before each repetition. If the expression is false, the
block is executed. If the expression is true, the block is not executed and that's the
end of the loop; execution resumes after the end repeat line. This construct is technically unnecessary, since the very same thing could have been achieved by reversing
the truth value of the condition of a repeat while block—that is to say, repeat until
is exactly the same as repeat while not.

```
set response to ""
repeat until response = "Enough!"
    set response to button returned of ¬
        (display dialog "Knock knock!" buttons {"Enough!", "Who's there?"})
end repeat
```

> Those accustomed to the do...until construct in other, C-like lan-
> guages should observe that it is possible for an AppleScript repeat
> until block not to be executed even once.

Repeat With

The syntax of a repeat with announcement line is as follows:

```
repeat with variableName from startInteger to endInteger [by stepInteger]
```

Here's how a repeat with works:

1. When the repeat with line is encountered for the first time, *startInteger* and
   endInteger (and *stepInteger*, if supplied) are evaluated once and for all, and
   coerced to integers if possible. (If it isn't possible, there's a runtime error.)

2. If *startInteger* is larger than *endInteger* (or smaller if *stepInteger* is negative),
   that's the end of the loop and execution resumes after the end repeat line.

3. The value *startInteger* is assigned to the variable *variableName*, which is created as a local if not in scope already.

> This fact is an exception to the rule that implicitly declared variables at
> top level are global ("Undeclared Variables" in Chapter 7).

4. The block is executed.

5. The value 1 (or *stepInteger* if supplied) is added to the value that *variableName* was assigned at the start of the previous repetition. If the resulting value is larger than *endInteger* (or smaller if *stepInteger* is negative), that's the end of the loop and execution resumes after the end repeat line. Otherwise, *variableName* is assigned this new value, and the block is executed and this step repeats.

If you read the description carefully, you will realize that:

- There's no extra overhead involved if any of the integers in the repeat with line are derived from handler calls or commands, since the evaluation is performed only once. This is in contrast to repeat while and repeat until.
- After a repeat with is all over, the variable *variableName* has the value it had when the last repetition terminated.
- Setting the variable *variableName* within a repeat with block affects the code that executes subsequently within the block, but it has no effect on the test performed at the top of the next repetition or on what value *variableName* will take on as the next repetition begins.

Here's a simple example of repeat with in action:

```
repeat with x from 3 to 1 by -1
    display dialog x
end repeat
display dialog "Blast off!"
```

Repeat With...In

The syntax of a repeat with...in announcement line is as follows:

```
repeat with variableName in list
```

This construct is much like a repeat with, but the variable *variableName* is assigned successively a reference to each item of the *list*.

When I say a reference, I mean it (see Chapter 11); nothing is copied from the list into *variableName*. So, for example, in this loop:

```
repeat with x in {1, 2, 3}
    -- ...
end repeat
```

the variable x takes on these successive values:

```
item 1 of {1, 2, 3}
item 2 of {1, 2, 3}
item 3 of {1, 2, 3}
```

In some contexts, the fact that *variableName* is a reference won't make a difference to your code, because references are transparently dereferenced much of the time. For example:

```
repeat with x in {1, 2, 3}
    display dialog x -- 1, 2, 3
end repeat
```

Here, the reference is implicitly dereferenced, and the value of each item is retrieved from the list. But things are different, for example, when you use the equality or inequality operator:

```
repeat with x in {1, 2, 3}
    if x = 2 then
        display dialog "2"
    end if
end repeat
```

The dialog *never appears*. That's because x is never 2. The second time through the loop, x is the reference item 2 of {1, 2, 3}; that's not the same thing as the integer 2, and AppleScript doesn't implicitly dereference the reference. The solution is to dereference it explicitly:

```
repeat with x in {1, 2, 3}
    if contents of x = 2 then
        display dialog "2"
    end if
end repeat
```

Here's another example; we'll retrieve each value and store it somewhere else:

```
set L1 to {1, 2, 3}
set L2 to {}
repeat with x in L1
    set end of L2 to x
end repeat
```

What do you think L2 is after that? If you said {1, 2, 3}, you're wrong; it's this:

```
L2 -- {item 1 of {1, 2, 3}, item 2 of {1, 2, 3}, item 3 of {1, 2, 3}}
```

L2 is not the same as L1. L1 is a list of values; L2 is a list of references. If you want L2 to end up identical to L1, you must dereference each reference:

```
set L1 to {1, 2, 3}
set L2 to {}
repeat with x in L1
    set end of L2 to contents of x
end repeat
L2 -- {1, 2, 3}
```

When, as here, *variableName* is a reference to an item of a list, you can use it to assign back into the original list:

```
set L to {1, 2, 3}
repeat with x in L
    set contents of x to item x of {"Mannie", "Moe", "Jack"}
end repeat
L -- {"Mannie", "Moe", "Jack"}
```

A loop can alter the value of an item of the list before encountering it, and it can increase the size of the list. Thus:

```
set L to {1, 2, 3}
repeat with x in L
```

```
        set beginning of L to contents of x
    end repeat
    L -- {1, 1, 1, 1, 2, 3}
```

Observe that this did not cause an infinite loop. AppleScript reads the size of the list once, before the first repetition; you won't repeat more times than that.

It can be important to be cognizant of the details of the references in the list. Recall the example from "Calculation and Repetition" in Chapter 1 where we renamed the files in a folder, first gathering their names like this:

```
    set allNames to name of every item of theFolder
    repeat with aName in allNames
```

Why didn't we cycle through the items of the folder directly, like this?

```
    repeat with anItem in theFolder
```

In the second formulation, the references in the list are to item 1 of folder..., item 2 of folder..., and so forth. But we're going to be changing the names of items in this folder while we're cycling, and changing the name of an item may alter the way the items are numbered. Thus we might not cycle through each item of the folder after all. Remember, a reference is a frozen expression, not a magic pointer ("Being Careful with References" in Chapter 11).

We now turn to considerations of efficiency. Here is some code that makes BBEdit capitalize every word that starts with "t":

```
    tell application "BBEdit"
        repeat with w in every word of window 1
            if contents of text of w begins with "t" then
                change case w making raise case
            end if
        end repeat
    end tell
```

It works, but we are sending at least twice as many Apple events as there are words in the document. Let's try to shorten the list to just the words that start with "t":

```
    tell application "BBEdit"
        repeat with w in (every word of window 1 ¬
            where contents of text of it begins with "t")
            change case w making raise case
        end repeat
    end tell
```

This fails with a runtime error. To see why, we investigate the successive values of w, and we learn something very interesting. It turns out that during the first repetition, w is a reference to this:

```
    item 1 of every word of window 1 of application "BBEdit" ¬
        whose contents of every text starts with "t"
```

We capitalize that word, and now we proceed to the next item, which is a reference to this:

```
item 2 of every word of window 1 of application "BBEdit" ¬
    whose contents of every text starts with "t"
```

This explains the runtime error. For example, if at the outset there were just two words beginning with lowercase "t", there is no such item as this, because we just capitalized one of those words, so there's now only *one* word in the window beginning with lowercase "t"! As we can see, w is being set to these curious references of the form item 2 of every word.... The expression every word...whose is thus being evaluated afresh every time through the loop. This, in addition to breaking our code, is a further source of inefficiency: we're making BBEdit perform this entire complicated boolean test each time through the loop, when it should suffice to perform it once.

The cause is a very odd feature of how AppleScript behaves when you say something like this:

```
tell some application
    repeat with x in every …
```

When AppleScript sees this form of repeat with announcement line, it responds by sending an Apple event to the target application. You might expect that this would be a request for a list of references; but it isn't. Instead, AppleScript merely asks the target application *how many* such references there are; it sends a count command, not a get command. Presumably AppleScript imagines it will be a lot more efficient to ask for one little number than for a list of who knows how many references.

The solution is to use get yourself:

```
tell application "BBEdit"
    repeat with w in (get every word of window 1 ¬
        where contents of text of it begins with "t")
        change case w making raise case
    end repeat
end tell
```

That works fine, because w is now set to values like this:

```
item 1 of {characters 11 thru 12 of text window 1 of application "BBEdit"}
```

And it's a lot more efficient too.

The implication seems to be that you should probably use get in constructs of this kind. In fact, if you don't use get, many applications won't be able to respond at all to what you say in the loop. The Finder is a good example. Suppose we want to gather the names of all folders. This doesn't run at all:

```
set L to {}
tell application "Finder"
    repeat with f in every folder
        set end of L to (get name of f) -- error
```

```
        end repeat
    end tell
```

This works fine:

```
set L to {}
tell application "Finder"
    repeat with f in (get every folder)
        set end of L to (get name of f)
    end repeat
end tell
```

The reason is that in the first form when you say get name of f, you're saying get name of item 1 of every folder and so on, and the Finder interprets this to mean, not the first item of a list of folders, but a list of the first items on disk inside each folder! In the second form, you start by gathering references to each individual folder; then you use each reference to ask for the name of that folder.

Repeat N Times

A repeat block where *whatKindOfRepeat* is an integer followed by the keyword times repeats that number of times. The integer can be a variable.

```
repeat 3 times
    display dialog "This is really boring."
end repeat
display dialog "ZZzzzz...."
```

An interesting use of this construct is to implement a workaround for AppleScript's lack of a next repeat keyword.* The problem is that you can short-circuit a repeat block by exiting it completely, but you cannot, as in many languages, short-circuit it by proceeding immediately to the next iteration. The workaround is to embed a one-time repeat block within your repeat block; an exit repeat within this one-time repeat block works as a next repeat with respect to the outer repeat block. This device doesn't accomplish anything you couldn't manage with an if block, but it can prove more legible and maintainable.

For example:

```
set L to {"Mannie", "Moe", "Jack"}
set L2 to {}
repeat with aBoy in L
    repeat 1 times
        if aBoy does not start with "j" then exit repeat
        set end of L2 to contents of aBoy
    end repeat
end repeat
L2 -- {"Jack"}
```

For another useful misuse of this construct, see "Blocks" in Chapter 6.

---

* This idea is suggested to me by Paul Berkowitz, who attributes it to Ray Robertson.

Being Careful with Loops

You probably think I'm about to say, "Watch out for infinite loops." You're wrong. Quite frankly, I don't care if your loops go on till Doomsday. But I do care if they do more work than they have to.

Keep in mind that Apple events are expensive, and some Apple events are *very* expensive. While I'm not a great believer in worrying about code optimization, you should probably take a little elementary care with your loops to see that your Apple events are as few and as simple as possible.

Observe, for instance, that the boolean expression at the top of a repeat while block must be evaluated before every repetition of the block, and then once more in order to decide not to repeat the block any further. This means that it should not contain any commands whose result will not change during the repetition, since this would be needless and wasteful overhead.

For example, it would be foolish to write this:

```
set x to 1
tell application "Finder"
    set f1 to folder "f1"
    set f2 to folder "f2"
    repeat while ((count items of f1) < (count items of f2))
        make new folder at f1 with properties {name:("f" & x)}
        set x to x + 1
    end repeat
end tell
```

That code sends the count message to the Finder six times when in fact we need only send it twice:

```
set x to 1
tell application "Finder"
    set f1 to folder "f1"
    set f2 to folder "f2"
    set c1 to count items of f1
    set c2 to count items of f2
    repeat while c1 < c2
        make new folder at f1 with properties {name:("f" & x)}
        set x to x + 1
        set c1 to c1 + 1
    end repeat
end tell
```

The example itself is rather a silly way to perform this task, but the lesson it illustrates is very real.

Our earlier example using BBEdit exposes the same issue. At first, you remember, we said this:

```
tell application "BBEdit"
    repeat with w in every word of window 1
```

```
            if contents of text of w begins with "t" then
                change case w making raise case
            end if
        end repeat
    end tell
```

This sets w each time to a reference of this form:

```
item 1 of every word of window 1 of application "BBEdit"
```

That code sends BBEdit two Apple events for every word in the window, one of which asks BBEdit to evaluate the concept *every word* afresh each time! If there are a thousand words and just two beginning with "t", that's a massive waste. The second version of our code was much better:

```
tell application "BBEdit"
    repeat with w in (get every word of window 1 ¬
        where contents of text of it begins with "t")
        change case w making raise case
    end repeat
end tell
```

If there are just two words beginning with "t", that code will send just three Apple events: one to gather the list of references to the two words, and then two more to change their case.

Also, be alert for the possibility that you might not have to loop at all. The target application might be smart enough do what you want with a single command. In the earlier Finder example, there was actually no need to gather a reference to every folder and then ask for the name of each; if that's all we wanted, it could have been done like this:

```
tell application "Finder" to set L to name of every folder
```

See "Properties of Multiple References" in Chapter 10.

Tell

A *tell block*, like an if block, comes in two forms: a genuine block and a single-line version. The block form is like this:

```
tell target
    -- code
end tell
```

The single-line version is like this:

```
tell target to command
```

A tell block performs two distinct functions:

- It determines (at runtime) the *target* of the commands in its code.
- It dictates (at compile time) the source that will be used for the resolution of the *terminology* that appears in its code.

The fact that tell does both these things makes a certain sense. After all, if you're going to be sending messages to the Finder, you're probably going to want to talk to the Finder in the Finder's own language. Nevertheless, the two functions are distinct, and it is possible to do either one without the other:

- To target an application without using its vocabulary, address it entirely by means of of, without using tell:

  ```
  get frontmost of application "Finder"
  ```

  That example compiles because the term frontmost is defined by AppleScript itself; it runs because the Finder adopts the same term.

- To use an application's vocabulary without targeting it, supply a terms block:

  ```
  using terms from application "Finder"
      tell me to get folder 1
  end using terms from
  ```

  That example compiles, but at runtime there's an error because our script doesn't understand the Finder's term folder.

On the determination of the target, see "Target" in Chapter 10. On the resolution of vocabulary, see Chapter 19.

Using Terms From

A *terms block* (as I call it) has the following structure:

```
using terms from application
    -- code
end using terms from
```

A terms block dictates what application's dictionary AppleScript should get the enclosed terminology from, without actually targeting that application. On the usual principle that the innermost block takes precedence, if multiple terms blocks are nested, only the innermost terms block containing a given line of code has any effect on that line. Similarly, a terms block overrides the dictionary-seeking function of an enclosing tell block. A terms block doesn't override an enclosed tell, but if an enclosed tell would not permit AppleScript to obtain a dictionary that it needs, a terms block may do so.

Thus, this will not compile:

```
tell application "Finder"
    using terms from application "Mailsmith"
        get name of folder 1 -- compile-time error
    end using terms from
end tell
```

The problem there is that AppleScript must seek `folder` in Mailsmith's dictionary, and doesn't find it. But this will compile:

```
using terms from application "Finder"
    tell application someVariable
        get name of folder 1
    end tell
end using terms from
```

AppleScript has no idea what `someVariable` will be at runtime, so it follows the instructions of the terms block and thus is able at compile time to obtain a dictionary that resolves the enclosed terminology. This, however, does not guarantee that the code will run. Perhaps `someVariable` will specify an application that knows what a `folder` is; perhaps not. Basically you're telling AppleScript to suspend judgment and just believe that the Finder's notion of a `folder` will work here. You could be lying. For example, this will compile, but it won't run:

```
tell application "Finder"
    using terms from application "Mailsmith"
        get mailbox 1
    end using terms from
end tell
```

It will compile because the terms block adduces Mailsmith to make the notion `mailbox` meaningful; but it won't run, because the Finder is the target, and when told to get a `mailbox` the Finder has no idea what this means.

The chief use of a terms block is to allow compilation of a script targeting a remote application. We have seen that AppleScript must be able to resolve all terminology at compile time, and that normally it attempts to do this by using the dictionary of the targeted application. When an application is on another computer, this might not be possible at the time the script is compiled: the remote machine might be unavailable, the remote application might not be running, or the script might specify the target machine dynamically. A terms block lets you get past these hurdles by specifying a local source for the terminology you're using.

In this example, I'll talk to my iBook in the next room using Rendezvous, having first turned on Remote Apple Events on the iBook in the Sharing preferences panel:

```
set whatMachine to text returned of ¬
    (display dialog "Machine to connect to:" default answer "eppc://")
-- I enter: eppc://little-white-duck.local
tell application "Finder" of machine whatMachine
    using terms from application "Finder"
        get name of disk 1 -- "OmniumGatherum"
    end using terms from
end tell
```

That script works equally well whether the tell block encloses the terms block or vice versa. (For more examples, see "Remote Applications" in Chapter 21.)

In this next example, we demonstrate how the target can be treated as a variable thanks to a terms block. There is no `tell` anywhere in this script, and the script has to determine the target entirely at runtime using a reference to the application, which is passed as a parameter. The main hurdle is getting the script to compile, since AppleScript must be able to resolve all terminology at compile time; we get over that hurdle with terms blocks:

```
global doThis
on getMailbox(whatApp)
    using terms from application "Mailsmith"
        get name of mailbox 1 of whatApp
    end using terms from
end getMailbox
on getFolder(whatApp)
    using terms from application "Finder"
        get name of folder 1 of whatApp
    end using terms from
end getFolder
on getTheRightThing(whatApp)
    if whatApp is application "Finder" then
        set doThis to getFolder
    else if whatApp is application "Mailsmith" then
        set doThis to getMailbox
    end if
    tell whatApp to my doThis(whatApp)
end getTheRightThing
getTheRightThing(application "Mailsmith") -- (drafts)
getTheRightThing(application "Finder") -- "Mannie"
```

If you tell AppleScript to look for a dictionary in an application that is a web URL, AppleScript won't actually look there, but will assume that this application is a SOAP or XML-RPC server. We can use this as a trick to treat the target as a variable when doing a SOAP call over the Internet. This example, based on a script distributed by Apple, shows how to write a general SOAP-calling handler. The handler, generalSOAP( ), contains no hardcoded information at all, except the application URL named in the terms block; this URL is a complete fake, and is intended only to satisfy the compiler that it's okay to use the call soap command. The actual parameters supplied in the last line fetch the current Apple stock price over the Internet:

```
on generalSOAP(u, m, s, a, p)
    using terms from application "http://www.apple.com/placebo"
        tell application u
            call soap ¬
                {method name:m, ¬
                method namespace uri:s, ¬
                parameters:p, ¬
                SOAPAction:a}
        end tell
    end using terms from
end generalSOAP
generalSOAP("http://services.xmethods.net:80/soap", ¬
    "getQuote", "urn:xmethods-delayed-quotes", ¬
    "", {Symbol:"AAPL"}) -- 18.8
```

See also "XML-RPC and SOAP" in Chapter 21.

With

A *with block* is used to modify Apple events sent within its code to target applications, specifying certain external attributes of those Apple events. Two types of with block are currently defined: a *timeout block* and a *transaction block*.

Timeout

Recall from "Apple Event" in Chapter 4 that during interapplication communications, the sender of an Apple event may attach to that Apple event a specification of how long it is willing to wait for a reply. This is the Apple event's *timeout* period. If the target does not reply within the specified timeout period, for whatever reason (the operation might be too lengthy, the target application might be otherwise engaged, and so forth), the System stops waiting for a reply and reports to the sender that the Apple event timed out. This report arrives as an error; your script can handle this error and proceed (see "Errors," later in this chapter).

This entire mechanism is valuable because, among other things, it saves the sender from hanging indefinitely while waiting for the target to reply; if the target takes too long to reply, the sender is able to proceed nonetheless. Of course, the sender must then do without any reply from the target; but the point is that a script can be written to take account of a problem of this kind, and reporting the problem to the user and proceeding or terminating in good order is certainly preferable to hanging or appearing to hang while waiting for a reply that is taking a long time to arrive and that may, indeed, never come.

All Apple events sent to target applications have a default timeout value of *one minute*. This is a good compromise between waiting sufficiently long for lengthy operations to complete and waiting so long (or not having any timeout at all) that a script can hang or appear to hang. If this value is acceptable to you, you don't need a timeout block to change it.

To change the timeout value temporarily using a timeout block, use this syntax:

```
with timeout of integer second[s]
    -- code
end timeout
```

This affects only code within the block; afterwards, Apple events revert to the default timeout value. To wait indefinitely, use an extremely large *integer*.

To illustrate, we'll command the Finder to perform an operation so long that without a timeout specification it probably wouldn't have time to reply—we'll ask it to cycle down the entire hierarchy looking for a certain kind of file:

```
with timeout of 100000 seconds
    tell application "Finder"
        get every application file of entire contents ¬
            of disk 1 where its creator type is "aplt"
```

```
        end tell
    end timeout
```

If we don't provide a timeout block, this code will time out before the Finder is finished, and we'll get an error: "Finder got an error: AppleEvent timed out." Even if the Apple event times out, the Finder will still be cycling down the entire hierarchy, and it will keep doing so until it finishes. So don't run that example unless you're not planning on using the Finder for a while.

Transaction

A problem that can arise with interapplication communications is that a target application is promiscuous. While you're being a sender and talking to a target application, some other sender can come along and talk to it as well. If this happens in the middle of a series of Apple events from you, it can alter the state of the target application, messing up what you're trying to accomplish.

The Apple event solution to this is the *transaction*. A transaction is a kind of permission slip allowing you to unify multiple commands. You start by asking for this permission slip, and the target application returns a transaction ID of some sort. You then continue sending the target application Apple events, showing it the transaction ID every time. When you're done, you tell the target that you're done (showing it the transaction ID, of course), and that transaction comes to an end. Not every scriptable application implements transactions (would that they did); a commonly used application that does is FileMaker Pro.

The target application itself is responsible for deciding how to implement the notion of a transaction. All you care about is that state should be conserved throughout the multiple commands of a single transaction. FileMaker's approach is to implement a transaction as monopolization: once you've asked for the permission slip and obtained the transaction ID, FileMaker will simply refuse to respond to any Apple event that does not show the transaction ID, until you tell it the transaction is over, at which point it returns to its normal state of promiscuity.

The way to obtain, show, and release the transaction ID is by wrapping your transactional communications in a transaction block, which looks like this:

```
with transaction
    -- code
end transaction
```

All the actual business of dealing with the transaction ID is handled transparently for you. The with transaction line causes an Apple event to be sent to the current target asking for the transaction ID. Then all the application-targeted Apple events inside the block are accompanied by this transaction ID. Finally, the end transaction line sends the current target one last Apple event accompanied by the transaction ID, telling it to leave transaction mode.

In this example, we monopolize FileMaker Pro long enough to create a Find request and perform it:

```
tell application "FileMaker Pro"
    with transaction
        tell database 1
            show every record
            set f to create new request
            set cell "lastname" of f to "neuburg"
            find
        end tell
    end transaction
end tell
```

There is one important thing to notice about that code: the transaction block is inside the tell block. It is essential to structure your code this way; the application with which you want to carry on a transaction must be the target when the with transaction line is encountered, so that AppleScript knows where to send that first Apple event asking for the transaction ID. Unfortunately, this means we run smack dab into a bizarre terminology problem. It turns out that FileMaker Pro's dictionary also implements the opening and closing transactional Apple events as the commands begin transaction and end transaction. This means that when you say end transaction inside a tell block addressed to FileMaker Pro, it is seen as FileMaker's end transaction command, not as the end of the transaction block. The script then won't compile. The workaround, which is terribly annoying, is to delete the word transaction from the end transaction line every time you are about to compile the script.

You might worry about what happens if something goes wrong in the middle of the transaction block. What if we say something that generates an error? We'll never reach the end of the transaction block, and that means we'll leave FileMaker Pro in a transaction state, refusing to respond to Apple events. You're perfectly right to worry about this; you certainly don't want to leave FileMaker Pro in transaction mode. If FileMaker Pro were to get into such a state, you couldn't even quit it, because the Quit menu item is implemented with an Apple event—and FileMaker Pro won't listen to that Apple event, because it doesn't supply the transaction ID! It turns out, though, that AppleScript solves this problem transparently. If an error is encountered during a transaction block, AppleScript sends the target the Apple event that ends the transaction. I suspect that the transaction block is wrapped in a sort of invisible try block. In any case, it's really all very nicely implemented.

Considering/Ignoring

There are two kinds of *considering/ignoring block*. One is the "ignoring application responses" block, which affects the nature of Apple events targeting an application. The other affects the details of string comparisons.

Ignoring Application Responses

Recall from "Apple Event" in Chapter 4 that during interapplication communications, the sender of an Apple event may specify that it has no intention of waiting around for a reply. It doesn't care what the result is; it doesn't care if there's an error. It just wants to send the Apple event and be done with it, proceeding immediately to its own next step. In AppleScript, here's how to send such an Apple event:

```
ignoring application responses
    -- code
end ignoring
```

Within the block, only Apple events sent to other applications are affected. Apple events sent to scripting additions, for example, are sent in the normal way and receive whatever replies they normally receive.

For an example, see "Reduction" in Chapter 1. The code that opens a URL from the clipboard is wrapped in an "ignoring application responses" block because I want the browser or mail client or whatever to open in the background and without my waiting for it; thus I can get on immediately with what I was doing.

Inside an "ignoring application responses" block, it is possible to override the block by embedding a "considering application responses" block. You might use this, for example, to ignore application responses from one application but not another.

String Considerations

String considerations are features of strings that may optionally come into play when performing a string comparison (see "Comparison Operators" and "Containment Operators" in Chapter 15). For example, string comparison may be case-sensitive or case-insensitive. You use a considering/ignoring block to govern this behavior.

Until recently there was no mechanism for making string considerations visible to a targeted application. This meant that string considerations could operate only within AppleScript; a string comparison performed as part of a boolean test element specifier, for example, could not be affected by string considerations (see "Boolean Test" in Chapter 10 and "Who Performs an Operation" in Chapter 15). This limitation has changed, but applications must be rewritten if they are to notice and take account of string considerations. See also "String and Clipboard" in Chapter 20 on the offset scripting addition command.

Here are the string considerations:

case

> If ignored, uppercase and lowercase variants of the same letter are taken to be equivalent. Ignored by default.

diacriticals

> If ignored, variants of the same letter with different accent marks (or no accent mark) are taken to be equivalent. Considered by default.

expansion

> If ignored, ligatures are taken to be equivalent to their component characters. Considered by default.

hyphens

> If ignored, hyphens are taken not to exist. Considered by default.

punctuation

> If ignored, word-boundary punctuation and quotation marks and apostrophes are taken not to exist. Considered by default.

white space

> If ignored, spaces, tabs, and line break characters are taken not to exist. Considered by default.

Here's the syntax for writing a string consideration:

```
considering | ignoring considerations
    [but ignoring | considering considerations]
    -- code
end considering | ignoring
```

Each set of *considerations* is any number of string considerations separated by comma; AppleScript will rewrite the last comma as and. Entire string consideration blocks may also be nested. So, for example:

```
ignoring hyphens, expansion and punctuation
    considering white space but ignoring case and diacriticals
        "a-" = "Å!" -- true
    end considering
end ignoring
```

Errors

An *error* is a message at runtime saying, in effect, that something bad has happened and execution cannot continue. The sender of such a message is said to *throw* an error. The message percolates up through the call chain looking for an error-handling block surrounding the line currently being executed; such a block is said to *catch* the error. If no block catches the error, it percolates all the way up to AppleScript, which puts up an error dialog, and the script terminates prematurely.

This entire mechanism is extremely nice, because it provides a target application, or AppleScript itself, with a way to signal that it's impossible to proceed and to interrupt the flow of code, while leaving it up to the caller whether and how to recover. Your script can implement no error handling, in which case any runtime error will bring the script to a grinding halt. Or your script can implement error handling in certain areas where it expects an error might occur. It can recover from some errors and re-throw others, allowing them to terminate the script. It can throw an error as a way of controlling the flow of code.

An error can be a positive thing, and can be built into the structure of a command's implementation. For example, display dialog throws an error if the user clicks the Cancel button in the dialog. This is not intended to kill your script. The expectation is that your script can just catch the error as a way of learning that the user has cancelled, and can then proceed in an appropriate manner.

I'll talk first about how to throw an error, then about how to catch one.

Throw

To throw an error, use the error command. It has five optional parameters:

```
error [messageString]
    [number shortInteger]
    [partial result list]
    [from anything]
    [to class]
```

Here are their default values:

messageString
Nothing

number
    -2700

partial result
    The empty list

from
    The currently executing script or script object

to
    The class item

You can use any of the parameters when throwing an error, but in real life you are likely to use only the first two. The others are present because this is also the structure of an error message from an application, which can supply this further information to help explain what the problem was.

If you throw an uncaught error, it will trickle all the way up to AppleScript and will be presented to the user as a dialog. The *messageString* is your chance to dictate what appears in that dialog. You will probably want to say something meaningful about what went wrong. For example:

```
error "Things fall apart, the centre cannot hold."
```

Figure 12-1 shows how that error is presented to the user in the Script Editor.

If an error is thrown in an applet, the applet puts up a similar dialog, which also offers a chance to edit the script. If this is a Stay Open applet ("Applet Options" in Chapter 24), the error does not cause it to quit.

Figure 12-1. An error dialog

If you don't supply any parameters at all to your error command, the error dialog reads: "An error has occurred." If you don't supply a *messageString* but you do supply an error number—let's say it's 32—the dialog reads: "An error of type 32 has occurred."

An error number is not highly communicative to the user, unless the user is supplied with a table of error numbers and their meanings; but it is certainly useful within code, particularly when you're implementing internal error handling. If different kinds of things can go wrong, you can use this number to signal which one did go wrong. An example appears in the next section.

Catch

The only way to catch an error is for that error to be thrown within a *try block*; this includes code that is ultimately called by code within a try block. The thrown error percolates up through the calling chain, and if it eventually finds itself within a try block, it may be caught.

There are two forms of try block. In the first, there is no actual error-handling code:

```
try
    -- code
end try
```

This form of try block handles the error by ignoring it. If an error is caught anywhere in the try block, the block terminates; execution resumes after the end try, and that's the end of the matter. Thus, you have no way to learn directly that an error was caught (though you can learn indirectly, because some code may have been skipped). But at least the error didn't bring your script to a halt. Here's an example:

```
set x to "Cancel"
try
    set x to button returned of (display dialog "Press a button.")
end try
display dialog "You pressed " & x
```

If the user presses the Cancel button, display dialog throws an error; without the try block, this code would then never reach the last line.

In this next example, we use a try block as a form of flow control. We want to get the name of every disk. (Ignore the fact that we could just ask the Finder for this information directly.) Instead of asking how many disks there are and looping that number of times, we loop forever but inside a try block. When we exceed the number of disks, the Finder throws an error and the loop ends.

```
set L to {}
set x to 1
tell application "Finder"
    try
        repeat
            set end of L to name of disk x
            set x to x + 1
        end repeat
    end try
end tell
```

In the second form of try block, you supply some error-handling functionality:

```
try
    -- code
on error [parameters]
    -- error-handling code
end try
```

If an error is caught anywhere in the try part, the try part terminates; execution resumes at the start of the error block. If no error is caught anywhere in the try part, the error block is skipped. The *parameters* are exactly the same as those for an error command, so your error block can capture and respond to any information that may have been included when the error was thrown. You don't have to include any parameters and you can include any subset of the parameters; thus you aren't forced to capture information you don't care about. Parameter variable names are local to the error block.

In this example, we have a handler that returns one error code if the user cancels a dialog and another if the user fails to enter the required information in that dialog:

```
on getFavoriteColor()
    try
        set r to display dialog "What is your favorite color?" default answer ""
    on error
        error number 1001
    end try
    set s to text returned of r
    if s = "" then error number 1000
    return s
end getFavoriteColor
set c to ""
repeat until c is not ""
    try
        set c to getFavoriteColor()
    on error number n
        if n = 1000 then
            display dialog "You didn't enter a color!" buttons "OK"
```

```
            else if n = 1001 then
                display dialog "Why did you cancel? Tell me!" buttons "OK"
            end if
        end try
    end repeat
    display dialog "Aha, you like " & c & ", eh?"
```

This example illustrates how errors and error handling help with the distribution of responsibilities. The handler getFavoriteColor( ) has just one job—to get the user's favorite color. If something goes wrong, it signals this with an error; that's all. It's up to the caller to decide how to proceed at that point. In this case, the caller is prepared for the possibility that two kinds of thing might go wrong, and has a different dialog ready to show the user in each case. The caller is perfectly prepared to loop all day until the user enters something in the dialog. But all of that is the caller's own decision; the handler itself just performs the single task for which it was written. Distribution of responsibilities makes for more reusable code, and the example shows how throwing errors contributes to this.

A common technique in an error handler is to handle only those errors that are in some sense yours, those that you expect and are prepared to deal with. Unexpected errors are simply allowed to percolate on up to AppleScript, causing the script to terminate; this makes sense because they're unexpected and you're not prepared to deal with them. There are two ways to accomplish this.

One way is to catch all errors and then rethrow any errors you aren't prepared to handle. If you're going to do that, you should probably use all the parameters, both in the on error line as you catch the error and in the error command as you rethrow it; otherwise you might strip the error of some of its information, which might reduce its value to the user (or to any code at some higher level that catches it).

In this example, we ask the user for the number of a disk to get the name of. If the number is not the number of an existing disk, the Finder throws error number -1728, so if we get an error and that's its number, we deliver a meaningful response. If we get any other error—for example, the user enters text in the dialog that can't be coerced to a number—we rethrow it.

```
set n to text returned of ¬
    (display dialog "What disk would you like the name of?" default answer "")
try
    tell application "Finder" to set x to name of disk (n as integer)
    display dialog x
on error e number n partial result p from f to t
    if n = -1728 then
        display dialog "I don't think that disk exists. " & e
    else
        error e number n partial result p from f to t
    end if
end try
```

The other approach is to use a *filtered error handler*. In this approach, some of the parameters in the on error line are not variable names but literals. AppleScript will call the error block only if all such literals are matched by the corresponding error parameter value. Otherwise, the error percolates up the call chain, of its own accord.

Thus, we can rewrite the error block from the previous example as follows:

```
on error e number -1728
    display dialog "I don't think that disk exists. " & e
end try
```

There's no way to list alternative literals; you can't write an error block that catches errors with either of just two particular error numbers, for instance. A workaround is to nest try blocks. Thus we can rewrite the second half of the earlier "favorite color" example like this:

```
set c to ""
repeat until c is not ""
    try
        try
            set c to getFavoriteColor( )
        on error number 1000
            display dialog "You didn't enter a color!" buttons "OK"
        end try
    on error number 1001
        display dialog "Why did you cancel? Tell me!" buttons "OK"
    end try
end repeat
display dialog "Aha, you like " & c & ", eh?"
```

If you don't like the look of literally nested try blocks ("lexical nesting"), you can nest them by means of the calling chain ("dynamic nesting"):

```
global c
set c to ""
on askUser( )
    try
        set c to getFavoriteColor( )
    on error number 1000
        display dialog "You didn't enter a color!" buttons "OK"
    end try
end askUser
repeat until c is not ""
    try
        askUser( )
    on error number 1001
        display dialog "Why did you cancel? Tell me!" buttons "OK"
    end try
end repeat
display dialog "Aha, you like " & c & ", eh?"
```

An expired timeout ("Timeout," earlier in this chapter) is an error like any other; this example shows a way to handle it:

```
try
    tell application "Finder"
        activate
        with timeout of 1 second
```

```
            display dialog "Press a button." giving up after 2
        end timeout
    end tell
on error number -1712
    activate
    display dialog "Ha ha, not fast enough!"
end try
```

Second-Level Evaluation

By "second-level evaluation" I mean constructing and executing code at runtime. AppleScript has no built-in way of performing second-level evaluation. However, you can achieve much the same effect through the use of the `run script` scripting addition command, which allows you to compile and run a string. (See "Compiled Script Files as Script Objects" in Chapter 9.)

The use of `run script` is rather resource-expensive, because it requires that a completely new instance of the AppleScript scripting component be generated and torn down. It's also rather slow, because it takes time to compile the string. Finally, it's rather clunky, because a string run in this way has no communication with its surroundings; indeed, because a new instance of the AppleScript scripting component is generated, it has no surroundings at all. In other words, it isn't like a script object that can "see" globals at the point where it is defined and run.

Nevertheless, there are things you can accomplish with `run script` that can be accomplished in no other way. For example, all terminology must be resolved at compile time, so the only way to construct completely dynamically, at runtime, a command involving terminology is by means of `run script`.

In this example, we permit the user to enter part of an expression to be evaluated by saying it to the Finder:

```
set d to "window 1"
set p to "What Finder object would you like the name of?"
set r to display dialog p default answer d
set s to text returned of r
set s to "tell app \"Finder\" to get name of " & s
try
    set res to run script s
    display dialog res
on error
    display dialog "Sorry, that didn't work."
end try
```

For another example of `run script` used for second-level evaluation, see "Record Properties" in Chapter 13.

Datatypes

A *datatype* is a classification of a value; every value is of one datatype or another. This is what AppleScript calls a class (see Chapter 10). For example, string is a datatype, integer is a datatype, and so forth. AppleScript provides a number of native datatypes; this chapter describes them.

Scriptable applications can extend the language by providing additional datatypes. For example, the Finder implements a folder datatype (or class). But such additional datatypes are confined to the application that defines them; a value returned by a scriptable application must be either a reference to an object belonging to that application, or one of AppleScript's native datatypes.

Some values can be mutated from one datatype to another. Such a mutation is called *coercion*. To put it more strictly: for some pairs of datatype, call them datatype 1 and datatype 2, it is the case that at least some values of datatype 1 can be coerced to a value of datatype 2. For example, the string "1" can be coerced to a number; when that happens, you get the number 1. What coercions are possible, and how they are performed, is explained in Chapters 14 and 15.

Boolean

A *boolean* is a datatype consisting of exactly two possible values, true and false.

```
class of true -- boolean
class of (1 < 2) -- boolean
```

The main use for a boolean is as a condition in a control statement, such as a repeat while block (Chapter 12). For the operators that generate and combine booleans, see Chapter 15.

Integer, Real, and Number

The *integer* and *real* datatypes are the numeric classes.

```
class of 1 -- integer
class of 1.1 -- real
```

A literal integer is a series of digits, possibly preceded by a minus sign. The maximum integer is 536870911, positive or negative, which, as everyone knows, is $2^{29}-1$. Any integer value outside this range is implicitly coerced to a real.

A literal real is a series of digits with a decimal point, possibly preceded by a minus sign. You may also use "scientific notation": that's a number followed by small or capital e, possibly followed by a plus sign or a minus sign, followed by an integer; AppleScript might rewrite a scientific notation number for you, but in any case it will always be a real. For example:

```
1e2 -- rewritten: 100.0
2.1e26 -- rewritten: 2.1E+26
```

You can't include a comma as a thousands separator in a literal number.

The class number is purely for purposes of coercion. In some situations you can use it to ask AppleScript to coerce to whichever numeric datatype, integer or real, is appropriate. This is nice because it saves *you* from having to worry about which is appropriate.

```
class of ("1" as number) -- integer
class of ("1.1" as number) -- real
```

However, number cannot be used in every situation where a numeric coercion is possible. For example, true as integer is legal, but true as number is not. I regard this as a bug.

An integer is four bytes. A dictionary may occasionally mention a class small integer, which is two bytes (ranging from -32768 to 32767). You can create one by coercion, but there should be little need to do so, since small integers are typically used transparently; they evidently become integers before you get a look at them:

```
set x to 4 as small integer
class of x -- integer
class of (ASCII number "a") -- integer, even though dictionary says "small integer"
```

There is also a class double integer, which is eight bytes. This is sometimes used when communicating with the System, and seems to be simply a real within the integer range. Again, there should be little need to create one; a double integer in your code is reported as a real. There are other rarely used numeric classes, transparently coerced to integer or real before you get hold of them; these include fixed, extended real, and so forth. For a full list, see Appendix A.

Date

A *date* is a date-time. For the practical limits on the range of dates that can be expressed, see the year property later in this section. AppleScript knows nothing of time zones, and assumes the Gregorian calendar even for dates before its invention.

A literal date is an object string specifier (see Chapter 10). In constructing a date, you may use any string value that can be interpreted as a date, a time, or a date-time; AppleScript (or more probably the System) is quite liberal in what it will accept, provided the string makes sense in terms of your date and time format settings in the International pane of System Preferences. AppleScript will supply missing values such as today's date (if you give only a time) or this year (if you don't give a year) or midnight (if you give only a date).

AppleScript presents a literal date specifier in long date-time format in accordance with your International settings. It does this even within your script, on decompilation, if you use a literal string in a date specifier:

```
date "5/25/2003" -- rewritten: date "Sunday, May 25, 2003 12:00:00 AM"
```

If the expression "5/25/2003" isn't a date according to your International preferences, this code won't compile. For example, if you have UK settings, you'd need to type date "25/5/2003".

Having obtained a date one way or another, you can then derive a new date from it in two ways. One is by date arithmetic, which involves adding and subtracting seconds. (See Chapters 15 and 17 for some constants that can help you calculate the desired number of seconds.) The other is to combine a new time part or date part with the existing date; this is done by an odd syntax that treats a date specifier as a property of another date:

```
date dateOrTimeString of date
```

For example:

```
set s to "2/25"
set d to date s -- February 25, 2003 12:00:00 AM
set d2 to date "10:30" of d -- February 25, 2003 10:30:00 AM
set d3 to date "1/24" of d2 -- January 24, 2003 10:30:00 AM
```

Again, notice that this code will compile but not run on a machine with UK settings. Scripts that form dates dynamically by coercing from a string are thus not very portable.

You can also alter a date in place by changing one of its properties. AppleScript (or more probably the System) will compensate when you change a property in a calendrically impossible way:

```
set s to "May 31"
set d to date s
set month of d to June -- July 1, 2003 12:00:00 AM
```

When you use set (as opposed to copy) to set a variable to a value which is a date, you set the variable *by reference*. This means that the date is not copied; the variable's name becomes a new name for the date, in addition to any names for the date that may already exist. The same is true when a date is passed as a parameter to a handler. This special treatment is in common between lists, records, dates, and script objects. (See "Pass By Reference" in Chapter 8 and "Set By Reference" in Chapter 9.)

For example:

```
set s to "May 31"
set d to date s
set d2 to d
set month of d2 to June
d -- July 1, 2003 12:00:00 AM
```

Date Properties

The following are the properties of a date value:

year
> A positive integer. You can't express BCE dates. The mathematical range limit on the year seems to be 100–9999.

month
> A constant (not a string!): January, February, and so on.

day
> A positive integer.

time
> An integer; the number of seconds since midnight represented by the date's time part.

weekday
> A constant (not a string!): Monday, Tuesday, and so on. In practice this property is read-only; there's no penalty for setting it, but trying to set a date's weekday to a weekday that isn't accurate for that date has no effect.

date string
short date string
time string
> A string consisting of just the date or time part of the date-time. In practice these properties are read-only; setting them results in a stack overflow (I'd have to call that a bug). They are formatted in accordance with your International preference pane settings.

The time string and date string are suitable for combining with an existing date to form a new date, using the syntax we saw earlier. For example:

```
set s to "5/25/2003"
set d1 to date s
set t to "4PM"
```

```
set d2 to date t
set d3 to date (time string of d2) of d1 -- May 25, 2003 4:00:00 PM
```

String

A *string* is the basic text datatype. A literal string is delimited by double quotation marks:

```
set s to "howdy"
class of s -- string
```

In typing a string literal, you may enter certain characters in "escaped" form; they are listed in Table 13-1. These are the only "escaped" characters; other untypeable characters may be concatenated into the string by means of the ASCII character scripting addition command. (See "Concatenation Operator" in Chapter 15 and "String and Clipboard" in Chapter 20.) After compilation, the tab, return, and linefeed characters are un-escaped and turned into whitespace: they remain intact, but you can no longer see directly what characters they are, which is a pity.

Table 13-1. "Escaped" string literals

What to type	ASCII equivalent	Result
\"	ASCII character 34	Quotation marks
\t	ASCII character 9	Tab
\r	ASCII character 13	Return
\n	ASCII character 10	Linefeed
\\	ASCII character 92	Backslash

Don't confuse AppleScript's built-in string type and its native manipulations of this type with how scriptable applications may implement their own string behavior. When you ask an application to perform manipulations on text of its own, it may behave differently from AppleScript. For example:

```
tell application "Tex-Edit Plus"
    set text of window 1 to "Now is the winter"
    get word after character 3 of text of window 1 -- "is"
end tell
get word after character 3 of "Now is the winter" -- error
```

In the tell block, everything belongs to Tex-Edit Plus; you're speaking of Tex-Edit's implementation of the text class, and you're dependent upon Tex-Edit's idea of a word and a character and what can be done with them. In the last line, you're working with a string and talking to AppleScript itself.

String Properties

The following are the properties of a string. They are read-only.

length
> The number of characters of the string. You can get this same information by sending the count message to the string.

quoted form
> A rendering of the string suitable for handing to the shell as an argument to a command. The string is wrapped in single quotation marks and internal quotation marks are escaped.

You probably shouldn't look at the result of quoted form, because you might not understand it; it's meant for the shell's eyes, not yours, and an extra level of (mis)representation is added by AppleScript as it shows you the string. For example:

```
quoted form of "life's a \"bowl\" of cherries"
-- "'life'\\''s a \"bowl\" of cherries'"
```

That looks pretty dreadful, but it's right, as you'll discover if you hand it to the shell:

```
set s to quoted form of "life's a \"bowl\" of cherries"
do shell script "echo " & s
-- "life's a \"bowl\" of cherries"
```

String Elements

The following are the elements of a string. Bear in mind that you can't set them; you cannot alter a string in place! Elements may be specified by index number, by range, or with every.

character
> A string representing a single character of the string.

word
> A string representing a single word of the string. It has no spaces or other word-boundary punctuation.

paragraph
> A string representing a single paragraph (or line) of the string. It has no line breaks. AppleScript treats a return, a linefeed, or the one followed by the other (CRLF) as a line break.

text
> A run of text. Its purpose is to let you obtain a single string using a range element specifier; see "Range" in Chapter 10. So, for example:
> ```
> words 1 thru 3 of "Now is the winter" -- {"Now", "is", "the"}
> text from word 1 to word 3 of "Now is the winter" -- "Now is the"
> ```

text item
> A "field" of text, where the field delimiter is AppleScript's text item delimiters property.

The text item property needs some explanation. There is a property of the Apple-Script script object (the parent of top-level script—see "The Implicit Parent Chain" in Chapter 9) called text item delimiters. You can set this to any string you like. (The documentation claims that the text item delimiters is a list of strings, but only the first item of the list is effective.) That string is used to "split" a string into text items. The number of text items a string has is always exactly one more than the number of times it contains the text item delimiters string. For example:

```
set the text item delimiters to ":"
text items of "xxx:Users:mattneub"
-- {"xxx", "Users", "mattneub"}
set the text item delimiters to "tt"
text items of "Matt"
-- {"Ma", ""}
set text item delimiters to "s"
set howMany to (count text items of "Mississippi") - 1
howMany -- 4, the number of s's in Mississippi
```

The value of the text item delimiters persists as long as this instance of the Apple-Script scripting component does. Since you might run more than one script in the presence of this scripting component, any of which might set the text item delimiters, it is wise to make no assumptions as to the value of the text item delimiters. In other words, don't use it without setting it. Apple's documentation makes a big deal of this, but it's really no different from any of the other AppleScript properties, such as pi (see Chapter 16).

Unicode Text

Unicode text is text in UTF-16 encoding, as opposed to string, which has the Mac-Roman encoding. Unicode is the native system-level encoding of Mac OS X, so text supplied by the System is often Unicode text rather than a string. For example:

```
tell application "Finder" to set x to (get name of disk 1)
class of x -- Unicode text
```

Similarly, some Mac OS X–native applications, such as TextEdit, return text values as Unicode text. Unicode is capable of expressing tens of thousands of characters, and in its fullest form will express about a million, embracing every character of every written language in history. Eventually we may expect that AppleScript will become completely Unicode-savvy; all AppleScript text will be Unicode text, and the old string type will fade into oblivion.

Unicode text is basically indistinguishable from a string; the differences between them are handled transparently. Whatever you can do to a string, you can do to Unicode text. If you get an element of a Unicode text value, the result is Unicode text. If you concatenate Unicode text and a string, the result is Unicode text (though if you concatenate a string and Unicode text, you get a string; this is troublesome and might change in a future version of AppleScript). You can explicitly coerce between a string and Unicode text, and AppleScript implicitly coerces for you as appropriate.

Nevertheless, Unicode text is currently still a second-class citizen in AppleScript, and can be hard to work with. You can't even type a Unicode text literal in AppleScript. Well, you can, but AppleScript will render it as MacRoman when you compile the script, so any characters outside the range of MacRoman are lost. And AppleScript's supplied string manipulation commands, such as the scripting addition command ASCII character, don't work outside the MacRoman range either.

One workaround is to construct a character as hex data (see "Data" later in this chapter) and coerce it to Unicode text. So, for example, the following code yields a z-hacek (ž), Unicode code point hex 017E:

```
set myZ to «data utxt017E» as Unicode text
```

Another approach is to write the data out to a file and read it back in. This works because AppleScript gives you a wide variety of ways to treat file data. Here's an example (on reading and writing files, see Chapter 20):

```
set f to a reference to file "myDisk:myFile"
open for access f with write permission
write 382 to f as small integer starting at 0
set s to read f as Unicode text from 0 to 1
close access f
```

After that, s is a z-hacek, because decimal 382 is hex 017E. There is also support for exchanging data with a file as UTF-8; but there is no internal support for AppleScript text in UTF-8 encoding, so if you read text as UTF-8, it is converted to UTF-16:

```
set f to a reference to file "myDisk:myFile"
open for access f with write permission
write "this is a test" to f as «class utf8» starting at 0
close access f
open for access f
set s to read f as «class utf8»
close access f
class of s -- Unicode text
```

Still another approach is to talk to the shell. This has the advantage that a good Unix scripting language, such as Perl, will let you express string data more conveniently than AppleScript will; it works because the do shell script scripting addition command returns Unicode text by default. So, for example:

```
set p to "use utf8;\n"
set p to p & "print chr(0x017E);"
set s to do shell script "perl -e " & quoted form of p
```

After that, s is a z-hacek. One must hope that some time soon these manipulations will cease to be necessary.

An older class, international text, is less likely to arise on Mac OS X. It was a way of representing text in accordance with a particular language and script (where "script" means a writing system); each language-script combination had its own rules (an encoding) for how particular sequences of bytes were mapped to characters (glyphs). The mess created by this multiplicity of encodings is the reason why Unicode is a Good Thing.

Styled Text

A *style* is an attribute of text, such as its font and size, whether it's underlined, that sort of thing. AppleScript defines a styled text class, but you can't manipulate it in any interesting way; in fact, you can barely even detect that it exists, because if you happen to encounter one and ask for its class, you're told it's a string. So you may as well treat it as such.

The styled text class isn't much used; most applications that provide scriptable text styling use a more sophisticated class that lets you access and manipulate the style information. Nevertheless, you might encounter styled text from time to time, especially when retrieving text data from the clipboard. You can detect that this has happened by coercing the text to a record, like so:

```
tell application "Finder"
    activate
    set x to (the clipboard)
end tell
x as record
-- {«class ktxt»:"test", ¬
«class ksty»:«data styl0001000000000000D000A00100000000C000000000000»}
```

As you can see, the string is actually made up of text information and style information. But the text information is all that AppleScript is normally willing to show you.

File

The built-in *file* class is AppleScript's way of letting you refer to a file or folder on disk. The literal form is an object string specifier using a pathname string:

```
file "xxx:Users:mattneub:"
```

AppleScript pathname strings are Macintosh-type paths, where you start with a disk name, and the delimiter between the disk name, folder names, and filename is a colon. A pathname ending in a colon is a folder or a disk. A partial pathname, one whose first element is not a disk, is taken to start inside the "current directory"; but the interpretation of this notion is unreliable, and partial pathnames should be avoided.

Alternatively, you can specify a file using a Unix-type (POSIX-type) path, where the delimiters are slashes and an initial slash means the top level of the startup disk. To do so, you must ask for a posix file instead of a file. AppleScript presents this, on decompilation or as a value, as a file specifier with the delimiters changed to colons. So, for example, if I write this:

```
posix file "/Users/mattneub/"
```

AppleScript changes it to this:

```
file "xxx:Users:mattneub:"
```

That looks like an ordinary file object, but behind the scenes it isn't; it's a different class, a file URL (class 'furl'). This class pops up in various contexts, lurking behind the file class. For example, the choose file name scripting addition is documented as returning a file object, and appears to do so, but in reality it's a file URL.

Just to confuse matters still further, some dictionaries mention a file specification class. For example, BBEdit's check syntax command requires a file specification parameter. This is a deprecated, outmoded class (class 'fss '), which the file class replaces transparently. So, this works, even though what you're forming is technically a file object and not a file specification, and a file specification comes back as part of the result:

```
tell application "BBEdit"
    set r to check syntax file "xxx:Users:mattneub:testing.html"
    class of result_file of item 1 of r -- file specification
end tell
```

You can even form a file specification object using an object string specifier; but don't. They can behave oddly; that's why they are deprecated. Stick to a file object and let the transparency work for you.

A file object constructed in your script can't be assigned directly to a variable (though, confusingly, a file URL can). Instead, you must assign a reference to the file object, like this:

```
set x to a reference to file "xxx:Users:mattneub:testing.html"
```

A file specifier is not resolved until the script actually runs. This means that the file on disk need not exist at compile time. At runtime, however, when the file specifier is handed to some command, either the file must exist, or, if the command proposes to create it, everything in the path must exist except for the last element, the file you're about to create. Otherwise the command will generate a runtime error. We've already met one command that accepts a file specifier to create a file—store script (for example, see "Context" in Chapter 9).

Don't confuse the AppleScript file object with the file class as defined by some scriptable application. For example, the Finder defines the file class with lots of elements and properties not defined in AppleScript itself:

```
tell application "Finder"
    get owner of file "xxx:Users:mattneub:myFile" -- mattneub
end tell
```

In that code, the owner property is defined by the Finder. The term file refers to the Finder's file class; the Finder allows you to use a pathname as the name, just as it does for item and folder and other classes. In fact, you can't hand an AppleScript file object to the Finder, as this example shows:

```
set f to a reference to file "xxx:Users:mattneub:myFile"
tell application "Finder"
    get owner of f -- error
end tell
```

An AppleScript file object *is* a viable medium of communication where a scripting addition or scriptable application doesn't define file objects of its own:

```
script x
    display dialog "howdy"
end script
set f to a reference to file "xxx:Users:mattneub:myFile"
store script x in f replacing yes
tell application "Script Editor" to open f
```

File Properties

You can obtain a POSIX pathname by forming a file specification and asking for its POSIX path. No element of the pathname need exist. For example:

```
POSIX path of file "alice:in:wonderland" -- "/alice/in/wonderland"
```

That, however, is a misuse of this feature; if you want it to behave properly, you need to behave properly. The POSIX path property does some useful things for you; for example, here it supplies the */Volumes* directory before the name of a nonstartup disk:

```
POSIX path of file "main:" -- "/Volumes/main/"
```

Again, it makes a difference whether you're talking to AppleScript or to some scriptable application. The Finder's file class, for example, has no POSIX path property.

You can obtain a host of useful information about a file, such as its creation date, whether it's invisible, whether it's a folder, how big it is, what application opens it, and lots of other cool stuff, with the info for scripting addition command:

```
info for file "xxx:Users:mattneub:someFile"
```

The result comes back as a record, which is easy to read and well-documented in the StandardAdditions dictionary, so I won't go into details here. You can obtain a list of the names of a folder's contents with the list folder scripting addition command. There are also commands for reading and writing a file, and there's even some interface for letting the user choose a file (see Chapter 20).

Alias

An *alias* object is very much like a file object. You can form an alias specifier in just the same way as you form a file specifier, and an alias object can often be used in the same places where a file object would be used. But there are some important differences:

- The item on disk represented by an alias specifier must exist at compile time.
- A pathname string or a file object can be coerced to an alias. (But a file specifier can't be coerced to an alias in the current Script Editor. I regard this as a bug, since it works fine in the old Script Editor.)
- An alias can be assigned directly to a variable as its value.
- An alias is an alias. That means it has the wonderful ability of a Macintosh alias to continue pointing to an item on disk even if the item is moved or renamed.

Alias objects are commonly used by scriptable applications as a way of returning a pointer to an item on disk. For example:

```
tell application "BBEdit"
    get file of window 1 -- alias "xxx:Users:mattneub:someFile"
end tell
```

In that code, the term file is merely the name of a window property, and has nothing to do with the file class from the previous section. (Well, almost nothing. Its raw four-letter code is the same as that of the file class. See Chapter 19.)

Again, don't be confused by classes belonging strictly to a particular scriptable application; the Finder's alias file class, for example, is not an alias.

There is a long-standing confusion in AppleScript about how to specify the file to which a new document is to be saved. AppleScript's Core Suite ("Suites" in Chapter 19) dictates that the save command takes an alias, and most applications' dictionaries therefore say the same. But this is impossible, because an alias must exist at compile time, and clearly it doesn't, since what you're trying to do is create it. Since the dictionary is lying, you must experiment in order to find out what the application really wants. For example:

```
tell application "GraphicConverter"
    set s to "xxx:Users:mattneub:Desktop:joconde"
    save window 1 in alias s as PICT -- error
end tell
```

That code fails with a runtime error, because the file doesn't exist. If you write the same code using a file specifier, it compiles and runs but the file isn't saved:

```
tell application "GraphicConverter"
    set s to "xxx:Users:mattneub:Desktop:joconde"
    save window 1 in file s as PICT -- no effect
end tell
```

After a great deal of banging around, you finally try this, and it works:

```
tell application "GraphicConverter"
    set s to "xxx:Users:mattneub:Desktop:joconde"
    save window 1 in s as PICT
end tell
```

Apparently the reliable way is simply to hand a pathname string to GraphicConverter. Indeed, more recent applications' dictionaries explicitly ask for Unicode text, implying that they expect a pathname. Even then you're not home free, because there are two forms of pathname string. Only experimentation will reveal, for example, that TextEdit wants a POSIX-style path:

```
tell application "TextEdit"
    save document 1 in "/Users/mattneub/someFile"
end tell
```

Application

The *application* class is used primarily to specify a target. You construct an application object using an object string specifier—the word application followed by a string representing the application's name or pathname. An abbreviation for application is app.

On Mac OS X, sometimes the application's name isn't what you think it is. The tendency is to glance at the Application menu at the upper left when the application is frontmost, or to look at the application's name in the Dock, and imagine that this shows you its real name; sometimes it doesn't. For example, Excel's name is "Excel" in both the Application menu and the Dock, but its real name is "Microsoft Excel".

If an application is targeted by a tell block, AppleScript must be able to find the application in order to compile the script. You can use a full pathname instead of just a name, to help it; but you shouldn't usually have to do this. (There is sometimes good reason to use a full pathname, though, such as to distinguish two versions of the same application on your machine.) If you get the name right, AppleScript searches for the application, and it usually finds it remarkably quickly. See "External Referents Needed at Compile Time" in Chapter 4 for what happens if you get the name wrong.

AppleScript may launch the application at compile time if it isn't already running. This is usually because otherwise it can't access the application's terminology (because its dictionary is marked as dynamic). See "Dictionary" in Chapter 4.

See Chapter 19 for more on resolution of terminology, and on the use of the application class to represent the top level of an application's object model.

Machine

The *machine* class is used to form a machine specifier, which appears in conjunction with an application specifier in order to target an application running on another computer. See "Remote Applications" in Chapter 21 for details.

Data

The *data* class represents raw data, a stream of bytes. It's a catchall for situations when results cannot be displayed in any other way. For example:

```
tell application "Finder"
    activate
    get (the clipboard)
end tell
-- {«data RECT0000000000B40075», ¬
    «data PICTFA480000000000B40075001102FF0C--... and so on for pages and pages
```

What was on the clipboard was a picture, and the Script Editor has no way to display it (though Script Debugger can); so it uses the data class and just shows you the data. The first four letters of this data can be informative, because they represent a resource type; clearly what's on the clipboard is a rectangle (probably the bounds of the picture) and a picture in PICT format.

It is also possible to form a data object yourself, by typing just the sort of thing you see here: the word data, a space, and then the resource type and the data, in guillemets (« »). However, this is an advanced technique and shouldn't arise much in real life (though an example of it was shown earlier in this chapter).

List

A *list* is a collection, corresponding roughly to what many other languages would call an array—it's an ordered set of values. These values are its *items*. Each value can be of any datatype (including a list).

A literal list is delimited by curly braces. Its contents can be literal values, variable names, or any other expressions that AppleScript can evaluate meaningfully; they are separated by commas. The literal empty list is just a pair of curly braces. So:

```
set empty to {}
set pep to {"Mannie", "Moe"}
set pep3 to "Jack"
set pep to pep & {pep3} -- {"Mannie", "Moe", "Jack"}
```

You can assign a list of values to a literal list of variable names or other references as a shorthand for performing multiple assignments. The assignments are performed pairwise in order: item 1 to item 1, item 2 to item 2, and so on. If the list of values is too long, the extra values are ignored; if it's too short, there's a runtime error. (See "Assignment and Retrieval" in Chapter 7 and "Multiple Assignments" in Chapter 10.) For example:

```
tell application "Finder"
    set {oldname1, oldname2} to {name of folder 1, name of folder 2}
    set {name of folder 1, name of folder 2} to {"f1", "f2"}
end tell
```

When you use set (as opposed to copy) to set a variable to a value that is a list, you set the variable *by reference*. This means that the list is not copied; the variable's name becomes a new name for the list, in addition to any names for the list that may already exist. The same is true when a list is passed as a parameter to a handler. This special treatment is in common between lists, records, dates, and script objects. (See "Pass By Reference" in Chapter 8 and "Set By Reference" in Chapter 9.) For example:

```
set L1 to {"Mannie", "Moe"}
set L2 to L1
set end of L1 to "Jack"
item 3 of L2 -- "Jack"
```

Unlike a string, a list can be modified in place. You can replace individual items, and you can add a new item to the beginning or end of a list. This is often a reason for using a list, instead of a string, for an extended series of operations, and then coercing to a string afterwards.

A list is stored internally as a data structure called a *vector*. This means that all the items of the list are accessible with equal efficiency; if a list has 100 items, it doesn't matter whether you refer to item 1 or item 100—AppleScript can access the item instantly. Under this vector implementation, setting an existing item of a list to a new value is efficient, because all that happens is that the new value is copied to the location in memory where the old value used to be.

```
set L to {"Mannie", "Moe"}
set item 1 of L to "Larry"
L -- {"Larry", "Moe"}
```

Also, setting the beginning or end of a list (as a way of appending to the list) is efficient. The reason for this is that nothing moves in memory except the new value, and the list is told it is one item longer than it was. So:

```
set L to {"Moe"}
set end of L to "Jack"
set beginning of L to "Mannie"
L -- {"Mannie", "Moe", "Jack"}
```

On the other hand, the vector implementation means that there is no efficient way to insert an item into the middle of an existing list, or to delete an item of a list, and there are no built-in commands for these operations. You'll probably want to arm yourself with a small arsenal of list utility handlers. For an item-deletion handler, see "LISP-likeness" in Chapter 5. See "Script Object as Handler Result" in Chapter 9 for a filter handler, and "Reference as Parameter" in Chapter 11 for a find-in-list handler. Here's an item-insertion handler:

```
on listInsert(L, what, ix)
    if ix = 1 then
        return {what} & L
    else
        return {item 1 of L} & listInsert(rest of L, what, ix - 1)
    end if
```

```
        end listInsert
    listInsert({"Mannie", "Jack"}, "Moe", 2) -- {"Mannie", "Moe", "Jack"}
```

A surprising feature of AppleScript lists is that they can recurse. This feature is actually a natural consequence of the foregoing. We know that when you use set to
assign a list as a value, you set by reference; you create a pointer to the existing list.
We know that a list item can be a list. So if a list item is created using set, it's a
pointer to a list. Well then, it can be a pointer to the *same* list. For example:

```
    set L to {"Mannie", "Moe", "Jack"}
    set end of L to L
    item 4 of item 4 of item 4 of item 4 of item 4 of L
    -- {"Mannie", "Moe", "Jack", {"Mannie", "Moe", "Jack", ...}}
```

Where did all those items of items of items come from? And what are those ellipses at
the end of the result? We've formed a recursive list. The fourth item of L is a pointer
to L itself. So if we look at the fourth item of L, we dereference this pointer and
presto, we're looking at L. The fourth item of that is a pointer to L itself—and so
forth. In other words, this is not an infinite list in the sense that it genuinely goes infi-
nitely deep or far in memory; if it were, flames would come out of your computer. It's
just a data structure of four items that goes round and round in a tight little circle.

Multiple lists can mutually recurse:

```
    set L1 to {"Mannie", "Moe", "Jack"}
    set L2 to {"Curly", "Larry"}
    set end of L1 to L2
    set end of L2 to L1
    L2 -- "Curly", "Larry", {"Mannie", "Moe", "Jack",
            {"Curly", "Larry", {"Mannie", "Moe", "Jack", ...}}}}
```

I don't know of any practical use for this curious feature, and I wouldn't count on its
being supported in future versions.

AppleScript contains a couple of built-in classes that are really just lists by another
name, along with some coercion rules. For example, bounding rectangle is a list of
four integers, rgb color is a list of three integers, and point is a list of two integers.
There may be others like this that I haven't stumbled upon.

List Properties

The following are the properties of a list. They are all read-only.

length
> The number of items in the list. You can get the same information by sending
> the list the count message.

rest
> Everything in the list except its first item.

reverse
> The list in reverse order.

List Elements

The following are the elements of a list:

`item`
> An item of the list, specified by index number, by range, or with every.

`classname`
> An item whose class is *classname*, specified by index number, by range, or with every. This is the closest thing a list has to a boolean test element specifier. For example, you can't say:
>
> ```
> item 2 of {23, "skiddoo", "catch", 22} whose class is integer -- error
> ```
>
> but you can say:
>
> ```
> integer 2 of {23, "skiddoo", "catch", 22} -- 22
> ```
>
> However, this does not work if the class you're asking about is class. This is a known bug.

Speed of List Access

When you access an element or property of a list, it is much faster to target a reference to the list, or the list as a script property, than to target the list directly. (Except when you set the beginning of and end of a list, that is. These operations are fast in any case because they have a special efficiency shortcut built in, as mentioned already.) Here's an adaptation of Apple's own example illustrating this point. Let's start with a version where we don't use a reference:

```
set L to {}
set total to 0
set bignum to 5000
repeat with i from 1 to bignum
    set end of L to i
end repeat
repeat with i from 1 to bignum
    set total to total + (item i of L)
end repeat
total -- 12502500, and it takes about 22 seconds to run on my machine
```

Now here's a version where we use a reference:

```
set L to {}
set refL to a reference to L
set total to 0
set bignum to 5000
repeat with i from 1 to bignum
    set end of L to i
end repeat
repeat with i from 1 to bignum
    set total to total + (item i of refL)
end repeat
total -- 12502500, and it took less than a second
```

That is an extraordinary speed difference. Now here's the really strange part: you don't actually have to form a value that's a reference; you can get the same speed bump by referring to the list as a script property:

```
set L to {}
set total to 0
set bignum to 5000
repeat with i from 1 to bignum
    set end of L to i
end repeat
repeat with i from 1 to bignum
    set total to total + (item i of my L)
end repeat
total -- 12502500, and it took less than a second
```

The key word in that code is my. Take it away, and the code takes 22 seconds to run; put it back, and the code runs in less than a second.

Now suppose all of that code is part of a handler, where L is a local variable. You can't take a reference to L, so you'd have to use the trick of making L a script property. Again, there is then no need to say a reference to explicitly; merely referring to the script property is sufficient:

```
on myHandler( )
    set L to {}
    script myScript
        property refL : L
    end script
    set total to 0
    set bignum to 5000
    repeat with i from 1 to bignum
        set end of L to i
    end repeat
    repeat with i from 1 to bignum
        set total to total + (item i of myScript's refL)
    end repeat
    return total
end myHandler
myHandler( ) -- 12502500, and it took less than a second
```

I have no clear explanation for this behavior. It appears that when you access a property of a list by simply using the name of a variable whose value is that list, AppleScript substitutes a copy of the literal value of the list; all that copying takes time when the list is large and there are many repetitions. Whatever the cause, complaints by users that AppleScript is slow are often attributable to a failure to use these techniques.

Record

A *record* is an unordered collection of name–value pairs. The values may be of any type. A literal record looks like a literal list except that each item has a name. The name is separated from the corresponding value with a colon. So:

```
set R to {who:"Matt", town:"Ojai"}
```

There is no such thing as an empty record. A record has no `item` elements, its items cannot be referred to by index number, and you can't talk about the `beginning` or `end` of a record.

You can assign a record of values to a literal record of variable names or other references as a shorthand for performing multiple assignment. The assignments are performed pairwise by name, independently. If the record of values includes names that aren't in the record of variables, the extra values are ignored; if it's missing any names that are in the record of variables, there's a runtime error. See "Assignment and Retrieval" in Chapter 7 and "List," earlier in this chapter. For example:

```
local who, town
set {who:who, town:town} to {town:"Ojai", who:"Matt"}
{who, town} -- {"Matt", "Ojai"}
```

When you use set (as opposed to copy) to set a variable to a value which is a record, you set the variable *by reference*. This means that the record is not copied; the variable's name becomes a new name for the record, in addition to any names for the record that may already exist. The same is true when a record is passed as a parameter to a handler. This special treatment is in common between lists, records, dates, and script objects. (See "Pass By Reference" in Chapter 8 and "Set By Reference" in Chapter 9.)

For example:

```
set R2 to {who:"Matt", town:"Ojai"}
set R1 to R2
set who of R2 to "Jaime"
R1 -- {who:"Jaime", town:"Ojai"}
```

In an existing record, you can replace the value of individual items by assigning to an item of a record using a name that already exists in that record. But if you wish to create an item with a name that doesn't already exist in that record, you must make a new record using concatenation. So:

```
set R to {who:"Matt", town:"Ojai"}
set who of R to "Jaime"
R -- {who:"Jaime", town:"Ojai"}
set R to R & {friend:"Steve"}
R -- {who:"Jaime", town:"Ojai", friend:"Steve"}
```

There is no penalty for concatenating an item with a name that already exists in a record, but it has no effect. For example:

```
set R to {who:"Matt", town:"Ojai"} & {who:"Jaime"}
R -- {who:"Matt", town:"Ojai"}
```

Clearly, order is all-important here, and you can use this fact to your advantage. Suppose you want to assign a friend value within a record. If the record already has such an item, you can do it by assignment. If it doesn't, you can do it by concatenation. But what if you don't know whether it has such an item or not? You can do it regardless by concatenating in the opposite order:

```
set R to {who:"Jaime", town:"Ojai"}
set R to {friend:"Steve"} & R
R -- {friend:"Steve", who:"Jaime", town:"Ojai"}

set R to {who:"Jaime", town:"Ojai", friend:"Matt"}
set R to {friend:"Steve"} & R
R -- {friend:"Steve", who:"Jaime", town:"Ojai"}
```

A record can recurse, for the same reason that a list can:

```
set R to {who:"Matt", town:"Ojai", cycle:null}
set cycle of R to R
R -- {who:"Matt", town:"Ojai", cycle:{who:"Matt", town:"Ojai", cycle:...}}
```

You can make records mutually recurse; you can even make a list and record that mutually recurse. Does anyone have an aspirin?

Record Properties

The following are the properties of a record:

length
> The number of items in the record. This property is read-only. You can get the same information by sending the record the count message.

The names of the items
> Every name of every item is a property of the record.

Please pretend now that I'm jumping up and down, waving a big red flag and screaming as I repeat, for emphasis: *the names of a record's items are properties*. The names are not strings; the names are not any kind of variable or value. They are effectively tokens created by AppleScript at compile-time, like the names of variables.

When you talk to a record, it is the target, and its item names are used to interpret the vocabulary you use. The first thing AppleScript does is look to see whether any of this vocabulary is the name of an item of the record. That's why you can't assign to a nonexistent item in a record—the name you're using for that item is meaningless. No terminological confusion normally arises, because the context is clear. So:

```
set town to "Ojai"
set R to {name:"Matt", town:null}
set town of R to town -- no problem
```

Of course, you can confuse AppleScript if you set your mind to it. This code just sets the existing value of the variable town to itself; the record is untouched:

```
set town to "Ojai"
set R to {name:"Matt", town:null}
tell R
    set town to town
end tell
R -- {name:"Matt", town:null}
```

But you know how to fix that—right?

```
set town to "Ojai"
set R to {name:"Matt", town:null}
tell R
    set its town to town
end tell
R -- {name:"Matt", town:"Ojai"}
```

There is no good way to obtain a list of the names of the items of a record. A record has no such introspective abilities. You (a human being) can see the names of the items of a record in AppleScript's display of the record's value. But your code can't see this information; the names of the items are not values of any kind, and cannot easily be turned into values. I have seen many elaborate attempts to work around this problem, but I'm not going to show you any of them. This is a big shortcoming of AppleScript itself, and it needs to be fixed on the level of AppleScript itself.

It is possible to fetch or assign to the value of an item of a record using a variable to represent the name, through a second level of evaluation. Here's a way to fetch an item's value:

```
global r
set r to {nam:"Matt", age:"49"}
on getWhat(what)
    set s to "on run {r}" & return
    set s to s & "get " & what & " of r" & return
    set s to s & "end"
    run script s with parameters {r}
end getWhat
getWhat("age")
```

It's a pity that such trickery is needed, and I don't really recommend this approach. See also "List Coercions" in the next chapter.

Coercions

A *coercion* is a conversion of a value of one datatype to a value of another datatype. This definition implies that there is some sort of equivalence or formula that determines the new value given the old value. In AppleScript, not just any old value can be turned into a value of just any old datatype. This chapter describes how coercions are performed and what coercions are possible.

Implicit Coercion

When you supply a value where a value of another datatype is expected, AppleScript may coerce silently if possible. This is called *implicit coercion*, and it takes place in connection with AppleScript's operators. These operators have definite rules about what datatypes they expect, and what implicit coercions they will perform if other datatypes are provided. Details appear in Chapter 15.

No implicit coercion takes place when assigning a value to a variable, because variables have no declared datatype; the variable simply adopts the new value.

No implicit coercion takes place when passing a parameter, because handlers and commands do not provide prototypes specifying a particular datatype. This is not to say that a handler or command cannot itself perform a coercion if it receives one datatype and prefers another. It can. But then the coercion is not necessarily implicit, and it isn't necessarily being performed by AppleScript.

For example, suppose you say this:

```
tell application "Finder"
    set name of folder 1 to 6
    -- error: "Can't make some data into the expected type."
end tell
```

The Finder's dictionary says very plainly what the Finder expects as the name of a folder—it expects Unicode text. But AppleScript does not look at the dictionary and then perform an implicit coercion; it just sends the Finder what you said to send it. It is then up to the Finder to decide whether it's happy with what was sent. In this particular case, the Finder is not happy, and it lets you know with an error.

Now suppose you say this:

```
tell application "Finder"
    set name of folder 1 to "6"
end tell
```

Now the Finder happily performs a coercion, and you never hear about it. The Finder expects Unicode text, and you sent a string. The Finder coerces the string to Unicode text, so the difference is never evident to you; it's all handled transparently.

An application's dictionary doesn't necessarily say what implicit coercions the application will perform. The Finder's dictionary didn't say, "I'd like Unicode text but I'll accept a string, and no numbers, please"; it said "Unicode text," period. Typically, to find out whether an application will accept a datatype other than what its dictionary specifies, you just have to try it and see ("Coercions" in Chapter 19).

Handlers that you write are not protected by any mechanism such as prototypes or datatype declarations in their definition from receiving parameters with undesirable datatypes. If your handler has reason to be choosy about what sorts of values it's willing to accept, then it needs to test those values and respond accordingly. For example:

```
on sendMeAString(s)
    if {class of s} is not in {string, Unicode text} then
        error "Can't make some data into the expected type."
    end if
    …
end sendMeAString
```

Explicit Coercion

Explicit coercion is performed with the as operator.

---

as   coercion

Syntax

value as *class*

Description

When you use the as operator, you're asking AppleScript to perform the coercion. If this is a coercion AppleScript is willing to perform (as described in the rest of this chapter), the result is a new value of the requested datatype. If not, there's a runtime error.

Examples

```
9 as string -- "9"
9 as boolean -- error
```

Even though a variable's value can be a class, you can't use a variable as the second operand in a coercion. This won't even compile:

```
set className to string
9 as className -- compile-time error
```

AppleScript must see a class name right there in the script at compile time, or it won't parse the line. (I regard this as a bug.)

Do not confuse a coercion with an object string specifier! (See "Object String Specifier" in Chapter 10.) This is a coercion:

```
"xxx:" as alias
```

This is an object string specifier:

```
alias "xxx:"
```

The distinction can be crucial. There are circumstances where the coercion will compile but the object specifier will not. You can't compile an alias specifier unless the file exists; but you can compile a coercion from a string to an alias, because the string is just a string. And there are circumstances where the object string specifier will compile but the coercion will not. You can form a file specifier using a pathname string, but you can't coerce anything, not even a pathname string, to a file object.

A special case of coercion arises when you say as in the context of a get, implicit or explicit, targeted at an application. When you do this, you are *not* using the as operator. You are using the get...as command, which is a very different thing. The as operator asks AppleScript to perform the coercion. The get...as command asks the target to return a particular class of value; in effect, you're asking the target to perform the coercion.

---

get...as   coercion by target

Syntax
[get] *attribute* as *class*

Example
```
tell application "Finder"
    folder 1 as string
end tell
```

An application may be willing to perform coercions of which AppleScript itself would be incapable. The preceding example demonstrates this. AppleScript itself can't coerce a folder to a string. It doesn't even know what a folder is. This is a request targeted entirely at the Finder, and it says: "Get folder 1, but please return a string as the result." It happens that the Finder has a way to do this, so it complies with this request—it returns the pathname of the folder.

You can be using the get...as command without realizing it if you become confused about who the target is. For example:

```
tell application "Finder"
    set f to folder 1
end tell
f as string
```

That looks like it shouldn't work. Having retrieved folder 1, we are no longer talking to the Finder. So when we try to coerce this folder to a string, we will be talking to AppleScript, and AppleScript won't know how to do it. Right? Wrong. The variable f isn't just a folder; it's a reference to a folder, a folder belonging to the Finder. (If this isn't clear to you, you should reread Chapter 11.)

```
tell application "Finder"
    set f to folder 1
end tell
f -- folder "myFolder" of desktop of application "Finder"
```

Therefore it's a complete and valid target. So when you say:

```
f as string
```

you're actually saying:

```
tell application "Finder"
    get (folder "myFolder" of desktop) as string
end tell
```

The target is the Finder and the get...as command is sent to the Finder.

If you ask an application to perform a coercion it isn't willing to perform, you'll receive the compulsory mysterious error message from the application:

```
tell application "Finder"
    set f to folder 1 as folder -- error: "Unknown object type."
end tell
```

Again, you usually have no way of knowing in advance what coercions an application is willing to perform for you, or what the rules of those coercions may be. The application's dictionary doesn't tell you. You just have to find out by experimentation.

Boolean Coercions

A boolean may be coerced to a string; depending on whether the boolean is true or false, this string will be either "true" or "false". A string may be coerced to a boolean. The string "true" (not case-sensitive) will be true; any other string will be false.

A boolean may be coerced to an integer; depending on whether the boolean is true or false, this integer will be either 1 or 0. The integers 1 and 0 may be coerced to a boolean, yielding true and false respectively; other integers can't be coerced to a boolean.

String, Number and Date Coercions

A class or enumerator may be coerced to a string; for example:

```
string as string -- "string"
```

A number may be coerced to a string. A string may be coerced to a number, provided it looks like a literal number; whitespace will be ignored, but nothing else will be. So for example "1a" can't be coerced to a number. But the empty string, or a string consisting solely of whitespace, will be coerced to 0.

An integer may be coerced to a real. A real may be coerced to an integer; it is rounded to the nearest integer. This is a new feature; in earlier versions of Apple-Script, a real could be coerced to an integer only if it *was* an integer. For example, 1.5 couldn't be coerced to an integer. The round scripting addition command can help here (see "Numbers and Dates" in Chapter 20), and can be used to dictate the desired rounding behavior.

A date may be coerced to a string; this is simply the string that appears in the literal date specifier after compilation. A string may be used to form a date specifier, but it cannot be coerced to a date. A month may be coerced to a string (because it is a class). A month may also be coerced to an integer; this is a new feature.

A string, Unicode text, and styled text may be coerced to one another. When coercing to a string, you can say as text instead of as string. This is confusing, since the class of the result is still string, and text is actually the name of a completely different class (string is 'TEXT', text is 'ctxt').

File Coercions

An alias can be coerced to a string representing its Macintosh pathname, and its POSIX path property is a string representing its POSIX pathname. An alias cannot be coerced to a file object, but a string can be used as an intermediary. A Macintosh pathname can be coerced to an alias. A file object cannot be coerced to a string, but it can be coerced to an alias (which can be coerced to a string). A file's POSIX path property is a string representing its POSIX pathname. A POSIX file can be coerced to a string representing its Macintosh pathname. A Macintosh pathname can be used to form a file specifier. A POSIX pathname can be used to form a POSIX file specifier. (I'm not making this up!)

I believe that the possibilities are summed up by the following code:

```
set colonPath to "main:reason:resources:"
set a to alias colonPath
set a to colonPath as alias
set colonPath to a as string
set posixPath to POSIX path of a
set f to a reference to file colonPath
```

```
set a to f as alias
set posixPath to POSIX path of f
set pf to POSIX file posixPath
set colonPath to pf as string
set posixPath to POSIX path of pf
set a to pf as alias
```

Just to make matters more confusing, coercion of a file specifier to an alias fails in the current Script Editor. To work around this, pass through a POSIX file:

```
set colonPath to "main:reason:resources:"
set f to a reference to file colonPath
set posixPath to POSIX path of f
set pf to POSIX file posixPath
set a to posixFile as alias
```

List Coercions

Anything may be coerced to a list, and will be treated as follows:

- If the thing you start with is not a collection, the result is a list of one item, and that item is the thing you started with.
- If the thing you start with is a list, the result is the very same list.
- If the thing you start with is a record, the result is a list of the values from the record.

Coercion to a list is very useful for making sure you have a list: if the thing you start with isn't a list, it becomes one, and if it is a list, it is unchanged.

Officially you can't coerce a list to a record, but there's a trick for doing it using a second level of evaluation. (Reread the warnings at "Second-Level Evaluation" in Chapter 12 before resorting to this trick; remember, it involves a lot of overhead.) Every odd item of the list becomes the name of the record item whose value is the corresponding even item of the list:

```
on listToRecord(L)
    script myScript
        return {«class usrf»:L}
    end script
    return run script myScript
end listToRecord
listToRecord({"yoho", "haha", "teehee", "giggle"})
-- {yoho:"haha", teehee:"giggle"}
```

A list of one item may be coerced to the datatype of that item, and the result will be that item. Of course, the result can then be coerced to any datatype that it can be coerced to, so you can also coerce a list of one item to that datatype in a single step. For example:

```
{true} as string -- "true"
```

That's possible because the list of one boolean is first coerced to boolean, and a boolean can be coerced to a string.

A list of multiple items may be coerced to a string, provided every individual item may be coerced to a string. This coercion is performed using the current value of the text item delimiters. (See "String" in Chapter 13.) The rule is that every item of the list is coerced to a string, and the resulting strings are joined into a single string with the text item delimiters value between each pair. The text item delimiters value can be the empty string; this is in fact its default value. If an item of the list is a list, it is coerced to a string by the same rule; so this coercion in effect flattens a list, to any depth, into a single string.

So, assuming the text item delimiters is the empty string:

```
{"Manny", {"Moe", "Jack"}} as string -- "MannyMoeJack"
```

Or, assuming the text item delimiters is a comma followed by a space:

```
{"Manny", {"Moe", "Jack"}} as string -- "Manny, Moe, Jack"
```

 A list can be implicitly coerced to a string. (See Chapter 15 for the situations in which this can occur.) Because the coercion is implicit, it can happen without your realizing it will happen; this means that the text item delimiters can be used without your expecting it. Therefore it is best not to leave the text item delimiters in a nonstandard state.

Also, bear in mind that the text item delimiters has a second use, namely to split a string into its text item elements ("String" in Chapter 13); a change in the value of the text item delimiters made for that purpose will affect any subsequent list-to-string coercions, and vice versa.

Unit Conversions

AppleScript provides a number of classes whose sole purpose is to allow you to perform measurement unit conversions. They are implemented as classes so that you can use the as operator to perform the conversion; that is, the conversion is really a coercion.

Because of this implementation, the way you have to speak in order to perform a conversion ends up looking fairly silly. You can't say 3 feet; you have to coerce 3 (a number) to the feet class, by saying 3 as feet. Now you coerce to the desired class; suppose this is yards. But now you have a value of the yards class. You can't do anything with it, so you have to coerce it to a number.

So, for example:

```
on feetToYards(ft)
    return ft as feet as yards as number
end feetToYards
feetToYards(3) -- 1.0
```

The implemented units are themselves a mixed lot. Many important units, such as acres and hectares, aren't implemented at all. Table 14-1 provides a list.

Table 14-1. Conversion unit classes

meters	inches	feet	yards
miles	kilometers	centimeters	square meters
square feet	square yards	square miles	square kilometers
liters	gallons	quarts	cubic meters
cubic centimeters	cubic feet	cubic inches	cubic yards
kilograms	grams	ounces	pounds
degrees Celsius	degrees Fahrenheit	degrees Kelvin	

A much better list of conversion units is built into Mac OS X by way of the Unix tool units. Here's a way to use it:

```
on convert(val, unit1, unit2)
    set text item delimiters to " "
    set conv to do shell script {"units", unit1, unit2} as string
    return val * (word 1 of paragraph 1 of conv as real)
end convert
convert(4, "feet", "meters") -- 1.2192
```

CHAPTER 15
Operators

An *operator* is a token that transforms a value or a pair of values into a new value. These transformations are *operations*, and the values operated upon are the *operands*. An operator with two operands is *binary*; an operator with one operand is *unary*.

That definition is pretty good, but it doesn't quite pick out what this chapter catalogues. Parentheses are also discussed here, because they determine the effects of the other operators; and some of the things I'm calling operators are thought of by AppleScript as language keywords. (For the coercion operator, as, see "Explicit Coercion" in Chapter 14; for the object containment operator, of, see Chapter 10.)

Binary operators can perform a limited range of implicit coercions. AppleScript's behavior in this regard is odd, and the error messages that result when a binary operator refuses to perform an implicit coercion are confusing. For example, if you say:

```
1 and 1 -- compile-time error
```

the compile-time error message says: "Can't make 1 into a boolean." But AppleScript *can* make 1 into a boolean, as you can prove by asking it to do so:

```
1 as boolean and 1 -- true
```

In that example, AppleScript refuses to coerce the first operand implicitly, but it happily coerces the second operand implicitly. But in this next example, AppleScript happily coerces both operands implicitly (to a number):

```
"3" + "4" -- 7
```

This chapter catalogues the rules governing this behavior. To learn what can be coerced to what in AppleScript, see Chapter 14.

Arithmetic Operators

As in most computer languages, multiplication and division take precedence over addition and subtraction (in the absence of parentheses). So, for example:

```
3 + 4 * 2 -- 11
3 * 4 + 2 -- 14
```

An operand that is a list consisting of one number will be coerced to a number. An operand that is a string, or a list consisting of one string, will be coerced to a number if possible.

+ addition

Syntax

```
number1 + number2
date + integer
```

Description

The addition operator is not overloaded to perform string concatenation; see on the ampersand operator (&) later in this chapter. A date plus an integer yields *date* increased by *integer* seconds.

The result is an integer if the first operand is an integer and if the second operand can be coerced to an integer without loss of information. Otherwise, the result is a real.

− subtraction; unary negation

Syntax

```
number1 - number2
date - integer
date - date
-number
```

Description

A date minus an integer yields *date* decreased by *integer* seconds. A date minus a date yields an integer, the number of seconds between them. For two numbers, see on addition (+).

Unary negation has very high precedence.

Example

```
-3 ^ 2 -- 9
```

---

* multiplication

Syntax

```
number * number
```

Description

For the class of the result, see on addition (+).

/ real division

Syntax

```
number1 / number2
```

Description

Both numbers are treated as reals, and the result is a real.

---

div

Syntax

number1 div *number2*

Description

Both numbers are treated as reals; the first is divided by the second, and the result is coerced to an integer by throwing away its fractional part. Notice that this is *not* the same as AppleScript's normal real-to-integer coercion behavior.

Example

```
4 div 5 -- 0
(4 / 5) as integer -- 1
```

mod

Syntax

number1 mod *number1*

Description

The first operand is divided by the absolute value of the second and the remainder is returned. For the class of the result, see on addition (+).

^

Syntax

number1 ^ *number2*

Description

Raises the first number to the power of the second. The result is a real.

Do not blame AppleScript for the phenomena inherent in doing floating-point arithmetic in any language on any computer. It is the nature of computer numerics that most values can only be approximated. Modern processors are extraordinarily clever about compensating, but rounding operations can easily expose the truth:

```
2.32 * 100.0 div 1 -- 231
```

Similarly, there may be situations where instead of comparing two values for absolute equality you will do better to test whether the difference between them lies within some acceptable small epsilon.

Boolean Operators

The second operand, but not the first, will be coerced from a string or an integer, or a list of one string or one integer, to a boolean. Either operand will be coerced from a list of one boolean to a boolean.

---

and

Syntax

boolean1 and *boolean2*

Description

Returns true if both operands are true. If the first operand is false, the second operand won't even be evaluated ("short-circuiting").

or

Syntax

boolean1 or *boolean2*

Description

Returns false if both operands are false. If the first operand is true, the second operand won't even be evaluated ("short-circuiting").

not

Syntax

not *boolean*

Description

Changes true to false and false to true.

Comparison Operators

The result is a boolean. The nature of comparisons involving strings can be influenced by a considering clause; see Chapter 12.

Lists are ordered, but records are not:

```
{1, 2} = {2, 1} -- false
{name:"Matt", age:"49"} = {age:"49", name:"Matt"} -- true
```

The equality (=) and inequality (≠) operators do *not* coerce their operands; operands may be of any datatype, and operands of different datatypes are unequal. So, for example:

```
{"2"} = 2 -- false
```

The first operand is a list; the second operand is a number; no coercion takes place; therefore the operands are not equal, and the comparison is false.

With the other comparison operators, operands must be a string, a number, or a date; the first operator is coerced to a string, a number, or a date, and then the second operator is coerced to match the datatype of the first:

```
{"2"} ≥ 2 -- true
```

The first operand is a list of one string, so it is coerced to a string. Now the second operand is coerced to a string; the two strings are equal and the comparison is true.

Thus, although you cannot use the equality operator to learn whether two values would be equal if implicitly coerced to the same datatype, you can work around the problem like this:

```
{"2"} ≤ 2 and {"2"} ≥ 2
```

= (is) equality

Syntax

operand1 = *operand2*

Description

No coercion is performed; operands of different datatypes are not equal. Synonym is equal to has abbreviations equal, equals, and equal to.

 This operator is not overloaded as an assignment operator; see "Assignment and Retrieval" in Chapter 7. It is not an error for a line of AppleScript code to consist of an equality comparison, like this:

```
x = 3
```

That line is an equality comparison, not an assignment! If you write a line like that, intending to write an assignment, your code will generate incorrect results that can be difficult to track down.

≠ (is not) inequality

Syntax

operand1 ≠ *operand2*

Description

No coercion is performed; operands of different datatypes are not equal. The not-equals sign is typed using Option-=. is not has abbreviation isn't. Synonym is not equal to has abbreviations is not equal, isn't equal, does not equal, and doesn't equal. There are no synonyms <> or !=.

< less than

Syntax

operand1 < *operand2*

Description

Synonyms are is less than (abbreviation less than) and comes before.

> greater than

Syntax

operand1 > *operand2*

Description

Synonyms are is greater than (abbreviation greater than) and comes after.

≤ less than or equal to

Syntax

operand1 ≤ *operand2*

Description

Abbreviation is <=, or the ≤ symbol may be typed using Option-comma. Synonym is less than or equal to has abbreviations omitting is, to, or both. There are also synonyms does not come after and is not greater than.

≥ greater than or equal to

Syntax

operand1 ≥ *operand2*

Description

Abbreviation is >=, or the ≥ symbol may be typed using Option-period. Synonym is greater than or equal to has abbreviations omitting is, to, or both. There are also synonyms does not come before and is not less than.

Containment Operators

Containment may apply to two strings, two lists, or two records. The result is a boolean. Containment implies comparison, and the nature of comparisons involving strings can be influenced by a considering clause; see Chapter 12.

The fact that in the case of list containment both operands must be lists is a little counterintuitive at first. Thus:

    {1, 2} contains {2} -- **true**

You might have expected to say:

    {1, 2} contains 2 -- **true**

You can say that, but only because 2 is coerced to {2} implicitly. In other words, the second operand is not an *element*; it's a *sublist*. Thus you can ask about more than one element at once. For example:

    {1, 2, 3} contains {2, 3} -- **true**

Lists are ordered, so the items of the sublist you ask about must appear consecutively and in the same order in the target list; these are false:

```
{1, 2, 3} contains {1, 3} -- false
{1, 2, 3} contains {3, 2} -- false
```

Since lists can contain lists, you may have to use an explicit extra level to say what you mean:

```
{{1}, {2}} contains {2} -- false
{{1}, {2}} contains {{2}} -- true
```

The first is false because 2 is not an element of the first list, and {2} is not going to be coerced to {{2}} for you—it's a list already so there's nothing to coerce.

In the case of record containment, both the label and the value must match for containment to be true. So:

```
{name:"Matt", age:"49"} contains {name:"Matt"} -- true
{name:"Matt", age:"49"} contains {title:"Matt"} -- false
{name:"Matt", age:"49"} contains {name:"Socrates"} -- false
```

Records are not ordered:

```
{name:"Matt", age:"49"} contains {age:"49", name:"Matt"} -- true
```

Since the containment operators are overloaded to apply to both strings and lists, the first operand is never implicitly coerced to a string, because AppleScript can't know that this is what you mean; it is coerced to a list unless it is a string. The second operand is then coerced to match the datatype of the first.

So, for example:

```
"49" contains 4 -- true; string containment, "49" contains "4"
49 contains 4 -- false; list containment, {49} doesn't contain {4}
```

It's important not to confuse the implicit coercion rules here with those for certain other operators. For example, your experience with arithmetic operators might lead you to expect a certain kind of implicit coercion:

```
{"7"} * 7 -- 49
```

The list of a single string is coerced to a single string and from there to a number. But that isn't going to happen with contains:

```
{"7"} contains 7 -- false
```

The first operand isn't coerced at all; the second operand is coerced to {7}, and that's the end. The second operand isn't a sublist of the first, so the comparison is false.

---

contains, does not contain, is in, is not in   containment

Syntax

```
string1 contains string2
string2 is in string1
list1 contains list2
```

list2 is in *list1*
record1 contains *record2*
record2 is in *record1*

Description

The is in synonyms reverse the operand order of the contains synonyms—that is, with is in, the second operand comes before the first operand (as deliberately shown in the syntax listings). This is relevant in the rules for implicit coercions.

---

begins with   initial containment

Syntax

string1 begins with *string2*
list1 begins with *list2*

Description

Same as contains with the additional requirement that the second operand come first in the first operand. Records are not ordered, so they aren't eligible operands. Synonym is starts with.

---

ends with   final containment

Syntax

string1 ends with *string2*
list1 ends with *list2*

Description

Same as contains with the additional requirement that the second operand come last in the first operand. Records are not ordered, so they aren't eligible operands.

Concatenation Operator

Concatenation may be performed on a pair of strings (resulting in a string), a pair of lists (resulting in a list), or a pair of records (resulting in a record). Implicit coercions are performed in exactly the same way as for the containment operators; see "Containment Operators," just previously.

So, for example:

```
"three" & 20 -- "three20"
3 & "twenty" -- {3, "twenty"}
```

This shows the difference the order of operands can make; the reason is perfectly obvious if you know the implicit coercion rules, baffling otherwise.

To turn string concatenation into list concatenation, it suffices to coerce the first operand to a list; this can be done simply by expressing it in list delimiters. So:

```
{"Mannie"} & "Moe" & "Jack" -- {"Mannie", "Moe", "Jack"}
```

Without the list delimiters, we'd end up with "MannieMoeJack".

Recall (from Chapter 14) that coercion of a list to a string is another way to concatenate. Thus concatenation of a string and a list concatenates the string with all the elements of the list, each coerced to a string and joined by the text item delimiters:

```
set text item delimiters to ""
"butter" & {"field", 8} -- "butterfield8"
```

Recall what was said in the previous section about both operands having to be of the same type, and what this implies for lists. Concatenation is a way to append one or more items to a list:

```
{1, 2, 3} & {4, 5, 6} -- {1, 2, 3, 4, 5, 6}
```

The result is not {1, 2, 3, {4, 5, 6}}; if that's what you wanted, you can use an extra level of list delimiters:

```
{1, 2, 3} & {{4, 5, 6}}
```

Recall (from Chapter 13) that a more efficient way to append a single element to a list is like this:

```
set L to {1, 2, 3}
set end of L to 4 -- {1, 2, 3, 4}
```

The operation set end of is more efficient than the concatenation operator for lists, and coercion of a list to a string is more efficient than the concatenation operator for strings, because no extra copies have to be made internally. So, instead of this:

```
set s to "anti"
set s to s & "dis"
set s to s & "establishment"
set s to s & "arianism"
```

it is more efficient to say this:

```
set text item delimiters to ""
set L to {}
set end of L to "anti"
set end of L to "dis"
set end of L to "establishment"
set end of L to "arianism"
set s to L as string
```

Concatenating records yields a record consisting of all the items of the first record along with just those items of the second record whose name isn't the name of any item in the first record (see Chapter 13):

```
set r to {who:"Jaime", town:"Ojai"} & {who:"Matt", friend:"Steve"}
r -- {who:"Jaime", town:"Ojai", friend:"Steve"}
```

Scripting additions can provide further interesting variations on the notion of concatenation. For example, the Satimage scripting addition's special concat command concatenates lists from items with the same name in different records:

```
special concat {who:{"Matt"}} with {who:{"Neuburg"}}
-- {who:{"Matt", "Neuburg"}}
```

Syntax

string1 & *string2*
list1 & *list2*
record1 & *record2*

Description

The result is a string, list, or record respectively.

Parentheses

Parentheses may be used to determine the order of operations at runtime:

```
3 + 4 * 2 -- 11
(3 + 4) * 2 -- 14
```

Parentheses can also help determine the order of interpretation of vocabulary at compile time. Thus they can make the difference between successful compilation and failed compilation. For example, this compiles fine, because all the expressions are legal:

```
set r to random number
round r rounding up
```

Now try to save a line by combining them:

```
round random number rounding up -- compile-time error
```

The problem is that random number is a command that can optionally take various labeled parameters, and rounding up isn't one of them. Instead of rethinking its interpretation ("So, maybe random number isn't taking any parameters here!"), AppleScript just gives up. You have to help it out, by using parentheses:

```
round (random number) rounding up
```

Sometimes AppleScript will insert parentheses for you, on compilation. For example, I didn't put any parentheses when I typed this code:

```
tell application "System Events"
    copy name of every process where it is frontmost to theProc
end tell
```

But AppleScript did, when it compiled:

```
tell application "System Events"
    copy (name of every process where it is frontmost) to theProc
end tell
```

The reason seems to be to delimit a phrase implying a get command. But if you actually use get explicitly here without parentheses, AppleScript refuses to compile at all:

```
tell application "System Events"
    copy get name of every process where it is frontmost to theProc -- compile error
end tell
```

The problem seems to be that AppleScript doesn't like the phrase copy get, which is two commands in a row. If you add the parentheses, AppleScript compiles:

```
tell application "System Events"
    copy (get name of every process where it is frontmost) to theProc
end tell
```

Parentheses can also make a difference at runtime. AppleScript will compile this, but it causes an error at runtime:

```
tell application "System Events"
    set L to name of every process
    the frontmost of process item 1 of L -- error
end tell
```

This runs fine:

```
tell application "System Events"
    set L to name of every process
    the frontmost of process (item 1 of L)
end tell
```

The moral is: if things don't seem to be working out, try playing with parentheses.

Who Performs an Operation

Some operations within an interapplication communications context can be performed by the target application rather than AppleScript. There are two cases to consider. The operation may appear as a bare expression (for example, the condition in an if clause); I will call this a *direct operation*. Or, the operation may be part of a boolean test element specifier.

Direct Operations

According to Apple's documentation, if the first operand of a direct operation is a reference to an object of the target application, the target application performs the operation. So, for example:

```
tell application "Finder"
    if the name of folder 1 contains "e" then
```

The comparison performed by the keyword contains is one of the operations that can be performed by the target application. The object the name of folder 1 is a Finder object, so in this case the Finder should perform the operation. In fact, though, experimentation shows that the Finder does *not* perform the operation; AppleScript does try to get it to do so, but the target application replies with an error indicating that it doesn't wish to perform that sort of operation. AppleScript thereupon adopts a new strategy: it asks the target application for the values in question, and performs the operation itself.

So, the way AppleScript first tries to deal with the operation in the previous example is by sending the Finder a single Apple event that means: "Please tell me whether the name of your folder 1 contains "e"." The Finder replies with an error message, so then AppleScript goes back to the Finder and sends it another Apple event that means: "Okay, never mind that, just tell me the name of your folder 1." The Finder complies, and now AppleScript looks, itself, to see whether the result contains "e".

This approach seems wasteful, but it is only wasteful the first time. The second time the same sort of code is encountered, the AppleScript scripting component remembers that the Finder doesn't do this sort of operation, and skips the first step; it just asks the Finder for the value of the operand and does the operation itself.

In fact, I have not found *any* application that appears willing to perform direct operations when AppleScript asks it to! The entire matter is therefore moot. One can see, all the same, that the mechanism is a good idea. Suppose both operands are objects belonging to the target application; for example, we might want the Finder to perform this comparison:

```
tell application "Finder"
    if the name of folder 1 is the name of folder 2 then
```

It would be efficient to be able to send the Finder a single Apple event saying: "Please tell me whether the name of folder 1 and the name of folder 2 are the same." As it is, AppleScript ends up sending the Finder two Apple events: one asking for the name of folder 1, the second asking for the name of folder 2. It then performs the comparison itself.

Boolean Test Element Specifiers

In a boolean test element specifier (see Chapter 10), the target application *always* performs the comparison itself. For example:

```
tell application "Finder"
    name of every folder whose name contains "E"
end tell
```

That is a single Apple event; the Apple event includes instructions to use contains "E" as the criterion for returning folder names, so the Finder must implement contains in order to obey.

Differences between an application's implementation of an operator and AppleScript's implementation can arise under these circumstances. This seems rather scary, but if the application is well-behaved, these differences should be minor. The primary case in point is the use of considering clauses. For example:

```
tell application "Finder"
    considering case
        name of every folder whose name contains "E"
    end considering
end tell
-- {"emptyFolder", "Test Me"}
```

The Finder gives the wrong answer; if you consider case, neither of these folder names contains "E". The Finder is simply ignoring the considering clause. In fact, I don't know of *any* application that considers considering clauses in a string comparison. See "String Considerations" in Chapter 12.

The workaround in a situation like this is to take a two-step approach: fetch all the values and then have AppleScript perform the test itself. AppleScript does not implement boolean test element specifiers for lists, so the test must be performed as a loop. So:

```
tell application "Finder"
    set L to name of every folder
end tell
set L2 to {}
considering case
    repeat with aName in L
        if aName contains "E" then
            set end of L2 to contents of aName
        end if
    end repeat
end considering
```

After that, L2 contains the right answer.

CHAPTER 16

Global Properties

This chapter catalogues the global script properties of the AppleScript language. These are implemented by the AppleScript scripting component, which is present as the parent of the top-level script (see "The Implicit Parent Chain" in Chapter 9). They are globally accessible, as if your entire script started with property declarations for them. In case of a naming conflict, they can also be accessed like the properties of any visible script object, using the term AppleScript as the script object's name. For example:

```
property pi : 3
display dialog AppleScript's pi -- 3.141592...
```

These are script properties like any other script properties, and as such:

- They are settable.
- Their values are in common to all scripts running under this instance of the AppleScript scripting component.
- They persist for as long as this instance of the AppleScript scripting component persists.

The status of the global script properties is thus somewhat counterintuitive. You can accidentally (or intentionally) change their values, and then scripts that rely upon them to have their default values will not work. You would probably have expected things like pi and tab to remain constant. That's not the case—you can change their values—and furthermore if you change such a value in one script in a script editor application, the new value affects all scripts run in that script editor application, until you quit the application.

Strings

return   "\r"

Description

Macintosh line break character. There does not seem to be any conflict with the keyword return ("Returned Value" in Chapter 8). The only place where a conflict could occur is when return is the first word of a line. The rule in that situation seems to be that if return is followed by an operator, it can't be the keyword, so it must be this property.

Example

```
"This is a line." & return & "This is another line."
```

tab   "\t"

Description

Tab character.

Example

```
"an item" & tab & "another item"
```

space   " "

Description

Space character.

Example

```
"word" & space & "otherWord"
```

text item delimiters   "" (the empty string)

Description

The text item delimiters has two uses. It is used to split a string into its text item elements ("String" in Chapter 13). And it is used to join list items when a list is coerced to a string ("List Coercions" in Chapter 14, and please reread the warning there).

Example

```
set text item delimiters to ":"
text item 1 of (path to system folder as string)
```

Numbers

The minutes property and its ilk are intended to help you convert to seconds. This is because date arithmetic uses seconds ("Date" in Chapter 13 and "Arithmetic Operators" in Chapter 15).

---

pi   3.14159265359

Description

The ratio of a circle's circumference to its diameter.

Example

```
set area to pi * (radius ^ 2)
```

---

minutes   60

Description

The number of seconds in a minute.

Example

```
(current date) + 30 * minutes -- half an hour from now
```

---

hours   3600

Description

The number of seconds in an hour.

Example

```
(current date) + 2 * hours -- two hours from now
```

---

days   86400

Description

The number of seconds in a day.

Example

```
(current date) + 2 * days -- two days from now
```

---

weeks   604800

Description

The number of seconds in a week.

Example

```
(current date) + 2 * weeks -- two weeks from now
```

Miscellaneous

version   "1.9.2"

Description

The version of AppleScript. This is actually the name of a class.

Example

```
display dialog AppleScript's version
```

CHAPTER 17

Constants

This chapter catalogues the constants of the AppleScript language. A *constant* is a reserved word representing a value. You cannot set the value of a constant; if you try, you'll get a compile-time error, "Access not allowed." You cannot create a variable whose name is that of a constant; if you try, you'll get a compile-time error, "Expected variable name or property but found application constant or consideration." The datatype (class) of a constant is usually constant; but as we shall see, some of them are a class instead.

The fixed value of a constant will appear to you as the name of the constant. For example, the value of yes is yes; it cannot be reduced to any other form. But a constant is meaningful to AppleScript behind the scenes. Also, a constant can be coerced to a string.

Constants are often implemented as *enumerations*, meaning a set of values any of which may occupy a certain syntactic slot. For example, the replacing clause of a store script command ("Compiled Script Files as Script Objects" in Chapter 9) may consist of any of the constants yes, no, or ask. Nothing stops you from supplying some other value, in which case it is up to the target to decide how it wants to respond. If you say replacing 42 in a store script command, the script will compile and run. If you try to set a date's weekday to yes, the script will compile but not run.

Applications are free to extend AppleScript's vocabulary by implementing constants of their own. For example, GraphicConverter can save an image file in many formats, and it needs a way to let you specify a format; it does this with some four dozen constants, such as PICT, TIFF, GIF, BMP, JPEG, and so forth. An application's dictionary will show you the constants that can be used in any connection with any command—though it probably won't tell you what they mean. See "Enumerations" in Chapter 19.

true, false

Description

Boolean values. See "Boolean" in Chapter 13 and "Boolean Operators" in Chapter 15.

Example

```
open for access f write permission true
```

yes, no, ask

Description

Options when saving a file. For a description of some typical behavior in response to these options, see "Compiled Script Files as Script Objects" in Chapter 9.

Example

```
store script s in f replacing yes
```

missing value

Description

This is actually a class, but it has no values; all you'll ever see is the class itself, so it works as if it were a constant. It seems to be a way for an application to return a value while signaling a nonvalue; it isn't an error, and it isn't a failure to return any value at all.

Example

```
tell application "Finder" to get clipboard -- missing value
```

In that example, the Finder's dictionary implements clipboard but warns that it isn't yet available; getting its value is not an error on the user's part, but the Finder can't comply either, so the Finder needs a way to reply apologetically, and missing value is its solution.

null

Description

Like missing value, this is implemented as a class with no values, and can be used as a placeholder to signal a nonvalue. I've never found a use for it in communicating with a scriptable application, nor have I ever seen an application return it as a result. But I do sometimes use it in my own scripts, as a way of giving a variable or record item a value to prevent it from being undefined (and causing an error), without its having any particular value belonging to a useful class.

Example

```
set aPerson to {name:null, age:null, town:null}
```

plain, bold, italic, outline, shadow, underline, superscript, subscript, strikethrough, small caps, all caps, all lowercase, condensed, expanded, hidden

Description

Text styles, available for use by applications that wish to speak of such things. The example here shows Tex-Edit Plus returning a text style record. (See "Pseudo-Classes" in Chapter 19.) This is a record consisting of two lists, the on styles (those that are applied to a piece of text) and the off styles (those that are not applied to a piece of text). The items of each list are text styles. The piece of text we're asking about here is underlined.

Example

```
tell application "Tex-Edit Plus"
    set tsr to style of word 4 of document 1
    on styles of tsr -- {underline}
end tell
```

case, diacriticals, white space, hyphens, expansion, punctuation

Description

String considerations; see "Considering/Ignoring" in Chapter 12.

Example

```
considering case
    "heyho" contains "H" -- false
end considering
```

application responses

Description

See "Considering/Ignoring" in Chapter 12.

Example

```
ignoring application responses
    tell application "GraphicConverter" to quit
end ignoring
```

current application

Description

The top-level object. See "The Implicit Parent Chain" in Chapter 9.

Example

```
name of current application -- Script Editor
```

Sunday, Monday, Tuesday, Wednesday, Thursday, Friday, Saturday

Description

Days of the week; see "Date Properties" in Chapter 13. These terms are actually implemented as class names (I don't know why).

Example

```
weekday of (current date) -- Wednesday
```

January, February, March, April, May, June, July, August, September, October, November, December

Description

Names of months; see "Date Properties" in Chapter 13. These terms are actually implemented as class names (I don't know why).

Example

```
month of (current date) -- May
```

CHAPTER 18

Commands

A *command* is basically a verb. This chapter catalogues the built-in commands of the AppleScript language—those that have not been described already. AppleScript defines very few verbs of its own, leaving it to other applications to define further commands by way of their dictionaries.

(On how to use a command, see Chapter 10. For set, copy, and get, see "Assignment and Retrieval" in Chapter 7. For run, see "Script Object's Run Handler" in Chapter 9. For error, see "Errors" in Chapter 12. For count, see "String Properties," "List Properties," and "Record Properties" in Chapter 13.)

Application Commands

A few commands may be sent to applications to start them up, bring them to the front, and make them quit. An application does not have to be scriptable to obey them (see Table 19-1 and the discussion there).

launch

Syntax

launch *application*

Description

Makes sure an application is running, without bringing it frontmost or making it perform any actions.

activate

Syntax

activate *application*

Description

Brings an application frontmost.

reopen

Syntax

```
reopen application
```

Description

Tells an application to behave as if it had been opened from the Finder. Some applications behave specially when told to do this. For example, in the case of the Finder, reopen makes a window open if no Finder windows are open at that moment; launch and activate don't.

quit

Syntax

```
quit application
```

Description

Tells an application to quit.

Logging Commands

These commands have to do with the script editor application's logging window or pane. They control the generation of the AppleScript messages that this window or pane is "watching" while it is open.

log

Syntax

```
log value
```

Description

If the event log pane or window is open, writes *value* to the log pane or window. This is useful for debugging. See Chapter 3 for an example.

stop log, start log

Syntax

```
stop log
start log
```

Description

If the event log pane or window is open, disables and enables automatic logging of Apple events sent between applications; has no effect on the log command.

Only the old version of Script Editor (version 1.9), and Script Debugger, implement stop log and start log properly. If you try to use them in Smile or in the current Script Editor, you get a runtime error.

AppleScript In Action

Part III is about AppleScript in practice. The previous section described the Apple-Script language; that is your sword. Now, wielding this sword, you will go forth to do battle; this section is about the battle—the practical side of actually using Apple-Script to get something done.

The chapters are:

CHAPTER 19

Dictionaries

A *dictionary* is a scriptable application's way of letting the world know how it extends AppleScript's vocabulary. This extended vocabulary is called the application's *terminology*. AppleScript itself defines few commands, and has few abilities of its own; its value emerges when it is used for communicating, by means of Apple events, with scriptable applications. A scriptable application provides powers that AppleScript lacks, along with terminology that permits the programmer to harness those powers. For example, AppleScript can't make a new folder on your hard drive, but the Finder can; and the Finder supplements AppleScript's vocabulary with terms such as make and folder so that you can use AppleScript to command it (the Finder) to do so. This supplementary terminology is made available through the Finder's dictionary.

A dictionary has two intended audiences:

The AppleScript programmer

> The AppleScript programmer studies a human-readable display of an application's dictionary to learn what English-like terms beyond those built into the AppleScript language itself may be used when targeting that application.

AppleScript

> AppleScript uses an application's dictionary at compile time to look up the terms that the programmer uses. In this way, AppleScript confirms that the terms really exist; since they don't exist within AppleScript itself, AppleScript cannot know without a dictionary that the programmer isn't just talking nonsense. AppleScript also uses the dictionary to *resolve* the terms into their corresponding Apple event form; otherwise, AppleScript wouldn't know what actual Apple event messages to send to the scriptable application at runtime. And it uses the dictionary when decompiling, to translate those Apple event terms back into English-like form for display to the programmer.

This chapter discusses both aspects of dictionaries. It explains how AppleScript uses dictionaries. It also describes the dictionary as experienced by the programmer, who will use it to learn how to talk to an application. Studying a dictionary to figure out how to use AppleScript to get an application to do your bidding (and combining that study with experimentation when the dictionary is insufficiently informative) is a major part of the typical AppleScript programming experience. See Chapter 3 for an example.

Certain details about how an application's dictionary is stored appear in the section "Dictionary" in Chapter 4. In the section "Target" in Chapter 10 we talked about how AppleScript decides what application it will be sending Apple events to. In the sections "Tell" and "Using Terms From" in Chapter 12 we discussed how Apple-Script decides what application's dictionary it will use to resolve terminology.

Resolution of Terminology

Example 19-1 consists of a little code exhibiting some common patterns of terminology usage; we will use it as an example to help us form a mental picture of Apple-Script's compilation process.

Example 19-1. Simple terminology resolution

```
tell application "Finder"
    set r to display dialog (get name of folder 1)
end tell
```

Compilation of code like Example 19-1 proceeds in two distinct stages. First the tell block causes AppleScript to locate a particular application and load its dictionary. Then the terms inside the tell block are resolved. Let's take these stages one at a time.

Loading the Dictionary

As AppleScript's compiler encounters a tell block targeting an application, it immediately attempts to locate this application, so that it can load its dictionary. If the compiler can't find the application, it will ask the user where it is; if the user cancels out of this process, refusing to choose an application, AppleScript will not compile the script.

(If the current instance of the AppleScript scripting component has already loaded a particular application's dictionary, it doesn't need to do so again, because it now has a copy of the dictionary cached in memory. This is one of the reasons why a script typically takes longer to compile the first time.)

AppleScript will proceed happily at this point, provided it can find the application, or the user chooses an application for it—*any* application. The compiler has not yet come to the point of trying to resolve any actual terminology, so it doesn't matter at this stage whether there is any terminology to resolve, or even whether the application has a dictionary. All that matters is that the application referred to in code should be identified with some actual application. See "External Referents Needed at Compile Time" in Chapter 4.

Example 19-1 consists of a single tell block, but there are other situations that will cause a dictionary to be loaded. The tell block might contain another tell block that names another application; in that case, that application's dictionary will also be loaded. The same thing happens if a terms block is encountered ("Using Terms From" in Chapter 12). The question of whether the running script will eventually target any of these applications is completely irrelevant; the dictionaries will be loaded anyhow.

Translating the Terms

Presume that the compiler has reached the interior of the innermost tell block or terms block that caused a dictionary to be loaded. The compiler now proceeds to resolve the actual terms of the block.

The innermost application dictionary

Only one application dictionary is involved in the resolution of terminology in a given context. This is the dictionary corresponding to the innermost surrounding terms block or tell block. Let's call this the *innermost application dictionary*.

So, for example, in the following code, it is the Finder's dictionary that is the innermost application dictionary, and it will be used to resolve the term folder (and this resolution will succeed):

```
using terms from application "Mailsmith"
    tell application "Finder"
        get name of folder 1
    end tell
end using terms from
```

In the following code, it is Mailsmith's dictionary that is the innermost application dictionary, and it will be used to resolve the term folder (and this resolution will fail, so that the code will not compile):

```
tell application "Finder"
    using terms from application "Mailsmith"
        get name of folder 1
    end using terms from
end tell
```

Hunting for each term

Every term used in a given context must be found in a dictionary in order to be resolved. But the innermost application dictionary is not the only place where

AppleScript may have to look, because some of the terms may be defined elsewhere. The hunt for terminology thus involves several steps. Here's how it goes:

1. At every step of the hunt, if a term is found as a property in a dictionary, and if it isn't linked to some object by of (or one of its synonyms), it is also sought as a variable in the current scope of the script itself; if it's found as a variable in the script, it is resolved as that variable.*

2. The term is sought in the innermost application dictionary.

3. The term is sought in AppleScript's own dictionary (described later in this chapter under "The 'aeut' Resource" and in Appendix A).

4. The term is sought in the dictionaries of any scripting additions that are present.

5. The term is sought in the script itself.

Let's trace the resolution of the terms in Example 19-1, according to these rules:

- The terms set and get are not defined in the dictionary of the Finder, so they are sought and found in AppleScript's own dictionary (rule 3).

- The term r isn't found anywhere, so it's sought in the script; that works fine in this syntactic context, because r is being used in a place where it can be the name of an implicitly defined local variable (rule 5).

- The term display dialog isn't found in the Finder's dictionary or in AppleScript's own dictionary, but it's defined in a scripting addition's dictionary (rule 4).

- The term folder is defined in the Finder's dictionary (rule 2).

- Definitions for the term name appear both in the Finder's dictionary and in AppleScript's own dictionary. The former is used in the present case (rule 2); the latter explains how name is resolved in the last line of the example on page 208.

(Example 19-1 did not illustrate the use of rule 1; this rule is rather tricky, and we'll explore it more fully in a moment.)

Substituting four-letter codes

Apple events are made up chiefly of *four-letter codes*. (See Example 4-1, where the four-letter codes have values like 'core', 'move', 'insh', 'insl', 'kobj', 'obj ', 'kpos', 'form', 'want', and 'seld'.) Having located a term in a dictionary, the compiler uses the term's dictionary definition to translate that term into a four-letter code so that it can build an Apple event.

---

* This rule is my attempt to codify a kind of short-circuiting that AppleScript performs in order to allow variables to be accessible even within a tell block (see "Names in Scope" in Chapter 10). Even after much experimentation I may still not quite have succeeded in formulating the rule perfectly.

These four-letter codes are actually integers. An integer is four bytes, while a character from the ASCII range is one byte; so an integer can express four "packed" characters. The expression of this integer as a four-letter string is simply a convenience for the human reader. The use of single quotes to delimit a four-letter code is a standard convention.

Think of a term as either a noun or a verb; a command is a verb, and everything else is a noun. These are fundamentally different grammatical entities in an Apple event just as they are in a human utterance, and the dictionary makes clear which is which. So, for example, the Finder's dictionary stipulates that eject is a verb, while folder is a noun. (Actually it says that eject is an *event*, while folder is a *class*. We'll talk more about these technical notions later in the chapter, under "What's in a Dictionary.")

The dictionary defines each verb as a pair of four-letter codes, and each noun as a single four-letter code. For example, the Finder's dictionary defines eject as 'fndr/ejct', and it defines folder as 'cfol'.

Thus, having found each term of a line of code in some dictionary, the compiler is able to use these four-letter codes, along with the line's grammar, to construct the Apple event that will eventually be sent to the application.

Resolution Difficulties

Having sketched a basic picture of how terminology is resolved, we can proceed to cover various complications that occasionally arise.

Conflict Resolution

Terms are sought in the dictionaries of the innermost application, of AppleScript itself, and of all scripting additions, as well as in the script. Given such a large namespace involving multiple independent entities, it is possible for conflicts to arise. Such a conflict is called a *terminology clash*. Either the programmer generates the clash by an unwise choice of variable names, or different dictionaries generate it by defining the same term in different ways.

Clash caused by the programmer

When the programmer causes a terminology clash, various things can happen. Sometimes the code won't compile; sometimes it won't run; sometimes it runs but gets an unexpected result; sometimes the clash is resolved sensibly and there's no problem.

When the compiler stops you from using a term, it is generally because the term is defined elsewhere as a certain "part of speech" and you're trying to use it in a different way. For example, this won't compile:

```
local container
tell application "Finder" to set container to 7 -- compile-time error
```

Within the context of a tell directed at the Finder, container is resolved as the Finder's term container, which is a class name; that's not something that can be assigned to, so the compiler balks.

You may be wondering what happened to rule 1 on page 300. Rule 1 didn't apply in that example, because container was resolved as a *class*. Rule 1 specifically applies only if a term is resolved as a *property*. So, for example:

```
local bounds
tell application "Finder"
    set bounds to (get bounds of item 1)
end tell
bounds -- {-33, -33, 31, 31}
```

The term bounds in the third line is found to be the name of a property defined by the Finder. But the first bounds in the third line is not followed by of and is matched by the name of a variable that's in scope at this point, so it is taken to be that variable, by rule 1. Thus there's no terminology clash.

The explicit declaration of bounds in the first line is crucial here; take it away, and the code won't run. With no existing variable bounds in scope during the third line, *both* occurrences of bounds in the third line are taken as a property in the Finder; so now the phrase set bounds in the third line is incorporated into an Apple event sent to the Finder, which replies with an error message because it doesn't know what it's supposed to set the bounds of.

This won't compile:

```
set sel to {length:2, offset:4} -- compile-time error
```

The error message from the compiler is so mysterious that it might take you a while to realize that the problem is a terminology clash. The trouble is that offset is defined as a command in a scripting addition. Because it's a command, you're trying to use a verb where a noun is expected. Observe that length doesn't cause a clash here, even though it's defined in AppleScript's own dictionary; that's because it's defined as a property, and you're using it as a property. (Remember, names of items of a record are properties; see "Record Properties" in Chapter 13.)

This won't compile:

```
local desktop -- compile-time error
```

Again, the problem is a scripting addition; desktop is part of an enumeration used in the path to command. (See "Enumerations," later in this chapter.)

Now let's look at a terminology clash where the compiler doesn't complain. This is potentially worse for the programmer than when the compiler does complain, because the code runs but it doesn't behave as expected:

```
local container, x
set container to "howdy"
tell application "Finder" to set x to container
x -- container, not "howdy"
```

In that example, container in the third line is the name of a class in the Finder; a class is a legitimate value for a variable, so the variable x ends up with that class as its value.

In a case like that, the compiler can give you one subtle hint that something might be wrong—in the way it formats the "pretty-printed" decompiled code. You can set AppleScript's pretty-printing preferences to distinguish dictionary terms from script-based terms such as variable and handler names, and this will let you see that container in the third line is being interpreted as a dictionary term.

If you are aware of a conflict caused by your choice of variable names, and you insist upon using those variable names, you can usually resolve the conflict, as explained earlier in the section "Me" in Chapter 10. You can use pipes to suppress Apple-Script's interpretation of something as a dictionary term. This works:

```
local container
tell application "Finder" to set |container| to 10
container -- 10
```

So does this:

```
set sel to {length:9, |offset|:4}
```

In the case of a handler call, you will have to retarget the message as well:

```
on container( )
    display dialog "Howdy"
end container
tell application "Finder" to my |container|( ) -- Howdy
```

In that example, if you omit my, the message is sent to the Finder instead of the script. If you omit the pipes as well, the compiler reinterprets the last line:

```
on container( )
    display dialog "Howdy"
end container
tell application "Finder" to get container {} -- error
```

The parentheses are (surprisingly) transformed at compile time into an empty list to be used as an index in an element specifier; an empty list is not an integer, so this fails at runtime.

Sometimes pipes aren't quite enough. This doesn't work:

```
local folder
set folder to 5
tell application "Finder" to set |folder| to 10
folder -- 5, not 10
```

The trouble is that folder is also defined in a scripting addition, as the name of a property. It's a property of the file information pseudo-class returned by the info for command. That in itself is a terminology clash, because the scripting addition defines folder as 'asdr', but the Finder defines it as 'cfol'. To use folder as a variable name successfully, if we are going to put pipes around it anywhere, we must put pipes around it *everywhere*, so that it isn't identified with this scripting addition property:

```
local |folder|
set |folder| to 5
tell application "Finder" to set |folder| to 10
|folder| -- 10
```

Clash between dictionaries

There's nothing wrong with an application's dictionary redefining an AppleScript-defined term, so long as the same English-like term and the same underlying four-letter code are both used (and, I should probably add, so long as they use the term as the same part of speech). For example, AppleScript defines the term name ('pnam') as a property of a script object; the Finder defines it as a property of an item. Since they both use the same English-like term and the same four-letter code, and they both use it as a property, this is not a conflict. If the Finder's name were defined as a different four-letter code, that would count as a conflict.

Even if an application's dictionary generates a terminology clash, at least the problem arises only if you're targeting that application; but when a scripting addition makes the same kind of mistake, it conflicts *everywhere*, and there's nothing you can do about it.

In general, a clash between dictionaries is completely out of your control; even if you know about it, you can't resolve it. The only dictionary you can refer to explicitly is the innermost application dictionary. You have no way to help AppleScript when there's a clash; you can't specify that a term should be interpreted in accordance with AppleScript's own dictionary or a particular scripting addition's dictionary.

We have already seen some examples of trouble caused by poor choice of terminology in an application's dictionary. The use of the term end transaction by File-Maker Pro as the English-like equivalent of the 'misc/endt' Apple event ("Transaction" in Chapter 12) conflicts with the AppleScript's own use of end transaction as the closing phrase of a transaction block. BBEdit's use of the term contents as a property of a text-object ("Dereferencing a Reference" in Chapter 11) conflicts with AppleScript's own contents of operator.

With scripting additions, there have historically been many instances of clashes. The real trouble lies in the nature of the scripting addition mechanism itself, which invites such clashes; this is one of the reasons why Apple discourages developers from writing scripting additions (see Chapter 20). Thoughtful scripting addition developers frequently give their terms unique, improbable names to reduce the likelihood of clashes. For example, the GTQ Script Library scripting addition sorts lists with the sort command, which is probably not a very wise choice of English-like term; the ACME Script Widgets scripting addition sorts lists with the ACME sort command, a term unlikely to recur elsewhere (see *http://www.osaxen.com/gtq_scripting_library.html* and *http://www.acmetech.com*). Even this doesn't prevent a four-letter code in the scripting addition from matching a four-letter code in some application; that sort of problem is hard for even a wary developer to guard against. With luck, some user notices the clash and notifies the scripting addition's developer, who responds by creating a new version of the scripting addition with an altered dictionary. But there are some scripting additions where terminology clash is simply part of the price of using them.

Invalid Apple Events

Aside from confirming that your terminology is defined, does the compiler use the dictionary to check that you're employing that terminology in a valid manner? It does to some extent, but not as much as one might wish; it is all too easy to form a nonsensical expression and get it past the compiler (which will then form a nonsensical Apple event, which will be sent to the application at runtime). In general, you should not expect that compilation can be used as "sanity check." It's up to you to know the language and to use it sensibly. This is one reason why I describe the contents of dictionaries in such detail later in this chapter ("What's in a Dictionary").

The compiler does largely enforce the difference between verbs and nouns, though it has various ways of expressing this, and it might not be obvious what it's doing. For example, this will compile:

```
tell application "Finder" to folder the item
```

It probably looks to you as if AppleScript has treated folder as a verb; but in fact AppleScript is supplying get, as it typically does if the verb is missing. AppleScript is parsing your words like this:

```
tell application "Finder" to get folder index item
```

It thinks you're asking for a folder by index (e.g., folder 1), except that you've put the class name item as your index instead of an integer value. The fact that a class name is not a valid index value doesn't seem to faze the compiler one bit, but of course the resulting Apple event is nonsense and causes a runtime error when sent to the Finder.

The compiler also checks that the terms following a verb match the labeled parameters of that verb as defined by the dictionary. For example, this won't compile:

```
tell application "Finder" to duplicate x by y -- compile-time error
```

because a command must be followed only by valid labeled parameters, and the duplicate command doesn't have a by parameter.

The compiler also won't let you say get name 1 or get left 1. Evidently, it knows that name is a property and that left is an enumeration (a constant), and that these are not the sorts of terms that can be used in an element specifier.

The compiler also displays some intelligence about singular and plural forms of a class name. The plural form of a class name is taken to be a synonym for the every element specifier; otherwise, if you use a plural where a singular is expected or vice versa, the compiler will usually change it for you, silently:

```
tell application "Finder"
    folder -- folder (the class name)
    folders -- {...}, a list of references to every folder
    folders 1 -- compiles as folder 1
    folder 1 thru 2 -- compiles as folders 1 thru 2
end tell
```

Now for the bad news: the dictionary describes certain definite relationships—this property is a property of this class, this element is an element of this class, this name is a class, this name is a property—but AppleScript largely ignores this information. As far as the compiler is concerned, property and element names are *not encapsulated* with respect to their class, and property names and class names are *not distinguished*. The result is a namespace mess; indeed, this is one reason why terminology clashes can so easily occur.

Here we use a class name where a property name is expected:

```
tell application "Finder" to eject the item of file 1
```

That's rank nonsense. The Finder's dictionary makes it clear that item isn't a property of file, and that it isn't a property name but a class name. But AppleScript's compiler ignores such matters; it will simply translate the line into an Apple event and (at runtime) send it, at which point it's up to the Finder to return an error message.

Here we use a property name where a class name is expected:

```
tell application "Finder" to make new extension hidden
```

But extension hidden isn't a class; it's a property. And it isn't a property of the application class. But the code compiles anyway.

Again, demonstrating the complete lack of encapsulation:

```
tell application "Finder" to get column 1 of desktop
```

That's also total nonsense; column is an element of the list view options class, not of the desktop, and of course there's an error at runtime.

Raw Four-Letter Codes

It is sometimes possible to resolve a term yourself, in code, in advance of compilation. Instead of an English-like term, you type the corresponding four-letter code. You are thus essentially doing what the compiler would do: you've looked up the English-like term in a dictionary and substituted the corresponding four-letter code yourself. This is a useful device in situations where, because of a terminology clash, the English-like term would be ambiguous, but the four-letter code is not.

This technique obviously requires a way to read the four-letter codes in a dictionary. There are various ways to do this. If the dictionary is a text file, you can read it in any text editor. If the dictionary is an 'aete' resource in a resource fork, you can read it with Eighty-Rez. The easiest way is to use Script Debugger, which lets you switch between the normal English-like view of a dictionary's terms and an Apple event view displaying the four-letter codes.

The notation is straightforward. Typically the term will be either a noun (a class) or a verb (an event), so you use the word class or event followed by a space, followed by the four or eight letters, respectively. The entire thing is wrapped in guillemets («»). On the U.S. keyboard layout, these are typed using Option-\ and Shift-Option-\ (backslash).

Let's look at an example. This won't compile:

```
tell application "BBEdit"
    tell window 1
        offset of "i" in contents of word 1 -- compile-time error
    end tell
end tell
```

The reason is that we're trying to use offset as defined in a scripting addition, but BBEdit's own implementation of offset is getting in our way. There is no way to target the scripting addition, so in this context, where BBEdit is specified as the innermost application dictionary, there is no way to inform AppleScript that we mean the scripting addition command offset and not BBEdit's offset.

One workaround is not to use the scripting addition command in the context of an innermost application dictionary that conflicts with it. All we have to do is use the scripting addition's offset outside the tell block:

```
tell application "BBEdit"
    tell window 1
        set w to contents of word 1
    end tell
end tell
offset of "i" in w -- 3 (word 1 is "this")
```

But we could use four-letter codes instead. BBEdit's offset is a noun, a property 'Ofse', while the scripting addition's offset is a verb 'syso/offs'. This means that with regard to the underlying Apple event representation the two are completely distinguishable. So, we type this:

```
tell application "BBEdit"
    tell window 1
        «event sysooffs» of "i" in (get contents of word 1) -- 3
    end tell
end tell
```

That's what we type, but it isn't what appears after compilation. The decompilation process involves translating terms from their raw four-letter codes back to their English-like equivalents. Thus, the compiled script ends up looking like this:

```
tell application "BBEdit"
    tell window 1
        offset of "i" in (get contents of word 1) -- 3
    end tell
end tell
```

Nevertheless, unlike the earlier attempt, this is the correct offset, the one defined by the scripting addition; the script compiles—and it runs, because when «event sysooffs» is sent to BBEdit, BBEdit can't deal with it and it is passed along to the scripting addition.

Unfortunately, because decompilation has removed our raw four-letter code, if we edit this script and compile it again, we are right back where we started. We must be prepared to enter «event sysooffs» into the code manually before every compilation if we want to use this solution.

Occasionally you'll see a four-letter code show up in a compiled script. Typically this is because the compiled script has lost track of an application; thus it can't find the application's dictionary, so it can't decompile the four-letter codes to the corresponding English-like terms. Therefore it just shows you the four-letter codes directly. For example, here's a script targeting Eudora:

```
tell application "Eudora"
    get subject of message 1 of mailbox "Trash"
end tell
```

Now I'll quit the Script Editor and throw Eudora away. When I try to open the script again, the Script Editor naturally can't find Eudora, so it asks me where it is; it's gone, so to get the script to open at all, I just pick an application at random (the Finder). This satisfies AppleScript's desire for a dictionary, but of course the terms subject, message, and mailbox aren't defined in that dictionary, so the raw four-letter codes are displayed (and the Finder is substituted for Eudora as the target of the tell block):

```
tell application "Finder"
    get «class euSu» of «class euMS» 1 of «class euMB» "Trash"
end tell
```

The same sort of thing can happen if you open an old compiled script whose application's dictionary has changed. It can happen with a dictionary, too; here's a line from BBEdit's dictionary:

cover page **«class lwec»** [r/o] -- *should a cover page be generated*
for the job and where should it be placed

Evidently, either the dictionary itself is defective because someone forgot to define the class 'lwec', or else at the time this dictionary was written, something (AppleScript itself, or a scripting addition) defined the class 'lwec' and no longer does.

A further use of raw four-letter codes in a script is described under "Pseudo-Classes," later in this chapter.

Multiple-Word Commands

Many terms, especially in scripting additions, consist of multiple words. An example frequently used in this book is `display dialog`. Such a term would seem to present extra challenges; but AppleScript seems to rise to them quite well. For example:

```
local clipboard, tester
set clipboard to "Mannie" -- sets the variable clipboard
set the tester to "Moe" -- sets the variable tester (ignoring "the")
set the clipboard to "Jack" -- sets the system scrap
```

That example illustrates AppleScript's ability to recognize the scripting addition command `set the clipboard to`, which is used in the last line. This works even though `set` is an AppleScript command, `clipboard` could be the name of a variable, and `the` is usually ignored. In this particular code, `clipboard` *is* the name of a variable, and we are able to set it, as the second line shows. The third line illustrates that AppleScript usually ignores `the`. Though I don't know the details, a natural explanation of AppleScript's success here would be that it tries the longest possible combinations of words first.

A multiple-word property name such as `text item delimiters` presents a special case in the context of an innermost application dictionary. To see why, contrast it with a single-word property such as `space`. Both are defined by AppleScript itself as global script properties (see Chapter 16), but they are treated differently. When you say this, no Apple event is sent to the Finder:

```
tell application "Finder" to get space
```

That's because, in accordance with rule 1 on page 300, AppleScript has resolved `space` as a name that's in scope in the script. But with `text item delimiters`, AppleScript can't do that, because a multiple-word name isn't a legal variable name. Thus, when you say this, an Apple event *is* formed and sent:

```
tell application "Finder" to get text item delimiters -- error
```

The Apple event tells the Finder to get its `'txdl'` property (because `'txdl'` is the four-letter code for `text item delimiters`). But the Finder has no `'txdl'` property, so it returns an error. To prevent this, you have to specify that the `text item delimiters` belongs to me, or AppleScript:

```
tell application "Finder" to get my text item delimiters
```

What's in a Dictionary

This section describes the contents of a dictionary. This is primarily so that you can interpret a dictionary when you read it in an application such as the Script Editor.

Enumerations

An *enumeration* is a value that must be one of a fixed list of four-letter codes. These four-letter codes are called *enumerators*; and the enumeration itself also has a four-letter code, identifying the entire set of its enumerators. Thus, by using the four-letter code of an enumeration, a dictionary can specify that a value must be one of the enumerators of that enumeration.

For example, BBEdit's dictionary entry for the close command reads, in part:

```
close reference [saving yes/no/ask]
```

The triad of values yes/no/ask is an enumeration. The dictionary actually just says here that the saving parameter is a 'savo'. That's the four-letter code for an enumeration. The script editor application, presenting this information in human-readable form, has looked up the 'savo' enumeration in the dictionary and has fetched the English-like equivalents of its three enumerators. The four-letter code for the enumeration itself, 'savo', has no English-like equivalent.

By and large, an enumerator is the same thing as a constant, as discussed in Chapter 17. If you ask AppleScript for the class of yes, it tells you it's a constant.

AppleScript uses this information to translate between English-like terms and four-letter codes, but the compiler does not check to see whether the value you actually supply is an enumerator of the specified enumeration.

Value Type

At various points in a dictionary, a *value type* is specified. For example, a command parameter is of some type; a command reply is of some type; every property of an object is of some type.

This notion corresponds to a datatype or class (Chapter 13). Thus, a value type is specified in a dictionary by means of the four-letter code for a class. An application can define classes beyond those that are native to AppleScript itself. There is also a wild-card value type ('****'), whose English-like rendering is "anything." A slightly less wild wild-card type ('obj ') may be used when the value is some object belonging to the application; the English-like rendering is "reference." A value type that is itself a class ('type') has the English-like rendering "type class."

A value type may be a list (since a list is a class); in the special case where the list is all of one class of item, there is a way to say so in the dictionary, and the English-like rendering for this is "a list of" followed by the name of the class. A value type may be an enumeration, or even a list of some one type of enumeration.

Here is part of the dictionary entry for the Finder's count command:

```
count reference -- the object whose elements are to be counted
    Result: integer -- the number of elements
```

The dictionary says that the parameter is an `'obj '` and the reply is a `'long'`. These are rendered as "reference" and "integer" respectively. A "reference" is a wild card denoting some object belonging to the Finder; "integer" is the built-in `integer` class ("Integer, Real, and Number" in Chapter 13).

Here is the dictionary entry for the Finder's make command:

```
make
        new type class -- the class of the new element
        at location reference -- the location at which to insert the element
        [to reference] -- when creating an alias file, the original item to create an alias to
                or when creating a file viewer window, the target of the window
        [with properties record] -- the initial values for the properties of the element
        Result: reference -- to the new object(s)
```

The new parameter is a "type class," meaning that its value is itself a class, so that the Finder knows what class of object to create. The to parameter, and the result, are a "reference." A "record" is the built-in `record` class ("Record" in Chapter 13). For "location reference" and the `insertion location` class, see "Relative" in Chapter 10.

In Mailsmith, a mail message's delivery path property appears in the dictionary like this:

```
delivery path a list of string [r/o]
```

A "string" is the built-in `string` class ("String" in Chapter 13). The dictionary actually says that this property's class is `'TEXT'`, and also specifies that the value type is a list. If you ask Mailsmith for the delivery path of a message, you'll see that it is indeed a list of strings, one for each "Received:" entry in the header.

In Mailsmith, a mail message's status property appears in the dictionary like this:

```
status a list of seen/answered/forwarded/redirected/deleted/flagged/draft/
        recent/sent [r/o] -- List of status flags
```

Mailsmith implements an enumeration called `'Eflg'` whose enumerators are the constants seen, answered, forwarded, and so forth. The dictionary actually says that the status property's class is `'Eflg'` and that its value type is a list. This makes sense, since the possible kinds of status are limited but a message might have more than one status.

This information is for the human reader only. The AppleScript compiler does not check to see whether the value you actually supply is of a specified type, and the runtime engine doesn't care what type of value a scriptable application returns.

Event

An *event* is a command. You can think of it as a verb; you can also think of it as an Apple event (hence the name). It is specified with two four-letter codes. The rendering of both codes together, separated by slash (or backslash) and delimited by single quotes, is a common convention. So, for example, the Finder's reveal command is the event `'misc/mvis'`. The dictionary lists the command's parameters; it specifies each parameter's value type, and whether the parameter is optional or required. The dictionary also specifies whether the command has a reply; if it does, the dictionary specifies the reply's value type.

There are two types of parameter. A parameter may be the command's *direct object* ("Direct Object" in Chapter 10). Every event listed in a dictionary must say whether the command has a direct object. For example, the Finder's quit command has no direct object:

```
tell application "Finder" to quit -- don't try this at home
```

The Finder's reveal command has a direct object:

```
tell application "Finder"
    reveal item 1 of desktop
    -- or, alternatively:
    tell item 1 of desktop
        reveal
    end tell
end tell
```

The other type of parameter is a labeled parameter ("Prepositional Parameters" in Chapter 8). For every labeled parameter, the label is specified as a four-letter code and as an English-like equivalent. From an Apple event point of view, a label is a property; when the command is sent as a message, the labeled parameters appear as items of a record. For example, recall that the Finder's make command appears in the dictionary like this:

```
make
    new type class -- the class of the new element
    at location reference -- the location at which to insert the element
    [to reference] -- when creating an alias file, the original item to create an alias to
        or when creating a file viewer window, the target of the window
    [with properties record] -- the initial values for the properties of the element
    Result: reference -- to the new object(s)
```

The command has parameters labeled new, at, to, and with properties. The first two parameters are required, and the second two are optional. So the following Apple-Script code:

```
tell application "Finder"
    make new folder at desktop with properties {name:"Jack"}
end tell
```

generates this Apple event:

```
core/crel{
    kocl:'cfol',
    insh:obj {
        form:'prop',
        want:'prop',
        seld:'desk',
        from:'null'()
    },
```

```
        prdt:{
            pnam:"Jack"
        }
    }
```

You can see the two four-letter codes specifying the event ('core/crel'), followed by a record where the names of the items are the four-letter codes for the three parameters we supplied: 'kocl', 'insh', and 'prdt' are the four-letter codes for new, at, and with properties.

You probably know enough by now to understand the rest of what's happening here too. 'cfol' is the four-letter code for the folder class; the last parameter is a record, and we've already mentioned that 'pnam' is the name property. The term desktop is a property, which is rendered as an object specifier, as mentioned in "Element Specifiers" in Chapter 10.

The AppleScript compiler enforces the rule that the only parameters following a command should be the direct object and the labeled parameters defined by that particular command. It knows nothing about required and optional parameters, however.

Classes

A *class* is a datatype (see Chapter 13). Applications are free to define new datatypes in addition to those provided by AppleScript. These will generally correspond to the various types of thing the application operates on. For example, the Finder is all about files and folders on hard drives; thus it has a file class, a folder class, and a disk class.

If a value type is of a particular class, the dictionary will say the name of the class. See "Value Type," earlier in this chapter, for the ways in which a value type may be expressed in the dictionary.

Plurals

For most classes defined by an application, the dictionary will provide both a singular and a plural form for the English-like term. So, for example, the Finder defines both file and files, both folder and folders, both disk and disks. In the dictionary, the mechanism for doing this is to list the class a second time, along with a pseudo-property marking it as a plural.

For example, in the Finder's dictionary, the listing for folder is immediately followed by a listing for folders. They both have the same four-letter code ('cfol'), and folders has the pseudo-property marking it as a plural. Therefore AppleScript knows that folders is the English-like plural of folder. The human-readable presentation in the Script Editor simply combines these into one listing:

```
Class folder: A folder
Plural form:
    folders
```

The only time a dictionary won't provide a plural form for a class name is when there is only one object of that class; you can't say every, because this class occurs only as a property, not an element. For example, the Finder provides only the singular for desktop-object, the class of the desktop. It is also possible for a class to be declared as its own plural (text does this, for example).

The compiler uses this information to treat singular and plural alternatives with some intelligence; see "Invalid Apple Events," earlier in this chapter.

Class inheritance

A dictionary can specify a class as *inheriting* from another class. The mechanism for this is a special pseudo-property; if a class has this property, the property's value is the class from which this class inherits. For example, in the Finder, there is a class item; both the file class and the container class have the pseudo-property stipulating that they inherit from item. We also say that item is the *superclass* of file and container, and that file and container are two of its *subclasses*. Similarly, the class folder is a subclass of container. Thus we have a hierarchy of inheritance.

The nature of this inheritance is that a subclass has all the properties and elements of its superclass. It may also implement some properties and elements that it doesn't inherit, and it passes these along to its own subclasses as well. For example, in the Finder, the item class has a name property; therefore, so does the container class, and so does the folder class. The container class has an entire contents property; therefore, so does the folder class.

Because of class inheritance, it is possible for a class to be *abstract*—that is, a class exists only as a way of encapsulating a set of elements and properties so that other classes can inherit them, and is not the class of any actual object to which the programmer will ever make or obtain a reference. For example, BBEdit's dictionary defines an item class to act as an ultimate superclass, just so that every other class will have an ID property inherited from it; there's no property or element anywhere in the dictionary whose class is item.

The Finder, too, has an item class that acts primarily as a superclass, though there's a slight difference: some classes do have an item element, so you can refer to the item class in this way. Nevertheless, the reference you wind up with is an item subclass, not an item; so it is reasonable to describe the Finder's item class as abstract. For example:

```
tell application "Finder"
    class of item 1 of desktop -- document file (not item)
end tell
```

The chief value of inheritance is that it makes the dictionary smaller. (Historically, in fact, this is why class inheritance in the dictionary was implemented; QuarkXPress's dictionary was too large to be displayed by the Script Editor, which had a 32K limit on the size of dictionary text.) For example, in the Finder, a file and a folder have lots of properties in common. Rather than having to list all these properties twice, once for the file class and once for the folder class, the dictionary simply lists them once, for the item class, and both file and folder inherit them from item.

Unfortunately for the human reader, a dictionary may be displayed in a way that makes inheritance more of a stumbling block than a convenience. In the Script Editor, for example, inheritance actually makes it harder for you to learn what a class's properties are. When you look at the listing for the Finder's file class, you see about five properties, preceded by a statement that the file class inherits from the item class. So if you want to know about the file class's other two dozen properties, you have to find the listing for the item class and look in that! You thus spend all your time slogging from class to class trying to remember what's in each one.

Script Debugger is much more helpful. The listing for a class optionally shows you its inherited attributes along with its own, so it suffices to look just in the listing for the Finder's file class to learn about all its properties, including those it inherits from item. And Script Debugger even displays the inheritance hierarchy graphically; Figure 19-1 shows its nice hierarchical display of some of the Finder's classes, including item, container, file, and folder.

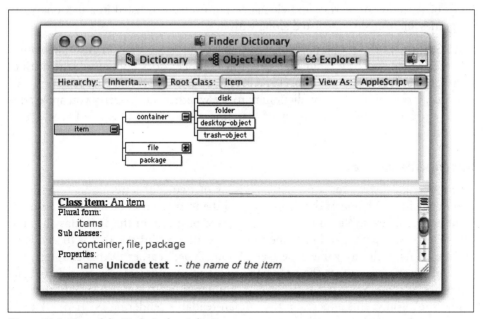

Figure 19-1. Part of the Finder's class inheritance structure

The implementation of inheritance of elements (as opposed to properties) is rather confusing. Most dictionaries behave as if there were no such thing. Thus, for example, in the Finder the elements of the folder class are the same as the elements of the container class, and folder inherits from container, but the identity of their elements is not a consequence of inheritance; their elements are stated separately in the dictionary, the same list of elements appearing twice. (This is not an artifact of the way the Finder's dictionary is presented to a human user in a script editor application; I'm describing the Finder's 'aete' resource.) If the Finder believed in inheritance of elements, it wouldn't need to do this, and more space would be saved. On the other hand, some applications, such as FrameMaker and Adobe Illustrator, do display element inheritance.

The truth is, however, that none of this matters much. The compiler doesn't enforce (or care about) encapsulation of property and element names with respect to their class ("Invalid Apple Events," earlier in this chapter), so class inheritance in the dictionary has no effect whatever on how AppleScript works. Class inheritance in the dictionary is merely a form of shorthand to save space; it is meaningless except to the human reader, and its chief effect upon that human reader is to make the dictionary harder to read.

Properties and Elements

Recall from "Properties and Elements" in Chapter 10 that an object can have two kinds of attribute: properties and elements. For every class listed in a dictionary, its properties and elements are listed along with it.

AppleScript uses the property listings to translate between their English-like names and their four-letter codes, but that's all. The compiler does not enforce the distinction between a property and an element, and does not enforce encapsulation (for example, it doesn't look in the dictionary to see whether the property you are ascribing to an object really is a property of that object). See "Invalid Apple Events," earlier in this chapter.

How properties are listed

The dictionary listing for a property consists of two four-letter codes—the four-letter code for the name of the property, and the four-letter code for the class of its value type. For example, in the Finder the name property of the item class has the four-letter code 'pnam', and its value type is specified as 'utxt', that is to say, Unicode text. As with any value type (see "Value Type," earlier in this chapter), the dictionary can specify that the property's value is an enumeration, or a list whose items are of some one particular class or enumeration. It can also specify that the value is read-only; this appears in the human-readable rendering as "[r/o]". Here's part of the listing for the Finder's item class:

```
Class item: An item
Properties:
    name Unicode text -- the name of the item
```

How elements are listed

The dictionary listing for an element is the four-letter code of a class—which must be defined elsewhere, of course—along with a list of the forms of specifier that may be used to refer to this element. (Naturally, there are four-letter codes for the element specifier forms.) For example, in the Finder the folder class has a 'file' element with specifier forms 'indx' and 'name'. The four-letter code 'file' is paired with the English-like term file elsewhere, namely at the point where the file class is defined. So this is a way of saying that a folder can have file elements which can be referred to by index or by name. This information appears in the human-readable rendering of the dictionary, which says, in part:

```
Class folder: A folder
Elements:
        file  by numeric index, by name
```

The object model

An object belonging to a scriptable application is of some class. That class can have properties and elements. All of the elements, and possibly some of the properties, represent objects belonging to the application as well. Thus, properties and elements together bind all of an application's objects into a hierarchy, whereby it should be possible to specify every object that actually exists. This is called the application's *object model*.

Much of the struggle of using a dictionary involves trying to work out the object model, so that you can refer to the object you want to refer to. (See Chapter 3.) This is another area where Script Debugger is particularly helpful. It charts the element hierarchy in a manner similar to the way it charts the class inheritance hierarchy (Figure 19-1); and it displays hierarchically all of an application's actual objects, telling you their values and how to refer to them (Figure 2-4).

Pseudo-Classes

A *pseudo-class* is a record that's listed as a class in the dictionary. This publicizes the names of the items of the record, making them part of the application's terminology, as well as informing the human reader about the structure of the record.

A good example is the text style info that some applications return as a description of how text is styled. Tex-Edit Plus is such an application. In its dictionary, there's a listing for a text style info class with properties on styles and off styles, each of which has a value that's a list of an enumeration ('styl'):

```
Class text style info: The on and off styles of a text object
Properties:
      on styles list of plain/bold/italic/underline/outline/shadow/
          condensed/expanded/strikethrough/all caps/
          all lowercase/hidden [r/o]
```

```
off styles list of plain/bold/italic/underline/outline/shadow/
          condensed/expanded/strikethrough/all caps/
          all lowercase/hidden [r/o]
```

Tex-Edit Plus's dictionary says that the text class has a uniform styles property whose class is text style info. But that's not really true; the dictionary does not distinguish between a real class and a pseudo-class. When you ask for a text object's uniform styles property, you get a record:

```
tell application "Tex-Edit Plus" to get uniform styles of the selection
-- {class:text style info, on styles:{bold, italic}, ¬
     off styles:{underline, outline, shadow, condensed, ¬
     expanded, strikethrough, all caps, all lowercase, hidden}}
```

However, AppleScript is able to characterize a record as being of a particular class; you can see this happening in the Apple event version of the result from the previous example ('tsty' is the four-letter code for the text style info pseudo-class):

```
tsty{
        onst:[
            'bold',
            'ital'
        ],
        ofst:[
            'undl',
            'outl',
            'shad',
            'cond',
            'pexp',
            'strk',
            'alcp',
            'lowc',
            'hidn'
        ]
    }
```

And within your script, the resulting record has been consequently endowed with an item whose name is class, so that if you ask about its class, you'll be told it *is* a text style info.

To retrieve items of a pseudo-class record outside of a tell block targeting the original application may require the use of raw four-letter codes (see "Raw Four-Letter Codes," earlier in this chapter). For example, this works:

```
tell application "BBEdit"
    set r to check syntax file "xxx:Users:mattneub:testing.html"
    get result_file of item 1 of r
end tell
```

But the following code doesn't, because AppleScript has no way to associate the term result_file with the four-letter code that identifies it internally within the record:

```
tell application "BBEdit"
    set r to check syntax file "xxx:Users:mattneub:testing.html"
```

```
end tell
get result_file of item 1 of r -- error
```

You can get around this error by using the raw four-letter code:

```
tell application "BBEdit"
    set r to check syntax file "xxx:Users:mattneub:testing.html"
end tell
get «class Efil» of item 1 of r
```

The reason why the same problem doesn't arise with text style info is that all the terms involved are defined within AppleScript's own dictionary (see "The 'aeut' Resource," later in this chapter, and Appendix A).

Suites

At the top level of a dictionary, events and classes are clumped into *suites*. What is a suite? In part, it's just a way of organizing the top level of a dictionary. This is supposed to make it easier for the human user to navigate the dictionary, but the result is often just the opposite. Typically, you don't get to see classes and events in alphabetical order; you don't get to see them in any order. They are clumped into suites, and within each suite they come in what seems an arbitrary order (it is whatever order the dictionary's designer felt like giving them).

Thus, suites can actually make it harder to find a particular class or event because you don't know what suite it's in or where it will appear within its suite. Once again, Script Debugger can be a big help here, because it lets you view all classes or events in alphabetical order, dispensing with suites altogether.

A suite also has a second use, behind the scenes. Suites are an attempt to bring some semblance of standardization to the anarchic world of terminology. Even before AppleScript was made public, back in the earliest days of System 7 when there were just Apple events, Apple began fostering an attempt to make Apple events more uniform from one application to another. Since it couldn't do this at System level, it resorted to a combination of propaganda and browbeating aimed at developers. An Apple event czar was appointed—the *Apple event registrar*—whose job was to organize and codify commonly used Apple events into a centralized database—the *Apple event registry*. The suites resulted from this codification.

You will thus see, recurring amongst applications, a few suites that have become informally conventional. An example is the Miscellaneous Suite, a frequent repository for commands like copy, cut, and undo. But Apple did more than just ask developers to implement and conform to the suites; they incorporated some suites into AppleScript's own dictionary (and you can see them in Appendix A, *The 'aeut' Resource*). They did this in such a way that there would be no breach of the freedom of developers to devise their own repertories of Apple events and their own dictionaries. The suites incorporated into AppleScript itself are mostly *voluntary*. An application may adopt none or any or all of these suites; it may adopt any suite in part, as a whole, or with extensions; it may adopt events and classes as is, or it may change them. In other words, the suites incorporated into AppleScript itself function as starting points.

Some of AppleScript's own suites, such as the Macintosh Connectivity Classes, are relatively obscure and rarely adopted, but others are frequently adopted by scriptable applications. The Standard Suite, sometimes referred to as the Core Suite, shows up quite a lot in one form or another; it contains terms like exists, make, and select. And the Text Suite, containing terms like word and text style info, is sometimes used as a starting point by applications that do that sort of thing.

There used to be a suite called the Required Suite; in the current implementation of AppleScript this is empty. It dates back to the invention of Apple events and System 7, where all applications, scriptable or not, had to respond to four particular Apple events or they couldn't exist as System 7–native applications at all. That's because these are fundamental Apple events sent by the Finder to the application in order to notify it that the user wants to do such things as launch it, open a document owned by it, or quit it. These Apple events now have analogues in the Standard Suite, but the original Required Suite Apple events are not listed, because it is certain that every application responds to them. They are shown in Table 19-1.

Table 19-1. The original Required Apple events

Command	Four-letter code	Effect
run	`'aevt/oapp'`	Launch the application
open	`'aevt/odoc'`	Open a document or documents
print	`'aevt/pdoc'`	Print a document or documents
quit	`'aevt/quit'`	Quit

The 'aeut' Resource

When terminology is resolved according to the rules in the earlier section "Translating the Terms," AppleScript itself is represented by a dictionary. This dictionary is the 'aeut' resource. The 'aeut' resource is loaded when the AppleScript scripting component comes into being. It looks just like any other dictionary. There's just one problem: you, the human reader, can't normally see it. Of the commonly used script editing programs, only Smile displays the 'aeut' resource. Therefore, I present it in Appendix A.

The appendix contains a representation of the 'aeut' resource as currently implemented by AppleScript on Mac OS X. You will be amazed when you see what's in there—basically, it's the entire AppleScript language as already described in this book, including comparison operators, prepositions for handler parameters, the global script properties, and so forth. There are even some terms not discussed in this book (because in practice they don't arise, or may never even have been implemented, like the upper case class). You can learn a lot from perusing the 'aeut' resource. For one thing, it shows you why certain variable names generate terminology conflicts. (It's because they're defined in the 'aeut' resource. How you're supposed to find this out without being able to *see* the 'aeut' resource is a mystery to me. AppleScript programming is often indistinguishable from guessing.)

Inadequacies of the Dictionary

One purpose of the dictionary is to show the human user how to speak AppleScript to a scriptable application in order to drive that application. But a dictionary, by its very nature, is not completely adequate to this task. A dictionary is merely a list of words. Knowing a lot of words is not the same as knowing a language. Languages refer to the real world, they develop under certain conventions of communication, and they have idioms. You might know every word of the English language, including the words "how," "you," and "do"; but nothing about these words, *qua* words, would tell you what "How do you do?" means, nor would anything about these words lead you to think of generating such a phrase at the appropriate moment. An AppleScript dictionary is like that. It tells you the building blocks of the phrases you can say, but it does not tell you *what to say*—how, as Austin famously put it, to *do things with words*. Yet this is exactly what you want to know.

This section lists the main types of problem you're likely to encounter. Forewarned, as they say, is forearmed. It is hoped that study of this section will make you a better reader of dictionaries and a wiser AppleScript programmer.

Defective Object Model

Since an application's object model (see "The object model," earlier in this chapter) is a hierarchy, essentially equivalent to the chain of ofs allowing you specify any of the application's objects, it's clear that it requires a starting point. If we are to specify any object, there must be some ultimate, top-level object in terms of which we will specify it. In an Apple event, that top-level object is null( ). But in AppleScript there is no way to express this null( ) explicitly; it is simply supplied for you as the end of the chain, whenever you specify an object. (You can see this happening in Example 4-1.)

By convention, in a well-written dictionary for a well-behaved application, the application class can be used to describe the top-level null( ) object. For example, the Finder's application class has a home property, and sure enough, you can refer to the home property as a property of the top-level object, with no further qualification:

```
tell application "Finder"
    get home -- folder "mattneub" of folder "Users" of startup disk ¬
        of application "Finder"
end tell
```

In reality, though, you never know quite what an application will do if you simply refer to a property or element with no further qualification. You can't find out from the dictionary; you just have to try it. A good example is what happens when you refer to a top-level element in the Finder:

```
tell application "Finder"
    get folder 1 -- folder "Moe" of desktop of application "Finder"
end tell
```

Since desktop is a property of the Finder's application object, it's a property of the top level; thus, a folder on the desktop is *not* an element of the top level. But the Finder permits you to speak as if it were; you can refer to a folder element without further qualification, and the Finder supplies the interpretation that this means a folder on the desktop. We say that the Finder supplies an *implicit subcontainer* (the desktop) when you speak of certain elements without qualification. That's convenient, but you have no way to know from the dictionary that it will do this.

Some applications are particularly badly behaved in this regard. A good example is Eudora. There is a mailbox class in Eudora, but how can you speak of any particular mailbox? The only place mailbox is listed is as an element of mail folder. But in fact not every mailbox in Eudora is in a mail folder, so that makes no sense. It turns out, however, that you can speak of a mailbox as an element of the top-level object:

```
tell application "Eudora" to count messages of mailbox "In"
```

Nothing about Eudora's dictionary informs you that this is legal. This is a good example of how an application can have an object model in its head, as it were, without showing it to you in its dictionary. In Eudora's dictionary, mailbox is an *orphan class*.

A dictionary may also simply omit pieces of the puzzle, such as not listing all of a class's elements. Much of the time in Chapter 3 was spent discovering, by experimentation, that in FrameMaker an anchored frame can be an element of a paragraph or of a document. This was a relief, and made our ultimate solution possible, but the dictionary said no such thing; only experimentation revealed it. In the Finder, too, a Finder window can have items, as if it were a folder, even though the dictionary doesn't list it as having any elements at all.

Defective Element Specifiers

There are many ways to refer to an element (see "Element Specifiers" in Chapter 10), but you can't be sure from the dictionary which ones are implemented for any particular element. The dictionary can list some element specifier forms as ways of accessing a particular element, but the list might not be correct. The programmer's difficulty here is closely related to the defective object model—how to work your way down the chain of ofs and tells to refer to some particular object or set of objects.

For example, as we saw earlier, the Finder lists only the 'indx' and 'name' specifier forms as ways of referring to a folder object's file elements. But this code both compiles and runs on my machine:

```
tell application "Finder" to get files 1 thru 2 of folder 1
```

That code doesn't use the 'indx' or 'name' specifier form; it uses the 'rang' (range) specifier form. So the Finder fails to list in its dictionary a specifier form that is valid. It also *does* list in its dictionary a specifier form that is *not* valid: it claims you can specify a folder by ID, but since you can't get a folder's ID, that's not true. So you often have to ignore the element specifier form information in a dictionary and just use good old trial and error to determine what specifiers are really possible.

Sometimes an application's implementation of element specifier forms (or lack thereof) is nothing short of astounding. Certain specifiers may work on the very same object in one context but not in another. In Eudora, you can say this:

```
tell application "Eudora" to get name of mailbox 1 -- "In"
```

but you can't say this:

```
tell application "Eudora" to get mailbox 1 -- error
```

and you can't say this:

```
tell application "Eudora" to get every mailbox -- error
```

or this, which amounts to the same thing:

```
tell application "Eudora" to count mailboxes -- error
```

As far as I know, there's no way to learn how many Eudora mailboxes there are; the only way to cycle through all mailboxes in Eudora is simply to keep cycling by index number, incrementing the index, until you get an error.

Boolean test specifiers are, of course, the most chancy. When a boolean test specifier works, it's a superbly elegant feature. We used this one in "Reduction" in Chapter 1:

```
tell application "System Events" to get process 1 where it is frontmost
```

If System Events didn't implement that boolean test, we would have had to get the list and then cycle through it ourselves:

```
tell application "System Events"
    repeat with p in (get every process)
        if frontmost of p then exit repeat
    end repeat
end tell
contents of p
```

That gets the same result, but it takes much longer and involves lots of Apple events.

Make

The verb make, used to create objects in AppleScript, poses many peculiar difficulties, so it's worth some individual attention. (See also the section "Relative" in Chapter 10.)

The first question is *what* to make. You might think, for example, that to make a new email message in Mailsmith—I mean a new outgoing message, one that you intend to populate with an address, a body, and so forth, so as to send it later—you'd ask to make a new message, but that creates a new *incoming* message (which makes no sense whatever). The way to make a new outgoing message is to ask for a new message window. Nothing in the dictionary would lead you to this solution.

Similarly, the way you create a new window in AppleWorks isn't to ask for a new window, which just gets you an incomprehensible error message, but to ask for a new document. The way you create a new window in the Finder isn't to ask for a new window but to ask for a new Finder window.

The verb make also often requires that you say *where* to create the new object. The dictionary lists this parameter:

at **location reference** -- *the location at which to insert the element*

Every application seems to have a different idea of what constitutes an appropriate location. In Eudora, for example, if you're trying to make an outgoing message, it turns out that the place to create it is at the end of the "Out" mailbox:

```
tell application "Eudora"
    make new message at end of mailbox "Out"
end tell
```

With Cocoa applications, the at parameter must typically refer to a collection (sometimes imaginary) of the same things you're trying to make one of. An example appears in the section "Application" in Chapter 2 (where the Cocoa application is AppleScript Studio). Here's another example; in the outliner NoteTaker, to make a new page, you have to say something like this:

```
tell application "NoteTaker"
    tell book 1
        tell section 1
            make new page at end of pages
        end tell
    end tell
end tell
```

If you target the wrong object, or if you don't say at end of pages, you get an error, or nothing happens, or NoteTaker crashes.

Not only the at parameter, but also the *meaning* of at, varies from application to application. This code inserts a new word *after* word 2:

```
tell application "BBEdit"
    tell window 1
        make new word at word 2 with data "howdy"
```

```
        end tell
    end tell
```

This code inserts a new word *replacing* word 2:

```
tell application "TextEdit"
    tell text of document 1
        make new word at word 2 with data "howdy"
    end tell
end tell
```

This code inserts a new folder *inside* folder 1:

```
tell application "Finder"
    tell desktop
        make new folder at folder 1 ¬
            with properties {name:"Cool new folder"}
    end tell
end tell
```

Then there's the with properties parameter. Sometimes you have to use this. For example, the way to add a recipient address to a Mailsmith message window is as follows:

```
tell application "Mailsmith"
    tell message window 1
        make new to_recipient at end ¬
            with properties {address:"matt@tidbits.com"}
    end tell
end tell
```

If you leave out the with properties parameter, you'll get a runtime error. Notice also the peculiar at end; you have to say it this way—you can't omit the at parameter, and you can't say something more sensible-sounding such as at end of to_recipients. None of this comes from the dictionary.

One more thing to know is that with the make command you can omit the word new; what follows the word make, where the direct object would go, is taken to be the new parameter. The dictionary fails to express this fact, which is hardcoded into the inner workings of AppleScript itself.

Idioms for Common Tasks

The commonest tasks are often the hardest to express using the terms the dictionary gives you. The object model is often not at all like the mental picture of the application you've built up from using it in the ordinary way. The verbs you think you need aren't there, or the verbs that are there don't do what you expect.

Take the problem of deleting a message in Eudora. You're used to simply selecting a message and deleting it (with the Delete key). This sounds like the delete event, so you try it:

```
tell application "Eudora"
    delete message 1 of mailbox "Out" -- error
end tell
```

The error message says, "Message 1 of mailbox 'Out' doesn't understand the delete message." So how on earth are you supposed to delete it? The solution is to move the message to the end of the trash:

```
tell application "Eudora"
    move message 1 of mailbox "Out" to end of mailbox "Trash"
end tell
```

Who would ever have thought of saying something like that? And the dictionary doesn't tell you to say it, so how are you supposed to find out?

Another good example is how you insert text into a BBEdit window. There is no insert verb, and make turns out to be unreliable. The best way turns out to be to position the selection where you want to insert the text and then say set the selection. You have to be careful, because set is not being used here quite the way you might suppose. For example, what do you think this code does?

```
tell application "BBEdit"
    tell window 1
        set selection to word 1
    end tell
end tell
```

If you expect that code to select the first word of the window, you're wrong; it changes whatever text is *currently* selected to the *same text* as the first word of the window. The way you "set the selection" in the sense of positioning the current selection point is with the select command.

To produce Fetch's shortcut window (a Fetch shortcut is like a bookmark in other Internet applications), you choose Fetch Shortcuts from the Window menu. How do you do it with AppleScript? There's a shortcut window class, so naturally you try various incantations based on make new shortcut window, but none of them work. Eventually you discover shortcut window listed as an element of the application class, and experimentation shows that you can say this:

```
tell application "Fetch 4.0.3" to open shortcut window 1
```

That makes no sense whatever. The application has only one Shortcut Window, after all. There is no shortcut window 1 (there are no shortcut windows at all, which is why you're trying to produce one), and you're never allowed to speak of shortcut window 2. This shouldn't be an element, but a property, and you should be using make, not open; but such is not Fetch's idiom. The dictionary didn't tell you what to do; you had to guess.

Events and Classes

A dictionary lists events (verbs) and classes (nouns), but it doesn't tell you *what* verbs apply to *what* nouns. The verb make creates a new object, but *what* objects am I allowed to create? The verb delete deletes things, but *what* objects am I allowed to delete? The dictionary doesn't say.

The problem is particularly acute when the dictionary entry for a verb doesn't provide any meaningful information. For example, here's how delete is listed in most dictionaries:

delete **reference** -- *the element to delete*

That could mean anything, so of course it means nothing. The only way to find out what it does mean is by trying it. If AppleScript or an application doesn't want to apply a particular verb to a particular object, it will usually return an error message that "such-and-such an object doesn't understand the so-and-so message." In other words: sorry, guess again.

Inconsistent Return Types

Dictionaries give no information about what sort of value will be returned when you use a verb that isn't defined in the dictionary (like get). As usual, experimentation is your best bet.

For example, when you ask the Finder for every folder (of any container), you get a list; but when you ask the Finder for every disk, you get a list unless there is only one disk, in which case you get a reference to a single disk object. Quite apart from the inconsistency, this is troublesome because it means a script like this can break:

```
tell application "Finder"
    repeat with d in (get every disk)
        -- do something here
    end repeat
end tell
```

The script will break in a subtle way: if you have more than one disk, then on every iteration of the repeat block, d represents a disk, but if you have just one disk, then on every iteration of the repeat block, d represents an item at the top level of that disk, and your script will behave very differently. What's more, if it just so happens that you have more than one disk, you have no way to find this out! You can test your script until you're blue in the face, believe that it works fine, and distribute it to others, only to learn later that it mysteriously breaks on someone else's computer.

Also, determining what sort of return value you've got is not always easy. Asking for its class doesn't necessary tell you what you want to know. The Finder, for example, simply lies to you about the class of the desktop, claiming that it's desktop when in fact it's desktop-object. But there is no desktop class! The problem is that the Finder's dictionary foolishly uses the same four-letter code for the desktop-object class and the application class's desktop property; when AppleScript tries to decompile that four-letter code, the term desktop comes first in the dictionary and hides the term desktop-object.

Coercions

Dictionaries don't list the coercions that can be performed by an application in response to get...as. (See "Explicit Coercion" in Chapter 14.) Only trial and error can give you this information.

A rare exception is the Finder, which defines a class alias list and almost tells you (but not quite) that the purpose of this class is to let you coerce to it:

```
tell application "Finder"
    get every disk as alias list
    -- {alias "xxx:", alias "main:", alias "second:", alias "extra:"}
end tell
```

A related problem is that dictionaries typically don't tell you about the implicit coercions that an application is willing to perform on a parameter of verb. We saw an example of this in "Alias" in Chapter 13, where it turned out that, even though GraphicConverter's dictionary says it expects an alias as the in parameter of the save command, a string would do:

```
tell application "GraphicConverter"
    set s to "xxx:Users:mattneub:Desktop:joconde"
    save window 1 in s as PICT
end tell
```

Ironically, the 'aeut' resource contains an alias or string class, expressly so that a dictionary has a way to convey to the user that an alias or a string is acceptable as a parameter. But GraphicConverter's dictionary fails to take advantage of this.

Enumerations

The way enumerations are presented in the human-readable version of a dictionary, there's no place for comments. There's no real reason for this, because in the dictionary itself, enumerators can and sometimes do have comments.

So, for example, in the 'aeut' resource, the enumerators of the 'savo' enumeration have comments:

```
yes -- Save objects now
no -- Do not save objects
ask -- Ask the user whether to save
```

But in the human-readable version of the dictionary, you aren't shown the enumeration in columnar form like this; instead, you see the English-like enumerators listed in their verb context. So, for example, GraphicConverter's dictionary entry for the verb close might be shown like this:

```
close reference -- the object to close
        [saving yes/no/ask]
        -- specifies whether to save currently open documents
```

In effect, the comments are thrown away. This isn't a big deal for yes/no/ask, since you can guess what they do; but there are lots of enumerations where comments would be more than welcome.

Borderline Syntax

Some syntactical constructions in AppleScript are of borderline legitimacy, and you can't be sure of what they'll do until you try them. A good example is the construction described in "Properties of Multiple References" in Chapter 10. This works:

```
tell application "Finder"
    name of every disk -- {"xxx", "main", "second", "extra"}
end tell
```

So does this:

```
tell application "BBEdit"
    contents of every word of window 1 -- {"this", "is", "a", "test"}
end tell
```

But this doesn't:

```
tell application "BBEdit"
    length of every word of window 1 -- 4
end tell
```

Instead of a list of lengths, we were given the length of the list (that is, the number of words in the window). This sort of inconsistency adds to the uncertainty of the programmer's task.

Bad Grammar

When developers decide on the English-like terminology for a dictionary, do they think about the experience of the users who will actually employ this terminology in typical AppleScript expressions? I sometimes wonder, when I find myself saying something like this:

```
if application file n is has scripting terminology then
```

The trouble is that has scripting terminology is the name of a property. Why would anyone make a property name a verb? If the name of this property were an adjective, such as scriptable, this expression would seem natural. The real trouble with this sort of mistake is that sooner or later the user will be misled by English into trying to write an expression that won't compile, such as this:

```
if application file n has scripting terminology then
```

See "The "English-likeness" Monster" in Chapter 5.

Lying Dictionary

If a dictionary wants to lie right to your face, it can. AppleScript has no way of checking to see whether the application's behavior matches the description in the dictionary.

The Finder's dictionary says that when you're using the make command, the new and at parameters are compulsory, not optional. That just isn't true; this works:

```
tell application "Finder" to make Finder window
```

In NoteTaker, the make command is said by the dictionary to return a reference to what has just been created. It should (since this is how most applications work), but it doesn't.

The StandardAdditions dictionary says that the POSIX file class's POSIX path property is a file; it's Unicode text. It say that list disks returns a list of aliases; it returns a list of strings. It says that do shell script returns plain text; it returns Unicode text.

StuffIt Expander's dictionary contains just one entry—the verb expand. The dictionary says that this verb returns an integer representing the number of files that were successfully expanded. It doesn't. It doesn't return anything at all. Just one term in the dictionary, and the folks who wrote the dictionary couldn't be bothered to tell the truth. I discovered this while trying to write the script for the section "Automatic Location" in Chapter 2. Naturally the script took much longer to write than it should have, because of the lying dictionary.

This is the sort of thing you must expect to encounter all the time. The road to AppleScript is strewn with the bodies of programmers who believed what the dictionaries told them. Be skeptical; you'll live longer.

Bad Comments

Because a dictionary, by its very nature, is inadequate in so many ways, its main chance to be informative is through its comments. Comments are just strings, so they are the developer's opportunity to say anything at all to the user. Unfortunately, many developers don't take advantage of this; they seem to feel that a comment should be terse and, if possible, opaque. AppleScript would be much easier to use if developers would take fuller advantage of the educational potential of comments in dictionaries.

My favorite example of this is Excel's dictionary, which in certain areas has no comments at all. (One area that has no comments is the Chart class; see "Combining Specialties" in Chapter 1 for some code written despite a complete lack of assistance from Excel's dictionary.) Excel has one of the weirdest dictionaries under the sun, along with one of the weirdest object models. The Microsoft folks have actually done a rather clever thing here: instead of working out an AppleScript scriptability implementation from scratch, they've simply taken the existing internal scripting implementation (Visual Basic for Applications) and exposed its entire object model, lock, stock, and barrel, to AppleScript. This is ingenious because it means that if you can drive Excel with Visual Basic you can drive it in just the same way with AppleScript, but it also means that if you don't know how to drive Excel with Visual Basic it's really hard to figure out how to drive it with AppleScript, since there are no comments to help you.

Here's an example of a good comment—the to parameter from the Finder's make command:

[to **reference**] -- *when creating an alias file, the original item to create an alias to*
    or when creating a file viewer window, the target of the window

That tells me exactly what this parameter is for; it's used on a limited set of occasions, and the comment says just what they are.

Here's an excerpt from Mailsmith's listing for the text_object class:

Class text_object: *abstract class describing a text object and its basic properties*
Properties:
    offset **integer** [r/o] -- *offset of a text object from the beginning of the document*
        (first char has offset 1)

That is really superb. The dictionary itself has no way to let you know a class is abstract, so the Mailsmith folks come right out and tell you in a comment. And the description of offset tells you how the characters are numbered—it all but gives you an example of how to use this property. Would that all comments were like these.

CHAPTER 20
Scripting Additions

A *scripting addition* is a compiled code fragment, typically written in a language such as C, that extends the AppleScript language. A scripting addition can't be targeted, and doesn't need to be; the commands that it implements are present as if built into AppleScript itself (see "Resolution of Terminology" in Chapter 19).

The scripting addition file *StandardAdditions.osax* is present on every machine. Therefore, even though AppleScript technically remains a "little language" with no ability to read files, put up dialogs, and so forth, such functionality is in fact essentially part of AppleScript (see "Scripting Addition" in Chapter 4).

This chapter provides some technical discussion of scripting additions generally, and then surveys the contents of the *StandardAdditions* osax. I'm not going to teach you how to write a scripting addition. If you're interested, see the vitally important Tech Note on the subject from Apple, *http://developer.apple.com/technotes/tn/tn1164.html*. See also *http://www.mactech.com/articles/mactech/Vol.10/10.01/ExtendApplescript/* and *http://www.latenightsw.com/technotes/ScriptingAddition/*.

Pros and Cons of Scripting Additions

In certain ways, scripting additions are clearly a Bad Thing, and Apple actively discourages them. As Apple puts it, "There are severe limitations to what you can do in the context of a scripting addition, and the system costs of managing large numbers of scripting additions are high." The main limitation is that a scripting addition cannot define any classes.* The system costs involve the global AppleScript namespace—we have already talked, in Chapter 19, about the terminology problems that scripting additions can cause—and certain technical considerations of memory management.

---

* A scripting addition can define events (commands). It can define pseudo-classes; see "Pseudo-Classes" in Chapter 19. It can also define coercions; this is not terribly common, but Jon's Commands defines some—see *http://www.seanet.com/~jonpugh/*. The Apple document I'm quoting here also says that scripting additions can't maintain state between calls, but this is no longer true.

Apple has tried to lead users away from scripting additions, in part through example, by installing faceless background applications in the same folder where the scripting additions live. On Mac OS 9, of the nine files present by default in the *Scripting Additions* folder, five are applications; under Mac OS X, of the seven files present in */System/Library/ScriptingAdditions*, five are applications. Such applications must be targeted explicitly; their vocabulary does not appear automatically as part of the AppleScript language. But applications don't suffer from any of the disadvantages of scripting additions, and as long as they are present on every machine, the commands they contain are universal.

On the other hand, there are some things that scripting additions do better than scriptable applications. An application must be running in order to be targeted; if it isn't running, it must be launched, which takes time. A scripting addition, on the other hand, once installed, is always present. If a scripting addition puts up some interface, that interface appears to be part of whatever application is being targeted at that moment. And communicating with an application is slower than calling a scripting addition command (though less so than formerly).

Scripting additions have a venerable history. Many generous developers have provided freeware or shareware scripting additions, and users have collected these with something approaching the fervor with which HyperCard users once collected XCMDs. (A popular and definitive repository of scripting additions is *http://www.osaxen.com*.) Scripting additions are a convenient way to provide AppleScript with system-level abilities and powers of rapid calculation that it otherwise lacks.

So it doesn't seem that scripting additions will be going away any time soon. One could argue that they aren't a very good idea, but they are a fact of life when you're using AppleScript.

Scripting Additions and Speed

One of the main reasons for using scripting additions is speed. For repeated trigonometric calculations, for example, it is certainly going to be a lot faster to use a scripting addition, such as the Satimage osax, than to roll your own calculation, as disingenuously suggested at Apple's web site. Similarly, a scripting addition that implements transformations to a list, such as returning a list with a particular element deleted, is going to be faster than coding the same operation in AppleScript (see "LISP-likeness" in Chapter 5).

Just how quickly a scripting addition is called, though, depends upon how you call it. The osax architecture is such that a scripting addition appears to be present "inside" whatever application is being targeted when the scripting addition command is called. This is noticeable, and useful, when a scripting addition puts up some user interface. For example, if the display dialog command is called from within a tell block targeting the Finder, the dialog appears within the Finder; it's as if you'd given the Finder a new dialog.

Behind the scenes, the way this works is that the application is sent the Apple event denoting a scripting addition command and can't deal with it; the message is then sent on up to the realm of scripting additions as a kind of fallback. This means that when you use a scripting addition command while targeting an application, it must go through an extra step. If you use a scripting addition command outside of any tell block, or within a "tell me" block, the message is sent directly to the scripting addition, which is faster by about an order of magnitude:

```
set t to the ticks
repeat 5000 times
    tell application "Finder" to get offset of "i" in "ticks"
end repeat
set t1 to (the ticks) - t
set t to the ticks
repeat 5000 times
    tell me to get offset of "i" in "ticks"
end repeat
set t2 to (the ticks) - t
return {t1, t2} -- {944, 71}
```

(The command the ticks comes from the Jon's Commands osax, and is good for timing things; a tick is about one-sixtieth of a second.)

Classic Scripting Additions

There is a difference between a scripting addition intended to be used with Mac OS 9 or before and a scripting addition intended to be used with Mac OS X. A Mac OS X–type osax will not work on Mac OS 9. A Mac OS 9–type osax will work on Mac OS X only if it has been Carbonized, meaning that internally its Toolbox calls have been linked against CarbonLib. In general, any particular osax file will probably be intended for one system or the other, not both. You may not be able to tell just by looking; if the Show Package Contents menu item appears in the Finder's contextual menu for an osax, it is certainly for Mac OS X, but otherwise you may need to consult the osax's documentation.

Classic implements AppleScript separately from Mac OS X, but the two are compatible and Apple events travel back and forth across the "system barrier." The Classic system contains osaxen, which are implemented by the Classic version of Apple-Script. This raises the question of how the presence of osaxen in Classic affects scripts running under Mac OS X.

The answer seems to be that when you run a script under Mac OS X, in code that targets a Classic application, any terminology that is resolved as belonging to a scripting addition is handled by a Classic scripting addition if possible. You can see this with a term like display dialog, because the dialogs put up by the Mac OS X and Classic versions of this command differ in appearance. So, for example:

```
tell application "Panorama" to display dialog "hello"
```

The dialog that appears is clearly a Classic dialog. (When I wrote this example, Panorama, my favorite database application, ran only in Classic.)

On my computer, it is impossible to use English-like terminology to call a Classic scripting addition command unless the same terminology is defined by an installed Mac OS X scripting addition. (The Apple documentation claims there's a way to do it with a terms block, but I have not gotten their way to work.) Fortunately, many commands are defined on both systems. But, for example, this will not compile:

```
min monitor depth -- compile-time error
```

and neither will this:

```
tell application "Panorama"
    min monitor depth -- compile-time error
end tell
```

The simplest solution is to employ the raw four-letter code to call the scripting addition command:

```
tell application "Panorama"
    «event aevtgmnd» -- 8 (same as min monitor depth)
end tell
```

But remember, you have to be targeting a Classic application for this to work. On its own, the same Apple event will fail:

```
«event aevtgmnd» -- error
```

Loading Scripting Additions

To be usable, a scripting addition must be present in the correct location on the machine where a script will compile or run. This means that scripts relying on third-party scripting additions are not particularly portable. You might write a script that depends on some scripting addition, and then distribute it to others without remembering to provide the scripting addition on which it depends. This can easily happen by accident, because scripting addition terminology appears to you, the programmer, to be part of the AppleScript language. Once again, Script Debugger is especially helpful here; it can list the scripting additions on which your script depends, and will even look them up on *http://macscripter.net* for you.

You might provide, along with your script, any third-party scripting additions on which the script depends. Two problems then remain:

- Osaxen are not loaded from just any old location; to be seen at all, they must be in a *Library/ScriptingAdditions* folder.
- Osaxen are loaded when the AppleScript scripting component instance is created and starts up.

So the user must install the extra scripting additions in the correct place *before* running your script. A script might, at runtime, move a scripting addition file into a *ScriptingAdditions* folder, but it's too late, since the AppleScript scripting component instance has already been created, and any scripting additions that are going to be loaded have already been loaded.

Under Mac OS X 10.3 ("Panther"), a solution to this problem has finally been provided. Save your script as an Application Bundle; then open the bundle with Show Package Contents and create *Contents/Resources/Scripting Additions*, and copy any needed osaxen into this folder. Now this applet will run on any Panther machine.

There is also a trick that allows your script to force osaxen to be loaded again, while the script is running. Here it is:

```
try
    tell me to «event ascrgdut»
end try
```

This raw Apple event, for which there is no equivalent English-like terminology, tells the current AppleScript scripting component instance to refresh its knowledge of scripting additions. It's enclosed in a try block because it will probably generate an error, but the error is spurious; the command works, and any osaxen that were installed since the scripting component was instantiated will be loaded.

So now we can write a script that installs a scripting addition on the fly and calls a command within it, all in one move. We still might not be able to call the scripting addition command using the English-like terminology, though, since the scripting addition was perhaps not installed at compile time. Here's an example using the Jon's Commands osax. If the osax isn't installed, we ask the user to find it for us, and we install it ourselves. We then call the ticks, a command within Jon's Commands, using the raw four-letter code:

```
try
    «event JonstikC»
on error -- evidently it isn't installed
    set jons to choose file with prompt "Please find Jon's Commands:"
    set sa to path to scripting additions from user domain
    tell application "Finder" to duplicate jons to sa
    try
        tell me to «event ascrgdut»
    end try
end try
display dialog («event JonstikC») -- 1974834
```

Standard Scripting Addition Commands

This section is a catalogue of the scripting addition commands present in a standard installation of Mac OS X.

For load script, store script, and run script, see "Compiled Script Files as Script Objects" in Chapter 9. For the POSIX file class, see "File" in Chapter 13 and "File Coercions" in Chapter 14. For digital hub scripting, folder action, and CGI events, see Chapter 24. For the do shell script command, see Chapter 23.

Dialogs

These scripting addition commands put up dialogs. The dialog will appear in whatever application is being targeted at the moment, or in the host application if no application is being targeted.

---

display dialog   general informational, text entry, and button-choice dialog

Description

A remarkably flexible little command. You can put up an information dialog, with a choice of standard icons. You can put up a text entry dialog, where the user can type a short string. You can dictate the names of up to three buttons, and learn which one the user pressed. The dialog can be set to time out if the user does not respond, and you can learn that this is what happened. By default, the buttons are "Cancel" and "OK". Returns a dialog reply record containing only the relevant items. If the user presses a button entitled "Cancel", an error is thrown (-128: "User canceled.").

Examples

```
set r to display dialog "Quick! Pick a Pep Boy!" buttons {"Mannie", "Moe", "Jack"} ¬
    with icon caution giving up after 3
set favoritePepBoy to button returned of r
if favoritePepBoy is "" and gave up of r then set notFastEnough to true
set whoIsIt to text returned of (display dialog "What is your name?" ¬
    default answer "" buttons {"OK"} default button "OK")
```

---

choose from list   listbox selection dialog

Description

Puts up a scrolling list of strings for the user to choose from. Returns a list of chosen strings, or false if the user cancels.

Example

```
choose from list {"Mannie", "Moe", "Jack"} with prompt "Pick a Pep Boy:"
```

---

choose file   file selection dialog

Description

Puts up a standard Open File dialog, with title "Choose File" and default button "Choose". Returns an alias. If the user cancels, an error is thrown (-128: "User canceled.")

Example

```
set f to choose file with prompt "Pick a text file:" of type "TEXT"
```

---

choose folder folder selection dialog

Description

Puts up a standard Choose Folder dialog, with title "Choose a Folder". The user can also create a new folder. Returns an alias. If the user cancels, an error is thrown (-128: "User canceled.")

Example

```
set f to choose folder with prompt "Pick a folder:"
```

choose file name file save dialog

Description

Puts up a standard Save File dialog (default button "Save"), with title "Choose File Name" and default prompt "Specify new file name and location". The user can also create a new folder. If the user types the name of an existing file, goes through the usual "Replace?" rigmarole. Returns a file URL (which appears as a file specifier). If the user cancels, an error is thrown (-128: "User canceled.") Does not actually save anything.

Example

```
set f to choose file name with prompt "Where shall I save this stuff?"
```

choose application application selection dialog

Description

Puts up a standard Choose Application dialog. The user can choose from a list of all applications, or can switch to browsing in a standard Open File dialog. Returns an application specifier, or an alias if requested; or a list of either, if multiple selections are allowed. If the user cancels, an error is thrown (-128: "User canceled.")

Example

```
set theApp to choose application as alias
tell application "Finder"
    set isScriptable to has scripting terminology of theApp
end tell
if isScriptable then display dialog "It's scriptable!"
```

choose URL URL selection dialog

Description

Puts up a standard Choose URL dialog (with a Connect button); this is the same as the Finder's Connect to Server dialog, useful for specifying servers on the local network, with an option to let the user choose various categories of server. The user can also just type a URL unless you prevent it; this can be basically any string at all. Does not actually connect! Returns a string. If the user cancels, an error is thrown (-128: "User canceled.")

Example

```
choose URL showing Remote applications -- "eppc://169.254.199.218:3031/"
```

choose color

Description

Puts up a standard Color Picker dialog, where the user may choose a color. Returns a color. A color is expressed as an `rgb color`, which is a list of three integers representing the red, green, and blue components. If the user cancels, an error is thrown (-128: "User canceled.") You can optionally specify a color that is selected initially when the Color Picker appears.

Example

```
choose color default color {9000, 10000, 50000} -- {50000, 9000, 10000}
```

Noises

The following commands can be invoked to produce a sound alert.

beep

Description

Plays the system beep sound.

Example

```
beep
```

set volume

Description

Sets how loud the speakers are, on a scale of 0 to 7.

Example

```
set volume 7
beep
```

say

Description

Performs text-to-speech, either speaking text or saving the synthesized speech as a sound file. Can also be used in conjunction with speech recognition to determine what text appears below the microphone window.

Example

```
tell application "SpeechRecognitionServer"
    set s to listen for {"yes", "no"} with prompt "Would you like me to beep?" ¬
        giving up after 10
end tell
if s is "yes" then
    say "Okay, I will beep now." displaying "Okay."
```

```
        beep
    else
        say "Okay, then I won't." displaying "Okay."
    end if
```

File and Machine Information

The following commands can be used to get information about a file or your system.

---

system attribute   gestalt and environment variables

Description
Returns the value of gestalt selectors.

Example
```
    set n to system attribute "sysv"
    set s to "print sprintf \"%1x\", " & n
    set v to do shell script "perl -e " & quoted form of s
    set L to characters of v
    set v to "." & item -1 of L
    set v to "." & item -2 of L & v
    set v to ((items 1 thru -3 of L) as string) & v
    display dialog "You are running system " & v & "!"
```

For a list of gestalt selectors, see *http://developer.apple.com/techpubs/macosx/Carbon/oss/GestaltManager/Gestalt_Manager/gestalt_refchap/ConstantsIndex.html*.

Also returns the value of user environment variables. To find out what they are, give the system attribute command with no parameters.

Example
```
    system attribute "SHELL" -- "/bin/tcsh"
```

For an example of the system attribute command used to fetch an environment variable, see Chapter 23.

---

path to   standard folder location

Description
Locates various standard folders, such as the system folder. Returns an alias (or string, if desired).

Example
```
    path to desktop -- alias "xxx:Users:mattneub:Desktop:"
```

If the designated folder is legal but doesn't exist, the path to command silently creates it unless you specify without folder creation, in which case an error is returned if the folder doesn't exist.

Because of a bug in the Script Editor's dictionary display, it can't display the complete list of standard folders available. So here it is:

```
application support
applications folder
desktop
desktop pictures folder
documents folder
favorites folder
Folder Action scripts
fonts
frontmost application
help
home folder
internet plugins
keychain folder
library folder
modem scripts
movies folder
music folder
pictures folder
preferences
printer descriptions
public folder
scripting additions
scripts folder
shared documents
shared libraries
sites folder
startup disk
startup items
system folder
system preferences
temporary items
trash
users folder
utilities folder
voices
apple menu
control panels
control strip modules
extensions
launcher items folder
printer drivers
printmonitor
shutdown folder
speakable items
stationery
```

Many standard folders aren't documented by the dictionary; these are accessed through four-letter codes as strings. For example, path to "cmnu" gives an alias to the Contextual Menu Items folder. For a list of these four-letter codes, see *http://developer.apple.com/ documentation/Carbon/Reference/Folder_Manager/folder_manager_ref/constant_6.html*.

For another way to access many standard folders, see "System Events" in Chapter 21.

This command also locates applications. Important undocumented uses are path to me and path to current application, which locate the host application.

Example

```
path to application "Finder" -- alias "xxx:System:Library:CoreServices:Finder.app:"
path to me -- alias "xxx:Applications:AppleScript:Script Editor.app:"
```

list disks
volume names

Description

Gets the names of all mounted volumes. Returns a list of strings (see "Lying Dictionary" in Chapter 19).

Example

```
list disks -- {"xxx", "main", "second", "extra"}
```

list folder
folder contents

Description

Gets the names of all items within a folder. Includes invisible files and folders if you don't prevent it. Returns a list of strings.

Example

```
list folder (path to home folder)
-- {".CFUserTextEncoding", ".DS_Store", ".Trash", "Desktop", ...}
```

info for
file/folder information

Description

Gets information about an item on disk. Returns a file information record packed with useful stuff.

Example

```
set uf to (path to home folder as string)
set L to list folder uf
set s to {}
repeat with f in L -- collect sizes of all items
    set end of s to size of (info for file (uf & f))
end repeat
set maxItem to 0
set maxVal to 0
repeat with i from 1 to (count s) -- find biggest size
    if item i of s > maxVal then
        set maxItem to i
        set maxVal to item i of s
    end if
end repeat
display dialog ¬
```

```
"The biggest thing in your home folder is " ¬
& item maxItem of L
```

If you ask for the info for a folder, the script may take some time to run, in order to sum the sizes of all the files within it.

File Data

These are scripting addition commands that read and write file data.

open for access
open file

Description

Opens a file for read access—optionally, for write access—creating the file as a text file if it doesn't exist (it does this even if you're opening for read access only; I regard this as a bug). Returns a file reference number that can be used with the other commands.

read
read data

Description

Reads data from a file, optionally coercing the data to a desired datatype. There are options for where to start (character positions are 1-based), how many characters to read, and what delimiter character to stop at.

The using delimiter parameter is poorly documented. This parameter is a list, as long as you like, of one-character strings. They are used to break the data into a single-level list of strings which will lack all the delimiter characters.

write
write data

Description

Writes data to a file, optionally coercing the data to a desired datatype. There are options for where to start and how much data to write.

The data coercion options for reading and writing allow you to store any kind of data in a text file and retrieve it later. The data is encoded, but it will be decoded correctly if you specify the same class when writing and when reading.

Example

```
open for access f with write permission
write {"Mannie", "Moe", "Jack"} as list to f
close access f
open for access f
set L to read f as list
close access f
L -- {"Mannie", "Moe", "Jack"}
```

On the whole, however, this approach is not very flexible; see "Data Storage" in Chapter 9.

get eof

Description

Returns the 1-based index of the last character of a file (which is also the size of the file).

Because character positions are 1-based, and because the eof is the position of the last character, if you want to append to a file you must start writing at a position one greater than the eof. That is the largest position at which you are permitted to start writing.

Example

```
write "Howdy" to f
set ourEof to get eof of f
write "Doody" to f starting at ourEof + 1
```

set eof

Description

Sets a file's size, truncating its data or filling the new excess with zeros.

close access

Description

Closes a file. Always close a file you have opened for access.

In general, the file data commands are smart about how they let you describe the file you want to operate on: they can take a file reference number returned by open for access, or a file specifier or alias.

When using the file data commands, you should ensure sufficient error handling so as not to leave a file open. If you do accidentally leave a file open, you might have to quit the current application (such as the Script Editor) in order to close it.

In this example, we use AppleScript to construct a miniature "database." We have some strings; taking advantage of the write command's starting at parameter, we write each string into a 32-character "field." The example perhaps overdoes the error handling, but it shows the general idea:

```
set pep to {"Mannie", "Moe", "Jack"}
set f to (path to current user folder as string) & "testFile"
try
    set fNum to open for access file f with write permission
on error
    close access file f
    return
end try
try
    set eof fNum to 0 -- erase if exists
    set eof fNum to (count pep) * 32
    repeat with i from 1 to (count pep)
```

```
            write item i of pep to fNum starting at (i - 1) * 32
        end repeat
        close access fNum
    on error
        close access fNum
    end try
```

Now we'll fetch the data from the "database." We take advantage of the fact that all data that isn't part of a string is null.

```
set f to choose file of type "TEXT"
try
    set fNum to open for access f
on error
    close access f
    return
end try
set L to {}
try
    set ct to (get eof fNum) / 32
    repeat with i from 1 to ct
        set end of L to read fNum from (i - 1) * 32 ¬
            before ASCII character 0 -- read up to but not including null
    end repeat
    close access fNum
on error
    close access fNum
end try
L -- {"Mannie", "Moe", "Jack"}
```

String and Clipboard

The following commands can be used to obtain a string or collect something from the Clipboard.

ASCII character
number to character

Description
Converts an ASCII numeric value to a one-character string.

Example
```
ASCII character 82 -- "R"
```

ASCII number
character to number

Description
Converts the first character of a string to an ASCII numeric value.

Example
```
ASCII number "Ribbit" -- 82
```

offset

Description

Reports the position of a substring within a target string. Character positions are 1-based. Returns 0 if the substring isn't found.

Example

    offset of "bb" in "Ribbit" -- **3**

The offset command's behavior used to be to consider case and ignore diacriticals, which is backwards from AppleScript's own defaults. In the current version, this is fixed, and string considerations are obeyed.

summarize

Description

Summarizes the content of a string or textfile, using the same technology as the Summarize Service.

set the clipboard to

Description

Sets the clipboard.

clipboard info

Description

Describes the contents of the clipboard as a list of class–size pairs.

Example

    clipboard info -- **{{string, 54}, {«class FMcl», 20}, {«class FMSC», 10240}}**

the clipboard

Description

Gets the clipboard text, or you can specify some other class (you'd use clipboard info to know what to specify).

Numbers and Dates

The following commands are used for working with numbers and dates.

round

Description

Rounds a real to an integer, in various ways.

Example
```
round 1.3 -- 1
```

---

random number
generate random number

Description

Generates a random number. This can be a real between 0 and 1, exclusive; or it can be an integer between two non-negative integers, inclusive. You can seed the generator to get it started; this is useful for generating a fixed pseudo-random sequence.

Example
```
random number
set L to {}
repeat 10 times
    if (random number 1) as boolean then
        set end of L to "heads"
    else
        set end of L to "tails"
    end if
end repeat
L -- {"heads", "tails", "heads", "heads", "heads",
    "tails", "heads", "heads", "heads", "heads"}
```

---

current date
now

Description

Generates a date object corresponding to the current date and time.

Example
```
time string of (current date) -- "10:41:13 AM"
```

---

time to GMT
time zone

Description

Reports the time zone that has been set via the Date & Time preference pane, as an offset from Greenwich time, in seconds.

Example
```
(time to GMT) / hours -- -7.0
```

Miscellaneous

These are scripting addition commands I couldn't categorize.

---

delay
wait

Description

Pauses a specified number of seconds. Starting with Panther, this number can be a real.

Example

```
delay 1
beep
```

mount volume

Description

Mounts an AppleShare volume (i.e., a machine where Personal File Sharing is turned on). The machine is specified as an afp URL; to avoid the dialog for choosing a particular volume, add the volume name as a second path element. Parameters can be used to avoid the username–password dialog (or you can include the username and password as part of the URL).

Examples

```
set s to choose URL showing File servers
mount volume s as user name "mattneub" with password "teehee"
mount volume "afp://little-white-duck.local" -- avoids no dialogs
mount volume "afp://little-white-duck.local/OmniumGatherum" ¬
    as user name "matt neuburg" with password "teehee" -- avoids all dialogs
```

If the machine is serving via AppleTalk (rather than TCP/IP), and if you have AppleTalk turned on in Mac OS X, you can mount the machine via AppleTalk using an AppleTalk URL, which looks, for example, like this: mount volume "afp:/at/LittleWhiteDuck". Note that you must use a name; the IP number doesn't apply here. You can specify volume, username, and password just as for a TCP/IP afp URL. Windows servers can be mounted using an smb URL.

scripting components

Description

Returns a list of strings giving the names of the installed OSA scripting components. One of these will be "AppleScript".

open location

Description

Hands the System a string representing a URL; the URL is opened with the appropriate helper application.

CHAPTER 21

Scriptable Applications

The chief virtue and purpose of AppleScript lies in its ability to communicate with scriptable applications by means of Apple events. This chapter summarizes the ways in which such communication is performed, and points out a few scriptable applications that might otherwise go unnoticed.

If you were hoping that this chapter would teach you all about how to script some particular application, I'm afraid you're going to be disappointed (see "The Scope of This Book" in the Preface). If the application comes with documentation or examples showing how to script it, start with that. For certain applications, there may be third-party books or web pages devoted to the topic. The application will in any case have a dictionary; see Chapter 19.

Targeting Scriptable Applications

To *target* a scriptable application is to aim Apple events at it, like arrows. This section catalogues the various ways to do it.

Tell and Of

The primary linguistic device for targeting an application in AppleScript is the tell block containing an application specifier. This actually has two purposes: it determines the target, if no other target is specified within the block, and it also causes a dictionary to be loaded, which may be used in the resolution of terminology. Instead of a tell block, the of operator (or its equivalents) can be used to form a target; this does not affect resolution of terminology.

(See "Target" and "Direct Object" in Chapter 10; "Tell" and "Using Terms From" in Chapter 12; "Application" in Chapter 13; and "Resolution of Terminology" in Chapter 19.)

Reference

A reference to an object belonging to an application can be used to target that application. The terminology within the reference has already been resolved (otherwise the reference could not have been formed in the first place); any further terminology prefixed to the reference when you actually use it will have to be resolved independently. (See Chapter 11.)

Local Applications

A *local application* is an application on the same computer as the script. The specifier for a local application may consist of a full pathname string (colon-delimited) or simply the name of the application; the name should usually be sufficient. Apple-Script builds into a compiled script enough information about the application that if the compiled script is moved to a different machine containing the same application, AppleScript on that machine will usually be able to find it. (But this mechanism does sometimes go wrong; see "Script Text File" in Chapter 4.) If AppleScript can't find a local application when compiling, decompiling, or running a script, it will put up a dialog asking the user to locate it.

(See "External Referents Needed at Compile Time" in Chapter 4 and "Loading the Dictionary" in Chapter 19.)

Remote Applications

A *remote application* is an application running on a different computer from the script. Communication is performed over IP (not AppleTalk, as in the past); this has the advantage that it works over the Internet, but it also means that even locally the remote machine needs an IP number (or a Rendezvous name). On the remote computer, Remote Apple Events must first be turned on; this can be done in the Sharing preference pane.

To the application specifier you append a machine specifier that uses an eppc URL. In Panther, the machine specifier can be just a Rendezvous name; in that case, Apple-Script will supply the *eppc://* prefix and the *.local* suffix on compilation. Connection requires a username and password; these will be requested in a dialog when the connection is first established, or you can avoid the dialog by means of username: password@ syntax in the URL. A terms block referring to a local application may be needed in order to resolve terminology at compile time (see "Using Terms From" in Chapter 12).

This example lets the user select the remote machine, supplies the username and password, and talks to the Finder on the remote machine. A terms block is needed because the machine is specified dynamically:

```
set u to choose URL showing Remote applications
set L to characters 8 thru -1 of u
```

```
set u to "eppc://mattneub:teehee@" & (L as string)
-- u is now e.g. "eppc://mattneub:teehee@169.254.168.138:3031/"
tell application "Finder" of machine u
    using terms from application "Finder"
        get name of disk 1
    end using terms from
end tell
```

As long as you're targeting an application on the remote machine, scripting addition commands you call are run on the remote machine. For example:

```
tell application "Finder" of machine "eppc://little-white-duck.local"
    say "Watson, come here, I want you."
end tell
```

When communicating with a remote machine, be careful with aliases. An alias is not a useful medium of communication between machines, because it will be resolved on the wrong machine. For example, don't ask the remote Finder for an alias list, and if you use the path to scripting addition command, ask for a string instead of an alias. For example:

```
tell application "Finder" of machine "eppc://little-white-duck.local"
    path to system folder as string
end tell
```

An even more devious variant of the same trick appears in the next example.

A remote application must already be running before you target it; you cannot target it and then launch it, as you can on a local machine. However, you can open an application from the remote Finder and then target it. If a tell block targets a literal application specifier for a remote application that isn't running, your script won't compile; so the trick is to put the name of the application in a variable, thus preventing AppleScript from trying to resolve the tell block until the script runs. By the time the tell block is executed, the application *will* be running. So, for example:

```
set m to "eppc://mattneub:teehee@little-white-duck.local"
tell application "Finder" of machine m
    set s to (run script "path to app \"System Events.app\" as string")
    open item s
end tell
set se to "System Events"
tell application se of machine m
    using terms from application "System Events"
        get every process
    end using terms from
end tell
```

XML-RPC and SOAP

XML-RPC and SOAP are web services allowing commands in a generalized form to be sent over the Internet by means of the http protocol, using a POST argument that contains XML structured according to certain conventions. This is clever because any CGI-capable web server can act as an XML-RPC server. The request is an ordinary POST request, and the server just passes it along to the appropriate CGI application, which pulls the XML out of the POST argument, parses it, does whatever it's supposed to do, and hands back the reply as a web page consisting of XML.

AppleScript can target XML-RPC and SOAP services through support built into the Apple Event Manager. The syntax is comparable to driving any scriptable application. You target the server by means of its URL, using a tell block. Within the tell block, you use either the call xmlrpc command or the call soap command; these terms are resolved only when the target is an http URL. Behind the scenes, the System acts as a web client: your command is translated into XML, the XML is shoved into the POST argument of an http request, the request is sent across the Internet, the reply comes back, the System extracts and interprets the XML from the reply, and this interpretation is returned as the result of the command.

The target can be expressed in this form:

```
tell application "http://www.xxx.com/someApplication"
```

or you can say this, which decompiles to the previous syntax:

```
tell application "someApplication" of machine "http://www.xxx.com"
```

The syntax for call xmlrpc is as follows:

```
call xmlrpc {method name: methodName, parameters: parameterList}
```

The syntax for call soap is as follows:

```
call soap {method name: methodName, ¬
    method namespace uri: uri, ¬
    parameters: parameterRecord, ¬
    SOAPAction: action}
```

You can omit an item of the record (such as method namespace uri or parameters) if it isn't applicable.

Now let's test these commands. There's a copy of UserLand Frontier on the Internet that is intended for users to test with XML-RPC and SOAP requests. By default, we access this server's XML-RPC functionality through a URL whose path is /rpc2. The server includes some simple test verbs, one of which is examples.getStateName. We can call this verb using AppleScript, as follows:

```
tell application "http://superhonker.userland.com/rpc2"
    call xmlrpc ¬
        {method name:"examples.getStateName", ¬
        parameters:30} -- "New Jersey"
end tell
```

Frontier is also a SOAP server. We can call the SOAP equivalent of the same verb using AppleScript, as follows:

```
tell application "http://superhonker.userland.com"
    call soap ¬
```

```
                {method name:"getStateName", ¬
                SOAPAction:"/examples", ¬
                parameters:{statenum:30}} -- "New Jersey"
    end tell
```

If you happen to have a copy of Frontier or Radio UserLand, you can test all this on
your own machine, without using the Internet. These programs run the very same
server on port 8080. So with Frontier or Radio UserLand running, you can substitute "http://localhost:8080/rpc2" and "http://localhost:8080" as the application
URLs for the tell block.

For further examples of call soap, see "Combining Specialties" in Chapter 1 and
"Using Terms From" in Chapter 12. In general, call xmlrpc and call soap are not
difficult to use; you'll just have to study the documentation for the service you're trying to call, and it may take a little trial and error to get the parameters just right.

Some Scriptable Applications

The purpose of this section is to alert you to some useful scriptable applications that
are part of Mac OS X but which you might not otherwise be aware of.

Finder

Okay, you're probably aware of the Finder. After all, you use it every day, and it is
the favorite target application for examples in this book. But I just wanted to remind
you about it one more time. The Finder concerns itself with the hierarchy of folders
and files on your hard drive. It's very good at such things as renaming files, copying
files, deleting files, creating folders and aliases, and describing the folder hierarchy.

If you're an old AppleScript hand, accustomed to scripting the Finder for other purposes, you'll want to read about System Events, later in this section.

Internet Connect

If you connect to the Internet via modem or PPPoE, Internet Connect is a good way
to query and manipulate your connection. A useful incantation is:

```
    tell application "Internet Connect" to get properties of status
```

The result is a record containing valuable information. For example, if its state is 0,
you're not connected to the Internet; if its state is 4, you are.

```
    tell application "Internet Connect"
        set r to properties of status
        if state of r is 4 then display dialog "You're connected!"
    end tell
```

System Events

In Mac OS 9 and before, the Finder was the locus of scriptability for a lot of System functionality that had nothing to do with files and folders, such as what applications were running. This was somewhat irrational, since the Finder wasn't really responsible for this other functionality; it was being used as a kind of stand-in for the System itself. In Mac OS X, scripting of such functionality has been moved to a faceless background application called System Events (located in the *CoreServices* folder, along with the Finder). Here are some of the things you can do with System Events:

- Sleep, restart, and shut down the computer.
- Manipulate login items—applications that are run automatically when the user logs in, which for most people means at startup. For example:

  ```
  tell application "System Events"
      make new login item at end of login items with properties ¬
          {path:"/Applications/Safari.app"}
  end tell
  ```

- Manipulate running processes, determining such things as which process is frontmost and which processes are visible.
- Access standard user folders.

System Events is also responsible for GUI scripting (Chapter 22) and for folder actions (Chapter 24). It is thus a very important application, and its dictionary deserves study. Examples of scripting System Events appeared in Chapter 1 and Chapter 2.

Speech Recognition Server

This application, hidden away in the Carbon framework, is the scriptable frontend for the System's built-in speech recognition functionality. For an example, see "Noises" in Chapter 20.

URL Access Scripting

This is a background-only application in the *ScriptingAdditions* folder. When it was invented (back in Mac OS 8.5, I believe), it was a very good thing, because it provided a way to download and upload via http and ftp across the Internet without the overkill of having to drive a full-featured client such as Netscape or Fetch. However, I personally find it undependable, and since we're now in the Unix-based world of Mac OS X, I recommend the use of do shell script and curl instead (see Chapter 23).

Keychain Scripting

This is another background-only application in the *ScriptingAdditions* folder, and acts as a scriptable frontend to the user's keychain, where passwords are stored. This is analogous to the functionality accessed through the Keychain Access utility. Keychain Scripting lets a script fetch a password from the keychain instead of hardcoding it in plaintext. For example:

```
tell application "Keychain Scripting"
    set k to (get key 1 of keychain 1 whose name is "mail.mac.com")
    tell k to set L to {name, account, password}
end tell
L -- {"mail.mac.com", "mattneub", "teehee"}
```

If, as in that example, you ask for the password of a key whose access control is set to require confirmation, the Confirm Access to Keychain dialog will appear (possibly twice—once for the Keychain Scripting application and once for the host application in which the script is running). You cannot script changes to the access control rules for a key through Keychain Scripting; I take it that this is a security measure.

Image Events

As this book was being written, Apple had begun work on a background-only application, Image Events, living in the same directory as the Finder and System Events. It will probably allow you to perform some basic manipulations on image files, such as scaling, rotating, and manipulating color profiles, as well as supplying information about monitors. For example:

```
tell application "Image Events"
    set f to (path to desktop as string) & "bigImage.eps"
    set f2 to POSIX path of (path to desktop) & "/smallerImage.eps"
    set im to open file f
    scale im by factor 0.5
    save im in f2
end tell
```

CHAPTER 22
Unscriptable Applications

Some applications are not scriptable; they have no repertory of Apple events to which they are prepared to respond. The developers simply omitted this feature, like the tinsmith who forgot to give the Woodsman a heart. You try to open the application's dictionary and you get an error. Other applications are scriptable, but they aren't scriptable in the way you'd like; the thing you'd like to make the application do isn't among its scriptable behaviors. In a case like this, how can you script the unscriptable?

On Mac OS 9 and before, the answer was to use a *macro program*. A macro program has the power to "see" an application's interface and to act as a kind of ghost user, pressing buttons, typing keys, and choosing menu items. Anything a user can do in an application can presumably be performed through some definable sequence of mouse and keyboard gestures; therefore it might be possible to emulate that sequence of gestures with a macro program. The result might not be as fast, elegant, or flexible as using AppleScript, but it could get the job done; plus, a macro program might itself be scriptable. (Three very strong macro programs that I often used on earlier System versions were QuicKeys, PreFab Player, and OneClick; see *http://www.cesoft.com/products/qkmac.html*, *http://www.prefab.com/player.html*, and *http://www.westcodesoft.com/index.html*.)

In the past, macro programs depended upon a feature of the System architecture whereby third-party code fragments called *system extensions* (or *INITs*) could be loaded into the System at startup in such a way as to modify the System's response to Toolbox calls. In essence, when the System was told to do a certain thing by any program (including itself), this code fragment would be called instead; usually it would also call the System's original functionality, so as not to break the computer altogether, but along the way it would interpose functionality of its own. (For a fine discussion of INITs, see Joe Zobkiw, *A Fragment of Your Imagination* [Addison-Wesley], Chapter 4.)

The trouble with this approach was that INITs were a threat to stability and reliability. They caused no end of headaches for users, who often found different INITs conflicted with one another, and for application developers, who would learn that their application misbehaved in the presence of some INIT. The ability of users to customize their own systems meant that every user's system could be essentially different from every other's.

On Mac OS X, INITs are abolished. In fact, that's part of the point of Mac OS X: at bottom, every system should be a clean system, and all machines should reliably work the same way. But without INITs, there's no way for a macro program to hook into the System's functionality at a level low enough for it to do the things that a macro program needs to do. This, in the early days of Mac OS X, made scripting the unscriptable next to impossible.

Recently, a solution to this quandary has emerged from Apple itself. As part of an effort to make Mac OS X accessible to people who may not be able to use a mouse and keyboard or see a computer screen, Apple has created the Accessibility API, a set of Toolbox commands that can do just what a macro program would do—"see" an application's interface and manipulate it like a ghost user wielding an invisible mouse and keyboard. Going even further, they have made the Accessibility API itself scriptable via AppleScript. Thus, you may be able to use AppleScript to drive the Accessibility API to manipulate the interface of a program that is not itself scriptable, or not scriptable in the way you desire. This technique is called *GUI scripting*.

Getting Started with Accessibility

If you want to script the unscriptable, you must first open System Preferences to the Universal Access pane and make sure that the "Enable access for assistive devices" checkbox is checked. This step is absolutely crucial, since the checkbox is unchecked by default; unless it is checked, the scripts in this chapter will fail (with a mysterious error message, of course).

You will now be able to use GUI scripting, by way of classes and events implemented in System Events, in the Processes Suite; here you'll see events such as click and keystroke and classes such as radio button and menu item. The classes in question are all UI element subclasses.

Given a particular task you'd like to perform in a particular application by means of the user interface, the problem is now to express the referenced interface elements in terms of the UI element object model. This is much the same problem that you always face with AppleScript—working out the target application's object model (see Chapter 3, and "The object model" in Chapter 19). But now there's an added twist, because the object model terminology within one application (System Events) must be used to express object relationships within another (the target application). There are various approaches that can help you:

- Use AppleScript. The UI element subclasses let you ask about the interface elements of a window or menu. Apple provides some scripts showing the sorts of thing you can say; look for one called *Probe Window*, for example.

- Use an application that will employ the Accessibility API directly to analyze a window or menu. Apple provides a utility that does this, the UI Element Inspector. At present this can be downloaded from *http://www.apple.com/applescript/uiscripting/02.html*, or (with source code) from *http://developer.apple.com/samplecode/Sample_Code/OS_Utilities/UIElementInspector.htm*. A more user-friendly dedicated application for studying the interface and expressing its elements in AppleScript terms is the inexpensive commercial utility PreFab UI Browser (see *http://www.prefab.com/uibrowser/index.html*).

GUI Scripting Examples

This section describes a couple of examples of GUI scripting from my own life.

Our first example will be to toggle File Sharing on or off. This is something I need to do quite often, and System Preferences isn't sufficiently scriptable to automate it. I have to open System Preferences, go the right pane, and press all the right buttons, every time; this, as they say, gets old real fast. But AppleScript can automate it for me, thanks to GUI scripting.

System Preferences *is* sufficiently scriptable to get us to the Sharing pane, so let's consider that problem solved. To write our script, then, the first step is to open the Sharing pane manually and explore it in terms of its UI element objects.

For example, we're initially interested in the Personal File Sharing row of the scrolling list in the Services tab. UI Element Inspector describes it this way:

```
<AXApplication: "System Preferences">
<AXWindow: "Sharing">
 <AXTabGroup>
  <AXScrollArea>
   <AXTable>
    <AXRow>
     <AXTextField>

Attributes:
   AXRole:  "AXTextField"
   AXRoleDescription:  "text field"
   AXHelp:  "(null)"
   AXValue (W):  "Personal File Sharing"
   AXEnabled:  "1"
   AXFocused:  "0"
   AXParent:  "<AXRow>"
   AXWindow:  "<AXWindow: "Sharing">"
```

```
        AXPosition:  "x=228 y=341"
        AXSize:  "w=195 h=18"
        AXSelectedText:  "(null)"
        AXSelectedTextRange:  "(null)"

    Actions:
        AXConfirm - AXConfirm
```

PreFab UI Browser displays the element hierarchy more graphically, using Apple-Script terminology; Figure 22-1 shows the result.

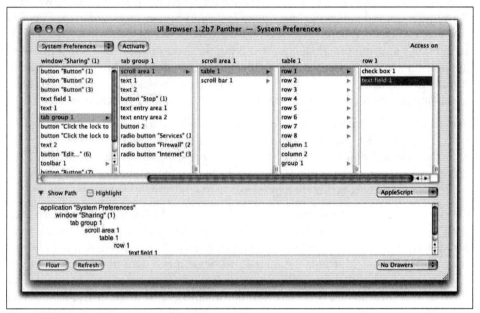

Figure 22-1. UI Browser describes a window

The procedure of exploration continues in just the same way, examining each interface item to which we might wish to send a message; I'll spare you the remaining details.

Once we know enough about the target window, we proceed to develop the actual script. This is generally quite straightforward because the repertory of actual commands is very small; you are pretending to be a mouse and a keyboard, after all, so the main things you can do are click and type. Here's the script:

```
tell application "System Preferences"
    activate
    set current pane to pane "com.apple.preferences.sharing"
end tell
tell application "System Events"
    tell application process "System Preferences"
        tell tab group 1 of window "Sharing"
            click radio button "Services"
```

```
            select row 1 of table 1 of scroll area 1
            click button 1
        end tell
    end tell
end tell
```

Let's sum up what happens in that example. First we open System Preferences and bring it to the front; then we open the Sharing pane. So much for System Preferences' own scriptability.

Now the Accessibility API takes over. Notice the structure of what follows: we target System Events, and *within the targeting of System Events we target the desired application process.* That's crucial. We target System Events because that's the locus of the terminology and the functionality for driving the Accessibility API. We speak of an application process, rather than an application, because we need to specify the application with actually targeting it! You can see that I also like to include a tell block specifying common UI elements, simply as a way of reducing the chain of ofs.

The rest is just a matter of doing programmatically what we would do in real life with the mouse. We click the Sharing tab (called a "radio button" in the dictionary) to make sure we're in the correct tab view, select the first row of the scrolling list, and click the button at the right. This might be captioned Start or Stop; that's why we refer to it by index rather than by name.

The next example has to do with Mailsmith. I've got Mailsmith set up to leave large mail messages on the server, so that they don't take up time and bandwidth when I'm checking my mail. If a large message is of interest, I later download it and delete it from the server. Unfortunately, there is no single menu item that lets me do this; I must manually choose a menu item to download the large message, wait until it has arrived, and then manually choose another menu item to delete it from the server. Since this is a frequent sequence of actions, I'd like to reduce it to a script. But although Mailsmith is pretty heavily scriptable, the developers neglected to define events for these actions. GUI scripting provides the solution:

```
tell application "Mailsmith" to activate
tell application "System Events"
    tell application process "Mailsmith"
        tell menu "Message" of menu bar 1
            click menu item "Get from Server"
            tell application "Mailsmith"
                delay 5
                repeat until not connection in progress
                    delay 2
                end repeat
            end tell
            click menu item "Remove from Server"
        end tell
    end tell
end tell
```

Observe the mixture of GUI scripting with normal scripting in that example. GUI scripting is used to choose the relevant menu items, but in between, normal scripting is used to wait until the connection with the server has had time to open and close, implying that the download is complete.

It should be noted, in closing, that GUI scripting is not a panacea. It doesn't work everywhere: a particular interface item, a window, or an entire application might not use the standard interface elements. In that case, the Accessibility API can do nothing for you. Also, even though it's a lot of fun, GUI scripting should be considered a workaround; real scriptability is always better. If you're reduced to using GUI scripting to accomplish some goal, and if the target application is still being actively developed, then consider writing to the developer and requesting that the application be made genuinely scriptable.

CHAPTER 23
Unix

AppleScript is a powerful way to get information and to make things happen through scripting on Mac OS X—but it's not the only way. Mac OS X is Unix, and comes with many Unix command-line tools, along with scripting languages such as Perl and Ruby. AppleScript and Unix are different worlds, but there's a communicating door between them, and it's open in both directions: you can call into the Unix shell from within AppleScript code, and you can call AppleScript from the Unix command line. That means you can combine the power of Unix with the power of AppleScript. This chapter talks about how to do it; see also "Unix" in Chapter 2.

Do Shell Script

The key to calling the Unix shell from your AppleScript code is the do shell script scripting addition command.

Apple provides an excellent Tech Note on this command, and your first step should be to read it (*http://developer.apple.com/technotes/tn2002/tn2065.html*). The direct object is a string representing the text you would type at the command-line prompt in the Terminal. But not quite, because your Terminal shell is probably bash or tcsh, whereas the default shell for do shell script is sh. Also, the default paths used by do shell script might not be the same as your own shell's default paths, so in order to specify a command you might have to provide a full pathname, such as /usr/bin/perl instead of just perl. (That's not a real example, though, since perl will probably work just fine.)

Optional parameters let you provide an administrator password. The result is whatever is returned from the command via stdout; Unix linefeed characters are converted to Mac return characters by default, but you can prevent this if you wish. If the command terminates with a nonzero result (an error), an error by the same number is thrown in your script, and you can use this number (along with the manpages for the command) to learn what went wrong.

For example, the following code requests a (decimal) number from the user and converts it to hex by means of the Unix `printf` command:

```
set theNum to text returned of (display dialog "Enter a number:" default answer "")
set s to "printf %X " & theNum
display dialog (do shell script s)
```

An important thing to remember about do shell script is that it does not set up an interactive shell. You give a command, you get the result, and that's all. In some cases where a tool is interactive, you can work around this problem. The tool may provide a noninteractive alternative. For instance, you might be able to pass through a file as intermediary. The following (rather silly) example illustrates the point; it converts a number to a hex string by way of bc, by writing out a small bc program file and calling bc to process it:

```
set theNum to text returned of (display dialog "Enter a number:" default answer "")
set t to path to temporary items
set posixT to POSIX path of t
set f to open for access file ((t as string) & "bctemp") with write permission
write "obase = 16\n" to f
write theNum & "\n" to f
write "quit\n" to f
close access f
set s to "bc --quiet " & quoted form of (posixT & "bctemp")
display dialog (do shell script s)
```

Similarly, if you wanted to call top, you could call it in a noninteractive form such as top -l1 and parse the result.

The hardest part of calling a Unix tool is dealing with the Unix parsing and quotation rules. To protect a string from the parsing rules, you can wrap it in single quotes. AppleScript makes this easy with the quoted form property of a string (see "String Properties" in Chapter 13), and you should use it, as in the previous example. This does not absolve you from AppleScript's own rules for forming literal strings (see Table 13-1). So, in the system attribute example in "File and Machine Information" in Chapter 20, double quotation marks are entered into the literal string in escaped form, to get AppleScript to do the right thing; then the entire string is munged with quoted form to get the shell to do the right thing.

When talking to Perl, using a file as an intermediary can simplify things. There is no problem forming a short Perl script and handing it to Perl directly by means of the -e switch; but if a longer Perl script is to be formed and executed on the fly, it might make sense to write it into a file and then tell Perl to run the file. And there may be no need to form the Perl script on the fly. Perhaps your script could consist of *two* scripts—one in AppleScript, one in Perl.

Here's an example. There's an excellent weekly online Macintosh journal called *TidBITS*, and their site has a web page where you can enter words to search for and get back a page of links to past articles containing those words (see *http://db.tidbits.com*).

We'll simulate this page, acting as a web client ourselves, with the help of curl. We know what the HTML of the results page looks like, so we've prepared a Perl script to parse it into the URLs and titles of the found articles. The Perl script expects as argument the pathname of the file containing the HTML:

```perl
$s = "";
while (<>) {
    $s .= $_;
}
$s =~ m{search results (.*)$}si;
$1 =~ m{<table(.*?)</table>}si;
@rows = ($1 =~ m{<tr(.*?)</tr>}sig);
for ($i=0;$i<$#rows;$i++) {
    ($links[$i], $titles[$i]) =
        ($rows[$i+1] =~ m{<a href="(.*?)">(.*?)</a>}i);
}
print join "\n", @links, @titles;
```

Now for the AppleScript code. First we put up a dialog where the user can enter some search terms. We URL-encode these terms in a primitive way (substituting a plus sign for any spaces) and assemble the POST data for the form submission. We use curl to submit this POST data to the TidBITS server. In essence, the TidBITS server receives exactly the same HTML it would receive if a user entered the same search terms in the first field of the TidBITS Search page and pressed the Submit button.

The results come back as a page of HTML, which curl writes out to a file. We now hand this file over to our Perl script for parsing. The results come back from the Perl script, and now we have a list which is really two lists: first the URLs of the found pages, then the titles of those same pages. We put up a list showing the titles; if the user chooses one, we ask the browser to display the corresponding URL.

```applescript
set t to text returned of ¬
    (display dialog "Search TidBITS for:" default answer "")
set text item delimiters to "+"
set t to (words of t) as string
set d to "'-response=TBSearch.lasso&-token.srch=TBAdv"
set d to d & "&Article+HTML=" & t
set d to d & "&Article+Author=&Article+Title=&-operator"
set d to d & "=eq&RawIssueNum=&-operator=equals&ArticleDate"
set d to d & "=&-sortField=ArticleDate&-sortOrder=descending"
set d to d & "&-maxRecords=20&-nothing=MSExplorerHack&-nothing"
set d to d & "=Start+Search' "
set u to "http://db.tidbits.com/TBSrchAdv.lasso"
set f to POSIX path of file ((path to desktop as string) & "tempTidBITS")
do shell script "curl -d " & d & " -o " & f & " " & u
set perlScript to POSIX path of ¬
    alias ((path to desktop as string) & "parseHTML.pl")
set r to do shell script "perl " & perlScript & " " & f
set L to paragraphs of r
set half to (count L) / 2
set L1 to items 1 thru half of L
```

```
set L2 to items (half + 1) thru -1 of L
set choice to (choose from list L2) as string
repeat with i from 1 to half
    if item i of L2 is choice then
        open location (item i of L1)
        exit repeat
    end if
end repeat
```

That code works well enough to demonstrate the principle, but one can't help feeling it's a pity that AppleScript doesn't let us present the user with some nicer interface. We'll rectify that little shortcoming in the next chapter, by building these same scripts into an AppleScript Studio application.

If you hesitate to use do shell script because you think it's scary or clumsy, stop hesitating. Unix tools are extremely valuable supplements to AppleScript's powers. I would much rather ask the shell to convert between decimal and hex, for example, than construct a handler in AppleScript alone to accomplish the same thing. I've already said (Chapter 21) that I'd rather use curl than the URL Access Scripting application. And being able to call on Perl to parse a string is sheer pleasure. The power of Unix tools is present on every Mac OS X machine; to ignore do shell script is to cut yourself off from the convenience and delight of having all this power at your command.

Osascript

Three command-line tools are provided for accessing AppleScript from Unix. The first, osalang, lists the scripting components present on your machine (see "The Open Scripting Architecture" in Chapter 4):

```
$ osalang -l
ascr appl cgxervdh  AppleScript
scpt appl cgxervdh  Generic Scripting System
```

If you have other OSA components installed, they will also appear. For example, if you use Script Debugger, you'll see AppleScript Debugger and JavaScript. These do in fact appear on my machine, but to reduce confusion, they are not shown here.

The two four-letter codes identifying each component are used by OSA programmers, but typically won't arise in the context of your AppleScript experience. Then comes a series of flags describing the capabilities of this scripting component (see the manpages for their meanings). Finally, we have the name of the component. The "Generic Scripting System" is the general front end to the OSA (what Chapter 4 calls the GSC); "AppleScript" is the AppleScript component in particular. You can use either of these two terms as a language specifier in calling the other two command-line tools, but their effect will be identical, since the GSC will treat AppleScript as the default component. In general, unless you are using other OSA scripting components, you'll have no need for osalang.

The osacompile command takes as argument a text file, or some text provided on the command line, and generates a compiled script file or applet. There are options letting you determine the characteristics of this file, such as its type and creator, but you typically won't need these. For example:

```
$ cat > textfile
display dialog "Hello, world!"
^D
$ osacompile -o compiledfile textfile
```

The result is a compiled script file *compiledfile* that opens into Script Editor when double-clicked in the Finder. We also generated an extra intermediate file, *textfile*. You can avoid this and type the script directly into osacompile:

```
$ osacompile -o compiledfile
display dialog "Hello, world!"
^D
```

The extension on the filename supplied in the -o parameter is used to determine the type of file that's created; this time we'll make an applet bundle:

```
$ osacompile -o appBundle.app
display dialog "Hello, world!"
^D
```

Further switches let you determine the applet's characteristics (see "Applet Options" in Chapter 24), so read the manpages.

The osascript command runs a compiled script file, a text file, or text provided from the command line. This command is the real key to bridging the gap between Unix and AppleScript from the Unix side. To enter text directly from the command line, you can use the -e switch, in which case the shell's usual quotational hoops will have to be jumped through; to enter the text of a multiple-line script from the command line in the Terminal, you can use the -e switch multiple times. For example:

```
$ osascript -e 'tell app "Finder"' -e 'activate' -e
'display dialog "Hello, world!"' -e 'end'
```

But you can also type the script as a series of lines, as in the osacompile examples earlier:

```
$ osascript
tell app "Finder"
activate
display dialog "Hello, world!"
end
^D
```

In languages such Perl and Ruby, you can conveniently construct a multiple-line script as text on the fly by means of a "here document" and then hand this off to osascript for execution:

```
$s = <<DONE;
    tell app "Finder"
        activate
        display dialog "Hello, world!"
    end
DONE
`osascript -e '$s'`;
```

Again, if you don't have to construct the script on the fly, then consider not doing so. There is nothing wrong with preparing a compiled script file beforehand and just calling it with osascript. This is faster than handing text to osascript, because there's nothing to compile, and it saves you from all the quotational headaches.

Unfortunately there's no way to call osascript with parameters to be handed to the compiled script. Consider, for example, the following Perl script:

```
print "What would you like me to say?\n";
$prompt = <STDIN>;
chomp $prompt;
$s = <<DONE;
    tell app "Finder"
        activate
        display dialog "${prompt}!"
    end
DONE
`osascript -e '$s'`;
```

We can call that script from the command line, as follows:

```
$ perl hello.pl
What would you like me to say?
Howdy
```

This works fine; the dialog saying "Howdy!" appears in the Finder. Now let's think about how we would move the AppleScript part of this Perl script off to a compiled script file and call it with the value of $prompt as a parameter. We can't do this in any direct way. AppleScript has no ARGV mechanism for retrieving arguments from the command line. The only place for incoming parameters in a compiled script file is through the run handler; but this would require us to call run script, which we can only do by way of osascript, at which point the overhead is even greater. The only real alternative is to leave the data in a "drop," that is, in some location where the compiled script expects to find it.

One such "drop" would be an environment variable. (Recall from Chapter 20 that the system attribute command can read Unix environment variables.) We can't tell the compiled script the name of the variable, of course, so it must be hardcoded both into the Perl script and the AppleScript code. So, for example, the chain of command might run like this—from the Terminal:

```
$ perl hello.pl
What would you like me to say?
Hello, world
```

to Perl (*hello.pl*):

```
print "What would you like me to say?\n";
$prompt = <STDIN>;
chomp($ENV{whatToSayInTheDialog} = $prompt);
`osascript Desktop/helloAS.scpt`;
```

to AppleScript (*helloAS.scpt*):

```
set p to system attribute "whatToSayInTheDialog"
tell application "Finder"
    activate
    display dialog p
end tell
```

Another approach would be to use a file to transfer the data. Again, the file path will have to be hardcoded in both scripts. Here's Perl (*hello.pl*):

```
print "What would you like me to say?\n";
$prompt = <STDIN>;
chomp $prompt;
chdir();
open OUT, ">Desktop/dataForHello";
print OUT $prompt;
close OUT;
`osascript Desktop/helloAS.scpt`;
```

And here's AppleScript (*helloAS.scpt*):

```
set f to (path to desktop as string) & "dataForHello"
set fNum to open for access file f
set p to read fNum
tell application "Finder"
    activate
    display dialog p
end tell
```

That technique may appear extraordinarily elaborate, but if the AppleScript file were lengthy, the shoe would be on the other foot. To create and compile the text of the AppleScript code entirely on the fly, merely in order to embed a single value in it from Perl, would be overkill—and slow. To compile the AppleScript code beforehand saves a lot of time, and handing off a parameter to it from Perl by way of an environment variable or a file is a perfectly reasonable technique.

Do not use any scripting addition commands that put up a user interface, such as display dialog, directly from within osascript. The problem is that osascript is not an application context, so it has no provision for user interactivity. The dialog appears, but you can't click the buttons to dismiss it! The only escape is to kill the osascript process. The solution is to make sure that your script targets an actual application and calls any user interface scripting addition commands from within that. That's why we targeted the Finder in the preceding examples.

Using the -ss switch with osascript presents the results as AppleScript would present them:

```
$ osascript -ss -e '{"Mannie", {"Moe"}}'
{"Mannie", {"Moe"}}
```

If you omit it, you wind up with a flat comma-delimited list:

```
$ osascript -e '{"Mannie", {"Moe"}}'
Mannie, Moe
```

The fact that these are strings, that there is a list, and that one of the list items is itself a list, is completely lost from the representation of the result. Nevertheless, this representation has its place, especially when you plan to use further shell commands to process the result. In this example, I find all persons who appear more than once in my Address Book:[*]

```
$ osascript -e 'tell app "Address Book" to get name of every person'
    | tr , "\n" | sort -bf -k2 | uniq -d
Mark Anbinder
Mary Byrd
Jeff Carlson
    ...
```

The example takes advantage of the fact that a comma is the delimiter between names in the output from the AppleScript command. See "Combining Specialties" in Chapter 1, "Unix" in Chapter 2, and Chapter 4 for more examples of osacompile in action.

---

[*] Thanks to Chris Nebel for this example.

CHAPTER 24
Writing Applications

Macintosh standalone applications are typically written in languages such as C, C++, Objective-C, or REALbasic. But you can write an application with AppleScript, and this chapter talks about the ways you can do it. You can write an applet or a droplet, essentially converting a script directly into an application; this application will be more or less faceless, but it's a true standalone application, it can accept drag-and-drop of files and folders onto its icon, and it's scriptable. Or you can wrap your script in a full-fledged Cocoa interface with AppleScript Studio.

This chapter also talks about writing CGIs and how AppleScript may be used to supplement a web server. It talks about digital hub scripting. And it talks about folder actions; a folder action is not really an application, but it is like an application in that it runs independently and spontaneously, and because it responds to certain events.

Applets

An *applet* is a compiled script wrapped up in a simple standalone application shell (see "Applet and Droplet" in Chapter 4). To make a script into an applet, save it from the Script Editor as an application instead of as a compiled script. You elect this choice in the Save As dialog. The result is a standalone application. If you open the application from the Finder (by double-clicking it, for example), the script runs.

Alternatively, you can now save a script as an application bundle. From the outside, the result looks and works like an applet, exactly as described in this chapter. Since it's a bundle, though, you can do things with it that you can't do with an old-style applet, such as storing extra resources inside it; for an example, see "Persistence," later in this chapter. Also, an application bundle can call scripting additions contained within itself; see "Loading Scripting Additions" in Chapter 20. Keep in mind that this format is not backward-compatible with earlier system versions.

A script still remains editable from inside the applet. The only trick is that now you must open the script for editing in a different way. You can't edit it by double-clicking it from the Finder, since that runs the applet. But the Script Editor can still open it. You can even have an applet open for editing in the Script Editor, save it without closing it, and then double-click it in the Finder to run it, as a way of testing while developing. (But you can't save an applet's script into the applet while the applet is actually running, for obvious reasons.) And there's another way to open an applet for editing, which we'll come to in a moment.

Applet Options

When you select Application (or Application Bundle) in the Save As dialog, some further options come into play. These options affect the way the application will behave.

One option is Show Startup Screen. If this is checked, the script's description is used to form a dialog which is displayed when the applet is started up, as a kind of introductory splash screen. In Script Editor, the description may be typed into the Description tab at the bottom of the window. It is styled text, and the styling is maintained in the startup screen dialog. The dialog offers the choice to run the applet's script or to quit without running it.

Another option is Stay Open. The default behavior of an applet is to run its script and then quit automatically. But if Stay Open is checked, it doesn't quit automatically after running. A Stay Open applet has a Quit menu item, so the user can quit it manually. (Actually, even a non–Stay Open applet has a Quit menu item, but one is unlikely to notice this unless its run handler takes a long time. This can confuse the user; see the next section.) It also has a File menu item that lets the user suppress the startup screen (if the applet was originally saved with Show Startup Screen checked), and an Edit menu item that lets the user open the applet's script in the Script Editor.[*]

An applet that was saved with the Show Startup Screen option unchecked, or whose startup screen has been suppressed by the user, can be forced to show its startup screen dialog by holding down the Control key as the applet starts up.

While the startup screen dialog is showing, the applet's menus are active. Thus, the user can always edit an applet's script, even if the applet is not set to Stay Open, by starting up the applet and holding down the Control key to bring up its startup screen dialog, then choosing the Edit menu item.

To prevent the applet from being editable by the user, you can save it as Run Only. Keep in mind that this means even *you* can no longer edit the applet; if you have no other copy of the script, you lose all ability to edit the applet's script forever.

---

[*] But the Edit menu item is not working for application bundles as of this writing.

Applet Handlers

Certain handlers in an applet script, if present, will be called automatically at certain moments in the lifetime of the applet. Because of their special status, none of these handlers takes parentheses in the first line of its definition; they are not called as handlers, but are responding to predefined commands (events):

run

> The run handler, whether implicit or explicit ("The Run Handler" in Chapter 8), is called when the applet is started up, either by the user opening it from the Finder or by a script targeting it. To start up an applet without calling its run handler, tell it to launch.

reopen

> A reopen handler, if present, is called when the already running applet is summoned to the front by such means as being double-clicked in the Finder or having its icon clicked in the Dock. Merely switching among applications with ⌘-Tab, or telling the applet to activate, does *not* send a reopen event.

idle

> An idle handler, if present, is called as soon as the run handler finishes executing, and then again periodically while a Stay Open applet is running. The value returned by the idle handler is a real representing the number of seconds before the idle handler should be called again. A return value of 0, or any other value that can't be coerced to a positive real, is treated as 30.

quit

> A quit handler, if present, is called when the applet is about to quit. If it is a Stay Open applet, this might be because the user has chosen its Quit menu item; if not, it might be because the applet has been started up and its run handler has finished executing. If the quit handler wishes to permit the applet to quit, it must give the continue quit command.

 An applet having a quit handler that does not give the continue quit command will appear to the user to be impossible to quit (except by force-quitting).

So, for example, here's an annoying little Stay Open applet:

```
on run
    display dialog "Howdy!"
end run
on quit
    display dialog "Farewell!"
    continue quit
end quit
on idle
    beep
    display dialog "Get to Work!"
```

```
        return 1 * minutes
    end idle
```

An applet is scriptable with respect to its handlers; that is, you can tell an applet to run, reopen, idle, or quit, and it will execute the respective handler if it has one. If you tell an applet to run and it has no run handler code, it simply starts up if it isn't running already. If you tell an applet to run and it does have a run handler, and it wasn't running already, the run handler will be called *twice*—once because you targeted it, and again because you told it to run. To prevent this, first tell the applet to launch, and then tell it to run. (To prevent the run handler from being called at all, tell the applet to launch and *don't* tell it to run.) If you tell an applet to quit and it has no quit handler, it simply quits. If you tell an applet to idle and it has no idle handler, or to reopen and it has no reopen handler, nothing happens (but the calling script may receive an error).

You are also free to add handlers of your own to an applet's script. If you do, then the applet becomes scriptable with respect to these handlers. You call them like ordinary handlers. For example, suppose we have an applet *howdy* whose script goes like this:

```
on sayHowdy(toWhom)
    activate
    display dialog "Howdy, " & toWhom
end sayHowdy
```

Then we can say in another script:

```
tell application "howdy"
    sayHowdy("Matt")
end tell
```

The value is returned as one would expect; here, the calling script receives the value {button returned:"OK"} if user presses the OK button.

An applet has no dictionary. This means that when you call an applet's handler from another script, AppleScript has no way of knowing whether the applet contains such a handler, or, if it does, what its parameters should be. But it doesn't need to know. Without attempting to resolve it as terminology, AppleScript converts your call into the Call•subroutine command ('ascr/psbr') (see Appendix A). Essentially, it just recodes your call as a record and throws that record at the applet. It is up to the applet to decide how to respond; and it decides this correctly, all by itself. If you call an applet handler that doesn't exist, or if you call an applet handler with parameters that are not in accordance with those of the handler definition, the applet returns an error at runtime. The need to be able to code a handler call as an Apple event that can be blindly sent from one process to another in this way helps to explain the peculiar rules of AppleScript's handler-calling syntax ("Syntax of Defining and Calling a Handler" in Chapter 8).

The idle handler should not be treated as ensuring a precise measure of time. The time interval returned is merely a request not to be called until after the interval has elapsed. I am not entirely clear on what the time interval is measured from;

experiments returning 0 seemed to suggest that it was measured from when the idle handler was last called, not from when it last returned, but this didn't seem to be true for other values. If your goal is to run a script at precise times or intervals, you might be happier using a utility to handle this for you. For example, see *http://www.sophisticated.com/products/ido/ido_ss.html* for iDo Script Scheduler, a commercial product that runs scripts at specified times.

The question arises of how to interrupt a time-consuming applet. Suppose the run handler takes a long time and the user wishes to stop it and quit. Even a non–Stay Open applet has a Quit menu item, both in the menu bar and in the Dock, so the user might try choosing one; but this won't work. The user can cause an error by pressing ⌘-Period, which your script can catch and respond by quitting; but the user might not think of this. The user can force-quit, but then any cleanup operations in your quit handler won't be performed. The best you can do is probably something like this:*

```
global shouldQuit
global didCleanup
on run
    set shouldQuit to false
    set didCleanup to false
    try
        -- lengthy operation goes here
        repeat with x from 1 to 10
            if shouldQuit then error
            say (x as string)
            delay 5
        end repeat
    on error
        tell me to quit
    end try
end run
on quit
    if not didCleanup then
        -- cleanup operation goes here
        say "cleaning up"
        set didCleanup to true
    end if
    set shouldQuit to true
    continue quit
end quit
```

While the run handler of that example is executing, here's what the user can do, and what our code will do in response:

- The user presses ⌘-Period. We catch the error, call our own quit handler, clean up, and quit in good order.
- The user chooses Quit from the applet's Application menu. This calls our quit handler, but when we say continue quit we don't succeed in quitting—we

---

* This example and the entire discussion of the problem come from Paul Berkowitz.

merely resume the run handler. Therefore we also set a global indicating that the user is trying to quit. The resumed run handler notices this, deliberately errors out as if the user had pressed ⌘-Period, and we catch the error and call our own quit handler, and quit in good order. We would perform our cleanup operations twice in this case, but that is prevented by another global.

- The user chooses Quit from the applet's Dock menu. This has no effect upon our applet. I regard this as a bug.

- The user force-quits our applet. This stops the applet dead, but of course there is no cleanup.

Droplets

A *droplet* is simply an applet with an open handler:

open
> An open handler, if present, will be called when items are dropped in the Finder onto the droplet's icon. It should take one parameter; this will be a list of aliases to the items dropped.

The open handler's parameter is a command parameter, not a handler parameter, so it does not have to be expressed in parentheses in the first line of the definition.

If a droplet is started up by double-clicking it from the Finder, then its run handler is executed and its open handler is not. But if it is started up by dropping items on it in the Finder, then it's the other way around: its open handler is executed and its run handler is not. Once a droplet is running (assuming it is a Stay Open droplet), the open handler can be executed by dropping items onto the droplet's icon in the Finder. The open handler is also scriptable, using the open command, whose parameter should be a list of aliases.

In this simple example, the droplet reports how many folders were dropped on its icon:[*]

```
on open what
    set total to 0
    tell application "Finder"
        repeat with f in what
            if kind of f is "folder" then set total to total + 1
        end repeat
    end tell
    display dialog (total as string) & " folder(s)"
end open
```

---

[*] This technique would have to modified in order to work on machines where the Finder's response to get kind of gives answers in a language other than English.

Persistence

Persistence of top-level entities (see "Lifetime of Variables" in Chapter 7 and "Persistence of Top-Level Entities" in Chapter 9) works in an applet. The script is re-saved when the applet quits, maintaining the state of its top-level environment.

So, for example, the following modification to the previous example would cause an applet to report the count of folders that had *ever* been dropped on it, not just the count of folders dropped on it at this moment:

```
property total : 0
on open what
    tell application "Finder"
        repeat with f in what
            if kind of f is "folder" then set total to total + 1
        end repeat
    end tell
    display dialog (total as string) & " folder(s)"
end open
```

On the other hand, this persistence ends as soon as the applet's script is edited. If you're still developing an applet, or likely to edit it further for any reason, you might like a way to store data persistently with no chance of losing it. The new application bundle format supplies a solution. An application bundle appears and behaves in the Finder just like an applet, but is in reality a folder. When it runs, path to me is the bundle's pathname. This means we can perform persistent data storage in a *separate* script file *inside the bundle*; the user won't see this separate file, and as long as we don't deliberately open it in the Script Editor, its data will persist even when we edit the applet's main script.

To illustrate, let's return to the example in "Data Storage" in Chapter 9. This code is just the same as in that example, except that we now assume we are an application bundle, and the first line has been changed to store the data inside the bundle:

```
set thePath to (path to me as string) & "myPrefs"
script myPrefs
    property favoriteColor : ""
end script
try
    set myPrefs to load script file thePath
on error
    set favoriteColor of myPrefs to text returned of ¬
        (display dialog "Favorite Color:" default answer ¬
            "" buttons {"OK"} default button "OK")
    store script myPrefs in file thePath replacing yes
end try
display dialog "Your favorite color is " & favoriteColor of myPrefs
```

Now we save the script as an application bundle, and we have a single file, an applet, which behaves correctly: the first time it runs, it asks for the user's favorite color; the next time it runs, it remembers the user's favorite color and presents it. And it doesn't forget the user's favorite color if we now edit this script.

Digital Hub Scripting

You probably have your computer set up so that when you insert a music CD, the application iTunes runs. This is one example of a general phenomenon called *digital hub scripting*: when a DVD, or a CD that doesn't consist of ordinary files, is inserted into your computer, the System can react by sending an Apple event to a designated application. You can interpose your own code in this process: instead of iTunes, when an event like this occurs, an applet of your choice is notified, and can react in any desired manner.

In the CDs & DVDs pane of System Preferences are the settings that determine how the System reacts to a disk-insertion event. You can determine what application should be notified when the disk is inserted. If this application is an applet, it should be prepared to receive an Apple event corresponding to what sort of disk was inserted. The terminology for these Apple events is defined in the dictionary of the *Digital Hub Scripting* scripting addition. (Therefore the parameter does not need to appear in parentheses at the start of the definition.)

Let's say we want to take charge of what happens when a music CD is inserted. We'll create an applet called *musicListener*. In the CDs & DVDs pane of System Preferences, we use the Open Other Application menu item to set *musicListener* as the target application to respond when a music CD being inserted. In *musicListener*, the music CD appeared handler will be called when a music CD is inserted.

To illustrate, let's offer the user a choice of playing just one track of the music CD:

```
on music CD appeared d
    set diskName to d as alias as string
    set text item delimiters to ":"
    set diskName to text item 1 of diskName
    tell application "Finder"
        set L to name of every file of disk diskName
    end tell
    set whichTrack to choose from list L
    tell application "iTunes"
        play file ({diskName, whichTrack} as string)
    end tell
end music CD appeared
```

Folder Actions

A *folder action* is a behavior that occurs automatically when certain events take place in a designated folder in the Finder. Folder actions are not implemented as applications, but as scripts (but they seem to have found their way into this chapter anyway). As with digital hub scripting, your script has certain handlers which, if present, will be called when the corresponding event takes place.

Any scripts to be used as folder action scripts should live in *~/Library/Scripts/Folder Action Scripts*. Alternatively they can live in */Library/Scripts/Folder Action Scripts*, and some example scripts are located there; but the former, the one in your user library, is the default.

Setting up a folder action involves the association of a script with a folder. To make such an association is to *attach* the script to the folder; to break the association is to *remove* the script from the folder. The script is not actually moved; attachment and removal are conceptual, not physical, and are performed through System Events (see "System Events" in Chapter 21), which ties a folder and a script together through a folder action object. It is up to System Events to maintain these folder action objects and to respond correctly when an appropriate action in the Finder takes place. So System Events must be running in order for folder actions to work; that is why, when you enable the folder actions mechanism, System Events is added to your Startup Items.

In general, you don't have to worry yourself with the details of scripting System Events to manipulate folder actions. Apple provides a straightforward user interface through the application *Configure Folder Actions*, located in */Applications/AppleScript*. Here you can turn the folder actions mechanism as a whole off and on; add and remove folders to the list of those that have folder actions; attach and remove scripts in association with any listed folder; enable and disable a particular folder or script; and open a script for editing.

Another interface is provided by a folder's contextual menu. This is a much simpler interface than the *Configure Folder Actions* application, because it is clear from the outset what folder is in question—it's the one whose contextual menu you're using—and so you're only manipulating scripts in connection with this one folder. You can attach a script to, and remove a script from, this particular folder, as well as edit an attached script. You can also enable or disable the folder actions mechanism, and open the *Configure Folder Actions* application.

There are also some scripts located in */Library/Scripts/Folder Actions*, which may be accessed directly or through the Script Menu (see "Script Runner" in Chapter 2). These are useful for study if you want to learn how to drive the folder actions mechanism by scripting System Events. Here is what they do:

Enable Folder Actions.scpt
> Turns on the folder actions mechanism.

Disable Folder Actions.scpt
> Turns off the folder actions mechanism.

Attach Folder Action.scpt
> Prompts the user for a script and folder and attaches the script to that folder as a folder action for it.

Remove Folder Actions.scpt
> Prompts the user for a folder and a script and removes that script from that folder so that it is no longer a folder action for it.

The latter two are especially interesting; look in particular at the use of the commands attach action to, attached scripts, and remove action from.

So much for how to associate a script with a folder. What about the code that goes into a folder action script? The terminology for the events to which a folder action script can respond is defined in the dictionary of the *StandardAdditions* scripting addition. Therefore the parameter in the first line of your handler definition doesn't have to be in parentheses. A folder action script can respond when a folder's window is opened, moved, or closed, or when items are added to or removed from the folder. An example appears at "Automatic Location" in Chapter 2. There are a number of educational examples in */Library/Scripts/Folder Action Scripts* as well.

CGI Application

A *CGI* application (for *common gateway interface*, if you must know) is a process that supplements a web server. When a request arrives for a page, instead of producing the page as a copy of a file on disk, the web server can turn to a CGI application and ask it for the page; the CGI application is expected to compose the entire HTML of the page, including headers, and hand it back to the web server, which passes it on to the client that made the request.

On Macintosh, the communication between a web server and a CGI application has conventionally been performed through Apple events. In particular, an Apple event usually known (for historical reasons) as the WebSTAR event is sent by the web server to the CGI application, describing the page request. The CGI application hands back the page as the reply to this Apple event (see *http://www.4d.com/products/wsdev/internetspecs.html*).

This means that an applet can be used as a CGI application; and such, indeed, is the traditional Mac OS approach. If you're using WebSTAR or some other web server that implements CGIs in this manner, you can use it directly with an applet. However, the web server that comes with Mac OS X, Apache, doesn't work this way. Apache is a Unix web server, and Unix doesn't have Apple events. In Unix, environment variables, along with stdin and stdout, are used as the communication medium between the server and the CGI process.

Therefore, in order to use an AppleScript applet as a CGI application with Apache, you need some intermediary application that swings both ways, as it were. On the one hand, this intermediary application must behave as an Apache-style CGI process, so that Apache has someone to talk to. On the other hand, this intermediary application must know how to translate a CGI request from Apache into an Apple event, send this Apple event to the correct applet, and receive the result. It must then translate the result into the form Apache expects, and pass it on to Apache.

Such an intermediary is James Sentman's *acgi dispatcher* utility. (See *http://www. sentman.com/acgi*.) Here, then, is a description of how to write and implement a basic CGI applet in AppleScript using *acgi dispatcher*.

Let's start with the applet. We'll write an "echo" CGI, whose job is to return a web page simply describing the original request. This is a valuable thing to have on hand because it can be used for testing and debugging, and it exemplifies the two basic tasks of a CGI applet, namely to receive the Apple event and to respond by constructing and returning a web page.

The terminology for the Apple event that's going to be arriving is defined in the *StandardAdditions* scripting addition, as the handle CGI request command. In defining our handle CGI request handler we can take advantage of this terminology, but there are some slight hiccups. The terminology speaks of an action parameter, but *acgi dispatcher* fails to provide this, so we must omit it. And *acgi dispatcher* includes one parameter that isn't mentioned in the terminology, and therefore has to be included by means of a raw four-letter code. (This extra parameter is a list of URL-decoded form elements, saving your applet the tedious job of parsing the form information. The example script ignores it.)

Apart from this the code is straightforward; here it is:

```
property crlf : "\r\n"
property http_header : "MIME-Version: 1.0" & crlf & ¬
    "Content-type: text/html" & crlf & crlf
property s : ""

on makeLine(whatName, whatValue)
    return "<p><b>" & whatName & ":</b> " & whatValue & "</p>" & return
end makeLine
on addLine(whatName, whatValue)
    set s to s & makeLine(whatName, whatValue)
end addLine

on handle CGI request path_args ¬
    from virtual host virtual_host ¬
        searching for http_search_args ¬
        with posted data post_args ¬
        using access method method ¬
        from address client_address ¬
        from user username ¬
        using password pword ¬
        with user info from_user ¬
        from server server_name ¬
        via port server_port ¬
        executing by script_name ¬
        of content type content_type ¬
        referred by referer ¬
        from browser user_agent ¬
        of action type action_path ¬
        from client IP address client_ip ¬
```

```
                with full request full_request ¬
                with connection ID connection_id ¬
                given «class TraL»:form_elements
        -- using action action -- not implemented by acgi dispatcher
        set s to http_header
        set s to s & ¬
            "<html><head><title>Echo Page</title></head>" & return
        set s to s & "<body><h1>Echo Page</h1>" & return
        addLine("virtual_host", POSIX path of virtual_host)
        addLine("path_args", path_args)
        addLine("http_search_args", http_search_args)
        addLine("post_args", post_args)
        addLine("method", method)
        addLine("client_address", client_address)
        addLine("username", username)
        addLine("password", pword)
        addLine("from_user", from_user)
        addLine("server_name", server_name)
        addLine("server_port", server_port)
        addLine("script_name", script_name)
        addLine("content_type", content_type)
        addLine("referer", referer)
        addLine("user_agent", user_agent)
        addLine("action_path", action_path)
        addLine("client_ip", client_ip)
        addLine("full_request", "</p><pre>" & full_request & "</pre><p>")
        addLine("connection_ID", connection_id)
        set s to s & "<hr><i>" & (current date) & "</i>"
        set s to s & "</body></html>"
        return s
    end handle CGI request
```

We start by defining the header that will precede our HTML. Then comes a pair of utility handlers that will make the code for generating each line of our HTML a bit less tedious; our plan for generating the HTML is to append line after line of this format:

```
<p><b>param_name:</b>param_value</p>
```

and these utilities make the job a bit more elegant. Finally we have the actual handler for the Apple event that will come from *acgi dispatcher*. In your own experiments, be sure to copy the parameters in the first line of the handler definition exactly as shown here, or the whole thing won't work! In the content of the handler you can do anything you like, but the result should be the header followed by some legal HTML.

Now let's talk about how to set up Apache to use this script as a CGI process. The directory where everything needs to go is */Library/WebServer/CGI-Executables*. Save the script as a Stay Open applet into that directory, calling it *echo.acgi*. Start up *echo.acgi*. Now open the *acgi dispatcher* folder and move the *dispatcher* application into that directory as well. Start up *dispatcher* and provide your admin password when requested. Finally, go into the Sharing pane of System Preferences and turn on

Personal Web Sharing. That's it! You're ready to test. Open a browser and ask for *http://localhost* just to make sure Apache is serving. If that works, then cross your fingers and ask for *http://localhost/cgi-bin/echo.acgi*. You should see a web page displaying your request; it will contain information such as your IP number and what browser you're using. At the bottom it will show the current date and time. You've just written your first AppleScript CGI.

A question that arises with CGI applets (or any applet, really) is what happens if a request arrives when the applet is already in the middle of running its handle CGI request handler in reaction to a pending request. AppleScript is not multithreaded, so execution of simultaneous requests must be taken in some definite order. In the latest version of AppleScript (1.9.2) and the System (Mac OS X 10.3), that order is FIFO—first in, first out. This means that requests are processed in the order in which they arrive; if a request arrives while another request is already being processed, the new request must simply wait its turn.

This is a big improvement over past systems, where the order was LIFO—last in, first out. Under LIFO ordering, if an Apple event arrives, all pending execution is put on hold until the execution triggered by this latest Apple event has finished. This means that if many requests arrive close to one another, it is theoretically possible for the first ones to be postponed a long time (so that, from the client's point of view, they time out).

AppleScript Studio

AppleScript Studio is a free development environment from Apple allowing you to write Cocoa applications using the AppleScript language. It would require an entire book to discuss AppleScript Studio adequately, so this section just explains how AppleScript Studio works, talks about its learning curve, and provides a brief illustration of AppleScript Studio in action. To begin at the beginning, we must be clear on what Cocoa is.

Cocoa

Cocoa is the name of a massive application framework included as part of Mac OS X. This framework knows how to do all the things that an application might typically wish to do. For example, it can put up windows, and in them it can display many different kinds of interface widgets for interacting with the user. It also provides very strong text capabilities and good graphics capabilities. Cocoa is a really great application framework, and makes it quite easy to write sophisticated, powerful applications. Cocoa applications can also be relatively small, because much of the work is done by the framework, which is part of the System and not present in the application itself.

How AppleScript Studio Relates to Cocoa

Cocoa is very big, and to use it fully one should learn the Objective-C language and study the framework as a whole. Objective-C is not hard, but the framework is big, and the effort involved is more than some will wish to make. Furthermore, AppleScript users are in rather a special position; you might easily have a script that works already, but would be enhanced by adding some user interface that is more sophisticated than AppleScript on its own is able to provide. So you don't want to learn all of Cocoa; you just want to leverage your existing script into a Cocoa application. AppleScript Studio provides a way out of these difficulties, making it possible for the user to wrap a Cocoa interface around AppleScript functionality with relative ease.

Cocoa is full of interface widgets and classes and objects, and it works through predefined messages that the programmer's code must be prepared to send and to receive in order to interact with the framework. For example, suppose there's a button in a window. If the programmer wants that button to change from being enabled to being disabled, there's a specific message that the programmer's code must send to the button; the connection between the programmer's code and the button is called an *outlet*, and it is up to the programmer to define this outlet and to know about the specific message that must be sent to change the button's enabled state. If the programmer wants to know when the user presses this button, the programmer's code must be prepared to receive a particular message that the button will send; the connection between the button and the programmer's code is called an *action*, and it is up to the programmer to define this action and to know what sort of information will arrive when the button is pressed. Furthermore, many events that take place over the lifetime of an application trigger other kinds of events that the programmer's code can register to receive, through mechanisms called *delegation* and *notification*. This is all very big stuff, and the documentation for it requires a lot of space on your hard drive.

AppleScript Studio itself, however, is quite small and light. It simplifies the programmer's view of Cocoa tremendously. In part, this is because it provides direct access to only a fraction of Cocoa's full power. But this is a deliberate design decision on the part of the Apple folks, and it's a good thing; if AppleScript Studio were too big and complicated, your eyes would glaze over and you'd never use it.

The link between AppleScript and Cocoa is accomplished behind the scenes by means of special glue code—you talk to AppleScript, and AppleScript turns what you say into Objective-C and passes it on to Cocoa. This linkage between AppleScript and Cocoa is often referred to as a *bridge*. So we may say that the Apple folks have bridged AppleScript to a certain area of Cocoa.

Furthermore, in the area where the Apple folks have bridged AppleScript to Cocoa, they have made Cocoa a lot easier to use than if you did it through Objective-C. You don't have to know about outlets and actions and delegation and notification, because that's all taken care of for you by AppleScript Studio and the bridging code. The consequence is that if your aims are restricted in the right way, if what you want to do with Cocoa from AppleScript lies within the scope of what is bridged, you can actually write a Cocoa application much more quickly and easily with AppleScript Studio than an Objective-C programmer could.

How Much Cocoa to Learn

In theory, it is perfectly possible to use AppleScript Studio without knowing any Cocoa at all. You simply confine yourself to the AppleScript language and to what the AppleScript Studio manual and dictionary tell you about the sorts of things you can say, and you can build a Cocoa application.

However, if you don't know any Cocoa at all, you might still be a little mystified about what's happening, and about how to achieve the effects you envision for your interface. In my opinion, therefore, the best way to climb the AppleScript Studio learning curve is to know at least some Cocoa. You will have a better sense of what's going on in AppleScript Studio, and you'll be able to use it with greater facility, the more you know about Cocoa itself. I'm not saying you should learn all of Cocoa; I'm merely suggesting that you should acquire some familiarity with the location of the Cocoa documentation on your hard drive, and that you might wish to have on hand a couple of good Cocoa books.

Furthermore, if you do know some Cocoa, you can do much more with AppleScript Studio than if you don't. That's because it's quite possible to find your programming desires banging up against a region where AppleScript is not bridged to Cocoa. At that point, you're going to find yourself in difficulties; and you can solve these difficulties only by giving up some of your desires, or else by learning some Cocoa and crossing the bridge yourself. You can do this by calling from AppleScript into Cocoa explicitly, perhaps even writing some of your application's code in Objective-C. Many AppleScript Studio users seem to feel daunted or even insulted by the fact that there are areas of Cocoa that AppleScript Studio does not hand them on a silver platter. They think that AppleScript Studio should be "pure," and that they should not need to get their hands dirty by using any Objective-C or even knowing what Cocoa is really up to behind the scenes. In my view, though, it's better to get things done with AppleScript Studio than to waste time and energy complaining about it; and that's just what knowing some Cocoa has allowed me to do. You don't have to adopt my philosophy in this matter, but I offer it for what it's worth.

Where and What Is AppleScript Studio

AppleScript Studio is like Los Angeles: it isn't actually anywhere. It isn't the name of a thing or a place; it's the name of a collection of things used in a certain way. So now we're going to talk about what those things are.

The Developer Tools

Step one in finding AppleScript Studio is to make sure it is present in the first place. If you haven't installed the Developer Tools, it isn't. The Developer Tools are on the mysterious extra CD that comes with some Mac OS X installers; but it is crucial to have the latest version, so the best way to get the Developer Tools is from Apple's site. First, you need to become a member of the Apple Developer Connection. You can join at the Online level, which is free (see *http://developer.apple.com/membership/online.html*). Then follow the links to the ADC Member Site and find the latest version of the Developer Tools. You can download them, if you have the bandwidth. Alternatively, it is possible to request the latest Developer Tools CD for a small fee. Then run the installer. The Developer Tools must be installed on your Mac OS X startup disk.

Interface Builder

In */Developer/Applications* is an application called *Interface Builder*. This is the program you will use to design your application's interface. Basically, you will draw the interface you want. You can experiment with Interface Builder if you like; start it up, choose the Cocoa Application starting point and press the New button, and presto, you've got a window. Press ⌘-/ to show the interface widgets palette if it isn't showing. Here you can select among sets of widgets; these sets have names like "Cocoa—Text" and "Cocoa—Controls." Drag some widgets into the window. Move them around. Resize them. You might even read the Interface Builder Help document at this point.

Xcode

Also in */Developer/Applications* is an application called *Xcode* (formerly known as Project Builder). This is the heart of the Cocoa development process. It is where you edit your code; it is also where you turn your code into an actual application. You can use Xcode whether you are writing a Cocoa application or an AppleScript Studio application, and it supports many other kinds of project as well. What makes your project an AppleScript Studio application, in particular, is that you say so when you create the project.

The fact that you design your interface in one application but edit your code and build the application in another is a tricky aspect of the Cocoa development experience, and takes some getting used to. For the most part the two applications communicate with one another in a reliable manner, but it's easy to confuse yourself, and it's possible to confound the connection between Interface Builder and Xcode. It is best to work on only one project at a time, to have both Interface Builder and Xcode running, and to hide whichever of them you're not using at that moment.

AppleScript Studio documentation and examples

The documentation for AppleScript Studio is in */Developer/Documentation/ AppleScript*. It consists of two books. One is an extended tutorial, well worth going through with your hands on the computer; it's in *Conceptual/StudioBuildApps*. The other is a reference manual, in *Reference/StudioReference*. You should probably skim the reference manual once at the outset and then be prepared to consult it pretty much constantly as you work. There are also lots of AppleScript Studio examples in */Developer/Examples/AppleScript Studio,* which explore and demonstrate just about all aspects of using AppleScript Studio to drive the user interface.

Cocoa itself is documented starting in */Developer/Documentation/Cocoa*. In the *Conceptual/ObjectiveC* folder is a splendid book about the Objective-C language. The file *Cocoa.html* is the major gateway to the Cocoa documentation. Among other things, it functions as a table of contents to a large number of highly readable, topic-oriented documents. These will prove helpful even to the AppleScript Studio programmer. For example, if you want to understand what a button really is, the different ways it can appear and behave, how it fits into the class architecture, and what it has to do with controls and cells, you'd click the "User Experience" link and from there you could read the "Buttons" document and the "Controls and Cells" document.

The nitty-gritty Cocoa reference material appears in *Cocoa.html* under "API Reference." The part you're likely to be interested in is the link that says "Application Kit Reference for Objective-C." This is where you would come to find out about all the Cocoa methods to which a built-in class responds. For example, if you wanted to know about buttons in the way that a Cocoa programmer knows about them, you'd go to "Application Kit Reference" and then "NSButton" (the Cocoa name for the button class) and read through this document, along with the chain of documents listed at the top about the classes from which NSButton inherits, namely NSControl, NSView, NSResponder, and NSObject (because anything they can do, NSButton can do too). You can also get to this document directly; it's in *Reference/ApplicationKit/ ObjC_Classic/Classes*.

Before you dismiss out of hand the idea that you, an AppleScript programmer, would ever want to read any of the Cocoa reference documentation, consider that, in general, everything you do with AppleScript Studio is a bridged version of something you could do with Cocoa, so that the Cocoa reference can function as a guide to what you're *really* doing. For example, the discussion of setState: in the Cocoa "NSButton" documentation is much clearer on what button "state" is all about than is the AppleScript Studio reference.

The dictionary

The bridge between AppleScript and Cocoa is implemented partly through files located in */System/Library/Frameworks/AppleScriptKit.framework/Resources*. Of these, the most important to you will be *AppleScriptKit.asdictionary*. This is the dictionary through which you will access the bridge terminology, the vocabulary that will allow you to talk to Cocoa. To examine it, just double-click it in the Finder, and it will open for reading in the Script Editor. (You don't have to find the dictionary like this every time; it also appears within your AppleScript Studio project in Xcode, as shown in Figure 24-2.) You'll see that this dictionary is full of exactly the terms that the Apple-Script Studio reference document is all about. Your job as an AppleScript Studio programmer is to harness these terms. This is how your AppleScript code will communicate with interface items, and how interface items and other Cocoa classes will communicate with your AppleScript code.

To understand what's going on in AppleStudio you will in general be using a combination of this dictionary, the AppleScript Studio reference documentation, and Interface Builder. The dictionary alone is inadequate for understanding how to communicate with Cocoa. As I mentioned earlier, Cocoa works in part through sending action messages, delegation messages, and notification messages to your code so that you can react to things that the user does, and to other things that happen during the lifetime of your application. In the dictionary, all these types of messages get lumped together, along with the messages that you can send to Cocoa, as events. You can't tell, just from looking at an event listing in the dictionary, whether this is something you say or something Cocoa will say to you. If it's something Cocoa will say to you, you can't tell from the dictionary precisely who will say it and when, and why you might want to put yourself in a position to listen. Thus you need the help of the documentation, and also of Interface Builder, which shows you what messages can be sent and received in connection with each widget of your interface.

AppleScript Studio Example

For our example, we'll return to the code developed in "Do Shell Script" in Chapter 23. In that code, we allow the user to enter search terms; we then go online to tell the TidBITS search engine to look for those terms. We receive some HTML that lists the pages found, we parse the HTML, and we present the results to the user. We have already developed some AppleScript code and some Perl code that work together to accomplish this task. Now we will embed this code in an application as a way of presenting the user with a nice interface. This is the sort of purpose for which AppleScript Studio is particularly appropriate: we already have some working AppleScript code, and now we want to leverage it and make it more comfortable to use by putting a Cocoa interface in front of it. The finished application is shown in action in Figure 24-1; the user has just searched for all TidBITS articles written by a certain favorite author.

My goal in what follows is not to teach you AppleScript Studio, nor to provide a hands-on step-by-step tutorial, nor even to show you the entire learning and development process for this particular example. I wish simply to highlight some aspects

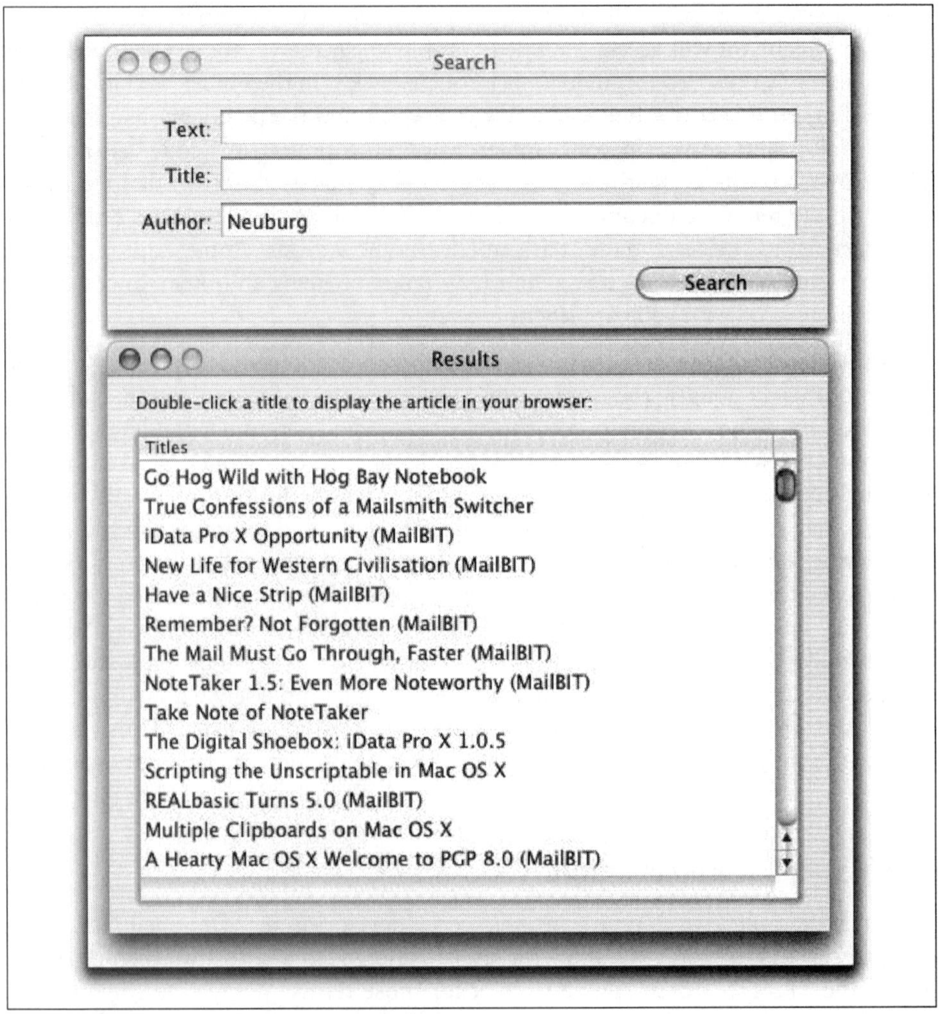

Figure 24-1. Our AppleScript Studio application in action

of the solution that are significant and typical, so that you gain some understanding of the workings of the whole, and a sense for what sorts of effort are generally involved in using AppleScript Studio to wrap a Cocoa interface around a script.

Create the project

The first step is to create the project, in Xcode. Choose File → New Project and select "AppleScript Application"; proceed through the creation steps to give the project a name and finish its creation. We'll call ours *SearchTidBITS*. A Cocoa project consists of a folder containing many files; the folder will be called *SearchTidBITS*, and within it the project itself will be represented by a file called *SearchTidBITS.xcode*. It is this file that now opens. It appears as the project window, and it acts as a table of contents to everything that's in the project. You would open this same file at a later time to continue working on any aspect of the project.

Incorporate extra bundle components

A Cocoa application is a bundle, meaning it's a folder that looks (in the Finder) like a single file. This means that we can store inside the application any ancillary files that it may require, such as images, help documentation, and so forth, and the user will not come into direct contact with these ancillary files or even be aware that they exist.

It happens that in this case we have such an ancillary file—the Perl script. To incorporate the Perl script, choose Project → Add Files. In the Open File dialog, find and select the Perl script, which is called *parseHTML.pl*, and elect in the next dialog to copy it into the project. Once it's listed in the left side of the project window, you can drag it to any location there; this has no effect in the real world, but merely organizes the project window in a nice way. I like to put it under "Other Sources," as shown in Figure 24-2.

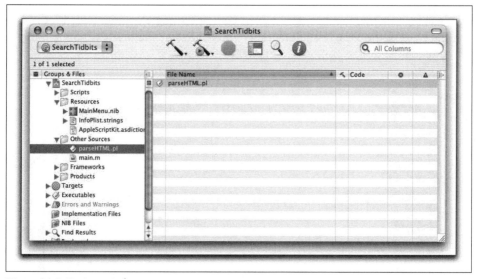

Figure 24-2. Project window

Create the interface

The next step is to create the interface. This is done by double-clicking *MainMenu.nib* in the project window (Figure 24-2). This opens Interface Builder; Interface Builder now knows it is dealing with an Xcode project, and coordinates its editing operations with Xcode.

My design for the interface consists of two windows. The first, the Search window, contains an NSForm displaying three fields the user can search on (text, title, and author) and a Search button, along with a progress indicator to provide feedback while we're talking to the Internet. The design is shown in Figure 24-3; the square thing in the lower left is the progress indicator (I'll explain later why it looks this way).

Figure 24-3. Search window

The second window, the Results window, contains a single-column table for displaying the titles of the found articles, along with some explanatory text telling the user what to do. The design is shown in Figure 24-4.

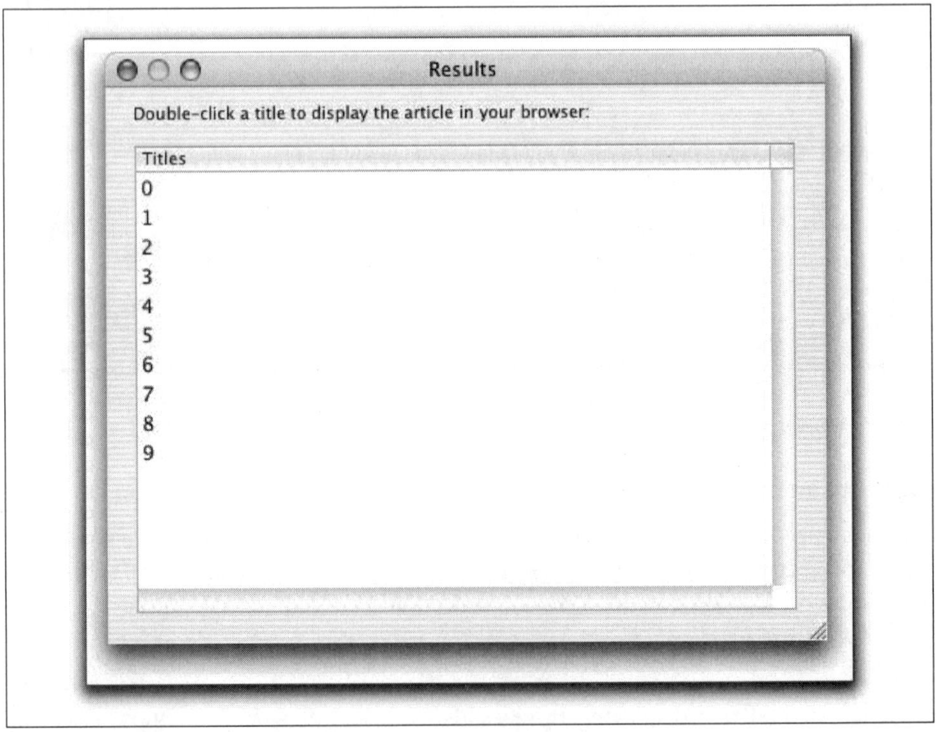

Figure 24-4. Results window

The last piece of the interface is the menus. Here I make two main changes. I remove the File menu and replace it with a Search menu consisting of a single menu item, New. And I add a Close menu item to the Window menu. The menu bar design is shown in Figure 24-5, displaying the Search menu.

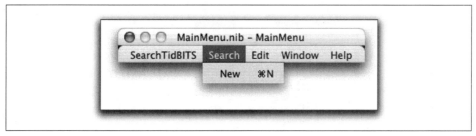

Figure 24-5. The menu bar

Add AppleScript names and handlers

Now comes the really interesting part. We will work in the AppleScript pane of the Interface Builder info window, which is shown when you select an interface item and press ⌘-7. (If you don't see the info window at all, press ⌘-Shift-I. The popup menu at the top lets you change panes.) This pane lets you do two important things.

First, it lets you give the interface item an AppleScript name. This is the name that will be used in your AppleScript code to refer to the item by name when forming an element specifier. So, for example, although the Search window has a title "Search," this is merely a matter of its appearance; it is not something you can use as an element specifier. The key step is to select the window and give it an AppleScript name (I call it search) in the info window. This is shown in Figure 24-6.

The other thing you do in the info window (also shown in Figure 24-6) is to explore and specify the notifications you wish to receive from this interface item. You'll recall that I said you'd be using Interface Builder to supplement the dictionary; I was referring to this. The Interface Builder info window lists the messages that the selected interface item is prepared to send to your code. As you design your application in Interface Builder, you select an interface item, look at the list of its events in the info window, look them up in the documentation, and think about which of them your code might need to receive. Then you use the checkboxes in the info window so that you *do* receive them. You check an event in the upper pane of the info window, and also check the name of the Xcode script file in the lower pane of the info window. In this example, we have only one script file, which has been created for us automatically; it is called *SearchTidBITS.applescript*. Checking the two checkboxes causes the correct handler to be created in the script when you save the Interface Builder file.

Figure 24-6. Info for the Search window

So now I'm going to run through the interface items of my project, giving some of them names and deciding what notifications I want to receive from each of them:

File's Owner

This icon in the main Interface Builder window represents the application as a whole. I want to know when the application has launched so that I can perform some initializations, so I select Application: launched.

Search → New menu item

I name this menu item newSearch. I want to know when the user chooses this menu item, so I select Menu: choose menu item.

Window → Close menu item

I name this menu item `closeWindow`. I want to know when the user chooses this menu item, so I select `Menu: choose menu item`.

Search window

I name this window `search`. I want to know when this window is about to open, because I want to make some interface adjustments; so I select `Window: will open`.

Search window: the Search button

I name this button `searchButton`. I want to know when the user clicks this button, so I select `Action: clicked`.

Results window

I name this window `results`.

Results window: the table view

I want to know when the user double-clicks a row of the table view, so I select `Action: double clicked`.

Results window: the table view's column

It's very important to give each column of a table view an AppleScript name. This table view has just one column, and I name it `titles`.

The code

We are now finished with Interface Builder, and it's time to work on our Apple-Script code. To access the code, just click the Edit Script button in the info window in Interface Builder. This causes Xcode to come to the front and to open the script file for editing. As you can see, the handlers that we specified in Interface Builder have been created. The terminology for these events is defined by the AppleScriptKit dictionary, so no parentheses appear in the first line of the handler definitions:

```
on will open theObject
    (*Add your script here.*)
end will open

on launched theObject
    (*Add your script here.*)
end launched

on choose menu item theObject
    (*Add your script here.*)
end choose menu item

on clicked theObject
    (*Add your script here.*)
end clicked

on double clicked theObject
    (*Add your script here.*)
end double clicked
```

Our task in Xcode is now to fill these in, and to add any further handlers of our own. Let's take a tour of the final code. I'll comment on what each part of the code does and on the various points about AppleScript Studio that it demonstrates.

Example 24-1 shows some top-level globals and the launched handler generated by the File's Owner object in Interface Builder. There is no particular reason for preferring script properties over global variables except as a matter of convenience: with script properties, I don't have to take any explicit action to initialize them. The globals L1 and L2 will be needed for maintaining state and communicating information between handlers. This use of globals is quite common in AppleScript Studio. It's true that as a rule I don't favor using globals for passing information around, but in the case of an application we have no choice, because different handlers will be called at different times, with our application lying idle in between, and during those idle periods we need a place to store information where the next handler to be invoked will be able to find it. The global perlScriptPath is really more like a script property, since I want to initialize it at startup and leave it alone after that, but I can't actually make it a script property, because in order to initialize it, I need to run some code after the application has started up. That code is what's in the launched handler.

Example 24-1. Globals and launched handler

```
property textSought : ""
property titleSought : ""
property authorSought : ""
global perlScriptPath
global L1
global L2

on launched theObject -- app started up, do initialization tasks
    set f to resource path of main bundle
    set perlScriptPath to POSIX path of POSIX file (f & "/parseHTML.pl")
    set perlScriptPath to quoted form of perlScriptPath
end launched
```

The launched handler will be called when the application starts up. Thus it is our earliest opportunity to perform initializations. The handler takes one parameter, theObject; this is the interface object that sent the event to our code. It happens that in this particular case I checked the launched event in Interface Builder for just one object, the File's Owner; so I know perfectly well what theObject is, and I don't bother with it. (In a moment we'll come to a spot in the code where we need to be more circumspect.)

My launched handler initialization involves setting the value of the global perlScriptPath, which is the path to the Perl script inside our application bundle. I will want to call this Perl script later, so I'll need to know where it is so I can tell Perl about it. The path is not known in advance, because the application bundle could be anywhere on the user's hard drive. The application object provides a main bundle property representing the application on disk, whose resource path property is the path to the *Resources* folder inside the application bundle. That's where the Perl script will be when the application is built, so I can use this information to construct a Unix path to the Perl script. The path needs to appear in its quoted form because it will be used as a command-line argument in a do shell script command.

Example 24-2 shows the on will open handler. This was created by the Search window, and will be called just before the window opens. Since I know this, I don't bother checking the value of theObject; I simply assume it is the Search window.

Example 24-2. The on will open handler

```
on will open theObject -- search window opening, set prog indic
    set p to progress indicator 1 of theObject
    call method "setStyle:" of p with parameter 1
    call method "setDisplayedWhenStopped:" of p with parameters {false}
end will open
```

The purpose of this handler is partly practical and partly pedagogical. The practical side is that I want to adjust some features of the progress indicator before the window appears. I don't actually have to do this in code, but that's where the pedagogical side comes in: I wanted an excuse to show you how one bridges between AppleScript and Cocoa when the bridging has not been provided by the Apple folks as part of the AppleScriptKit dictionary. It's done with the call method command. This command allows just about any Objective-C method to be translated into AppleScript.

In this case, we wish to use code to set the progress indicator to be a spinning progress indicator. AppleScript Studio has not provided the progress indicator object with any properties that let us do this. But in Objective-C Cocoa it's easy to do. Looking in *NSProgressIndicator.html*, we find that we would like to say the equivalent of this Objective-C code:

```
[theProgressIndicator setStyle: NSProgressIndicatorSpinningStyle];
[theProgressIndicator setDisplayedWhenStopped: NO];
```

The two call method commands in Example 24-2 are the exact equivalents of these two lines of Objective-C. Now, I'm not saying that arriving at these equivalents requires no thought; but it isn't very difficult either. The AppleScript Studio documentation tells you what to do. If an Objective-C method has a colon in its name, that colon must appear in the name as quoted in the call method command; also, Objective-C method names are case-sensitive, so we must get the case right. The only slightly difficult part of translating these particular methods was arriving at the parameter value to represent the constant NSProgressIndicatorSpinningStyle. This is actually an integer value, and in order to pass it from AppleScript I had to find out what that integer is. To do so, I looked in the header file *NSProgressIndicator.h*; one convenient way to open this file is directly from the project window, as shown in Figure 24-7.

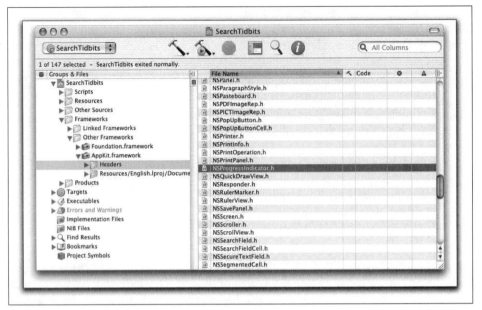

Figure 24-7. Accessing headers from the project window

Example 24-3 shows the choose menu item handler. This handler was generated both by our Search → New menu item and our Window → Close menu item, and will be called when the user chooses either of these two menu items. I've architected the application this way to show you that more than one interface item can have an event with the same name, and so the very same handler can be called by more than one interface item. You will typically want the various interface items that call the same handler to do different things, so your first task in such a handler must be to distinguish which of the interface items is calling (that is, which of them is theObject).

Example 24-3. The choose menu item handler

```
on choose menu item theObject
    set which to (name of theObject)
    if which is "newSearch" then
        hide window "results"
        show window "search"
        tell matrix 1 of window "search"
            set string value of cell 1 to ""
            set string value of cell 2 to ""
            set string value of cell 3 to ""
        end tell
    else if which is "closeWindow" then
        hide window 1
    end if
end choose menu item
```

Thus, in our choose menu item handler, we do two different things, depending which menu item it is. This is why we gave the menu items names—it was so that we could easily distinguish them at this point. If it's the `newSearch` menu item, we show just the Search window and empty the NSForm, ready for the user to enter new values for a new search. If it's the `closeWindow` menu item, we close the frontmost window.

Example 24-4 shows the `clicked` handler. This is created by the Search button, and will be called when the user clicks it. This, obviously, is the heart of our application. To make the code clearer, I've broken the functionality out into some ancillary handlers.

Example 24-4. The clicked handler and associated utilities

```
on clicked theObject
    if name of theObject is "searchButton" then
        startNewSearch( )
    end if
end clicked

on startNewSearch( )
    tell matrix 1 of window "search"
        set textSought to string value of cell 1
        set titleSought to string value of cell 2
        set authorSought to string value of cell 3
    end tell
    urlEncodeStuff( )
    doTheSearch( )
end startNewSearch

on urlEncode(what)
    set text item delimiters to "+"
    return (words of what) as string
end urlEncode

on urlEncodeStuff( )
    set textSought to urlEncode(textSought)
    set titleSought to urlEncode(titleSought)
    set authorSought to urlEncode(authorSought)
end urlEncodeStuff
```

The `clicked` handler simply calls the `startNewSearch` handler. The `startNewSearch` handler copies the three user entries from the NSForm into the three script properties set aside for them, and calls `urlEncodeStuff` to URL-encode them in our simpleminded way (replacing any spaces with plus signs). It then calls the `doTheSearch` handler, which is shown in Example 24-5.

In Example 24-5 we first have a handler, `feedbackBusy`, which is intended purely to provide some user feedback. The idea is that we're going to be talking to the Internet by way of `curl`, and while we're doing so, nothing is going to be happening. The user might think that the application is idle or broken. Therefore we spin the progress indicator and disable the Search button to give the user a sense that the application is busy and that he should keep his hands off while it does whatever it's doing. The handler is called with a boolean parameter telling whether to begin or end this feedback.

Example 24-5. The doTheSearch handler

```
on feedbackBusy(yn)
    tell window "search"
        if yn then
            set enabled of button "searchButton" to false
            start progress indicator 1
        else
            set enabled of button "searchButton" to true
            stop progress indicator 1
        end if
    end tell
end feedbackBusy

on doTheSearch( )
    set d to "'-response=TBSearch.lasso&-token.srch=TBAdv"
    set d to d & "&Article+HTML=" & textSought
    set d to d & "&Article+Author=" & authorSought
    set d to d & "&Article+Title=" & titleSought
    set d to d & "&-operator"
    set d to d & "=eq&RawIssueNum=&-operator=equals&ArticleDate"
    set d to d & "=&-sortField=ArticleDate&-sortOrder=descending"
    set d to d & "&-maxRecords=2000&-nothing=MSExplorerHack&-nothing"
    set d to d & "=Start+Search' "
    set u to "http://db.tidbits.com/TBSrchAdv.lasso"
    set f to "/tmp/tempTidBITS"
    feedbackBusy(true)
    try
        do shell script "curl -s --connect-timeout 15 -m 120 -d " ¬
            & d & " -o " & f & " " & u
        set r to do shell script ("perl " & perlScriptPath & " " & f)
        feedbackBusy(false)
        set L to paragraphs of r
        set half to (count L) / 2
        set L1 to items 1 thru half of L
        set L2 to items (half + 1) thru -1 of L
        displayResults( )
    on error
        feedbackBusy(false)
        beep
    end try
end doTheSearch
```

At last we come to doTheSearch. This should seem astoundingly familiar; it is almost unchanged from the first part of the code on page 364. The main differences are as follows:

- The variable d, expressing the search as a POST argument, now incorporates values for the three NSForm fields the user is allowed to fill out.

- The variable d asks for 2,000 articles instead of 20. The reason is that we're hoping to capture the titles of all the found articles. The search was originally constructed so that its results could be displayed in a web page, where you're supposed to find the first 20 results, then ask for another page showing the next 20, and so forth. I originally thought of trying to emulate this in our application. But then it struck me that we've got this nice scrolling table view to play with, and displaying a large number of titles is no problem, so we may as well gather lots of them in one search and be done with it.

- Feedback is provided to the user through calls to feedbackBusy before and after the call to curl.

- The call to curl now has a few more parameters—we provide some timeout values, because the TidBITS search server can be rather slow—and the intermediary file is now located in */tmp* where the user won't see it and it will be deleted when the user logs out.

- Error handling has been added. It's primitive—if there's a problem, we beep—but this is enough to prevent any evil error messages from appearing before the user's eyes. The problem will usually be either that no results were obtained from the search or that the search was never run because we couldn't connect to the server. In real life it might be nice to distinguish these cases and to provide nice error messages, but this is left as an exercise to the reader (meaning that I was too lazy to do it myself).

If all goes well, the Perl script has now parsed the HTML results from our curl call, and we proceed to the next step, which is to display the parsed results to the user. This is done by calling the displayResults handler, which is shown in Example 24-6. We have, at this point, two lists in global variables: L1 is a list of the URLs of the found articles, L2 is a list of their titles. We proceed to load L2 into the table view of the Results window, and then show the window. The code itself is almost exactly the same as the code we used to accomplish the same task in "Application" in Chapter 2.

Example 24-6. The displayResults handler

```
on displayResults( )
    set ds to make new data source at end of data sources
    set tv to table view 1 of scroll view 1 of window "results"
    set col to make new data column at end of data columns of ds ¬
        with properties {name:"titles"}
    repeat with aName in L2
        set aRow to make new data row at end of data rows of ds
        set contents of data cell "titles" of aRow to aName
    end repeat
    set data source of tv to ds
    show window "results"
end displayResults
```

The chain of events started by the user pressing the Search button has now ended; the application is idle, and the user is confronted with the Results window containing a list of titles in its table view. If the user double-clicks a line of the table view, our on double clicked handler is called; it is shown in Example 24-7. We assume that theObject is the table view, and we find out the index of the row that the user clicked. We then, just as at the end of the original code on page 364, use this index number to get the corresponding URL from L1, and hand this off to the open location scripting addition command to be opened in the user's preferred browser.

Example 24-7. The on double clicked handler

```
on double clicked theObject -- user double-clicked in results table
    tell theObject
        set r to clicked row
        if r ≤ (count L1) then
            open location (item r of L1)
        end if
    end tell
end double clicked
```

Final steps

When you have designed and saved your interface in Interface Builder, and when you have written your code in Xcode, you can try out the application by choosing Build → Build and Run. Xcode constructs your application and starts it up, so you can test it. If you want to make modifications, just quit your application, edit your code, and do it again. When you're all done developing your application and are ready to loose it upon the world, select your project in the project window and click the Info button at the top of the window to bring up the Project Info window; in the Styles tab, switch the Build Style from Development to Deployment (Figure 24-8). Then choose Build → Clean All Targets and then Build → Build. The result is a more compact application with the script saved as run-only so that curious users can't read it.

Scriptability

A pleasant consequence of writing an AppleScript Studio application is that the resulting application is scriptable. It's as if the AppleScriptKit dictionary were your application's dictionary, so the way you talk to the application from outside (driving it from a script) is much the same as the way you talk to it from inside (writing the application's own code). This facility can be used to script your finished application, and it can also be used to explore your application during the development process; in other words, you can use the Script Editor together with Xcode as part of your arsenal of development tools.

For example, suppose I've forgotten the AppleScript name of the Search button in the Search window. I could figure it out by looking in Interface builder, but another way would be to ask my running application, using the Script Editor:

```
tell application "SearchTidbits"
    get name of every button of window 1 -- {"searchButton"}
end tell
```

Figure 24-8. Changing build styles

A problem is that you can't call handlers for events that are intended to be called by Cocoa; but you can sometimes work around this. For example, there's a `perform action` command that lets you tell a button to generate its call to the `clicked` handler. So, for example, the following code brings the Search window to the front, fills out the NSForm with a new search, and presses the Search button:

```
tell application "SearchTidBITS"
    activate
    show window "Search"
    tell window "Search"
        tell matrix 1
            set string value of cell 1 to ""
            set string value of cell 2 to "Catch Conflict"
            set string value of cell 3 to ""
        end tell
        perform action button "searchButton"
    end tell
end tell
```

As of this writing, Apple is starting to expose the scripts inside an AppleScript Studio application by means of an interface item's script property, so the future may hold some interesting possibilities. Already one can say things like this:

```
tell application "SearchTidbits"
    set s to (get script of button 1 of window 1)
    tell s
        set its titleSought to "Catch Conflict" -- set a script property
        urlEncode("ha ha") -- call a handler
    end tell
    set script of window 1 to 5
end tell
```

This amounts to dynamic development—we can actually alter features of a script inside an AppleScript Studio application while it is running. Observe that what we get when we obtain an item's script is a copy; that is why we must explicitly save the changed script back into our application. This is very exciting, but to explore it further would take us outside the scope of this book.

PART IV

Appendixes

Part IV contains this book's appendixes.

The appendixes are:

    Appendix A, *The 'aeut' Resource*
    Appendix B, *Tools and Resources*

The 'aeut' Resource

This appendix contains AppleScript's 'aeut' resource, which is used for resolution of terminology as explained in Chapter 19.

The 'aeut' resource is divided into suites. The AppleScript Suite is automatically visible to the compiler; these are the global terms that make AppleScript work. The Type Names Suite is automatically visible to the compiler as well. So, for example, you can always use the activate command (see Chapter 18) because it is defined in the AppleScript Suite; and the rotation class is always recognized, even if you can't usually do anything with it, because it is defined in the Type Names Suite. Applications may implement their own version of the Type Names Suite. It has the special feature that it is suppressed from the human-readable display of the application's dictionary, so this is a place for terms that must be defined for compilation but that the user never needs to see.

The Standard Suite (also called the Core Suite) and the Text Suite are automatically visible to the compiler too, but they can be overridden and extended by individual applications, and terms within them don't necessarily have any functional implementation in and of themselves, though some of them do. So, for example, the count command, defined in the Standard Suite, works on lists and strings. But the exists command, although it is defined in the Standard Suite and is recognized when you compile a script, does not actually do anything in AppleScript itself; many scriptable applications, on the other hand, implement exists so as to give it some functionality (so that you can, for example, say exists disk 1 to the Finder).

Other suites and their contents are not implemented except voluntarily by individual applications; they are not seen by the compiler except when an application that implements them is being targeted.

```
AppleScript Suite
    EVENTS:
        activate: Bring the targeted application program to the front
            activate
        log: Cause a comment to be logged
            log string
        stop log: Stop event logging in the script editor
            stop log
        start log: Start event logging in the script editor
            start log
        idle: Sent to a script application when it is idle
            idle
            Result: integer -- the number of seconds to wait for next idle event
        launch: Start an application for scripting
            launch
        tell: Record or log a 'tell' statement
            tell
        end tell: Record or log an 'end tell' statement
            end tell
        error: Raise an error
            error [anything]
                [number small integer] -- an error number
                [partial result list] -- any partial result occurring before
                    the error
                [from anything] -- the object that caused the error
                [to anything] -- the desired class for a failed coercion
        Call•subroutine: A subroutine call
            Call•subroutine [anything]
                [at anything]
                [from anything]
                [for anything]
                [to anything]
                [thru anything]
                [through anything]
                [by anything]
                [on anything]
                [into anything]
                [onto anything]
                [between anything]
                [against anything]
                [out of anything]
                [instead of anything]
                [aside from anything]
                [around anything]
                [beside anything]
                [beneath anything]
                [under anything]
                [over anything]
                [above anything]
                [below anything]
                [apart from anything]
                [about anything]
                [since anything]
                [given anything] -- parameter:value pairs, comma-separated
```

            [with **type class**] -- *formal parameter set to true if*
                matching actual parameter is provided
            [without **type class**] -- *formal parameter set to false if*
                matching actual parmeter [sic] is provided
        Result: **anything**
=: *Equality*
        = **reference**
        Result: **anything**
≠: *Inequality*
        ≠ **reference**
        Result: **anything**
+: *Addition*
        + **reference**
        Result: **anything**
-: *Subtraction*
        - **reference**
        Result: **anything**
*: *Multiplication*
        * **reference**
        Result: **anything**
÷: *Division*
        ÷ **reference**
        Result: **anything**
div: *Quotient*
        div **reference**
        Result: **anything**
mod: *Remainder*
        mod **reference**
        Result: **anything**
^: *Exponentiation*
        ^ **reference**
        Result: **anything**
>: *Greater than*
        > **reference**
        Result: **anything**
≥: *Greater than or equal to*
        ≥ **reference**
        Result: **anything**
<: *Less than*
        < **reference**
        Result: **anything**
≤: *Less than or equal to*
        ≤ **reference**
        Result: **anything**
&: *Concatenation*
        & **reference**
        Result: **anything**
starts with: *Starts with*
        starts with **reference**
        Result: **anything**
ends with: *Ends with*
        ends with **reference**
        Result: **anything**

```
    contains: Containment
          contains reference
          Result: anything
    and: Logical conjunction
          and reference
          Result: anything
    or: Logical disjunction
          or reference
          Result: anything
    as: Coercion
          as reference
          Result: anything
    not: Logical negation
          not reference
          Result: anything
    negate: Numeric negation
          negate reference
          Result: anything
CLASSES:
    boolean -- A true or false value
    booleans (Plural)
    integer -- An integral number
    integers (Plural)
    real -- A real number
    reals (Plural)
    number -- an integer or real number
    numbers (Plural)
    list -- An ordered collection of items
          Properties:
          length integer -- the length of a list
          reverse list -- the items of the list in reverse order
          rest list -- all items of the list excluding first
    lists (Plural)
    linked list -- An ordered collection of items
          Properties:
          length integer -- the length of a list
    linked lists (Plural)
    vector -- An ordered collection of items
          Properties:
          length integer -- the length of a list
    vectors (Plural)
    record -- A set of labeled items
    records (Plural)
    item -- An item of any type
          Properties:
          id integer -- the unique ID number of this object
    items (Plural)
    script -- An AppleScript script
          Properties:
          name string -- the name of the script
          parent script -- its parent, i.e. the script that will handle events that
                      this script doesn't
    scripts (Plural)
    list or record -- a list or record
```

```
list or string -- a list or string
number or string -- a number or string
alias or string -- an alias or string
list, record or text -- a list, record or text
number or date -- a number or date
number, date or text -- a number, date or text
class -- the type of a value
classes (Plural)
event -- an AppleEvents event
events (Plural)
property -- an AppleEvents property
properties (Plural)
constant -- A constant value
constants (Plural)
preposition -- an AppleEvents preposition
prepositions (Plural)
reference form -- an AppleEvents key form
reference forms (Plural)
handler -- an AppleScript event or subroutine handler
handlers (Plural)
data -- an AppleScript raw data object
text -- text with language and style information
international text (Plural)
international text -- text that begins with a writing code
string -- text in 8-bit Macintosh Roman format
strings (Plural)
styled text (Plural)
styled text -- text with font, size, and style information
styled Clipboard text (Plural)
styled Clipboard text -- clipboard text with font, size,
     and style information
Unicode text (Plural)
Unicode text -- text in the Unicode format
     (cannot be viewed without conversion)
styled Unicode text (Plural)
styled Unicode text -- styled text in the Unicode format
encoded string -- text encoded using the Text Encoding Converter
encoded strings (Plural)
C string -- text followed by a null
C strings (Plural)
Pascal string -- text up to 255 characters preceded by a length byte
Pascal strings (Plural)
character -- an individual text character
characters (Plural)
text item -- text between delimiters
text items (Plural)
writing code -- codes that identify the language and script system
writing code info -- script code and language code of text run
     Properties:
     script code small integer -- the script code for the text
     language code small integer -- the language code for the text
writing code infos (Plural)
<blank> -- the undefined value
```

missing value -- *unavailable value, such as properties missing from*
    heterogeneous classes in a Whose clause
missing values (Plural)
reference -- *an AppleScript reference*
references (Plural)
anything -- *any class or reference*
type class -- *the name of a particular class (or any four-character code)*
RGB color -- *Three integers specifying red, green, blue color values*
RGB colors (Plural)
picture -- *A QuickDraw picture object*
pictures (Plural)
sound -- *a sound object on the clipboard*
sounds (Plural)
version -- *a version value*
file specification -- *a file specification as used by the operating system*
    Properties:
    POSIX path **string** -- *the POSIX path of the file*
file specifications (Plural)
alias -- *a file on a disk or server. The file must exist*
    when you check the syntax of your script.
    Properties:
    POSIX path **string** -- *the POSIX path of the file*
aliases (Plural)
machine -- *a computer*
machines (Plural)
zone -- *an AppleTalk zone*
zones (Plural)
keystroke -- *a press of a key combination on a Macintosh keyboard*
    Properties:
    key **character** -- *the character for the key was pressed*
        (ignoring modifiers)
    modifiers **A list of 'eMds'** -- *the modifier keys*
        pressed in combination
    key kind **'ekst'** -- *the kind of key that was pressed*
keystrokes (Plural)
seconds -- *more than one second*
date -- *Absolute date and time values*
    Properties:
    weekday **weekday** -- *the day of a week of a date*
    month **month** -- *the month of a date*
    day **integer** -- *the day of the month of a date*
    year **integer** -- *the year of a date*
    time **integer** -- *the time since midnight of a date*
    date string **string** -- *the date portion of a date-time value as text*
    time string **string** -- *the time portion of a date-time value as text*
dates (Plural)
month
months (Plural)
January
February
March
April
May
June

```
July
August
September
October
November
December
weekday
weekdays (Plural)
Sunday
Monday
Tuesday
Wednesday
Thursday
Friday
Saturday
metres
meters
inches
feet
yards
miles
kilometres
kilometers
centimetres
centimeters
square metres
square meters
square feet
square yards
square miles
square kilometres
square kilometers
litres
liters
gallons
quarts
cubic metres
cubic meters
cubic centimetres
cubic centimeters
cubic feet
cubic inches
cubic yards
kilograms
grams
ounces
pounds
degrees Celsius
degrees Fahrenheit
degrees Kelvin
```
upper case -- *Text with lower case converted to upper case*
app -- *Short name for application*
application

```
                    Properties:
                    result anything -- the last result of evaluation
                    space character -- a space character
                    return character -- a return character
                    tab character -- a tab character
                    minutes integer -- the number of seconds in a minute
                    hours integer -- the number of seconds in an hour
                    days integer -- the number of seconds in a day
                    weeks integer -- the number of seconds in a week
                    pi float -- the constant pi
                    print length integer -- the maximum length to print
                    print depth integer -- the maximum depth to print
                    text item delimiters list -- the text item delimiters of a string
                    AppleScript script -- the top-level script object
            applications (Plural)
ENUMERATIONS:
        'cons'
            case
            diacriticals
            white space
            hyphens
            expansion
            punctuation
            application responses
        'boov'
            true
            false
        'misc'
            current application
        'eMds'
            option down
            command down
            control down
            shift down
            caps lock down
        'ekst'
            escape key
            delete key
            tab key
            return key
            clear key
            enter key
            up arrow key
            down arrow key
            left arrow key
            right arrow key
            help key
            home key
            page up key
            page down key
            forward del key
            end key
            F1 key
            F2 key
```

```
                    F3 key
                    F4 key
                    F5 key
                    F6 key
                    F7 key
                    F8 key
                    F9 key
                    F10 key
                    F11 key
                    F12 key
                    F13 key
                    F14 key
                    F15 key
```

Required Suite
Standard Suite
    EVENTS:

        open: *Open the specified object(s)*

           open **reference** -- *list of objects to open*

        run: *Run an application.*

           Most applications will open an empty, untitled window.

           run -- *no direct parameter required*

        reopen: *Reactivate a running application.*

           Some applications will open a new untitled window
           if no window is open.

           reopen -- *no direct parameter required*

        print: *Print the specified object(s)*

           print **reference** -- *list of objects to print*

        quit: *Quit an application*

           quit
               [saving yes / no / ask] -- *specifies whether to save*
                        currently open documents

        close: *Close an object*

           close **reference** -- *the object to close*
               [saving yes / no / ask] -- *specifies whether changes*
                        should be saved before closing
               [saving in file] -- *the file or alias in which to save the object*

        count: *Return the number of elements of an object*

           count **reference** -- *the object whose elements are to be counted*
               [each **type class**] -- *if specified, restricts counting to*
                        objects of this class
           Result: **integer** -- *the number of elements*

        delete: *Delete an object from its container. Note this does not work*
           on script variables, only on elements of application classes.

           delete **reference** -- *the element to delete*

        duplicate: *Duplicate one or more objects*

           duplicate **reference** -- *the object(s) to duplicate*
               [to **location**] -- *the new location for the object(s)*
               [with properties **record**] -- *the initial values for properties*
                        of the new object that are to be different from the original
           Result: **reference** -- *to the duplicated object(s)*

        exists: *Verify if an object exists*

           exists **reference** -- *the object in question*
           Result: **boolean** -- *true if it exists, false if not*

        make: *Make a new element*

```
make
        new type class -- the class of the new element
        [at location] -- the location at which to insert the element
        [with data anything] -- the initial data for the element
        [with properties record] -- the initial values
                for the properties of the element
        Result: reference -- to the new object(s)
move: Move object(s) to a new location
        move reference -- the object(s) to move
                to location -- the new location for the object(s)
        Result: reference -- to the object(s) after they have been moved
save: Save an object
        save reference -- the object to save, usually a document or window
            [in file] -- the file or alias in which to save the object
            [as type class] -- the file type of the document in which
                    to save the data
select: Make a selection
        select reference -- the object to select
data size: (optional) Return the size in bytes of an object
        data size reference -- the object whose data size is to be returned
            [as type class] -- the data type for which the size
                    is calculated
        Result: integer -- the size of the object in bytes
suite info: (optional) Get information about event suite(s)
        suite info type class -- the suite for which to return information
            [in 'intl'] -- the human language and script system
                    in which to return information
        Result: a list of type suite info -- a record containing
                the suites and their versions
event info: (optional) Get information about the Apple events in a suite
        event info type class -- the event class of the Apple events
                for which to return information
            [in 'intl'] -- the human language and script system
                    in which to return information
        Result: a list of type event info -- a record containing
                the events and their parameters
class info: (optional) Get information about an object class
        class info type class -- the object class about which
                information is requested
            [in 'intl'] -- the human language and script system
                    in which to return information
        Result: type class info -- a record containing
                the object's properties and elements
CLASSES:
    application -- An application program
        Properties:
        name international text -- the name of the application
        frontmost boolean -- Is this the frontmost application?
        selection selection-object -- the selection visible to the user.
                Use the 'select' command to set a new selection;
                use 'contents of selection' to get or change information
                in the document.
        clipboard A list of anything -- the contents of the clipboard
                for this application
```

```
            version version -- the version of the application
        applications (Plural)
        document -- A document of a scriptable application
            Properties:
            modified boolean -- Has the document been modified
                since the last save?
        documents (Plural)
        file -- a file on a disk or server
            Properties:
            POSIX path string -- the POSIX path of the file
        files (Plural)
        alias -- a file on a disk or server. The file must exist when you
            check the syntax of your script.
            Properties:
            POSIX path string -- the POSIX path of the file
        aliases (Plural)
        selection-object -- A way to refer to the state of the current
            of the selection. Use the 'select' command to make a new selection.
            Properties:
            contents anything -- the information currently selected.
                Use 'contents of selection' to get or change information
                in a document.
        window -- A window
            Properties:
            bounds bounding rectangle -- the boundary rectangle
                for the window
            closeable boolean -- Does the window have a close box?
            titled boolean -- Does the window have a title bar?
            index integer -- the number of the window
            floating boolean -- Does the window float?
            modal boolean -- Is the window modal?
            resizable boolean -- Is the window resizable?
            zoomable boolean -- Is the window zoomable?
            zoomed boolean -- Is the window zoomed?
            visible boolean -- Is the window visible?
        windows (Plural)
        insertion point -- An insertion location between two objects
        insertion points (Plural)
COMPARISON OPS:
    starts with
    contains
    ends with
    =
    >
    ≥
    <
    ≤
ENUMERATIONS:
    'savo'
        yes
        no
        ask
    'kfrm'
        index -- keyform designating indexed access
```

```
                 named -- keyform designating named access
                 id -- keyform designating access by unique identifier
        'styl'
                 plain
                 bold
                 italic
                 outline
                 shadow
                 underline
                 superscript
                 subscript
                 strikethrough
                 small caps
                 all caps
                 all lowercase
                 condensed
                 expanded
                 hidden
Text Suite
    CLASSES:
        character
                 Properties:
                 <inheritance> text
        line
                 Properties:
                 <inheritance> text
                 justification 'just' -- the justification of the text
        lines (Plural)
        paragraph
                 Properties:
                 <inheritance> text
        paragraphs (Plural)
        text (Plural)
                 Elements:
                 Character by numeric index
                 Line by numeric index
                 Paragraph by numeric index
                 Text by numeric index
                 Word by numeric index
                 Properties:
                 color RGB color -- the color of the first character
                 font text -- the name of the font of the first character
                 size fixed -- the size in points of the first character
                 writing code 'intl' -- the script system and language
                 style text style info -- the text style of the first character
                        of the first character
                 uniform styles text style info -- the text styles
                        that are uniform throughout the text
                 quoted form text -- the text in quoted form
        text flow -- A contiguous block of text.
                 Page layout applications call this a 'story.'
                 Properties:
                 <inheritance> text
                 name international text -- the name
```

```
            text flows (Plural)
            text style info
                Properties:
                on styles A list of 'styl'-- the styles that are on for the text
                off styles A list of 'styl' -- the styles that are off for the text
            text style infos (Plural)
            word
                Properties:
                <inheritance> text
            words (Plural)
    ENUMERATIONS:
            'just'
                left
                right
                center
                full
            'styl'
                plain
                bold
                italic
                outline
                shadow
                underline
                superscript
                subscript
                strikethrough
                small caps
                all caps
                all lowercase
                condensed
                expanded
                hidden
QuickDraw Graphics Suite
    CLASSES:
        arc -- An arc
                Properties:
                arc angle fixed -- the angle of the arc in degrees
                bounds bounding rectangle -- the smallest rectangle
                    that contains the entire arc
                definition rect bounding rectangle -- the rectangle
                    that contains the circle or oval used to define the arc
                fill color RGB color-- the fill color
                fill pattern pixel map -- the fill pattern
                pen color RGB color -- the pen color
                pen pattern pixel map -- the pen pattern
                pen width small integer -- the pen width
                start angle fixed -- the angle that defines the start of the arc,
                    in degrees
                transfer mode 'tran' -- the transfer mode
        arcs (Plural)
        drawing area -- Container for graphics and supporting information
                Properties:
                background color RGB color -- the color used to fill in
                    unoccupied areas
```

background pattern **pixel map** -- *the pattern used to fill in*
    unoccupied areas
color table **color table** -- *the color table*
ordering **A list of reference** -- *the ordered list of*
    graphic objects in the drawing area
name **international text** -- *the name*
default location **point** -- *the default location of*
    each new graphic object
pixel depth **small integer** -- *the number of bits per pixel*
writing code **'intl'** -- *the script system and language*
    of text objects in the drawing area
text color **RGB color**-- *the default color for text objects*
default font **international text** -- *the name of the default font*
    for text objects
default size **fixed** -- *the default size for text objects*
style **text style info** -- *the default text style for text objects*
update on change **boolean** -- *Redraw after each change?*
drawing areas (Plural)
graphic line
    Properties:
    start point **point** -- *the starting point of the line*
    end point **point** -- *the ending point of the line*
    dash style **A list of dash style** -- *the dash style*
    arrow style **'arro'** -- *the arrow style*
graphic lines (Plural)
graphic object
graphic objects (Plural)
graphic shape
graphic shapes (Plural)
graphic text -- *A series of characters within a drawing area*
    Properties:
    color **RGB color** -- *the color of the first character*
    font **text** -- *the name of the font of the first character*
    size **fixed** -- *the size in points of the first character*
    uniform styles **text style info** -- *the text styles that are*
        uniform throughout the text
graphic group
graphic groups (Plural)
oval
ovals (Plural)
pixel
    Properties:
    color **RGB color** -- *the color*
pixels (Plural)
pixel map
pixel maps (Plural)
polygon
    Properties:
    point list **A list of point** -- *the list of points that define*
        the polygon
polygons (Plural)
rectangle
rectangles (Plural)
rounded rectangle

```
            Properties:
            corner curve height small integer -- the height of the oval
                used to define the shape of the rounded corners
            corner curve width small integer -- the width of the oval
                used to define the shape of the rounded corners
        rounded rectangles (Plural)
    ENUMERATIONS:
        'tran'
            copy pixels
            not copy pixels
            or pixels
            not or pixels
            bic pixels
            not bic pixels
            xor pixels
            not xor pixels
            add over pixels
            add pin pixels
            sub over pixels
            sub pin pixels
            ad max pixels
            ad min pixels
            blend pixels
        'arro'
            no arrow
            arrow at start
            arrow at end
            arrow at both ends
```

QuickDraw Graphics Supplemental Suite

```
    CLASSES:
        drawing area -- Container for graphics and supporting information
            Properties:
            rotation rotation -- the default rotation for objects
                in the drawing area
            scale fixed -- the default scaling for objects in the drawing area
            translation point -- the default repositioning for objects
                in the drawing area
        drawing areas (Plural)
        graphic group
        graphic groups (Plural)
```

Table Suite

```
    CLASSES:
        cell
            Properties:
            formula text -- the formula of the cell
            protection 'prtn' -- Indicates whether value or formula in the cell
                can be changed
        cells (Plural)
        column
            Properties:
            name international text -- the name of the column
        columns (Plural)
        row
        rows (Plural)
```

```
                table
                tables (Plural)
        ENUMERATIONS:
                'prtn'
                        read only
                        formulas protected
                        read/write
Macintosh Connectivity Classes
        CLASSES:
                device specification -- A device connected to a computer
                        Properties:
                        properties record -- property that allows getting and setting
                                of multiple properties
                        device type 'edvt' -- the kind of device
                        device address 'cadr' -- the address of the device
                device specifications (Plural)
                address specification
                        Properties:
                        properties record -- property that allows getting and setting
                                of multiple properties
                        conduit 'econ' -- How the addressee is physically connected
                        protocol 'epro' -- How to talk to this addressee
                address specifications (Plural)
                ADB address
                        Properties:
                        <inheritance> -- address specification
                        ID small integer -- the Apple Desktop Bus device ID
                ADB addresses (Plural)
                AppleTalk address
                        Properties:
                        <inheritance> -- address specification
                        AppleTalk machine string -- the machine name part of the address
                        AppleTalk zone string -- the zone part of the address
                        AppleTalk type string -- the type part of the AppleTalk address
                AppleTalk addresses (Plural)
                bus slot
                        Properties:
                        <inheritance> -- address specification
                        ID small integer -- the slot number
                bus slots (Plural)
                Ethernet address
                        Properties:
                        <inheritance> -- address specification
                        ID integer -- the Ethernet address
                Ethernet addresses (Plural)
                FireWire address
                        Properties:
                        <inheritance> -- address specification
                        ID small integer -- the FireWire device ID
                FireWire addresses (Plural)
                IP address
                        Properties:
                        <inheritance> -- address specification
                        ID string -- the address in the form "127.201.0.1"
```

```
                DNS form string -- the address in the form "apple.com"
                port string -- the port number of the service or client
                    being addressed
        IP addresses (Plural)
        LocalTalk address
            Properties:
            <inheritance> -- address specification
            network small integer -- the LocalTalk network number
            node small integer -- the LocalTalk node number
            socket small integer -- the LocalTalk socket number
        LocalTalk addresses (Plural)
        SCSI address
            Properties:
            <inheritance> -- address specification
            SCSI bus small integer -- the SCSI bus number
            ID small integer -- the SCSI ID
            LUN small integer -- the SCSI logical unit number
        SCSI addresses (Plural)
        Token Ring address
            Properties:
            <inheritance> -- address specification
            ID small integer -- the Token Ring ID
        Token Ring addresses (Plural)
        USB address
            Properties:
            <inheritance> -- address specification
            name string -- the USB device name
        USB Addresses (Plural)
ENUMERATIONS:
        'edvt'
            hard disk drive
            floppy disk drive
            CD ROM drive
            DVD drive
            storage device
            keyboard
            mouse
            trackball
            trackpad
            pointing device
            video monitor
            LCD display
            display
            modem
            PC card
            PCI card
            NuBus card
            printer
            speakers
            microphone
        'econ'
            ADB
            printer port
            modem port
```

```
                modem printer port
                LocalTalk
                Ethernet
                Token Ring
                SCSI
                USB
                FireWire
                infrared
                PC card
                PCI bus
                NuBus
                PDS slot
                Comm slot
                monitor out
                video out
                video in
                audio out
                audio line in
                audio line out
                microphone
        'epro'
                serial
                AppleTalk
                IP
                SCSI
                ADB
                FireWire
                IrDA
                IRTalk
                USB
                PC card
                PCI bus
                NuBus
                bus
                Macintosh video
                SVGA
                S video
                analog audio
                digital audio
                PostScript
Type Names Suite
    CLASSES:
                type class info
                type event info
                plain text (Plural)
                plain text
                string
                bounding rectangle
                point
                fixed
                location reference
                application dictionary
                color table
                dash style
```

```
double integer
extended real
fixed point
fixed rectangle
long fixed
long fixed point
long fixed rectangle
long point
long rectangle
machine location
menu
menu item
null
pixel map record
PostScript picture
RGB16 color
RGB96 color
small integer
small real
system dictionary
rotation
scrap styles
TIFF picture
version
unsigned integer
type property info
type element info
type parameter info
type suite info
```

Tools and Resources

This appendix provides sources for tools and further reading on various topics mentioned in this book. Some of this information has appeared earlier in the book but is gathered here for reference purposes.

Scripting Software

- Script Debugger, a commercial script editing and debugging environment with many powerful features to assist development; without it, I couldn't write any AppleScript code, and wouldn't have been able to write this book:

  http://latenightsw.com/sd3.0/index.html

- JavaScript OSA, a free OSA component file that adds JavaScript as a System-wide scripting language on your machine, complete with the ability to send and receive Apple events:

  http://latenightsw.com/freeware/JavaScriptOSA/index.html

- Gary McGath's EightyRez, a free 'aete' resource editor; this book could not have been written without it:

  http://www.panix.com/~gmcgath/EightyRez.html

- Smile, a free script editing environment:

  http://www.satimage.fr/software/en/softx.html

- FastScripts, a replacement for Apple's Script menu:

  http://www.red-sweater.com/RedSweater/FSFeatures.html

- Big Cat, a contextual menu script runner:

  http://ranchero.com/bigcat

- QuicKeys, a macro program:

  http://www.quickeys.com/products/qkx.html

- iKey, Keyboard Maestro, and DragThing, programs that let you run a script by typing a keyboard shortcut:

    http://www.scriptsoftware.com/ikey
    http://www.keyboardmaestro.com
    http://www.dragthing.com

- iDo Script Scheduler, a commercial product for running scripts at specified times:

    http://www.sophisticated.com/products/ido/ido_ss.html

Other Software Mentioned in This Book

For free software from Apple, the URL is "somewhere on your hard drive." Remember that for AppleScript Studio (Xcode, Interface Builder) you must install the Developer Tools.

- HyperCard, an overpriced, out-of-date, Classic-only, unsupported, but historically insanely great Mac scripting and interface construction environment:

    http://store.apple.com (and then search on "HyperCard")

- UserLand Frontier, and its inexpensive little brother Radio UserLand, a brilliant, powerful scripting environment with its own scripting language and built-in persistent storage, great interapplication communications, and Internet server/client capability:

    http://www.userland.com

- BBEdit, a scriptable text editor:

    http://www.barebones.com/products/bbedit/index.shtml

- Mailsmith, a scriptable email client:

    http://www.barebones.com/products/mailsmith/index.shtml

- Eudora, a scriptable email client:

    http://www.eudora.com/email/index.html

- Microsoft Word, a word processor with extensive internal (Visual Basic) scriptability:

    http://www.microsoft.com/mac/products/wordx/wordx.aspx

- Microsoft Excel, a spreadsheet program with extensive internal (Visual Basic) scriptability and strange but powerful AppleScript scriptability:

    http://www.microsoft.com/mac/products/excelx/excelx.aspx

- FileMaker Pro, a scriptable database program:

    http://www.filemaker.com

- REALbasic, an application development environment:

  http://www.realbasic.com
- GraphicConverter, a scriptable image processing program:

  http://www.lemkesoft.com/en/graphcon.htm
- Tex-Edit Plus, a scriptable styled text editor:

  http://www.tex-edit.com
- Fetch, a scriptable FTP client:

  http://www.fetchsoftworks.com
- NoteTaker, a scriptable outliner:

  http://www.aquaminds.com
- Panorama, a database program:

  http://www.provue.com/panorama.html

Apple Documentation

- The main AppleScript page, including a number of example scripts and other resources:

  http://www.apple.com/applescript/
- The AppleScript Language Guide, still the primary official documentation, and an important source of information, even though it often obfuscates more than it explains and is valid only to Version 1.3.7:

  http://developer.apple.com/techpubs/macosx/Carbon/interapplicationcomm/ AppleScript/AppleScriptLangGuide/
- Incremental release notes and change notes post-dating the Language Guide:
  - AppleScript 1.4 change notes:

    http://developer.apple.com/technotes/tn/tn1176.html#applescript
  - AppleScript 1.4.3 change notes:

    http://docs.info.apple.com/article.html?artnum=75073
  - AppleScript 1.5.5 change notes:

    http://developer.apple.com/technotes/tn/tn2010.html#applescript
  - AppleScript 1.6 change notes:

    http://docs.info.apple.com/article.html?artnum=60835
  - AppleScript 1.7–1.9.2 release notes (at this point Apple seems at last to have recognized the importance of gathering and linking to the release notes from a single location):

    http://www.apple.com/applescript/release_notes/

- A superb detailed historical record of AppleScript changes, maintained by Bill Cheeseman:

    http://www.applescriptsourcebook.com/applescript.html
- GUI Scripting:

    http://www.apple.com/applescript/uiscripting/
- AppleScript Studio:

    http://developer.apple.com/documentation/AppleScript/Conceptual/ StudioBuildingApps/index.html
- Scripting on Mac OS X:

    http://developer.apple.com/techpubs/macosx/Cocoa/TasksAndConcepts/ ProgrammingTopics/Scriptability/Concepts/ScriptingOnOSX.html
- XML-RPC and SOAP:

    http://developer.apple.com/techpubs/macosx/Carbon/interapplicationcomm/ soapXMLRPC/index.html
- *Inside Macintosh*, Apple events and Scripting:

    http://developer.apple.com/documentation/mac/IAC/IAC-2.html
- The Open Scripting Architecture:

    http://developer.apple.com/documentation/Carbon/Reference/Open_Scripti_ Architecture/index.html
- Making a Cocoa application scriptable:

    http://developer.apple.com/documentation/Cocoa/Conceptual/Scriptability/ index.html
- Glossary of AppleScript/Apple event terms:

    http://developer.apple.com/documentation/Cocoa/Conceptual/Scriptability/ Concepts/ScriptabilityTerms.html

Portals, Instruction, and Repositories

It's better to list a few web sites that between them contain virtually all important links than to try to list all those links, so here they are:

- ScriptWeb, a web portal to all things scripting-related:

    http://www.scriptweb.org
- MacScripter, a live collection of news items, examples, and links; now also incorporates AppleScriptCentral:

    http://macscripter.net
- MacScripter's scripting additions repository:

    http://osaxen.com

- Bill Cheeseman's encyclopedic site of history, examples, instruction, links, and more:

    http://www.applescriptsourcebook.com/home.html
- Main portal for XML-RPC and SOAP servers:

    http://www.xmethods.net

Mailing Lists

Mailing lists remain an important source of assistance, and are often haunted by Apple employees and by users of wisdom and experience:

- Apple's AppleScript list:

    http://lists.apple.com/mailman/listinfo/applescript-users
- Dartmouth's venerable MacScrpt list (in whose name the "i" is not only silent, it's downright absent):

    http://www.lsoft.com/scripts/wl.exe?SL1=MACSCRPT&H=LISTSERV. DARTMOUTH.EDU
- Apple's list for developers writing scriptable applications:

    http://lists.apple.com/mailman/listinfo/applescript-implementors
- Apple's AppleScript Studio list:

    http://lists.apple.com/mailman/listinfo/applescript-studio

Books

- Danny Goodman's ground-breaking *AppleScript Handbook*; outdated and out of print, it remains a classic, and is now available through print-on-demand direct from the publisher:

    http://www.dannyg.com/pubs/index.html
- Ethan Wilde, *AppleScript for the Internet: Visual QuickStart Guide* (Peachpit Press: 1998):

    Currently out of print, but check *http://www.amazon.com/exec/obidos/ASIN/ 0201353598/* for a used copy.
- Ethan Wilde, *AppleScript for Applications: Visual QuickStart Guide* (Peachpit Press: 2001):

    http://www.peachpit.com/books/
- Shirley Hopkins, *AppleScripting InDesign* (Dtp Connection: 2000):

    http://www.amazon.com/exec/obidos/ASIN/0970726511/
- Shirley Hopkins, *AppleScripting QuarkXPress* (Dtp Connection: 2000):

    http://www.amazon.com/exec/obidos/ASIN/0970726503/

- Ethan Wilde, *Adobe Illustrator Scripting with Visual Basic and AppleScript* (Adobe: 2002):

    http://www.amazon.com/exec/obidos/ASIN/0321112512/

- Matt Neuburg, *Frontier: The Definitive Guide* (O'Reilly & Associates, 1998); contains some helpful technical discussion of AEPrint format and of how object references are structured as Apple events:

    http://pages.sbcglobal.net/mattneub/frontierDef/ch00.html

Unix Scripting

Since the Unix shell command line and the Unix scripting languages Perl and Ruby are mentioned in this book, here are some suggestions for further reading:

- Dave Taylor and Brian Jepson, *Learning Unix for Mac OS X* (O'Reilly & Associates: 2002)

- Larry Wall et al., *Programming Perl*, Third Edition (O'Reilly & Associates: 2000)

- "Programming Ruby," an excellent online book:

    http://www.rubycentral.com/book/

Index

Symbols

{ } (curly braces)
  delimiting lists, 256
  empty lists, 45
  enclosing lists, 44
( ) (parentheses)
  determining order of operations, 281
  in comment delimiters, 56
& (ampersand), concatenation operator, 56,
  279–281
* (asterisk)
  comment delimiters (* *), 56, 109
  multiplication operator (*), 273
  wildcard value type ('****'), 310
\ (backslash)
  entering in a literal string, 247
  escaping variable names enclosed in
    pipes, 119
` (backtick) operator, 37
: (colon)
  in named parameters, 148
  in records, 261
, (comma), separating items in lists, 44
/ (division) operator, 273
= (equals sign)
  equality operator, 275, 276
^ (exponentiation) operator, 274
> (greater than) operator, 277
- (hyphens)
  in single-line comments, 109
  string consideration, 236
< (less than) operator, 276

- (minus sign), subtraction and unary
  negation operator, 273
+ (plus sign), addition operator, 273
" (quotation marks)
  delimiting literal strings, 247
  empty strings, signifying, 47
  escaping for AppleScript in FileMaker
    Pro, 26
  escaping in strings, 247
  inside comment delimiters, 109
  strings, AppleScript in VBA, 25
  strings formatted for osascript, 37
| (vertical bars)
  inside comment delimiters, 109
  interpretation as dictionary term,
    suppressing, 303
  resolving names in script vs. target
    object, 195
  variable names, surrounding with, 119
≤ (less than or equal to) operator, 277
≥ (greater than or equal to) operator, 277
≠ (inequality) operator, 275, 276
¬ (continuation character), 82
« » (guillemets), 256, 307

A

a reference to operator, 149, 209
abbreviations, 110
  equal, equals, and equal to (for is equal
    to), 276
  into (for to), 114
  is not, isn't, does not, and doesn't equal
    (for is not equal to), 276

We'd like to hear your suggestions for improving our indexes. Send email to *index@oreilly.com*.

M

Mac OS 9
  rebooting into, 8
  saving script as Mac OS X applet, 89
  scripting additions, 334
machine class, 255
machine-language code, 80
Macintosh Connectivity Classes, 320,
  420–422
Macintosh line breaks (\r), 104, 247, 286
MacRoman text encoding, 249
macros, 356
  QuicKeys program, 424
macros, Microsoft Word, 24
MacScript function, 24
mailing lists, 428
Mailsmith, 425
  comments in dictionary, 331
  creating new outgoing message, 14
  defective object model, 325
  dictionary inadequacies
    make command, 324
  FileMaker Pro, using with, 25
  GUI scripting, 360
  references, identifying, 214
  spam-reporting feature, 7
  targeting by a message, 184, 188
  translating terms from, 299
  using terms from, 230
make command, 324
me (keyword)
  getting polymorphism to operate, 180
  lists, speeding up access to, 260
  representing current script, 194
measurement unit conversions, 270
  Unix units tool, using, 271
menus
  Script Menu, 28
  script runner, 29
messages
  commands vs., 184
  error, 237
  handler calls as, 191
Microsoft Entourage, 29
Microsoft Excel (see Excel)
Microsoft Word, 425
  AppleScript code, constructing in
    VBA, 24
minutes property, 287
Miscellaneous Suite, 319
missing value constant, 290
mod operator, 274

month (date property), 246
month name constants, 291
mount volume command, 348
multiple steps, combining into single
  operation, 8
multiplication operator (*), 273
mutable datatypes, 149
my (see me)

N

\n (newline character)
  escaping in strings, 247
  Unix line breaks, 104
name property, 198
named (keyword), 198
named parameters for handlers, 148
names
  element specifier, 198
  record items, 262
  variables, 117
    forcing illegal name to be legal, 119
nesting
  target object specifications, 188
  try blocks, 241
next repeat command, 226
no constant, 290
noises, scripting addition commands for, 339
not operator, 275
NoteTaker, 324, 330, 426
NSAppleEventDescriptor class, 36
NSAppleScript class, 35
null( ) (top-level object), 321
null constant, 290
number class, 244
numbers
  coercion of, 268
  global properties
    days property, 287
    hours property, 287
    minutes property, 287
    pi, 287
    weeks property, 287
  integer and real datatypes, 244
  scripting addition commands for, 346
numeric abilities, AppleScript, 5
numeric classes, 244

O

obj value type, 310
object model, 63, 317
  defective, in dictionary contents, 321

white space (string consideration), 236
whitespace
    in AppleScript code, 104
    bytecode decompilation and, 82
    in strings, 247
    in variable names, 119
whose (keyword), 202
wildcard value type ('****'), 310
will open handler, 395
Windows line break (\r\n), 104
with blocks, 232–234
    timeout, 232
    transactions, 233
with or without (handler parameters), 147
word (string element), 248
write command, 343
writing applications, 370–402
    AppleScript Studio, using, 382–402
        Cocoa, 382–384
        example application, 387–402
        where/what it is, 384–387

applets, 370–376
    droplets, 375
    handlers for, 372–375
    options, 371
    persistence, 376
CGI, 379–382
digital hub scripting, 377
folder actions, 377

X

Xcode, 31, 385
    project, creating, 388
XML text files (Cocoa application
        dictionaries), 90
XML-RPC and SOAP services, 14, 351–353,
        427

Y

year (date property), 246
yes constant, 289, 290

About the Author

Matt Neuburg started programming computers in 1968, when he was 14 years old, as a member of a literally underground high school club, which met once a week to do timesharing on a bank of PDP-10s by way of primitive teletype machines. He also occasionally used Princeton University's IBM-360/67, but gave it up in frustration when one day he dropped his punch cards. He majored in Greek at Swarthmore College, and received his PhD from Cornell University in 1981, writing his doctoral dissertation (about Aeschylus) on a mainframe. He proceeded to teach Classical languages, literature, and culture at many well-known institutions of higher learning, most of which now disavow knowledge of his existence, and to publish numerous scholarly articles unlikely to interest anyone. Meanwhile he obtained an Apple IIc and became hopelessly hooked on computers again, migrating to a Macintosh in 1990. He wrote some educational and utility freeware, became an early regular contributor to the online journal *TidBITS*, and in 1995 left academe to edit *MacTech Magazine*. In August 1996 he became a freelancer, which means he has been looking for work ever since. He is also the author of two books for O'Reilly & Associates, Inc., *Frontier: The Definitive Guide* and *REALbasic: The Definitive Guide*.

Colophon

Our look is the result of reader comments, our own experimentation, and feedback from distribution channels. Distinctive covers complement our distinctive approach to technical topics, breathing personality and life into potentially dry subjects.

The animal on the cover of *AppleScript: The Definitive Guide* is a Boston terrier. The youngest breed in the American Kennel Club (AKC), the Boston is a cross between various types of bulldogs and bull terriers. Originally bred in England, the breed stabilized in the United States, where it was initially favored as a fighter in the underworld rat pits of the seedier areas of late eighteenth- and early nineteenth-century Boston. By the late nineteenth century, however, people started to admire the beauty of the breed's compact, elegant build—the "American Gentleman," as the Boston terrier is now known, had been discovered.

In 1889, the AKC rejected the Stud Book applications put forth by the "American bull terrier" owners only to accept the breed in 1893 under its new name, Boston terrier. Today, its gentle yet playful and protective nature combined with its willingness to be trained make it a popular family pet—especially, of course, in Boston, the metropolitan area in which O'Reilly maintains a large editorial and production staff. Though the Boston terrier's fighting days are in its past, the sportsmen and -women at Boston University evoke the breed's heritage each time they take the field or ice.

Genevieve d'Entremont was the production editor and proofreader for *AppleScript: The Definitive Guide*. Nancy Kotary was the copyeditor; Claire Cloutier and Phil Dangler provided quality control. Mary Agner provided production assistance. Ellen Troutman-Zaig wrote the index.

Ellie Volckhausen designed the cover of this book, based on a series design by Edie Freedman. The cover image is an original illustration created by Susan Hart. Emma Colby produced the cover layout with QuarkXPress 4.1 using Adobe's ITC Garamond font.

Melanie Wang designed the interior layout, based on a series design by David Futato. This book was converted by Julie Hawks to FrameMaker 5.5.6 with a format conversion tool created by Erik Ray, Jason McIntosh, Neil Walls, and Mike Sierra that uses Perl and XML technologies. The text font is Linotype Birka; the heading font is Adobe Myriad Condensed; and the code font is LucasFont's TheSans Mono Condensed. The illustrations that appear in the book were produced by Robert Romano and Jessamyn Read using Macromedia FreeHand 9 and Adobe Photoshop 6. The tip and warning icons were drawn by Christopher Bing. This colophon was written by Sarah Jane Shangraw.

Want To Know More About Mac OS X?

The Apple Developer Connection offers convenient and timely support for all your Mac OS X development needs.

Developer Programs

The Apple Developer Connection (ADC) helps developers build, test, and distribute software products for Mac OS X. ADC Programs provide direct, affordable access to Mac OS X software, along with many other products and services, including:

- Pre-release software seeds
- Apple hardware discounts
- Code-level technical support

Programs range in price from $0 (free) to US$3500 and are available worldwide.

Developer Tools

All ADC Program members receive free Mac OS X Developer Tools such as Project Builder, Interface Builder, and AppleScript Studio.

Getting Started is Easy

The ADC web site offers a variety of reference materials including in-depth articles, tutorials, sample code, and FAQs. You'll also find student developer resources, open source projects, mailing lists, and more. Our electronic newsletter keeps members notified with up-to-the-minute information on new releases and documentation.

Join today!

Visit http://developer.apple.com/membership/

Related Titles Available from O'Reilly

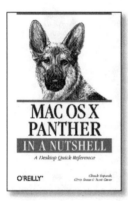

Macintosh

Appleworks 6: The Missing Manual

The Best of the Joy of Tech

iMovie 3 and iDVD: The Missing Manual

iPhoto2: The Missing Manual

iPod: The Missing Manual

Mac OS X Panther in a Nutshell

Mac OS X Panther Pocket Guide

Mac OS X: The Missing Manual, *Panther Edition*

Mac OS X Unwired

Macintosh Troubleshooting Pocket Guide

Office X for the Macintosh: The Missing Manual

Running Mac OS X Panther

Switching to the Mac

Mac Developers

Building Cocoa Applications: A Step-By-Step Guide

Cocoa in a Nutshell

Learning Carbon

Learning Cocoa with Objective-C, *2nd Edition*

Learning Unix for Mac OS X Panther

Mac OS X for Java Geeks

Mac OS X Hacks

Mac OS X Panther for Unix Geeks

Objective-C Pocket Reference

Programming Quartz 2D

RealBasic: The Definitive Guide, *2nd Edition*

Keep in touch with O'Reilly

1. Download examples from our books

To find example files for a book, go to:

www.oreilly.com/catalog

select the book, and follow the "Examples" link.

2. Register your O'Reilly books

Register your book at *register.oreilly.com*

Why register your books?
Once you've registered your O'Reilly books you can:

- Win O'Reilly books, T-shirts or discount coupons in our monthly drawing.
- Get special offers available only to registered O'Reilly customers.
- Get catalogs announcing new books (US and UK only).
- Get email notification of new editions of the O'Reilly books you own.

3. Join our email lists

Sign up to get topic-specific email announcements of new books and conferences, special offers, and O'Reilly Network technology newsletters at:

elists.oreilly.com

It's easy to customize your free elists subscription so you'll get exactly the O'Reilly news you want.

4. Get the latest news, tips, and tools

www.oreilly.com

- "Top 100 Sites on the Web"—PC Magazine
- CIO Magazine's Web Business 50 Awards

Our web site contains a library of comprehensive product information (including book excerpts and tables of contents), downloadable software, background articles, interviews with technology leaders, links to relevant sites, book cover art, and more.

5. Work for O'Reilly

Check out our web site for current employment opportunities:

jobs.oreilly.com

6. Contact us

O'Reilly & Associates, Inc.
1005 Gravenstein Hwy North
Sebastopol, CA 95472 USA

TEL: 707-827-7000 or 800-998-9938
        (6am to 5pm PST)

FAX: 707-829-0104

order@oreilly.com
For answers to problems regarding your order or our products. To place a book order online, visit:

www.oreilly.com/order_new

catalog@oreilly.com
To request a copy of our latest catalog.

booktech@oreilly.com
For book content technical questions or corrections.

corporate@oreilly.com
For educational, library, government, and corporate sales.

proposals@oreilly.com
To submit new book proposals to our editors and product managers.

international@oreilly.com
For information about our international distributors or translation queries. For a list of our distributors outside of North America check out:

international.oreilly.com/distributors.html

adoption@oreilly.com
For information about academic use of O'Reilly books, visit:

academic.oreilly.com

O'REILLY®

Our books are available at most retail and online bookstores.
To order direct: 1-800-998-9938 • *order@oreilly.com* • *www.oreilly.com*
Online editions of most O'Reilly titles are available by subscription at *safari.oreilly.com*